A N

M E D I A

G R O U P

P U B L I C A T I O N

C0-AON-503

AGORA

Digital Marketplace

Talent Sourcebook

The Fastest Way

to find Computer Services

and Solution Providers

APPLE DEVELOPER GROUP

SiliconGraphics
Computer Systems

Morph's
Outpost
ON THE DIGITAL FRONTIER

RES NOVA
SOFTWARE INC.

RE:SOURCE
NETWORK SOLUTIONS

PAC TEL
Electronic Publishing Services

✳ MZ Media Group is a new media publishing and information services company founded in 1986 by Mansoor Zakaria, *Chairman* and *CEO*. Its main business units are described below:

AGORA

Business Information Division

The Business Information Division is a national forerunner in producing business research for the news media across the country. It has produced research and source-books for clients and partners including: *The Wall Street Journal*, *The Los Angeles Times*, the *Miami Herald*, the *Philadelphia Inquirer*, the *Boston Globe*, the *Houston Chronicle*, the *San Francisco Examiner*, the *Atlanta Journal & Constitution*, the *Cleveland Plain Dealer*, the *Rocky Mountain News*, the *Tampa Tribune*, *Ft. Worth Star Telegram*.

Today's new media aren't mass. They're targeted. Individualized. Customized.

New Media Markets Division

By focusing on new technology solutions, the New Media Markets Division builds digital marketplaces. This business unit produces and publishes information products that provide solutions for acquiring and integrating digital technology. Current publishing projects include *Re:Source Network Solutions*, a joint product with Pacific Bell Information Services. This quarterly multimedia CD-ROM magalog comprises a digital bazaar for networking solutions and includes a magazine, catalog and purchasing venue all in one CD-ROM publication. The *AGORA Digital Marketplace* also falls under the purview of this market division. Previously published products include *Macintosh Services Directory* and *Network Solutions Guide*.

Call, write or fax or e-mail us if you want to:

✳ Advertise in the next edition of AGORA;

✳ Become a member of the AGORA Referral Network;

✳ Order additional copies of the AGORA directory

EXECUTIVE

Mansoor Zakaria
Founder & Publisher

Kim Daus
Editor & General Manager

Mike Aiello
Director of Systems & Products

Geoff Workman
Director of Strategic Alliances

Sheryl Hamlin
General Manager, Business Information Division

JoAnn Lopez
Manager, Database Resources

Jeff Wright
Vice President of Finance & Administration

SALES & SERVICE

Michael Delaney
Douglas Hamar
Gary Parsons
Andrea Waterstreet
Will Webster

DESIGN & PRODUCTION

John Goodchild
Elena Maya Welch
Art Direction & Design

Mason Deal
Robin Benjamin
Production

Garrett Cobarr, Lingua Service Associates
Cover Art and Category Design

DATABASE ADMINISTRATION

Cameron Causey, Michael Delaney
Database Managers

Michelle Henry
Database Coordinator

Jamie Seidel
Dyane Villalobos
Database Assistants

AGORA Digital Marketplace
221 Main Street, Suite 700
San Francisco, CA 94105
Phone: 415-543-8290, ext. 140
Fax: 415-543-5613
AppleLink: AGORA
Internet: agora@delphi.com

WELCOME TO THE AGORA DIGITAL MARKETPLACE, and the premiere edition of the AGORA Talent Sourcebook. This Sourcebook seeks to connect buyers and sellers of computer related services and is the only multi-platform directory of its kind, featuring thousands of service providers that are most needed today. Our entire economy seems to be redefining itself with each passing day. With the new media revolution constantly forging new horizons, more than ever before we find ourselves charting courses into unknown territories. While frontiering new geographies or even galaxies is not new, this is the first time new space or technology exploration has literally been handed to the masses. It is clear that those who integrate new computer technology into current business models will help chart the future.

To incorporate new media into current systems, development teams and individuals must include creative and technical resources one never thought about in days gone by. And while product functionality remains as cri- tical as ever, it is becoming ever more critical to present the user with an easy, enjoyable computing experience. What's more, developing for the content rich, networked nineties involves bringing together more **We are experiencing a new era unfolding** resources from far flung disciplines to work in an integrated way.

As multimedia, the "hottest" piece of the industry pie, moves towards mainstream, just making pretty pictures on screen for demos is not enough. Sound and video have to be incorporated into modern networked business systems in a way that makes applications easier to learn and use while concurrently raising productivity levels for the entire organization. To meet this challenge, assembling the right team for the job has become complex.

Take a journey with us as we browse the ancient Western AGORA, back to the dawn of history, and then travel through modern times peering into the cyber marketplace that lies before us. We think you'll discover the thrill and opportunities of the new era that is unfolding. Within our AGORA, you are witnessing the initial launch of a digital bazaar that will demonstrate the electronic future of commerce. Take advantage of it to position yourself powerfully for the future.

Very truly yours,

Mansoor Zakaria

Mansoor Zakaria

3

35

Custom Solutions

This section highlights specialized computing solutions from service providers who integrate hardware, software and services to create custom solutions for clients.

Document Management 36
Finance/Accounting   36
Human Resources   36
**Manufacturing/
    Production   37**
Marketing & Sales   37
Mobile Computing   38
Project Management   38

4I

Development/ Programming

This section covers solution providers who develop a range of industry-specific applications, provide contract programming, interface design, product localization and other services pertaining to designing and developing software applications. Within each category are sub-sections which further define the listed solution providers by

application specialty and programming languages, etc.

Applications Development   43
   Accounting 58
   Architecture 60
   Business 60
   CAD 63
   Courseware Authoring 63
   Education 64
   Engineering 65
   Entertainment 69
   Financial 70
   Government 71
   Legal 72
   Manufacturing 72
   Medical 73
   Publishing/Graphics 75
Contract Programming 78
   Assembler 85
   C++, Object Oriented 85
   C, Pascal 90
   HyperTalk 90
   THINK 92
Database Programming 92
   4th Dimension 95
   DAL 99
   DBase 99
   Filemaker Pro 99
   FoxBASE 101
   Helix 102
   Omnis 7 103
   Oracle 104
   Paradox 105
   SQL 106
   Sybase 106

**Multiplatform
    Development   106**
Product Localization   108
User Interface Design   109
   Human Interface 109
   Screen Graphics 112
Virtual Reality   112

II5

Marketing & Distribution

In this section you will find expert help in marketing and distributing your product, from initial conception to final release. Each category contains service providers with specific areas of expertise.

Marketing   116
   Advertising 116
   Business Presentations 116
   Consulting 117
   Copywriting 118
   Demo Disks 118
   Direct Mail 118
   Graphic Design 119
   International 120
   Market Research 120
   Public Relations 120
   Sales 121
   Trade Show Services 121

Package Design 121
Product Testing 122
Software Distribution 123
Catalog/Retail 123
Value Added Resellers 123

127

Multimedia

This section contains artists and producers who specialize in a broad spectrum of multimedia development services.

Multimedia 129
Animation 143
Audio 144
Content Development 146
Database Development 147
Graphics/Interface 147
Legal Services 148
Marketing & Sales 148
Video 148

Multimedia Producers 149
Education & Training 150
Entertainment 151
Information 152

CD ROM 152
Archiving Services 152
Development 152
Duplication 153
Photo CD 153

157

Networking

Client server network experts, both solution providers and systems integration vendors, can be found here under specific categories which define their area of expertise.

Client/Server 159
Network & Systems Integration 159
Design 163
Enterprise Network Solutions 165
Installations 165
System Integration 166
Training 167

Network Systems & Protocols 167
Network Services 168
Networks 168

171

Publishing

For publishing and production needs, from computer publishers to technical writers, look under these specific categories.

Desktop Publishing 172
Design & Layout 172
Training 174

Disk Duplication 175
Imaging 175

Information & Online Services 175
Publishing 175
CD ROM Publishers 175
Computer Book Publishers 176
Editors/Proofreaders 176
Electronic Publishing 176
Prepress 177
Software Publishing 177

Technical Writing/ Documentation 178
End User 178
Technical 179

183

Support

Look here for technical service providers, as well as associations, user-groups and training experts, each within their pertinent category.

Associations/User Groups 185

Data Conversion/ Recovery/Security 186
Data Conversion 186
Data Recovery 186
Data Security 186

Equipment Rental/ Leasing/Repair 187
Technical Support 187
Training 188
Developer 188
User 189

Publisher's Letter 3
AGORA Referral Network 14
Telephone Index 193
Geographic Index 229

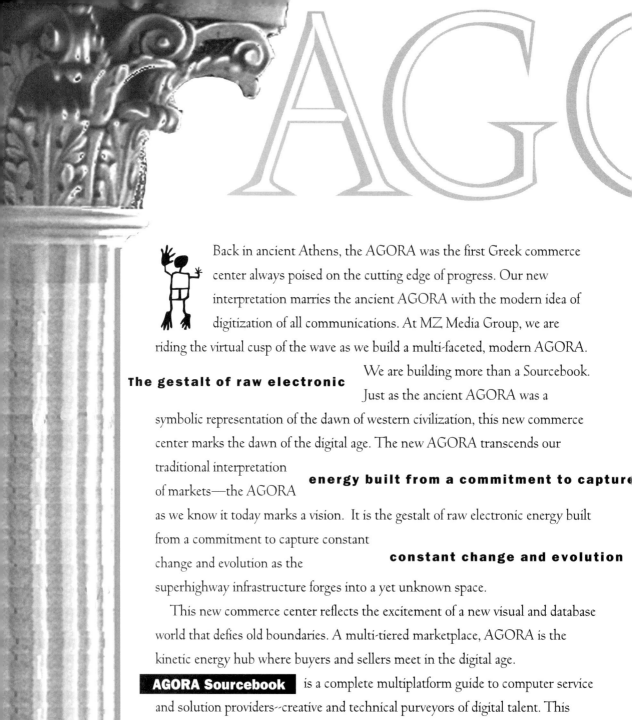

Back in ancient Athens, the AGORA was the first Greek commerce center always poised on the cutting edge of progress. Our new interpretation marries the ancient AGORA with the modern idea of digitization of all communications. At MZ Media Group, we are riding the virtual cusp of the wave as we build a multi-faceted, modern AGORA.

The gestalt of raw electronic

We are building more than a Sourcebook. Just as the ancient AGORA was a symbolic representation of the dawn of western civilization, this new commerce center marks the dawn of the digital age. The new AGORA transcends our traditional interpretation of markets—the AGORA **energy built from a commitment to capture** as we know it today marks a vision. It is the gestalt of raw electronic energy built from a commitment to capture constant change and evolution as the **constant change and evolution** superhighway infrastructure forges into a yet unknown space.

This new commerce center reflects the excitement of a new visual and database world that defies old boundaries. A multi-tiered marketplace, AGORA is the kinetic energy hub where buyers and sellers meet in the digital age.

AGORA Sourcebook is a complete multiplatform guide to computer service and solution providers--creative and technical purveyors of digital talent. This Talent Sourcebook is a printed directory of service providers from more than one hundred categories within such industry segments as multimedia, development and programming, networking, marketing, publishing, and custom

There are several delivery and distribution

solutions. It provides everything a developer, entrepreneur, MIS or marketing exec might need when piecing together the team for projects in the digital age.

AGORA Referral Network is an on-demand service where buyers request specific technical and creative skills and sellers present their wares, or talent portfolios. Within the AGORA, there are several delivery and distribution channels for matching service provider talent with buyer or project needs.

channels for matching service provider talent

This includes custom searches, personal referral counseling and completely automated perusal or browsing through the digital talent base.

AGORA OnLine is a cyber marketspace that lets the user navigate through digital talent providers' qualifications and permits users to experience providers' work portfolios in an entirely new, interactive way.

The AGORA Digital Marketplace brings thousands of creative and technical solution providers together to create a multi-tiered, modern marketplace. This Sourcebook is just the

with project requirements

first phase of our vision. As the industry defines itself with each passing day, we plan to keep the AGORA Digital Marketplace on the cusp of progress as we surf the wave that takes us toward a new digital domain. 🏃🏃

history & metaphor

The word "Agora" comes from fourth century BC Athens as the height of its legendary democracy was unfolding. The city spent untold amounts of civic funds on glamorous architectural wonders of the Acropolis—the Parthenon, Erektheion and Propylaia. However, the citizens of Athens spent most of their time milling around the town square located at the base of the Acropolis hill — the Agora. In more ancient times, the Agora was originally a sort of farmer's market where

The AGORA was the political center, merchants, slaves and various artisans gathered

to sell their goods and services. As Athens increased in size, wealth and political sophistication, the Agora became more and more of a social meeting ground where political influence, popular philosophies, and gossip were exchanged along with the more traditional goods and services.

As the Athenian democracy **and it was also the economic heart** expanded in breadth and

bureaucracy, savvy politicians were quick to respond by building up the Agora; in fact, improving the Agora became a primary vote-getting strategy. In 510 BC, or so,

Kleisthenes began this trend with **of the city for trading goods and services.** the grand, state-financed Stoa (long,

roofed colonnades) that bound the northwestern square of the Agora. By the time the great leader and reformer, Pericles, held sway during Athens' golden years of

today's
technologies
collapse
time

democracy, the Agora had gained the Bouleuterion; Council Chambers of the Athenian Senate, the Tholos; the administrative headquarters that housed clerks and scribes, the Strategeion; where the annually chosen military leaders met, and various law courts and secular temples.

While the Agora was the primary political center of Athens, it was also the economic heart of the city. Products and services were provided by small businessmen operating out of booths. Alongside the potters, sculptors, physicians, and such existed a slightly seedier brand of tradesmen (and

History, within context, makes even the most tumultuous change sensible.

women), such as slaves contracting themselves out for day-labor, musicians, dancers, actors, and, of course, the subversively influential hetairoi. These were the courtesans/prostitutes whose chief clients were the more powerful and wealthy politicians, who presumably divulged many state secrets in their frequent trysts. All in all, the Agora was a crowded, noisy gathering of who's who in Athenian society. To walk through it

We're not sure who discovered water, but we're sure it wasn't the fish.

promised an assault on all sides of vendors hawking their fares, political machinery in motion, and, most importantly, a kinetic exchange of information.

So, how does this ancient concept merge with our modern world of computer service and solution providers? To stretch the Athenian metaphor, one can compare the pristine, imposing structures of the Acropolis where, in more ancient times, the city of Athens had been bound, to the teeming,

Whether in fourth century BC or in twentieth century AD, the AGORA promises a flow of vital advice and information.

sprawling Agora or New City, in the same manner one compares the previously monolithic platform giants to the new community of independent digital solution and service providers. When the who's who of Athenian society needed to shop for goods, bargain for services, or at least catch some hot gossip, they would step out into the bustling din of the Agora. When you, citizen of the global village, need to tap into the vast wealth of talent and information contained in the new realm of service and solution providers, you can enter the cyberspace of the thoroughly modern, vital AGORA Digital Marketplace.

Hanging out in the AGORA, whether in fourth century BC or in twentieth century AD, promises a flow of useful advice and information. After calling a platform company's support line for the hundredth time and still not getting the

Morphing toward the millennium

answer you wanted, take a stroll into AGORA, and look for your Custom Applications Developer busily writing code in the Tholos. Or, step into the law courts for some expert advice on the protocols for your business's new Network. Or, wander through the galleries of the Stoa as you look for the creative genius of Multimedia folk to pump up your company's next business presentation.

In the Athenian Agora, a government-managed group of officials called the agoranomoi supervised the quality of the goods sold and services provided by the marketplace denizens. In the

Imagine a world in which advertising is selected by the customer, where marketing dollars are spent not in waging war for the customer's fleeting attention, but in engaging in a dialogue with customers.

Digital AGORA, you have easy access to pre-screened service and solution providers through the AGORA Referral Network, the agoranomoi of 1994. At MZ Media Group, we hope to make your experience in the new AGORA Digital Marketplace as useful, entertaining, informational, and above all, as productive as it was for the citizens of Classical Athens. 🏃🏃

a word about our sponsors

 As architects and builders of digital marketplaces, MZ Media Group is in the business of crafting commerce centers that transcend traditional models. In this new age that unfolds before us, out on the digital frontier, we are witnessing the birth of an entire new market structure. To craft the AGORA Digital Marketplace — to transform visions into "real time" ideas — MZ Media Group has aligned with visionary market leaders. These sponsors contributed to ideas that have resulted in our new AGORA and our vision of electronic commerce.

 In their unique ways, the following companies are leading the pack venturing into as yet undiscovered digital terrain. Together and collectively, we are not only envisioning, but also implementing "superhighway" applications that have practical uses and benefits in the marketplace of today.

 Just as the heart and soul of Classical Athens was the ancient AGORA, so too is our modern adaptation at the core of the electronic future of commerce. The collective insight, energy, and daring attitudes of founding sponsors and advertisers have not only supported the AGORA, but have also helped craft this one-of-a-kind digital bazaar. To learn more about the group of digital leaders who made this AGORA possible, please contact us by phone, fax, or email.

- ☐ Apple Computer Developer Group
- ☐ Morph's Outpost on the Digital Frontier
- ☐ Pacific Telesis Electronic Publishing Services
- ☐ ResNova Software
- ☐ Silicon Graphics Developer Program

AGORA / MZ Media Group, Inc.
221 Main Street, Suite 700
San Francisco, CA 94105

 12

PHONE:
415.543.8290
x. 140

FAX:
415.543.5613

EMAIL:
agora@delphi.com

IT IS THE BUSINESS
OF THE FUTURE
TO BE DANGEROUS.

AGORA DIGITAL MARKETPLACE

GET INVOLVED

800.927.1200

referral network

Your client needs the product a month earlier than planned. How can you slice a month off the schedule and manage the other projects without compromising? Your regular vendors are starting a six month contract in Uruguay and can't be reached. Your doctor says you need a rest. The boss says management is considering cutbacks. You need help. There is not time to meet and analyze a variety of vendors who might get the job done. There's only one thing to do: Call the AGORA Digital Marketplace.

AGORA Digital Marketplace emerges in the wake of an increasingly fragmented computer industry and diminishing support channels. The complexities of each individual project and the diversity and geographic dispersement of service providers can make

Connecting Buyers and Sellers

your talent search an ordeal — but one you can't afford to compromise. With AGORA, gone are the days of projects waiting on hold because it lacks the right developer, project team or multimedia animator. AGORA's referral network provides custom searches of computer professionals who have passed a rigorous application process. This database allows us to put businesses in touch with professionals who fall

within the skill set, experience and price range that

in the Digital Age

your project needs. The Referral Network members showcased here comprise a select group of talent assembled to fill digital service gaps. You can locate these

Accessing the Network members alphabetically on the following roster

or identify them by the icon located below their name throughout the directory. Simply enter the AGORA marketplace by calling the Digital Talent Hotline at 800-927-1200.

800 927-1200

Step One - Call 1-800-927-1200.

Step Two - Select either automated or personalized service.

Step Three - If you choose automated service, recorded instructions will direct your search. If you choose our premiere personalized referral service, an AGORA Referral Counselor will personally handle your need. Here's how it works:

A Referral Counselor personally builds a Client Profile by identifying the type of project, specific technical requirements, skills required, geographical preferences, time constraints, budget limits—all the elements allowing us to make an exact match from our digital talent database.

We search our talent database for members whose skills match the project needs.

Through an alliance with M2, a San Francisco Bay Area executive placement firm, we personally interview service providers who match the project parameters.

We confirm the placement with both client and service provider, coordinating all forms including reports, payment agreements and signatures.

How to Become a Member of the AGORA Digital Marketplace

Simply fill out the preliminary questionnaire on the business reply card and fax or mail it to MZ Media Group. Additional applications can also be obtained by calling directly (800) 927-1200.

Announcing an alliance to provide customized, service-driven solutions for those clients who need more help securing the right professional digital talent in the San Francisco Bay Area. Together AGORA and M2 will help define your needs, structure the project, identify the best consultant or team to get the job done, negotiate the transaction and evaluate performance. Call us for personalized, professional assistance.

referral network

▣ CUSTOM SOLUTIONS ▣

Art & Logic   **818-501-6990**
Justin Souter
P.O. Box 56465
Sherman Oaks, CA 91413
Skills: C++, C, 680x0, UI design, hardware interfacing.

Bear River Associates, Inc. **510-644-9400**
Anthony Meadow
P.O. Box 1900
Berkeley, CA 94701
Skills: C++, C, Windows, A/UX, UNIX, VAX/VMS, IBM, Pascal, FORTRAN, LISP, COBOL.

Bizware Corporation **201-816-9271**
Alex Cooper
210 Sylvan Avenue
Englewood Cliffs, NJ 07632

Creative Enterprises **310-987-3450**
Sonni Cooper
5354 East 2nd Street, Suite 200
Long Beach, CA 90803
Skills: Multimedia, 2 D and 3D graphic screen applications, multilingual, technical backgrounds, cultural and minority interests.

Nelson Laffey Associates, Inc. **314-436-9725**
Bud Schilling
1919 Park Avenue
St. Louis, MO 63104
Skills: C, C++, OOPs, financial process controls for manufacturing, MRP and inventory programming.

New Media, Inc.   **216-481-7900**
Leonard Pagon Jr.
503 E. 200th Street, Suite 202
Cleveland, OH 44119
Skills: Object-oriented design and development, client/server design and development, graphic interface design.

TurnKey Computer Systems, Inc. 212-779-8445
David Seidman
401 2nd Avenue, Suite 25D
New York, NY 10010
Skills: Alpha IV, Clipper and FoxPro database applications. PowerSoft object-oriented client/server applications. Languages: Assembly, BASIC, C, C++, COBOL, FORTRAN, Pascal, and Tandem TAL. Novell NetWare Engineer: (Novell OS 2.1x, 2.2x, and 3.1x). Operating systems: DOS, NextStep, Novell, Tandem TACL/ Comint, and Windows.

Waverly Software Design **415-322-4414**
Matt Brown
159 Waverly Street
Palo Alto, CA 94301
Skills: Object-oriented programming in NewtonScript/C, UI design, and project management.

▣ DEVELOPMENT & PROGRAMMING ▣

1-Up Computing   **719-488-0125**
Christopher Magnuson
1330 Deby Place
Colorado Springs, CO 80921
Skills: C, C++, MacApp, THINK/Symantec, MPW, assembly, MS Windows, UNIX, XII, Motif, DSP, embedded systems, electronic design.

---

members

AceNet   818-405-0087
Jerven R. Carver
424 N. Catalina Avenue, Suite 1
Pasadena, CA
*Skills: Custom computer programming in BASIC, Pascal, C,
and C++. Custom database system development.
Information flow analysis. Productivity enhancement, systems
design, and implementation. Training.*

Alamo Computers   510-820-1399
Michael Ambrose
P.O. Box 875
Alamo , CA 94507
*Skills: Macintosh Communications Toolbox, System 7
programming, QuickTime, THINK C, Symantec C++, MPW,
AOCE/PowerTalk programming, PowerPC.*

Antley Business Systems   612-542-9651
Bob Antley
5217 Wayzata Blvd., Suite 213
Minneapolis, MN 55416
*Skills: Helix Express, database design and construction, user-
friendly interface design.*

Applied Technology   713-981-4747
Associates, Inc.
T.L. Pontius
9301 S.W. Freeway, Suite 465
Houston, TX 77074
*Skills: ATA develops software in C, C++, FORTRAN, and
Assembler.*

Arborworks, Inc.   800-346-6980
John Van Rockel
431 Virginia Avenue
Ann Arbor, MI 48103
Skills: THINK C, C++, Pascal, assembly language.

Ariel Software Consultants, Inc.   312-764-3434
David J. Cowen
2827 W. Sherwin Avenue
Chicago, IL 60645-1239
Skills: Database analysis, design, and programming.

Art & Logic   818-501-6990
Justin Souter
P.O. Box 56465
Sherman Oaks, CA 91413
Skills: C++, C, 680x0, UI design, hardware interfacing.

B & L Associates, Inc.   800-594-7494
Bob Greenblatt
2 Northfield Court
Lambertville, NJ 08530
*Skills: Multiplatform applications development using
Microsoft Excel.*

Bear River Associates, Inc.   510-644-9400
Anthony Meadow
P.O. Box 1900
Berkeley, CA 94701
*Skills: C++, C, Windows, A/UX, UNIX, VAX/VMS, IBM,
Pascal, FORTRAN, LISP, COBOL.*

Boxes & Arrows Inc.   904-446-4908
Frank Sweet
5111-6 Baymeadows Rd., Suite 255
Jacksonville, FL 32217
Skills: C++, MPW, Pascal, MacApp 2+3, DOS.

Braided Matrix, Inc.   914-657-6411
Lincoln Stoller
148 DuBois Road
Shokau, NY 12481
*Skills: 4th Dimension programming and software design,
systems specification and development*

Bruce, Bruce & Bruce   410-526-3791
David Champney
4100 Butler Road
Glundon, MD 21071
Skills: 4th Dimension, COBOL, SAS, BASIC, IBM, OS/MVS.

Business Brothers, Inc.   612-853-3024
David B. Kingsman
3105 E. 80th Street, Suite C270
Bloomington, MN 55425-1507
Skills: 4th Dimension (primary), other supporting languages as necessary for externals to 4th Dimension.

CF Software   708-824-7180
Rogers Faden
2454 E. Dempster
Des Plains, IL 60016
Skills: PC to mainframe connectivity experts, specializing in data transfer.

Charles Cooper Consulting   317-892-4588
Charles S. Cooper
P.O. Box 206
Pittsboro, IN 46167
Skills: 4th Dimension design and programming.

Cheshire Group   707-887-7510
Shirley Grant
321 S. Main Street, #36
Sebastapol, CA 95472
Skills: C and C++ programming; PostScript and Acrobat PDF programming; Macintosh and Windows development.

Christopher Gross   813-572-1149
Christopher Gross
2333 Feather Sound Drive, #A701
Clearwater, FL 34622
Skills: C, C++, Assembler-Animation, sound, user interface, programming, design.

Complete Data Solutions   512-329-6161
Marianne Linde
1301-B Capital of Texas Highway, Suite 123
Austin, TX 78746
Skills: CDS specializes in developing and integrating multiplatform client/server solutions. Our skills include Oracle, Sybase, Omnis 7, 4th Dimension, FileMaker Pro, Blacksmith.

COMPUTER: Applications Inc.   919-846-1411
Steve Pierce
12813 Lindley Drive
Raleigh, NC 27614
Skills: Assembly, C, C++ Object, Pascal, layout.

Computer Science Innovations, Inc.   407-676-2923
Jeffrey Seebeck
1235 Evans Road
Melbourne, Fl 32904
Skills: Computer aided dispatch, automatic meter reading, software development, integrating text, GUI development, RDBMs, mathematical analysis, pattern recognition, neural networks, knowledge-based expert systems.

members

Concurrent Engineering   **602-464-8208**
Tools, Inc.
Bob Tipton
1115 N. Delmar Street, Suite B
Mesa, AZ 85203
Skills: C++, Object Pascal, System 7, Scripting, AE Object model, Macintosh OS (CDEVs, DRVRs, trap patches, etc.), radar scattering, radar signal processing, 3D graphics, AppleTalk & PPC, AOCE, PostScript.

Consulting Solutions, Inc.   **718-275-8976**
Steven S. Gold
100-25 Queens Boulevard
Forest Hills, NY 11375
Skills: DBase, Clipper, Visual BASIC, COBOL, C, communications, Windows, OS/2, NetWare, advanced relational database design, systems analysis.

Copious Systems   **805-528-2685**
Richard Leddy
P.O. Box 6703
Los Osos, CA 93412
Skills: C++, software design, numerical math, AI optimization, symbolic programming, real-time programming.

CORGROUP   **203-458-9363**
Ralph Bosson
P.O. BOX 1265
Madison, CT 06443
Skills: Object-oriented, prograph CPX environment.

Creative Enterprises   **310-987-3450**
Sonni Cooper
5354 East 2nd Street, Suite 200
Long Beach, CA 90803
Skills: Multimedia, 2 D and 3D graphic screen applications, multilingual, technical backgrounds, cultural and minority interests.

Data Solutions, Inc.   **303-444-7969**
Scott Roy
1790 30th Street, Suite 308
Boulder, CO 80301
Skills: Experts in Paradox PAL, Paradox Windows, OPAL, Quattro Pro.

DataMasters   **301-831-0183**
Bruce L. Brossart
6121 Ridgeline Drive
Mt. Airy, MD 21771
Skills: Case Tools (e.g. ERD), SQL, OS/2, PL/1, REXX.

Demometricka   **310-390-6380**
Diane Ahlem, Charles Swartz
P.O. Box 66689
Los Angeles, CA 90066
Skills: Data analysis employing demographic and statistical techniques; PAL programming: programming Paradox applications using PAL in conjunction with WaitPlus Pro; SAS programming; systems design and analysis for single and multiple platform applications; system and end user documentation.

Desjardin Consulting   **510-659-1546**
Bill Desjardin
43643 Skye Road
Fremont, CA 94539
Skills: 4th Dimension custom programming.

---

referral network

DFC Enterprises Inc.   714-497-0611
Jay Rubin
985 Coast View Drive
Laguna Beach, CA 92651
Skills: Custom programming FoxPro/FoxBase Windows, DOS and Macintosh, individual training.

Digital Information Gallery   716-832-2861
Philip T. Glinski
2316 Delaware Avenue, Suite 293
Buffalo, NY 14216
Skills: Object-oriented application development: visual user interface design; multimedia content production and integration. Languages include C, C++, SmallTalk, Visual BASIC, and others. Cross- platform development.

EDR Consulting Services, Inc.   801-797-7318
Emil Ratti
P.O. BOX 172
Fair Lawn, NJ 07410
Skills: Programming RPG, RPG/400, OCL systems design and implementation.

Edu-Tech Associates, Inc.   407-952-0745
Doris Hertzberg
228 Loggerhead Drive, P.O. Box 510340
Melbourne Beach, FL 32951
Skills: Word processing, graphics, desktop publishing, spreadsheets, customized databases, accounting.

Exodus Software   513-522-0011
Edward M. Lutz, Jr.
800 Compton Road, Suite 9240
Cincinnati, Ohio 45231-3848
Skills: Database development, C, assembly, MacApp, PostScript, Object Pascal development, HyperCard/SuperCard development, mainframe connectivity.

Fresh Software and Instructional Design   510-524-0852
Bill Hofmann
1640 San Pablo Avenue, #C
Berkeley, CA 94702
Skills: Software specification development (C, C++, Assembler, Macintosh Communications Toolbox, PowerPC), technical training development and delivery.

Good Northwest   206-842-7164
Bill Good
321 High School Road, Suite 325
Bainbridge Island, WA 98110
Skills: Software development (project management, design, coding, testing, documentation) C++ and FORTRAN, Oracle database, video production, multimedia applications, geophysical data acquisition, geophysical data processing and interpretation, geographical information systems.

Heritage Computer Consulting & Services   913-268-1469
Arlene Watkins
6314 Acuff
Shawnee, KS 66216
Skills: Object PAL, COBOL, Visual BASIC, Wang 220, BASIC 2.

Honeybee Software Inc.   800-667-1233
James McBeath
5 East 47th Street
New York, NY 10017
Skills: 4th Dimension, Pascal, C++ programming, MIS services, software support, accounting, software development, Apple Events, AppleScript programming, DTP, design, support.

members

HyperActive Software   612-724-1596
Jacqueline Landman Gay
5226 W. Nokomis Parkway
Minneapolis, MN 55417
*Skills: HyperCard (HyperTalk), SuperCard, multimedia,
FileMaker Pro, MS Word, PageMaker, applications
development, programming.*

Information Systems   708-887-1911
Technology, Inc.
Martin Volk
911 N. Elm Street, Suite 310
Hinsdale, Illinois 60521
*Skills: Programming languages: Assembler, C++, MPW,
THINK C, Watcom C, LabView, Mathlab, FORTRAN, DOS,
Windows, signal/image processing, PC/Macintosh hardware
development.*

International Accessability   408-454-0200
Corporation
Susan Chester
500 Chestnut Street, Suite 200
Santa Cruz, CA 95060-3602
*Skills: Software localization, development, engineering,
desktop publishing.*

InterOptica Publishing   415-788-8788
Limited
Victor Medina
300 Montgomery Street, Suite 201
San Francisco, CA 94104

IronMike Software   404-687-9646
Miles Waldron
1015 Eastlake Drive
Decatur, GA 30030
*Skills: Five years experience with C, two years experience
with C++, OOPs, publishing, journalism, object- oriented
programming and design.*

Jonoke Software   403-448-3647
Development, Inc.
Jody Bevan
10123-99th Street, Suite 580
Edmonton, Alberta T5J 3H2 Canada
Skills: Networking, system integration, 4th Dimension.

Karow Associates, Inc.   410-276-4016
Charles Karow
2208 E. Baltimore Street
Baltimore, MD 21231 2001
Skills: C, C++, Visual BASIC, DBase, Clipper.

Knowledge Factory   612-890-8292
Jeff Iverson
2800 Selkirk Drive, Suite C-104
Burnsville, MN 55337-5662
Skills: Oracle, PowerBuilder, Authorware, HyperCard.

Le Blanc Consulting Group   203-849-7737
Paul LeBlanc
324 Main Avenue, Suite 204
Norwalk, CT 06851

MacSourcery   619-747-2980
James Roberts
P.O. Box 461537
Escondido, CA 92046
*Skills: Macintosh programming: C, C++, PowerPC, and
testing.*

MacXperts, Inc.   804-353-7122
Karen Cauthen
3228 L. West Cary Street
Richmond, VA 23221
*Skills: Specialize in writing custom Macintosh and Newton
software.*

---

referral network

Master Software, Inc. 510-975-0650
Meryl Natchez
1148 Alpine Road, #204
Walnut Creek, CA 94596
Skills: C, C++, THINK C, SmallTalk, MitemView,
HyperCard, COBOL, SCOBOL, DAL, RSC, Object PAL,
Visual BASIC, Visual C++, SQL, Oracle, IBM Utilities, etc.

McGilly Information 514-933-2323
Systems, Inc.
Richard McGilly
4030 Saint-Ambroise, #440
Montreal, Quebec H4C 2C7 Canada
Skills: Client/server application development using Omnis 7.
Macintosh and Windows multiplatform development.

Medical Database Systems 619-558-2002
Tony Loeffler
6450 Lusk Boulevard, Suite E104
San Diego, CA 92121

Metafact Technology Inc. 604-244-9662
Michael Lo
155-10751 Shellbridge Way
Richmond, BC V6X 2W8 Canada
Skills: Localization, AppleGlot, ResEdit, Macintosh System
7.1, 7.1TC, 7.1SC, 7.1K, 7.1J, MPW C++, C, Pascal,
Assembler, THINK C, MacBug.

MicroWorks Businessworld, Inc. 212-932-0001
305 Riverside Drive, Suite 4A
New York, NY 10025

Mindstorm, Inc. 510-644-3902
Burt Johnson
88 Oak Ridge Road
Berkeley, CA 94705
Skills: C, C++, SQL.

Montage Software 203-834-1144
Systems Inc.
Jim Alonso
228 Dan Built Road, P.O. Box 7574
Wilton, CT 06897-7574
Skills: 4th Dimension, cross-platform integration,
client/server, some C for external development.

Nelson Laffey Associates, Inc. 314-436-9725
Bud Schilling
1919 Park Avenue
St. Louis, MO 63104
Skills: C, C++, OOPs, financial process controls for
manufacturing, MRP and inventory programming.

New Media, Inc. 216-481-7900
Leonard Pagon Jr.
503 E. 200th Street, Suite 202
Cleveland, OH 44119
Skills: Object-oriented design and development, client/server
design and development, graphic interface design.

Northwest Data Services, Inc. 206-252-7287
Jack Wilson, Jr.
2418 California Avenue, Suite A
Everett, WA 98201
Skills: NDS supports Open Systems Technology compliance
guidelines under the MS-DOS and UNIX based operating
system platforms. Development languages supported
include Informix 4gl, MS FoxPro for DOS, Macintosh and
UNIX, MS Visual BASIC and Visual C++. Cross-platform
development.

PaperClip Products   800-497-5508
Kirk Kerekes
4308 S. Peoria, #763
Tulsa, OK 74105
Skills: Interface design, THINK C and C++. Extensions and definition procedures, translating engineering concepts into software, hardware/software integration.

Pinpoint Solutions   415-962-9857
Charles L. Lloyd
2095 Landings Drive
Mountian View, CA 94043
Skills: Visual BASIC, Visual C++, Access BASIC, PAL, Object PAL, C, C++.

PMS Microdesign, Inc.   412-731-4004
Phillip M. Sauter
1904 Brushcliff Road
Pittsburgh, PA 15221
Skills: Engineering-microcomputer, analog, digital, software (Assembler, BASIC, scripting, OSA), circuit board layout, multimedia production, virtual reality system design, virtual reality product design.

PowerHouse Programmers   510-946-0904
Leonard Barton
P.O. Box 2147
Walnut Creek, CA 94595
Skills: C, C++, PowerPC Macintosh programming, 68K assembly, Macintosh Communications Toolbox, RISC, THINK C, MetroWerks, MPW, Projector, DSP, MS Windows, graphics.

Prototype Systems, Inc.   201-998-5850
Yung Lin
10 Woodland Avenue, Suite 31
Kearny, NJ 07032-1968
Skills: FoxPro, Novell NetWare (CNE) consulting service.

Rae Technology, Inc.   408-725-2850
Norman Gilmore
19672 Stevens Creek Blvd.
Cupertino, CA 95014
Skills: 4th Dimension, C++, Visual BASIC, MacApp.

Reusable Solutions Inc.   503-223-6892
Karen Gillis
1130 S.W. Morrison Street, #318
Portland, OR 97205
Skills: Object-oriented databases, client/server design, object-oriented languages, analysis, project management.

Rhyton Software   408-626-1250
Les Vogel
10 Mal Paso Road
Carmel, CA 93923

Shapiro & Company   805-962-8109
Harv Shapiro
1650 Loma Street
Santa Barbara, CA 93103-2022
Skills: SQL, REXX, C, C++, DB2/2.

Shell Systems, Ltd.   910-996-1757
Jill Merriam-Knotts
471 Buckhurst Drive
Kernersville, NC 27284
Skills: Omnis 5, Omnis 7, Omnis 72, PageMaker, MS Word, MS Excel, OS2, Knowledgeware/ADW, Microfocus Workbench, Windows, PowerBuilder, Sybase, MVS/XA, TSO/SPF, OS/VS COBOL, VS COBOL, VS COBOLII, CICS/VS, BMS, Natural, DYL280, SAS, ADABASE/Adamint, Assembler, Easytrieve Plus, IMS/DLI, IMS/CICS, Telon,DB2, QMF, KBMS, Quickjob.

referral network

Simetra Systems   **310-640-6878**
Margaret Cook
P.O. Box 998-1013
El Segundo, CA 90245
Skills: Database design and implementation; H/W design and implementation; business graphics automation

SoftEngine   **619-549-0907**
Paul Stannard
9777 Caminito Pudregal
San Diego, CA 92131
Skills: Product design and specification; Macintosh Communications Toolbox programming; MS Windows programming; C programming

Southern Horizons   **404-552-6875**
Corporation
Jerry West
325 North Peak Drive
Alpharetta, GA 30202 5269
Skills: Paradox PAL heavy, Object PAL medium.

SpectraLogic, Inc.   **404-874-4200**
Chris Tyburski
430 Tenth Street, Suite 206
Atlanta, GA 30318
Skills: Applications development, systems integration, multiplatform development.

Stonecutter Software   **209-966-3066**
Don Sawtelle
2748 Cricket Hill Road
Mariposa, CA 95338
Skills: MACAPP, TCL, C++, NewtonScript, Macromedia Director, Prograph, SmallTalk, Object Pascal, SQL, Common USP, HyperTalk, various databases and database servers, etc. Computer control of hardware (Laser Disk, VTR, etc.). TCP/IP, Internet, and Macintosh e-mail based client/server applications.

STR Corporation   **703-758-1100**
Pat Kaczmarek
10700 Parkridge Blvd
Reston, VA 22091
Skills: 3GL/4GL software development, database development, database training, artificial intelligence, operations research, factory and industrial automation.

Strategic Micro Systems   **717-871-9126**
Lisa Ressler
310 Windgate Court
Millersville, PA 17551
Skills: PAL, COBOL, Clipper, Object PAL, Pascal, NetWare.

The SU5 Group   **817-870-2557**
Kenneth Clark
1701 River Run Road, #603
Fort Worth, Tx 76107
Skills: C, C++.

The Visaeon Corporation   **914-939-2579**
Paul Merriam-Knotts
33 Greenwood Avenue
Port Chester, NY 10573
Skills: C, C++, Visual BASIC, DBase, MS Access, AS/400 COBOL.

Turning Point Software   **617-332-0202**
Ken Carson
One Gateway Center
Newton, MA 02158

Unlimited Access   **415-255-8958**
Bren Besser
529 Noe Street
San Francisco, CA 94114
Skills: 4th Dimension, SQL, HyperTalk, Advanced Revelation, Visual BASIC.

members

Vintage Consulting Group   707-939-8387
Jay Hill
P.O. Box 1805
Sonoma, CA 95476
Skills: System design, project management, Visual BASIC, XBase, SQL, C, Pascal, Paradox, Crystal Reports.

Visions Software   617-246-6260
Giorgio Pironi
338 Main Street, Suite 303
Wakefield, MA 01880
Skills: MacApp, MFC, TCL, Visual BASIC.

ViviStar Consulting   602-483-3123
Jonathan Hess
7015 E. Aster Drive
Scottsdale, AZ 85254
Skills: Object-oriented design and programming, structured analysis and design (SA/SD), event language programming, automatons, lex, yacc, and many 3D graphic techniques.

Wizdom Micro Systems, Inc.   602-567-5011
James Trammell
P.O. Box 5444
Lake Montezuma, AZ 86342
Skills: C, Pascal, BASIC, SQL, 4th Dimension, graphic design.

Workplace   818-407-0010
Leon Rubins
21550 Oxnard Street, 3rd Floor
Woodland Hills CA 91367

▣ MARKETING & DISTRIBUTION ▣

Fortune & Associates   415-494-9919
Daniel Fortune
3962 Nelson Court
Palo Alto, CA 94306
Skills: Design, writing, communications, project management, innovations in development and production, translating complex tasks into easy, friendly product.

Scott Satovsky, Sat's Graphics   810-354-4333
Scott Satovsky
28455 North Western Highway
Southfield, MI 48034

▣ MULTIMEDIA ▣

21st Century Media   818-848-4543
James Lambert
1066 Clybourne Avenue
Burbank, CA 91505
Skills: Layout, HyperTalk, SuperTalk.

21st Century Media   414-771-8906
Nancy Cavanaugh
1224 A Glenview Avenue
Milwaukee, WI 53213
Skills: Layout, HyperTalk, SuperTalk.

850 Productions Inc.   312-642-8520
Manny Medelson
10 East Ontario, #4507
Chicago, IL 60611
Skills: World class composer, orchestrator, sound design.

referral network

Aaron Marcus &   510-601-0994
Associates, Inc.
Aaron Marcus
1144 65th Street, Suite F
Emeryville, CA 94608 1109
Skills: Lingo scripting, usability analysis, graphic design, icon/symbol design, technical editing, illustration, map/chart/diagram design, information design.

Art & Logic   818-501-6990
Justin Souter
P.O. Box 56465
Sherman Oaks, CA 91413
Skills: C++, C, 680x0, UI design, hardware interfacing.

Claire Moore   716-645-2085
Instructional Design
Claire Moore
1256 Shirley Way
Lincoln, CA 95248
Skills: Instructional design, Authorware Pro, CBT design production and presentation.

DigitalFacades Corporation   310-208-0776
John Lin
1140 Westwood Blvd
Los Angeles, CA 90024
Skills: Layout, interface design, animation, 3D modeling, CAD, packaging design, desktop video, brochure design, presentation design.

Dolphin Multimedia, Inc.   415-354-0800
Cynthia Kondratieff
2440 Embarcadero Way
Palo Alto, CA 94303
Skills: Presentation design and objectives, audience definition; video preproduction, production, and post-production; multimedia from concept to delivery.

Honeybee Software Inc.   800-667-1233
James McBeath
5 East 47th Street
New York, NY 10017
Skills: 4th Dimension, Pascal, C++ programming, MIS services, software support, accounting, software development, Apple Events, AppleScript programming, DTP, design, support.

InfoUse   510-549-6520
Lewis Kraus
2560 Ninth Street, Suite 216
Berkeley, CA 94710
Skills: Programming, graphics, videography, video editing, instructional design.

Kamen Audio Productions/   212-575-4660
CD Archives
James Barry
701 7th Avenue, 6th Floor
New York, NY 10036
Skills: Audio programming, video encoding, 3D graphic design. Presentation layout, MPEG encoding, QuickTime.

KMS Systems, Inc.   713-363-9154
George Mallard
P.O. Box 7857
The Woodlands, TX 77887
Skills: Programming, system design and installation.

Lingua Service Associates   206-448-8404
Garrett Cobarr
66 Bell Street, #101
Seattle, WA 98121 1600
Skills: Authoring in all major Macintosh multimedia animation and asset production for other platforms, image manipulation/photo enhancement.

members

Media Direct, Inc.   201-894-5548
David Kaplan
P.O. Box 302
Tenafly, NJ 07670
Skills: Needs analysis, system design, programming, writing.

Media Kinematics   510-674-1282
Kime H. Smith, Jr.
900 San Simeon Drive
Concord, CA 94518
Skills: Object-oriented design and programming for Macintosh and UNIX. Rapid applications prototyping for Macintosh and UNIX. User interface design and conceptual design.

NB Engineering   410-721-5725
Karl Von Schwartz
2110 Priest Bridge Drive
Crofton, MD 21114
Skills: Custom "C" language development under a variety of O/s: DOS, Windows, Os/2, Novell.

On-Line Design, Inc.   404-325-2977
Greg Weil
1006 North Crossing Way
Decatur, GA
Skills: Authorized Macromedia Developer. Authorized Apple Multimedia Developer.

Paradigm Interactive, Inc.   910-768-7844
Ron Jones, Matt Dalia
1531-D Westbrook Plaza Drive
Winston-Salem, NC 27103
Skills: Programming; design (information, interface, graphics); sound editing; video editing; networking.

Perkins/Boyer   415-346-8820
Digital Productions
T.D. Perkins
1377 Fulton, Suite #3
San Francisco, CA 94117
Skills: Macromedia Director authoring, copywriting, script story boards, marketing, direct mail, design, animation, video capture and editing, packaging and project management.

PMS Microdesign, Inc.   412-731-4004
Phillip M. Sauter
1904 Brushcliff Road
Pittsburgh, PA 15221
Skills: Engineering-microcomputer, analog, digital, software (Assembler, BASIC, scripting, OSA), circuit board layout, multimedia production, virtual reality system design, virtual reality product design.

Presentation   404-393-3820
Technologies, Inc.
Pierre Thiault
30 Basswood Circle
Atlanta, GA 30328
Skills: 3D and 2D animation, sound and video, CD-ROM, kiosk development, multimedia programming.

The Human Element, Inc.   513-745-9204
Joseph P. Lanham
7842 Cooper Road
Cincinatti, OH 45242
Skills: Multimedia development, graphics, animation, instructional design, interactive design.

The Voice Emporium   718-522-7533
Dan Ogden
505 Court Street, Suite 6J
Brooklyn, NY 11231
Skills: Voiceover artist. Multimedia audio, animation characters.

referral network

TouchMedia   **804-464-2191**
Jim Bain
4950 Lauderdale Avenue
Virginia Beach, VA 23455-1328
Skills: Project management, programming, interface design, media integration.

Treehouse Computer Services   **713-356-7926**
Brian Hecht
40310 Three Forks Road
Houston, TX 77355
Skills: C, C++, ToolBook, Visual BASIC, Multimedia Viewer, RoboHelp (online documentation), database/local area network integration, client/server, DOS/Windows development, Windows authoring and graphic development, Apple/PC cross-platform applications.

Unlimited Access   **415-255-8958**
Bren Besser
529 Noe Street
San Francisco, CA 94114
Skills: 4th Dimension, SQL, HyperTalk, Advanced Revelation, Visual BASIC.

Wildware   **415-322-9086**
Tom Neuman
307 Grayson Court
Menlo Park, CA 94025
Skills: Macromedia Director, Lingo Programming, HyperCard, HyperTalk programming, Illustrator, Painter, KAIS Power Tools, Ray Dream Designer, 3D, Logomotion, add-depth, instructional design, project management, interface design.

▣ NETWORKING ▣

Alan M. Gordon Consulting   **516-374-6414**
Alan Gordon
51 Valley Lane East
North Woodmere, NY 11581
Skills: FilemakerPro database programming, system troubleshooting and repair.

Arcom Electronics, Inc.   **408-452-0678**
Jim Vye
1735 N. First Street, Suite 101
San Jose, CA 95112
Skills: Technical services, consultation/design, installation, contractors' certification, maintenance, service, and support.

Crossroad Systems   **800-435-7636**
Robert Kinnin
20 Garden Street, Suite 6
Rhinebeck, NY 12572
Skills: Database design, document imaging, network integration.

Gordian   **714-850-0205**
John Kalucki
20361 Irvine Avenue
Santa Ana Heights, CA 92707
Skills: Total product development—hardware and software design and implementation, circuit board layout, gate array design, operating systems, multiprocessor design, protocol stacks, GUIs, documentation, production support, etc.

Greenline Electronics   **617-422-8644**
James Green
10 Post Office Square, #600
Boston, MA 02109
Skills: Installation of cross-platform networks, hardware, software.

members

Integrated Management   **508-897-7064**
Resources, Inc
Michael Maynard
119 Adams Drive
Stow, MA 01775
Skills: Systems design and analysis, business systems process analysis, management consulting, interim management, systems development, and implementation.

KMS Systems, Inc.   **713-363-9154**
George Mallard
P.O. Box 7857
The Woodlands, TX 77887
Skills: Programming, system design and installation.

Nelson Laffey Associates, Inc.   **314-436-9725**
Bud Schilling
1919 Park Avenue
St. Louis, MO 63104
Skills: C, C++, OOPs, financial process controls for manufacturing, MRP and inventory programming.

New Media, Inc.   **216-481-7900**
Leonard Pagon Jr.
503 E. 200th Street, Suite 202
Cleveland, OH 44119
Skills: Object-oriented design and development, client/server design and development, graphic interface design.

Software Engineering   **910-855-0922**
Consultants, Inc.
RaeAnn Dixon
5710-K High Point Road, Suite 155
Greensboro, NC 27407

South Sound Software   **206-456-4103**
Art Carter
5937 44th Way NE
Olympia, WA 98516
Skills: OOP, systems design, systems analysis.

Warever Computing, Inc.   **800-WAREVER**
Jeff Sherman
10961 Palms Boulevard
Los Angeles, CA 90034-6130

Zocalo Engineering   **510-540-8000**
Bill Woodcock
2355 Virginia Street
Berkeley CA 94709-1315
Skills: Interface design, layout, and flow control on a wide range of platforms. Interface element creation and rendering. General bitmap and object-oriented illustration and rendering. Icon-based, frame, and QuickTime animation.

▣ PUBLISHING ▣

Curves   **510-601-1032**
Gail Holian
4124 Shafter Ave.
Oakland, CA 94609
Skills: Corporate identity programs, newsletters, advertising campaigns, direct mail.

PEMD Education Group   **707-894-3668**
Ernest Rosenberg
35000 Highway 128
Cloverdale, CA 95425
Skills: Information services, educational consulting, programming (Object Pascal, MacApp, HyperTalk, BASIC).

referral network

Software Solutions, Inc.   510-426-6751
Mark Van Alstine
4269 Garibaldi Place
Pleasanton, CA 94566
Skills: THINK C, MPW C, PostScript, QuickDraw GX, System 7, THINK C++, Mac Easy Open, XTND, printer drivers, INIT, Debuggers.

Tech Prose   510-975-0660
Meryl Natchez
1725 Springbrook Road
Lafayette, CA 94549

◙ SUPPORT ◙

DriveSavers, Inc.   415-883-4232
Scott Gaidanol
400 Bel Marin Keys Blvd.
Novato, CA 94949
Skills: Data recovery/repair of hard drives, opticals, and removables.

DT & T Macintosh Services   800-622-7977
TD
586 Weddell Drive, Suite 1
Sunnyvale, CA 94089
Skills: Components level repair for all Macintosh products.

New Ledger   619-558-0222
Elizabeth Fields
4350 La Jolla Village Drive, #300
San Diego, CA 92122

Porter & Porter   708-350-9090
Vivienne Porter
1069 Bryn Mawr Avenue
Bensenville, IL 60106

STR Corporation   703-758-1100
Pat Kaczmarek
10700 Parkridge Blvd
Reston, VA 22091
Skills: 3GL/4GL software development, database development, database training, artificial intelligence, operations research, factory and industrial automation.

Tech Prose   510-975-0660
Meryl Natchez
1725 Springbrook Road
Lafayette, CA 94549

**Wong, Pamela L.,
Macintosh Consulting**   415-388-0668
Pamela Wong
116 Carlotta Circle, #9
Mill Valley, CA 94941

AN Mz MEDIA GROUP PUBLICATION

AGORA
Digital Marketplace

Talent Listings

The Fastest Way

to find Computer Services

and Solution Providers

High technology

New media

This is not new.

San Francisco   Red Sky Interactive   415 421 7332

35
Custom Solutions

*This section highlights specialized
computing solutions from service providers
who integrate hardware, software and
services to create custom solutions for clients.*

Document Management 36

Finance/Accounting 36

Human Resources 36

**Manufacturing/
  Production** 37

Marketing & Sales 37

Mobile Computing 38

Project Management 38

BEAR RIVER ASSOCIATES, INC.
P.O. Box 1900
Berkeley, CA 94701-1900
Contact: Rodney Smith, Anthony Meadow
Phone: 510-644-9400
Fax: 510-644-9778
AppleLink: BEARRIVER
Skills: Programming, systems integration, training, and consulting for Macintosh, Windows, and Newton platforms. Complete range of services, from product development to in-house systems. Curriculum includes Macintosh technology, OOP, AppleTalk, Newton, and VITAL.

ELB CONSULTING
P.O. Box 30056
Tucson, AZ 85751
Contact: Emile Bourdelier
Phone: 602-886-2646
Fax: 602-298-5419
Skills: PRINT AUTOMATION: Improve the effectiveness of your data processing printing operation. Analysis, requirements, cost-benefit, equipment selection, configuration, layout.

TURNKEY COMPUTER SYSTEMS, INC.
401 Second Avenue, Suite 25D
New York, NY 10010-4057
Phone: 212-779-8445
Fax: 212-696-4527
Internet: turnkeysys@delphi.com
Projects: We are committed to providing professionally designed and supported software for businesses. We assist businesses in selecting the proper combination of packaged and custom software and hardware that best fits their requirements. Member ICCA/IEEE.

DOCUMENT MANAGEMENT

Bear River Associates, Inc.
Berkeley, CA   510-644-9400
Please See Company Highlight Page 36.

Cordant Imaging Systems
W. Boxford, MA   508-352-5500

Data Flow Systems
Dallas, TX   214-746-4882

ELB Consulting
Tucson, AZ   602-886-2646
Please See Company Highlight Page 36.

GenText, Inc.
Dallas, TX   214-691-0300

Go Technology, Inc.
San Gabriel, CA   818-281-9409

Infrastructures for Information Inc.
Toronto, ON Canada
                      416-920-6489

Interlinear Technology, Inc.
Alameda, CA   510-748-6850

Montgomery Consulting Group, Inc.
Blue Springs, MO   816-224-4100

Southern Computer Systems
Birmingham, AL   205-251-2985

Wessex Corporation
Richardson, TX   214-384-2894

FINANCE/ACCOUNTING

Account Ware Distributors.
Concord, ON Canada
                      905-738-4508

American Software
Mesa, AZ   602-834-1579

Bizware Corporation
Englewood Cliffs, NJ 201-816-9271

Bottom Line Consulting
Weston, CT   203-454-1727

Darmstadter Designs
Lufkin, TX   409-632-3549

Micro Business Software
Plainview, NY   800-354-MICR

Tab Computer Systems
Bloomfield, CT   203-286-8410

Tanner Software Development
Greenwood Village, CO
                      303-689-0720

Task Force, Inc.
New York, NY   212-777-4280

TurnKey Computer Systems, Inc.
New York, NY   212-779-8445
Please See Company Highlight Page 36.

HUMAN RESOURCES

Cyborg Systems, Inc.
Chicago, IL   312-454-1865

Pierian Spring Software
Portland, OR   503-222-2044

RSG International
San Diego, CA   619-259-6890

Skunk Works Multimedia, Inc.
Collegeville, PA   610-489-0895

Solo Systems
Plano, TX   214-612-8425

**Technoliteracy
Development Company**
Mt. Vernon, WA   206-856-6080

William M. Mercer, Inc.
Deerfield, IL   708-317-7615

MANUFACTURING/ PRODUCTION

LRM Consultants International, LC
Glendale, AZ

Manex SPRL
Boncelles, Belgium   32 41 380 368

Nelson Laffey Associates, Inc.
St. Louis, MO   314-436-9725
Please See Company Highlight Page 37.

TurnKey Computer Systems, Inc.
New York, NY   212-779-8445

MARKETING & SALES

Appropriate Solutions, Inc.
Peterborough, NH   603-924-6079

Blenks International
Germany   31-41-13 3333

CCS Enterprises, Inc.
Easton, MD   410-820-4670

**CIS Communication and
Information Services**
Boone, NC   704-264-5643

Consensus
Cheshire, England
          44-0625-537777

Larry Wisch Associates
San Francisco, CA   415-495-4959

NELSON LAFFEY ASSOCIATES, INC.
1919 Park Avenue
St. Louis, MO 63104
Contact: Linda Laffey,
General Manager
Phone: 314-436-9725
Fax: 314-436-1629
Skills: C, C++, LISP, OOP, Major
Networks, Paradox, FileMaker
Pro, OS/2, Windows, A/UX, Excel,
S/I.
Projects: Networking computers
and data communications
projects; factory floor automation;
electronic transmittal and receipt
of data; quality control and status
software; subscription control
system.
Clients: Ralston Purina, Edward
D. Jones & Co., Optec Sales of
America, C.BIS Federal, Pulsar
Data Systems, Saddle and Bridle
magazines.

NEW MEDIA, INC.
503 E. 200th Street, Suite 202
Cleveland , OH 44119-1543
Contact: Leonard W. Pagon, Jr.,
President
Phone: 216-481-7900
Fax: 216-481-1570
AppleLink: NEWMEDIA
Skills:We offer a full range of
client/server and workflow
development and certified training
with tools such as PowerBuilder,
Visual BASIC, Access, Windows
NT, SQL server, Lotus Notes, C++.
We are a certified Public
PowerBuilder education site and
development partners.

DOCUMENT
MANAGEMENT

FINANCE/
ACCOUNTING

HUMAN RESOURCES

MANUFACTURING/
PRODUCTION

MARKETING &
SALES

MOBILE COMPUTING

PROJECT
MANAGEMENT

ART & LOGIC
P.O. Box 56465
Sherman Oaks, CA 91413
Contact: Justin Souter, Partner
Phone: 818-501-6990
Fax: 818-995-8669
AppleLink: J.SOUTER
Skills: C++, assembly, MacApp,
MFC, and OWL.

BEAR RIVER ASSOCIATES, INC.
P.O. Box 1900
Berkeley, CA 94701-1900
Contact: Rodney Smith, Anthony
Meadow
Phone: 510-644-9400
Fax: 510-644-9778
AppleLink: BEARRIVER
Skills: Programming, systems
integration, training, and
consulting for Macintosh,
Windows, and Newton platforms.
Complete range of services, from
product development to in-house
systems. Curriculum includes
Macintosh technology, OOP,
AppleTalk, Newton, and VITAL.

CREATIVE ENTERPRISES
5354 East 2nd Street, Suite 200
Long Beach, CA 90803
Contact: Sonni Cooper, President
Phone: 310-987-3450
Fax: 310-987-3449
AppleLink: CREATIVE
Skills: Cross-platform
multimedia—all relevant current
tools. Macromedia, Apple Media
Tool. Pen-based (AST, Toshiba,
Samsung, Newton) developers.
Microsoft Network member. Visual
BASIC, C++, Object
Pascal, others.

LeadingWay Corporation
Irvine, CA   714-453-1112

National Management Systems
Vienna, VA   703-827-0797

New Media, Inc.
Cleveland, OH   216-481-7900
Please See Company Highlight Page 37.

Ra Data A.S.
Tonsberg, Norway   47 33317707

SaleMaker Corporation
Salem, NH   603-893-2422

Teknowledgy
Eden Prairie, MN   612-946-0106

Trilogy Development Group
Austin, TX   512-794-5900

MOBILE COMPUTING

Art & Logic.
Sherman Oaks, CA   818-501-6990
Please See Company Highlight Page 38.

Avalon Engineering, Inc.
Boston, MA   617-247-7668
Please See Ad Page 37.

Bear River Associates, Inc.
Berkeley, CA   510-644-9400
Please See Company Highlight Page 38.

Commstalk
Herts, England   0727-827146

corder associates, inc.
Phoenix, AZ   602-993-8914

Creative Enterprises
Long Beach, CA   310-987-3450
Please See Company Highlight Page 38.

INFO grafix, Inc.
Atlanta, GA   404-607-1970

Magna
San Jose, CA   408-282-0900.

Rod Williams Resource Group
Aptos, CA   408-685-9431

The Alternate Approach
Agoura Hills, CA   818-889-6035

Waverly Software Design
Palo Alto, CA   413-322-4414

PROJECT MANAGEMENT

Agie Seife Associates, Inc.
Upper Nyack, NY   914-358-5707

Comacon, Inc.
Wilmington, DE   302-764-1984

Dipl.-Ing. Thomas Gamisch
Holzkirchen, Germany
                    49-8024-7380

InfoServices, Inc.
Grand Rapids, MI   616-530-2767

Los-Lawrence Computer Systems
Short Hills, NJ   201-379-1547

Phoenix Management, Inc.
Portland, OR   503-297-8720

Robert E. Nolan Company
Dallas, TX   214-248-3727

The Ansar Group
Columbia, MD   410-997-0436

DOCUMENT
MANAGEMENT

FINANCE/
ACCOUNTING

HUMAN RESOURCES

MANUFACTURING/
PRODUCTION

MARKETING & SALES

MOBILE COMPUTING

**PROJECT
MANAGEMENT**

DEVELOPMENT & PROGRAMMING

4I

This section covers solution providers who develop a range of industry-specific applications, provide contract programming, interface design, product localization and other services pertaining to designing and developing software applications. Within each category are sub-sections which furthur define the listed solution providers by application specialty and programming languages, etc.

Applications Development   **43**

  Accounting 58
  Architecture 60
  Business 60
  CAD 63
  Courseware Authoring 63
  Education 64
  Engineering 65
  Entertainment 69
  Financial 70
  Government 71
  Legal 72
  Manufacturing 72
  Medical 73
  Publishing/Graphics 75

Contract Programming 78

  Assembler 85
  C++, Object Oriented 85
  C, Pascal 90
  HyperTalk 90
  THINK 92

Database Programming 92

  4th Dimension 95
  DAL 99
  DBase 99
  Filemaker Pro 99
  DAL 99
  DBase 99
  Filemaker Pro 99
  FoxBASE 101
  Helix 102
  Omnis 7 103
  Oracle 104
  Paradox 105
  SQL 106
  Sybase 106

Multiplatform Development 106

Product Localization 108

User Interface Design 109

  Human Interface 109
  Screen Graphics 112

Virtual Reality 112

APPLICATIONS DEVELOPMENT

1-Up Computing
Colorado Springs, CO
719-488-0125
Please See Company Highlight Page 43.

Abacot Information Systems
Tucson, AZ   602-795-6817

AceNet
Pasadena, CA   818-405-0087

Adaptive Machine Technologies, Inc.
Columbus, OH   614-486-7741

Admiral
New York, NY   212-744-1101

Advanced Decisions Inc.
Orange, CT   203-795-6255

Alan George & Associates, Inc.
Chicago, IL   312-909-2509

Alexus Group Limited
Edina, MN   612-832-9930

Alpha Omega Systems Corporation
Anaheim, CA   714-939-7777

Anzus
Yardley, PA   215-321-0249

Apple Computer Development Group
Cupertino, CA   408-974-4897
Please See Inside Back Cover.

Applied Computer Solutions, Inc.
Columbia, MD   301-490-5575

Applied Imagination Inc.
New York, NY   212-645-7199

Applied Technology Associates, Inc.
Houston, TX   713-981-4747

Ariel Publishing, Inc.
Pateros, WA   509-923-2249

Art & Logic
Sherman Oaks, CA   818-501-6990
Please See Ad Page 43.
Please See Company Highlight Page 44.

Assembled Solutions, Inc.
Cedar Rapids, IA   319-363-1030

Avalon Engineering, Inc.
Boston, MA   617-247-7668
Please See Company Highlight Page 44.

B & L Associates, Inc.
Lambertville, NJ   609-397-8410
Please See Company Highlight Page 45.

Bear River Associates, Inc.
Berkeley, CA   510-644-9400
Please See Ad Page 44.

1-UP COMPUTING
1330 Deby Place
Colorado Springs, CO 80921
Contact: Chris Magnuson, Project Manager
Phone: 719-488-0125
Fax: 719-488-0125
AppleLink: ONE.UP
Internet: oneup@oneup.com
Skills: Macintosh and PowerPC, C/C++, MacApp, THINK/Symantec, Apple MPW, Assembly, Microsoft Windows, UNIX, X11, and Motif.
Projects: Digital audio filtering, SCSI drivers, device drivers, graphical user interfaces (GUI), embedded systems design, custom applications and control panels, network applications, technical writing.
Clients: Hewlett-Packard, Sonic Foundry, Los Alamos National Laboratories.

APPLICATIONS
DEVELOPMENT

Accounting
Architecture
Business
CAD
Courseware
Authoring
Education
Engineering
Entertainment
Financial
Government
Legal
Manufacturing
Medical
Publishing/
Graphics

ART & LOGIC

P.O. Box 56465
Sherman Oaks, CA 91413
Contact: Justin Souter, Partner
Phone: 818-501-6990
Fax: 818-995-8669
AppleLink: J.SOUTER
Skills: C++, assembly, MacApp, MFC, and OWL.
Projects: Digital audio editor, motion animation editor and scheduler, film sound auto assembly system, magazine layout application, and prepress scan/record system.
Clients: Manufacturers and service providers in the entertainment and media arts industries.
▣

AVALON ENGINEERING, INC.

45 Newbury Street, Suite 208
Boston, MA 02116
Contact: Michael Bonnette, Vice President, Marketing
Phone: 617-247-7668
Fax: 617-247-7698
AppleLink: AVALON
CompuServe: 70541,2000
Skills: Newton, OOD/OOP, imaging algorithms, color calibration, QuickTime, Photoshop, Quark, SCSI/Serial drivers.
Projects: PresenterPad for Newton, PCS100 color workstation, KCMS developer toolkit, QuickTime digitizer, color photo-retouch package, CD-ROM data retrieval application, PIM database.
Clients: Kodak, Scitex/IRIS, ON Technology, Pastel, Data Translation, MicroRetrieval. Publishing Graphics

Bishop Development
Irvine, CA   714-857-6618

Blank-Hitchcock Associates
Bend, OR   503-385-8998

Boca On-Line Systems, Inc.
Boca Raton, FL   407-395-0242

Bootstrap Enterprises Inc.
Charlotte, NC   704-521-9167

Brainchild Corporation
Cincinnati, OH   513-831-8451

Brinkmann Consultants
Charlestown, MD   410-287-6743

Broughton Systems Inc.
Richmond, VA   804-672-1122

Business Brothers, Inc.
Bloomington, MN   612-853-3024
Please See Company Highlight Page 45.
▣

Business Tools, Inc.
Chapel Hill, NC   919-932-3068

Camsoft Data Systems, Inc.
Baton Rouge, LA   504-752-4391

Candes Systems Inc.
Harleyville, PA   215-256-4130

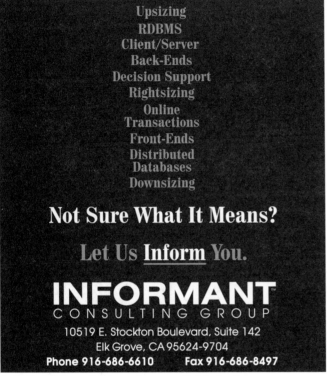
Castle Rock Software Development
Woodacre, CA   415-488-1563

CDBS-The Software Wizards
Pasadena, CA   818-441-4045

Cellular Hotline
Maryland Heights, MO
                      314-993-0050

Central Coast Software
Santa Cruz, CA   408-458-0272

CF Software
Des Plaines, IL   708-824-7180
回

Christopher Gross
Clearwater, FL   813-572-1149
回

Chronos Software, Inc.
San Francisco, CA   415-920-6900

Claude J. Pany
Sunnyvale, CA   408-922-0207
Please See Company Highlight Page 46.

Clear Access-Fairfield Software
Fairfield, IA   515-472-7077

Colin-Data
Lochristi, Belgium   32 9 355 75 07

B & L ASSOCIATES, INC.
2 Northfield Court
Lambertville, NJ 08530-1309
Contact: Bob Greenblatt
Phone: 609-397-8410
Fax: 609-397-4021
AppleLink: BANDL
CompuServe: 71540,3362
Projects: Specialists in innovative multiplatform solutions using Microsoft Excel. Total project services for financial, sales and marketing, scientific, and manufacturing systems.
Clients: ABB, AT&T, Bellcore, Delta Financial, Ernst & Young, ISK Magnetics, and Simmons Market Research. Microsoft Certified Professional, Solution Provider, and Excel Consulting Partner. Professional member of Macintosh Consultants Network.
回

BUSINESS BROTHERS, INC.
3105 E. 80th Street, Suite C270
Bloomington, MN 55425-1571
Contact: David Ringsmuth, President
Phone: 612-853-3024
Fax: 612-853-3592
AppleLink: D2348
CompuServe: 7200,1306
Skills: We specialize in rapid software development, guaranteed software solutions, micro to massive 4th Dimension development, and connectivity solutions.
回

DEVELOPMENT & PROGRAMMING

APPLICATIONS DEVELOPMENT

Accounting
Architecture
Business
CAD
Courseware Authoring
Education
Engineering
Entertainment
Financial
Government
Legal
Manufacturing
Medical
Publishing/ Graphics

CLAUDE J. PANY
P.O. Box 62318
Sunnyvale, CA 94088
Contact: Claude Pany,
Independent Software Developer
Phone: 408-922-0207
AppleLink: D2252
Skills: Applications—video
telephony, video digitizing,
image processing, graphics,
communications; environment—
Macintosh Communications
Toolbox/OS, THINK C/C++
(with TCL), MPW C/C++ (with
MacApp 3.x).

COPIOUS SYSTEMS
P.O. Box 6703
Los Osos, CA 93412
Contact: Richard Leddy, Owner
Phone: 805-528-2685
AppleLink: COPIOUS.SYS
Skills: Languages (C, C++,
HyperTalk) MPW, MacApp, THINK
C. TCP/IP experience. Algorithm
design research and development:
AI, Numerics, etc.
Projects: Involve real-time
organization, database management
and presentation graphics.
Clients: Previous employment with
large technical organizations.
Presently helping small businesses
with corporate clients as well as
small family businesses.

DATA SOLUTIONS, INC.
1790 30th Street, #308
Boulder, CO 80301
Contact: Scott Roy, President
Phone: 303-444-7969
Fax: 303-444-7846
CompuServe: 71202,520
Skills: Paradox database systems
for manufacturing, sales,
accounting, medical, legal,
communications, and transportation
industries. Clients include Comtel,
General Cable, state of Colorado,
and Lutheran Medical Center.

Compare Technologies, Inc.
Schaumburg, IL   800-482-8824

Complete Data Solutions
Austin, TX   512-329-6161

Computer Applications Corporation
Memphis, TN   901-458-8630

**Computer Associates
International, Inc.**
Islandia, NY   800-CALL-CAI

Computer Hyphenation Ltd.
Bradford, England   44-02747-33317

Computer Presentations, Inc.
Cincinnati, OH   513-281-3222

Computer Science Innovations
Melbourne, FL   407-676-2923

Computer Solutions!
Holyoke, MA   413-534-2420

Computer Solutions, Ltd.
Iowa City, IO   319-351-7549

Comshare
Ann Arbor, MI   809-922-7979

Concept Information Systems
Stamford, CT   203-363-2060

Conure Software
Norristown, PA   215-277-9071

Prototype Systems, Inc.

Yung S. Lin
Executive Consultant

10 Woodland Avenue, Suite 31 Kearny, NJ 07032 Tel./Fax. 201-998-5850

Copious Systems
Los Osos, CA   805-528-2685
Please See Company Highlight Page 46.
▣

Coral Research
Stateline, NV   702-831-9346

Cornerstone Data Systems
Anaheim, CA   714-772-5527

Costanza & Associates
Langhorne, PA   215-752-5115

Cottage Micro Services
Waxahachie, TX   214-435-2446

Creative Consulting Associates, Inc.
Summit, NJ   908-273-8607

Creative Enterprises
Long Beach, CA   310-987-3450
▣

Cressey Consulting & SW
Bernardston, MA   413-648-9936

Crisp Computer Corporation
Mill Neck, NY   516-922-4056

Current Music Technology
Malvern, PA   215-647-9426

Custom Software Inc.
Irvine, CA   714-261-1188

Cutting Edge Computer Consulting
Tarrytown, NY   914-631-2322

CVSI
Marshall, TX   903-938-7776

D & A Infosystems Inc.
Hempstead, NY   516-538-1240

d-Log
Taverny, France   33-1-30-40-04-04

Data Solutions, Inc.
Boulder, CO   303-444-7969
Please See Company Highlight Page 46.
▣

Databasics, Inc.
Atlanta, GA   404-873-0064

Decision Software Systems
Willow Grove, PA   215-657-1448

Deltam Systems, Incorporated
San Mateo, CA   415-571-0551

Desktop Paging Software, Inc.
Williamsville, NY   716-634-9010

DIGITAL APPLICATIONS, INC.
207 S. 5th Street
Darby, PA 19023-2883
Contact: Mark Gavin, Vice President
Phone: 215-534-8495
Fax: 215-284-4233
AppleLink: DIGAPP
Skills: MPW assembly, C, Pascal. Macintosh Communications Toolbox, MacApp, SCSI, NuBus, XTND, XCMDs, and XCFNs.
Projects: Custom and commercial Macintosh applications. Socket-level DECnet, TCP/IP, and ADSP communications, serial communications, backup software for SCSI tape drives, network updating of Macintosh computers across wide area networks. APIs, drivers, and INITs.
Clients: SmithKline Beecham, E.I., DuPont, GE Aerospace, FMC.

EMERGENT BEHAVIOR
635 Wellsbury Way
Palo Alto, CA 94306
Contact: Stephen Wilson, Partner
Phone: 415-494-6763
Fax: 415-494-0570
AppleLink: WILSON6
Skills: Genetic algorithms, OOP, C++, framework programming, simulation software.
Projects: Makers of MicroGA: object-oriented C++ framework for genetic algorithms. Makers of QuickApp C++ applications framework.
Clients: GoodYear, John Deere, HBO, Canadian Space Agency.

APPLICATIONS DEVELOPMENT

Accounting
Architecture
Business
CAD
Courseware Authoring
Education
Engineering
Entertainment
Financial
Government
Legal
Manufacturing
Medical
Publishing/ Graphics

Digital Applications, Inc.
Darby, PA   215-534-8495
Please See Company Highlight Page 47.

Digital Information Gallery
Buffalo, NY   716-832-2861

Digital Science Corporation
San Diego, CA   619-792-8833

Digital Systems Consulting, Inc.
Hauppange, NY   516-435-3959

DMP Associates
E. Douglas, MA   508-476-7014

Doktor Einrik's Software
Corvallis, OR   503-757-8499

DRAC'S Technologies
Melen, Belgium   32-41-772-444

DreamTime™
San Diego, CA   619-236-1341

DRW, Inc.
Trenton, NJ   609-581-1425

Dubl-Click Software Corporation
Woodland Hills, CA 818-888-2068

Ecosophon®
Basel, Switzerland   6-272-5038

EDP Consulting, Inc.
Oakland, CA   510-530-6314

EDR Consulting Services, Inc.
Fair Lawn, NJ   201-797-7318

ELEX Computer, Inc.
Seoul, Korea   82-2-780-4545

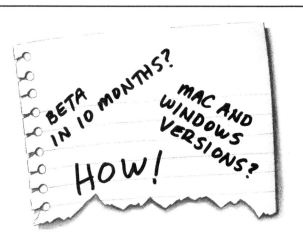

TURN TO TURNING POINT

For a very simple reason - We understand the business of software product development and we've been doing it successfully since 1983.

Our approach to project management insures proper controls, scheduling and budgeting. With a full time Quality Assurance and experienced Software Engineering staff, we have the technical excellence and proven track record to get your product done right. Plus, our experience in Macintosh®, MS-Windows® and DOS cross platform development is unparalleled.

Turning Point Software, the one to turn to for software product development services at its best.

Call or write for a free portfolio.

TPS Turning Point Software

One Gateway Center
Newton, Massachusetts 02158
617-332-0202

Emergent Behavior
Palo Alto, CA   415-494-6763
Please See Company Highlight Page 47.

Engineering Resources, Inc.
Sussex, NJ   201-875-7916

ESOFT
Cypress, CA   310-865-4078

ESS Development Company
Fullerton, CA   714-528-8958

Eureka Software
Pittsburgh, PA   412-521-6303

Evolution Computing
Tempe, AZ   602-967-8633

Excel Software
Marshalltown, IA   515-752-5359

Exodus Software
Cincinnati, OH   513-522-0011

F1 Consulting Services
Sudbury, ON Canada
          705-524-4357

Fain & Co.
Atlanta, GA   404-876-4668
Please See Company Highlight Page 47.

Fifth Generation Systems
Baton Rouge, LA   504-291-7221

FAIN & CO.
957 Blue Ridge Avenue
Atlanta, GA 30306
Contact: David Fain, President
Phone: 404-876-4668
Fax: 404-876-4085
AppleLink: D6620
Skills: Computer assisted training, database and multimedia development, AVC, C, HyperCard, Director, Omnis 7, Premier, QuickTime, SuperCard, ToolBook, and others.
Projects: Medical and business applications covering training, databases, testing, and presentations.
Clients: Educational software publishers, healthcare clients, post-production houses.

IN PHASE CONSULTING
337 West California, #4
Glendale , CA 91203
Contact: William Woody,
Phone: 818-502-1424
Fax: 818-502-1467
Internet:woody@
alumni.cco.caltech.edu
Skills: C, C++, Microsoft Windows, user interface, computer graphics, QuickTime, Apple Events, networking, technical writing, and user documentation for all our projects.

APPLICATIONS DEVELOPMENT
Accounting
Architecture
Business
CAD
Courseware Authoring
Education
Engineering
Entertainment
Financial
Government
Legal
Manufacturing
Medical
Publishing/ Graphics

LeBlanc
CONSULTING GROUP, INC.
✓ *Specializing in Macola Accounting Software*
MACOLA ®
SOFTWARE
PC Magazine Editor's Choice '87, '89, '91, '93
✓ *Custom design of financial systems*
✓ *Timeslips, ACT!, Foxpro, Paradox*
✓ *Network design and installation - Novell and LANtastic*
✓ *Headed by a CPA with 10 years consulting experience*
1-800-448-8483
324 Main Ave., Norwalk, CT 06851
Tel. (203) 849-7737 Fax (203) 849-0733

MAGNA
332 Commercial Street
San Jose, CA 95112
Contact: Cindy Johnson,
Marketing Coordinator
Phone: 408-282-0900
Fax: 408-275-9147
AppleLink: MAGNA
Projects: Magna develops and
markets a family of Macintosh
security software: Empower I
prevents unauthorized use of
PowerBooks; Empower II protects
data and programs stored on
shared Macintosh computers;
Empower Remote remotely
administers security options
across
Macintosh networks.
Clients: Apple Computer, Inc.;
Eli Lilly; Bank of America; Bell
Atlantic; Motorola; Northern
Telecom.

MASTER SOFTWARE INC.
1725 Springbrook Road
Lafayette, CA 94549
Contact: Meryl Natchez
Phone: 510-975-0650
Fax: 510-930-7304
Skills: C, C++, THINK C,
SmallTalk, MitemView,
HyperCard, TAL, COBOL,
SCOBOL, DAL, RSC, ObjectPAL,
Visual BASIC, Visual C++, SQL,
Oracle, IBM Utilities, etc.

ForeFront Long Island
Lindenhurst, NY   516-225-0179

**Frederic M. Fowler &
Associates, Inc.**
Sunnyvale, CA   408-720-9456

Freewood Computer Services Inc.
Brick, NJ   908-255-8241

**Fresh Software &
Instructional Designs**
Berkeley, CA   510-524-0852

G'Day Software, Inc.
Plano, TX   214-424-6164

G141J Systems Inc.
Plano, TX   214-424-5038

GEOPOINT Software
San Francisco, CA   415-957-1560

**Greystone Computer
Management, Inc.**
Kansas City, MO   816-471-5550

**Heritage Computer
Consulting & Services**
Shawnee, KS   913-268-1469

Honeybee Software Inc.
New York, NY   800-667-1233

HotCode Ltd.
Lincoln, MA   617-259-8520

HRF Associates, Inc.
Stamford, CT   203-961-1199

Hyper Active Software
Minneapolis, MN   612-724-1596

IDR UniCom, Inc.
Plymouth Meeting, PA
                     610-825-6500

**IMS Information Management
Solutions, Inc.**
St. Louis, MO   314-432-0997

In Phase Consulting
Glendale, CA   818-502-1424
Please See Company Highlight Page 49.

Infinity Digital, Inc.
Lakewood, CO   303-232-6906

Infinity Systems
Columbia, MD   301-596-7741

Info Systems
Toronto, ON Canada 416-665-7638

Info Systems, Inc.
Boone, NC   204-264-1948

Informant Communications Group
Elk Grove, CA   916-686-6610
Please See Ad Page 45.

**Information Systems
Technology, Inc.**
Hinsdale, IL   708-887-1911
▣

Infotech Information Services
Barrington, IL   708-381-3837

Innovative Systems & Solutions
Little Falls, NJ   201-256-9036

Instant Information Inc.
Tualatin, OR   503-692-9711

INTE-GREAT Corporation
Bethesda, MD   301-654-9100

Integra Technologies Inc.
Santa Clara, CA   408-980-1371

Integration
Montreal, QC Canada
                     514-284-2284

Interactive Software Engineering
Goleta, CA   805-685-1006

**International Software
Consultants Inc.**
Durant, OK   405-924-6888

Inventure Inc.
San Francisco, CA   415-282-0280

ITech, Inc.
Herndon, VA   703-709-1244

J.W.G. Enterprises, Inc.
Durham, NC   919-286-9859

James Hays
Seattle, WA   206-328-8188

Jirokichi & Company, Ltd.
Kamakura, Japan 81-467-32-2237

Karow Associates, Inc.
Baltimore, MD   410-276-4016
▣

Knowledge Based Systems Inc.
College Station, TX 409-696-7979

Land Lord Software Inc.
Frederick, MD   301-695-1544

**MILLENNIUM COMPUTER
CORPORATION**

642 Kreag Road
Pittsford, NY 14534
Contact: Joel Reiser, President
Phone: 716-248-0510
Fax: 716-248-0538
AppleLink: D0466
Skills: MacApp, C++, THINK C
and TCL, MPW, Pascal, FoxBASE,
QuickTime, AppleTalk, UNIX,
DAL, TCP/IP, Sybase OpenClient,
PC-DOS/Windows ports.
Projects: Specialty in color
graphics/image processing,
client/server, linguistic/text
applications, and
compression/decompression.
Projects include WordFinder,
SpellFinder, INFODesk, NutriCalc,
Photo CD.
Clients: Kodak, Microlytics, Claris,
LVT, Iona College.

MLT SOFTWARE, INC.
P.O. Box 19787
Portland, OR 97280
Contact: Michael Trigoboff, Ph.D.,
President
Phone: 503-452-0652
AppleLink: MLT.SOFTWARE
Skills: Prograph, HyperCard,
THINK C/C++, TCL, MPW,
Assembler, LISP.
Projects: Decision tree analysis,
patient medical records, medical
decision making, Sun Clock,
StartUp Manager (part of Now
Utilities), Claris PipeLines
prototype, Puppet Playhouse.
Clients: Palo Alto Software, Inc.,
Oregon Health Sciences
University/Biomedical Information
and Computing Center, Portland
Veterans Administration,
MedChartz Inc., Claris, Now
Software, CompuTeach.

**APPLICATIONS
DEVELOPMENT**

Accounting

Architecture

Business

CAD

Courseware
Authoring

Education

Engineering

Entertainment

Financial

Government

Legal

Manufacturing

Medical

Publishing/
Graphics

MOLECULAR ARTS CORPORATION

Hanover Corporate Center,
1532 E. Katella Avenue
Anaheim, CA 92805-6627
Contact: Jeff Marusin, President
Phone: 714-634-8100
Fax: 714-634-1999
AppleLink: MAC.COM.TECH
CompuServe: 71644,3626
Internet: info@molecules.com
Skills: New products, cross-platform strategies, interface design, conversions/update, 3D graphics, technical/business applications, networks.
Languages include C, C++, OOP, assembly, Pascal, FORTRAN; all major development environments.
Platforms: Macintosh, Windows, MS-DOS, UNIX.
Projects: Publishing, data visualization, telecommunications, education, entertainment software.
Clients: Publishing houses, pharmaceuticals, government agencies, chemicals.

Language Engineering Corporation
Belmont, MA   617-489-4000

Le Blanc Consulting Group, Inc.
Norwalk, CT   203-849-7737
Please See Ad Page 49.

Le Groupe Micro-Intel Inc.
Montreal, QC Canada 514-528-1905

Liberty Computer
Blaine, MN   612-755-0351

(M)agreeable software, inc.
Plymouth, MN   612-559-1108

M.I.B. Chock
Santa Monica, CA   310-828-4788

MacPeak
Austin, TX   512-327-3211

Magna
San Jose, CA   408-282-0900
Please See Company Highlight Page 50.

Marisys Inc.
Delray Beach, FL   407-272-3490

Marubeni America Corporation
New York, NY   212-599-3750

Master Software Inc.
Lafayette, CA   510-975-0650
Please See Company Highlight Page 50.

Mastersoft Inc.
Scottsdale, AZ   800-624-6107

Maui Software
Makawao, HI   808-572-0673

Mayfield Information Services
Ponca City, OK   405-765-5330

McClure Consultants Ltd.
Barrington, IL   708-382-6233

Mesa Graphics, Inc.
Los Alamos, NM   505-672-1998

Meyer Software
Hatboro, PA   215-675-3890

Michael Ericksen PC
Schaumburg, IL   708-330-6328

Micro Consulting S.A.
Le Mont, Switzerland   21 653 2400

MicroAge Computer Center
Richland, WA   509-946-4230

Microlytics Inc.
Pittsford, NY   716-248-9150

Microstar
Derry, NH   603-425-2553

MicroWorks
New York, NY   212-794-4466

Millennium Computer Corporation
Pittsford, NY   716-248-0510
Please See Company Highlight Page 51.

Millennium Software Company
Dallas, TX   214-314-2688

Mind & Motion
Hood River, OR   503-388-9114

Minuti Software Consulting, Inc.
Condia, NH   603-483-5819

MLC Computer Services
Fort Lauderdale, FL   305-424-9514

MLT Software, Inc.
Portland, OR   503-452-0652
Please See Company Highlight Page 51.

Molecular Arts Corporation
Anaheim, CA   714-634-8100
Please See Company Highlight Page 52.

MonkWorks
Homewood, AL   205-879-9867

MTEC
Marion, IL   618-997-6461

n Dimensions Software House
Aptos, CA   408-662-9703

Napa Valley Computing Company
Napa, CA   707-259-1349

New Media, Inc.
Cleveland, OH   216-481-7900
Please See Company Highlight Page 53.
回

New Visions
Oklahoma City, OK 405-239-6411

NHG Inc.
Charlotte, NC   704-531-7654

Northstar Systems, Inc.
Amherst, NH   603-673-5040

Northwest Data Services, Inc.
Everett, WA   206-252-7287
回

NOVA Electronics & Software
Riverside, CA   714-781-7332

OakTree Software Specialists
Altamonte Springs, FL
                   407-339-5855

Ocean Beach Communications
San Diego, CA   619-523-1182

OGDEN Bio Services
Rockville, MD   301-309-8280

OITC, Inc.
Melbourne Beach, FL 407-984-3714

Open Systems Associates, Inc.
Reston, VA   703-758-6708

OS Systems Group
Trumbull, CT   203-452-9043

PaperClip Products
Tulsa, OK   800-497-5508
回

Paradise Software Corporation
Phoenix, AZ   602-759-0335

PC Consulting Services, Inc.
Mountlake Terrace, WA
                   206-670-1570

Prana Computing Inc.
Marina Del Rey, CA 310-826-4687

Precision Computer Systems
Tempe, AZ   602-829-3131

Precision Data Corporation
Memphis, TN   901-682-0732

Productive Systems, Inc.
Hilliard, OH   614-777-1748

Productivity Point
Atlanta, GA   404-816-5833

Productivity Through Technology
Union City, CA   510-471-2776
Please See Ad Page 51.

Professional Systems International
Fremont, CA   510-659-8144

Progressive Computing, Inc.
Arlington, TX   817-572-6567

Prompt, Inc.
Tariffville, CT   203-651-8710

NEW MEDIA, INC.
503 E. 200th Street, Suite 202
Cleveland, OH 44119-1543
Contact: Leonard W. Pagon, Jr., President
Phone: 216-481-7900
Fax: 216-481-1570
AppleLink: NEWMEDIA
Skills: PowerBuilder, Visual BASIC, 4th Dimension, FoxPro, Lotus Notes, Omnis 7, Visual C, C++, MacApp, SQL server, Oracle, Windows NT.
Projects: We offer a full range of application development and education services focusing on graphical, client/server, workflow, OOP, and cross-platform technology areas. We assist as organizations migrate toward emerging technologies such as client/server and workgroup computing, and provide planning, education, and development to facilitate knowledge transfer. Typical projects include: marketing support, financial reporting, decision support, EIS, sales automation, customer service, order entry, project tracking for Fortune 1000 companies.
回

PROSOFT ENGINEERING INC.
942 Finovino Court
Pleasanton, CA 94566
Contact: Greg Brewer, President
Phone: 510-462-8935
AppleLink: PROSOFT
Skills: SCSI, Ethernet, Token Ring, Assembler, C, C++, Pascal, HyperCard, MPW, THINK, INIT, CDEV, DA, XFCN, and XCMD.
Projects: Custom software for graphics, databases, scheduling, data backup, sound editing, communications, printers, plotters, fax modems, and interapplication communications.

APPLICATIONS DEVELOPMENT

Accounting
Architecture
Business
CAD
Courseware Authoring
Education
Engineering
Entertainment
Financial
Government
Legal
Manufacturing
Medical
Publishing/ Graphics

SOFTENGINE

SoftEngine's principals have been developing for graphical user interfaces since 1983, and are some of the most experienced professionals in the field. They have completed more than a dozen published applications, and several mission-critical applications for in-house use by large organizations.

We offer a comprehensive development service from concept to follow-on support. We can design, code, test, document, and support your application either working alongside your engineers, or as a separate development team. Also, by using our reusable software modules, or software "engines," SoftEngine can offer a quicker and more reliable development cycle for your application.

SOFTENGINE
9777 Caminito Prudregal
San Diego, CA 92131
Phone: 619-549-0907
Fax: 619-549-2830
AppleLink: D2212

Prosoft Engineering Inc.
Pleasanton, CA   510-462-8935
Please See Company Highlight Page 53.

Prototype Systems, Inc.
Kearny, NJ   201-998-5850
Please See Ad Page 47.
Please See Company Highlight Page 55.

Q Technologies, Inc.
Evanston, IL   708-864-8505

QLS (Int.) Inc.
Trail, BC Canada   604-364-1921

Quantum Solutions, Inc.
Gahanna, OH   614-855-0265

Rajni Malik
West Haven, CT   203-931-7722

Read Technologies, Inc.
Irvine, CA   714-551-2049

Revelar Software
Salt Lake City, UT   801-485-3291

Revision
Edmonds, WA   206-382-6607

Rhythm Technology
Foster City, CA   415-574-8312

Richard Soohoo Associates, Inc.
Floral Park, NY   516-531-1953

Right Click!
Chicago, IL   312-248-6072

RISM
Shawnee Mission, KS 913-642-5600

RJM Systems, Inc.
San Francisco, CA   415-731-2884

Robertson Associates
Menlo Park, CA   415-322-5335

RWD Technologies, Inc.
Columbia, MD   404-551-8198

San Francisco Canyon Company, Inc.
San Francisco, CA   415-398-9957

Scientific Placement Inc.
Houston, TX   713-496-6100

SCV Consulting, Inc.
Fridley, MN   612-572-2425

Selfware
McLean, VA   703-506-0400

Sentient Software
San Carlos, CA   415-595-2523

Sequel Development Corporation
Cupertino, CA   408-366-6900

Sequent Associates
San Jose, CA   408-436-0111

Sheridan Software
Freeland, WA   206-331-1868

Shuger Software Services
Des Plaines, IL   708-228-2959

Silicon Graphics Computer Systems
Mountain View, CA   800-770-3033
                    415-390-3033
Please See Inside Front Cover.

Simon/Ross & Associates, Inc.
Toronto, ON Canada 416-960-5647

**Simple Software
Development Company**
Mill Valley, CA 415-381-2650

Skees Associates Inc.
Fairfax Station, VA 703-250-0862

Skye Solutions Inc.
Hoboken, NJ 201-222-9006

Slippery Disks
Los Angeles, CA 310-274-3600

SoftAnswer
Cupertino, CA 408-725-4041

SoftEngine
San Diego, CA 619-549-0907
Please See Ad Page 54.
▣

Software By Design, Inc.
Natick, MA 508-650-4273

Software & Consulting
Wiesbaden, Germany
49-611-400142

Software Corporation
Boca Raton, FL 407-995-8436

Software Engineering Consultants
Greensboro, NC 910-855-0922
▣

THE SU5 GROUP

We are an experienced team of Macintosh application developers. The products we have written range from a vertical market lighting equipment controller interface to a horizontal market charting application with an estimated 400, 000 copies sold. Our programming and advice helped turn someone's drawing application into a major product in the desktop presentation market. Let us transform your idea into a quality software product. Write, call, fax, or e-mail.

THE SU5 GROUP
1701 River Run Road, #603
Fort Worth, Tx 76107
Phone: 817-870-2557
Fax: 817-870-2610
AppleLink: D1176
Internet: su5@rahul.net

PROTOTYPE SYSTEMS, INC.
10 Woodland Avenue, Suite 31
Kearny, NJ 07032-1968
Contact: Yung S. Lin,
Executive Consultant
Phone: 201-998-5850
Fax: 201-998-5850
CompuServe: 74013,1033
Skills: FoxPro, Novell NetWare
(CNE) consulting services,
with extensive programming
experience in C, C++, Windows
SDK, MS-DOS. Past experience:
mainframe COBOL, CICS/DB2,
MVS/TSO. Interfacing PCs to
mainframe: MicroFocus COBOL,
CICS/PC, xdb, LAN.
Projects: Payroll, customer report
information center, military sales
business system.
Clients: UPS, AT&T, Naval Air
Engineering Center.
▣

THE ALTERNATE APPROACH
29757 Strawberry Hill Drive
Agoura Hills, CA 91301
Contact: Rose Quesada, Project
Development
Phone: 818-889-6035
Fax: 818-889-4788
CompuServe: 71161,2352
Skills: Macintosh, IBM, UNIX,
and Newton. C/C++, Assembly,
Prolog, NTK, etc. Apple Certified
Developer. See Brockman
Consulting for consulting services.
See also listing under Custom
Solutions; Mobile Computing..

DEVELOPMENT & PROGRAMMING

**APPLICATIONS
DEVELOPMENT**

Accounting
Architecture
Business
CAD
Courseware
Authoring
Education
Engineering
Entertainment
Financial
Government
Legal
Manufacturing
Medical
Publishing/
Graphics

ZEIK CONSULTING
76 North Maple Avenue, Suite 277
Ridgewood, NJ 07450
Contact: Stephen Zeik
Phone: 201-444-5800
Fax: 201-444-8831
AppleLink: ZJS57
Skills: MPW C, C++, THINK C, MacApp, XCMD. Application development expertise in financial applications, educational software, spreadsheets, databases, and scheduling software.

BRAIDED MATRIX, INC.
P.O. Box 339
Shokan, NY 12481
Contact: Lincoln Stoller, Ph.D., President
Phone: 914-657-6411
Fax: 914-657-6411
AppleLink: BRAIDMATRIX
CompuServe: 76662,2357
Skills: 4th Dimension Accounting.
Projects: 4th Quarter® Accounting is a complete, ready-to-run, integrated accounting package and a unique development platform. Because it is built on a modular source code and reconfigurable file structures that are fundamental to all accounting-based systems, 4Q™ can be easily extended to support enterprise systems of any kind. 4Q™ is designed exclusively as a client/server application and provided as source code.

Software Farm
Berkeley, CA   510-843-3331

Software Productivity Strategists, Inc.
Rockville, MD   301-670-2837

Software Systems Group
Arlington, VA   703-534-2297

Softweaver
Middletown, CA   707-987-9000

SoluProbe Limited
Westminster, CO   303-460-8264

Sonalysts Inc.
Waterford, CT   203-442-4355

SophSupp Inc.
Brooklyn, NY   718-253-0444

Spentech, Inc.
Silver Spring, MD   301-622-1076

Spring Branch Software
Manchester, IA   319-927-6537

Steam Radio Limited
London, England   44 71 267 2561

Stonecutter Software
Mariposa, CA   209-966-3066

Stow Lake Software
San Francisco, CA   415-665-9005

HONEYBEE SOFTWARE, INC.

Programming and integration services for creative companies of all sizes, Honeybee has become the cutting edge in technology with job management and accounting solutions for the Macintosh. With 5 years of experience in the design, agency, public relations, and multimedia industries, products and services are offered to reengineer the way service-oriented companies manage their workflow. Honeybee offers needs-analysis custom programming, MIS services, installation, training, and support as a full turnkey Macintosh bureau. Honeybee offers full programming for all multimedia platforms including Apple Media Tool and Macromind Director. See also listings under Development and Programming; Database Programming and Multimedia; Multimedia: General.
Skills: 4th Dimension, AR, AP, GL, and job cost, time billing applications development.

HONEYBEE SOFTWARE INC.
5 East 47th Street
New York, NY 10017
Phone: 800-667-1233
Fax: 514-875-2940
AppleLink: CDA0270

Strategic Directions, Inc.
Davie, FL   305-473-4161

Suick Bay Technologies
Maple Grove, MN   612-425-7025

Sundgau Software Development
Rodersdorf, Switzerland
                   416-175-1302

Superset '93 Inc.
San Diego, CA   619-587-6003

Symantec Corporation
Cupertino, CA   800-441-7234

Synthesis Software
Charlotte, NC   704-394-3094

Systems Data Processing Associates
Nashua, NH   603-881-3107

Tangram Enterprise Solutions
Raleigh, NC   919-851-6000

The Alternate Approach
Agoura Hills, CA   818-889-6035
Please See Company Highlight Page 55.

The Computer Factory Limited
Berkshire, England   44 488 57035

The Dawson Group
Phoenix, AZ   602-496-6848

The DesignSoft Company
Wheaton, IL   800-426-0265

The Intelligent Games Company
Near Newbury, England
                   44-635-248042

The Interface Experts
Los Angeles, CA   310-474-3850

The Maverick Group, Inc.
Edmonds, WA.   206-672-2000

The MEGA MAC Company
Augusta, ME   207-582-2442

The Stepstone Corporation
Sandy Hook, CT   203-426-1875

The SU5 Group
Fort Worth, TX   817-870-2557
Please See Ad Page 55.

The Technical Edge
Scotts Valley, CA 408-438-2524

The Willowplace Group
Burnsville, MN   612-435-8025

TNT Computing
Upland, CA   909-984-5775

Total Automation, Inc.
New Hope, MN   612-535-2968

TransPac Software
San Jose, CA   408-261-7550

Trix Systems
Vegby, Sweden   46-302-464 79

True Ware
Edmonton, AB Canada
                   403-483-5934

TSP Software
Irvine, CA   714-731-1368

Tuesday Software
Santa Barbara, CA 805-962-7889

Tuffet AntiGravity Inc.
London, ON Canada 519-672-5120

Tulip Software
Andover, MA   508-475-8711

HONEYBEE SOFTWARE INC.
5 East 47th Street
New York , NY 10017
Contact: James McBeath,
Phone: 800-667-1233
Fax: 514-875-2940
AppleLink: CDA0270
Skills: 4th Dimension, job cost,
estimating billing, purchasing,
time-billing development.

WORKPLACE
21550 Oxnard Street, 3rd Floor
Woodland Hills, CA 91367
Contact: Leon Rubins, Principal
Phone: 818-407-0010
Fax: 818-407-1641
Skills: AppWare development for
interior, architectural, and creative
firms. Project specifying/financial
management automating:
proposals, invoicing, purchasing,
project tracking, client/vendor
information, transmittals.

DEVELOPMENT & PROGRAMMING

APPLICATIONS DEVELOPMENT

Accounting

Architecture

Business

CAD

Courseware Authoring

Education

Engineering

Entertainment

Financial

Government

Legal

Manufacturing

Medical

Publishing/ Graphics

TURNING POINT SOFTWARE

Founded in 1983, Turning Point Software is a consulting firm specializing in the design and development of a wide varitey of Macintosh, MS-Windows, and DOS software products. The company offers a full range of services including new product development, cross-platform development, multimedia development, conversions, and systems software. In addition to strong technical expertise, the company has a mature technical management and organizational structure. Turning Point is one of the largest, independent product development companies in the industry and employs a large, full-time staff of software engineers, technical managers, and quality assurance engineers. The company has a proven track record of success in commercial product development.

Skills: Product design/development, multimedia, cross platform, systems software, conversion, C, C++, Assembler, MS-Windows, MS-DOS.

Clients: Microsoft, Lotus, Broderbund.

TURNING POINT SOFTWARE, INC.
One Gateway Center
Newton, MA 02134
Phone: 617-332-0202
Fax: 617-332-1121
AppleLink: D0621

Turning Point Software
Newton, MA   617-332-0202
Please See Ads Pages 48, 58.
回

Twilight & Barking
Phoenix, AZ   602-759-0857

Universal Imaging Corporation
West Chester, PA   215-344-9410

Universal Management Accounting
Northridge, CA   818-366-8344

Urban Software
Seattle, WA   206-720-0590

Vanguard Research Inc.
Fairfax, VA   703-934-6300

Vineyard Software
Ontario, CA   714-930-1724

Vinko Enterprises
Oakville, ON   905-338-7836

Visions Software, Inc.
Wakefield, MA   617-246-6260
Please See Ads Pages 67, 84.
回

White Oak Software
San Carlos, CA   415-637-0222

White Pine Software, Inc.
Nashua, NH   603-886-9050

Willow Solutions
New Haven, CT   203-777-5634

WillStein Software, Inc.
Wilmette, IL   708-256-2895

Winthrop-Lawrence Corporation
Agawam, MA   413-786-0041

WMP NJ Software
Longview, WA   206-578-9597

Work Improvement Technologies Inc.
Morris Plains, NJ   201-292-2736

WOW Control Technology
Eindhoven, The Netherlands
                   040-511-662

Xperience Consulting Inc.
Santa Clara, CA   408-983-1177

**Yoh Information
Technology Associates**
San Jose, CA   408-956-1611

Z Mac Software Solutions
Kirkland, WA   206-448-4929

Zeik Consulting
Ridgewood, NJ   201-444-5800
Please See Company Highlight Page 56.

Accounting

Acumen, Inc.
Santa Fe, NM   505-983-6463

Antley Business Systems, Inc.
Minneapolis, MN   612-542-9651

回

Bob Harris Consulting
Inverness, CA   415-669-7702

Braided Matrix, Inc.
Shokan, NY   914-657-6411
Please See Company Highlight Page 56.
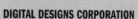

Datadesigns
San Antonio, TX   210-697-0780

Emanuele Corso & Associates, Inc.
Penasco, NM   505-587-1022

Freagra
Suffolk, England   0473 230202

Honeybee Software Inc.
New York, NY   800-667-1233
Please See Ad Page 56.

Human Line Inc.
Liege, Belgium   32-41-210238

Island Micro Solutions, Inc.
Honolulu, HI   808-833-6048

JAG Enterprises
New York, NY   212-627-0058

LCS-Lawrence Computer Systems
Short Hills, NJ   201-379-1547

MICROWORKS BUSINESSWORLD, INC.

MicroWorks Businessworld Inc. is a custom database developer and consulting firm, specializing in complete business management systems based on either customized databases or previous software development in the 4th Dimension language. Existing systems provide accounting, inventory management, sales lead tracking, customer service, office automation, personnel expertise. MicroWorks can provide the most complete and powerful inventory control system available today in "BOSS," an extensive program for which simple "configuration" rather than "customization" can provide clients with operational, tailored solutions within 4 to 6 weeks. Principal clients for BOSS are distributors, wholesalers, importers, exporters in the food, apparel, electronics, gift industries, and sales and service areas. Clients for general custom database work in 4th Dimension include Fortune Magazine, Ernst & Young, Chase Bank.

MICROWORKS BUSINESSWORLD, INC.
305 Riverside Drive, Suite 4A
New York, NY 10025
Phone: 212-932-0001
Fax: 212-316-0399

BEAR RIVER ASSOCIATES, INC.
P.O. Box 1900
Berkeley, CA 94701-1900
Contact: Rodney Smith, Anthony Meadow
Phone: 510-644-9400
Fax: 510-644-9778
AppleLink: BEARRIVER
Internet: info@bearriver.com
Skills: Programming, systems integration, training, and consulting for Macintosh, Windows, and Newton platforms. Complete range of services, from product development to in-house systems. Curriculum includes Macintosh technology, OOP, AppleTalk, Newton, and VITAL.

DIGITAL DESIGNS CORPORATION
2505 S. Jefferson Avenue
Sioux Falls, SD 57105
Contact: David Knoflicek,
Phone: 605-334-1588
Fax: 605-335-4312
AppleLink: D4064
Skills: 4th Dimension single-user and client/server applications.
Projects: General accounting and retail management service systems, medical billing systems for clinics, wholesale/retail/manufacturing inventory control, multilevel automated pricing systems, development of integrated customized applications.

APPLICATIONS DEVELOPMENT

Accounting
Architecture
Business
CAD
Courseware Authoring
Education
Engineering
Entertainment
Financial
Government
Legal
Manufacturing
Medical
Publishing/Graphics

Lincoln Software, Inc.
Lincoln, MA   617-259-4135

Lipschultz Brothers, Levin & Gray
Northbrook, IL   708-272-5300

Masterplans
San Anselmo, CA   415-459-7574

MicroWorks Businessworld, Inc.
New York, NY   212-932-0001
Please See Ad Page 59.
🔳

Phase II Consulting Inc.
Cumberland, RI   401-333-4536

Pinehill Software Corporation
Falmouth, MA   508-548-4470

Reiter Consulting Services
Riva, MD   301-261-4505

The MIS Group Inc.
Shelton, CT   800-303-7339

Wayne Norman Inc.
Pacifica, CA   415-738-8475

WM Associates
Redwood City, CA   415-366-1548

Working Computer
Oceanside, CA   619-945-4334

WSC, Inc.
Tampa, FL   800-776-5924

Architecture

Honeybee Software Inc.
New York, NY   800-667-1233
Please See Company Highlight Page 57.
🔳

HR Hi-Tech Inc.
Oakville, ON Canada 416-829-2290

Seaborne Woodworking
Petaluma, CA   707-778-3474

Shoestring Engineering
San Francisco, CA   415-647-4107

The VITAL Consulting Network
Cupertino, CA   408-255-6456

WorkPlace
Woodland Hills, CA 818-407-0010
Please See Company Highlight Page 57.
🔳

Business

A. A. Gole, Consulting
Glen Rock, NJ   201-612-1070

Aardvark Research Group
Burlington, VT   802-658-2030

Accountasystems Ltd.
W. Bloomfield, MI   313-737-0031

Advantage Software Inc.
Mississauga, Canada 416-891-2901

Ahmac Associates, Inc.
Oyster Bay, NY   516-922-4145

Allied Support
San Francisco, CA   415-386-2242

Arabic Information Systems
Cairo, Egypt   202-711-684

Augment, Inc.
Durham, NC   919-489-9041

Bear River Associates, Inc.
Berkeley, CA   510-644-9400
Please See Company Highlight Page 59.
🔳

Binary Techniques Inc.
Somerville, MA   617-628-7200

Blankenship Systems Consulting, Inc.
Elmhurst, IL   708-530-2399

Blueridge Technologies, Inc.
Flint Hill, VA   703-675-3015

Boston Systems Group Inc.
Boston, MA   617-423-1670

Boxes & Arrows Inc.
Jacksonville, FL   904-446-4908
🔳

TO ORDER ADDITIONAL COPIES OF THE

AGORA DIGITAL MARKETPLACE
TALENT SOURCEBOOK
CALL

1-800-927-1200
EXT. 140

Brio Technology Inc.
Mountain View, CA   415-961-4110

BSO Management Support
The Hague, Holland
0031-70-3245555

Bunder Computer Services
Greenville, SC   803-268-7063

C.T.A. Inc.
New Haven, CT   203-786-5828

Campagne Associates Ltd.
Nashua, NH   800-582-3489

Catalyst Computer Systems
Hanover Park, IL   708-289-0797

Cederblom & Associates
Seattle, WA   206-772-0371

CEI Systems, Inc.
Osseo, MN   612-425-1167

CMJ Computers Inc.
Big Sandy, MT   406-378-2302

Cognitive Systems Inc.
Boston, MA   617-742-7227

Colleague Business Software Inc.
Austin, TX   800-926-9965

Computed Designs
Bloomington, IN   812-876-6923

**Computer Consultants &
Service Center, Inc.**
St. Louis, MO   314-647-8891

CONSTAR
San Diego, CA   619-581-0459

CORGROUP
Madison, CT   203-458-9363
▣

Coyne Company
Mission Viejo, CA   714-855-4689

Daniel L. Roudelbush
Kailua-Kona, HI   808-326-2025

Database Associates
Needham, MA   617-449-8387

Database International Inc.
Boston, MA   617-859-8579

Decision Technologies
Overland Park, KS   913-681-6640

Digital Designs Corporation
Sioux Falls, SD   605-334-1588
Please See Company Highlight Page 59.

Dimension Consulting, Inc.
Coral Springs, FL   305-341-7077

Dimensional Insight, Inc.
Burlington, MA   617-229-9111

Doblin Group
Chicago, IL   312-443-0800

Electronic Catalog Corporation
Cincinnati, OH   800-777-7770

Fashoro Langhill Inc.
Danville, CA   510-736-7634

FIT Software
Santa Clara, CA   408-562-5990

Flashpoint, Inc.
Somerville, MA   617-625-3100

FoodStar Inc.
Tampa, FL   813-281-2705

Franklin Estimating Systems
Salt Lake City, UT   801-355-5954

THE SLEETER GROUP
952 San Jose Street
San Leandro, CA 94577-3833
Contact: Don Sleeter, Partner
Phone: 510-614-8148
CompuServe: 71101,2130
Skills: HyperTalk, WindowScript, XCMDs, C++, MacApp, Visual BASIC, database programming.

DEVELOPMENT &
PROGRAMMING

**APPLICATIONS
DEVELOPMENT**

Accounting
Architecture
Business
CAD
Courseware
Authoring
Education
Engineering
Entertainment
Financial
Government
Legal
Manufacturing
Medical
Publishing/
Graphics

Goldsoft Corporation
Sherman Oaks, CA   818-501-2837

Good News Marketing Inc.
Arlington, MA   617-643-7131

Green Shades Software, Inc.
Jacksonville, FL   904-260-7766

Hechtsoft
Muenchen, Germany   089-884248

Human Resource Microsystems
San Francisco, CA   800-972-8470

HyperDEX
Bellingham, WA   206-738-0541

Inspiration Software, Inc.
Portland, OR   503-245-9011

ISIS International, Inc.
Sherman Oaks, CA   818-788-4747

Jeddak
San Jose, CA   800-982-6900

Kansas Bay Systems, Inc.
Oakland, CA   510-339-7300

Keep It Simple Software
Helena, MT   406-442-3559

Kjell Ingvarsson Konsult hb
Skurup, Sweden   46-411 40184

Les Logiciels SYSTAMEX Inc.
Montréal, QC Canada 514-932-4431

MacHelp Associates, Inc.
Dover, DE   302-734-7491

Macintosh Applications Consultants
Fort Lauderdale, FL   305-776-6777

Mainstay
Agoura Hills, CA   818-991-6540

Maxim Software SA
Buenos Aires, Argentina
54-1-325-9281

MData Inc.
Phoenix, AZ   800-426-4963

Menlo Business Systems, Inc.
Los Altos, CA   415-948-7920

MG Management Group
Southeastern, PA   610-644-2833

Micro Dynamics Ltd.
Silver Spring, MD   301-589-6300

Micro Planning International Ltd.
Bristol, England   272 509 417

MicroWorks Businessworld, Inc.
New York, NY   212-932-0001
Please See Ad Page 59.

Miller/Burns Associates, Inc.
Springfield, IL   217-789-4430

Minder Technologies, Inc.
New Berlin, WI   414-789-7433

Navaco
Erie, PA   814-833-2592

North Communications
Santa Monica, CA   310-828-7000

NoteTaker Software
Truckee, CA   916-587-7450

Optimization Alternatives
Austin, TX   512-479-4140

PCX Consulting
Pittsburgh, PA   412-471-7500

Peachtree Software
Norcross, GA   800-247-3224

Pensee Corporation
Scottsdale, AZ   602-494-7075

Phillips Associates
Redmond, WA   206-881-2856

R & L Office Systems
Pittsburgh, PA   412-856-8707

Ron Wallace Enterprises Inc.
Peoria, IL   309-685-4843

Ruigrok Innovations Inc.
Vancouver, BC Canada
604-683-5599

Sales Dominator Ltd.
Wayzata, MN   612-544-1800

Sensible Business Systems
Cortland, NY   607-753-9482

ShopKeeper Publishing International Inc.
Tallahassee, FL   904-222-8808

Sign Equipment Engineering Inc.
Bellevue, WA   206-747-0693

Simetra Systems
El Segundo, CA   310-640-6878

Simulate Inc.
Bala Cynood, PA   215-664-7433

Somerville Associates
Dover, DE   302-678-8100

Sterling International/ Ambush Productions
Mooresville, NC   704-664-8400

Strategic Management Group Inc.
Philadelphia, PA   215-387-4000

Systems Engineering Solutions Inc.
Dunn Loring, VA   703-573-4366

Telicon Aps
Odenses, Denmark   45 65959444

The Design Office
Jupiter, FL   407-747-9884

The Farrell Company
Plymouth, MA   508-747-3565

The Management Services Group, Inc.
Valley Cottage, NY   914-358-0070

The Pacific Group
Aptos, CA   408-662-2325

The Sleeter Group
San Leandro, CA   510-614-8148
Please See Company Highlight Page 61.

Turning Point Software
Newton, MA   617-332-0202
Please See Ad Page 58.
▣

Turtle Creek Software
Spencer, NY   607-589-4471

Varcon Systems Inc.
San Diego, CA   619-563-6700

Viscon
Plano, TX   214-422-8313

Western Software Associates
Walnut Creek, CA   510-932-3999

White Crow Software Inc.
Burlington, VT   802-658-1270

Working Software Inc.
Santa Cruz, CA   408-423-5696

CAD

Automated Analysis Corporation
Raleigh, NC   919-876-1450

Digital Vision Design & Automation
Irvine, CA   714-852-8660

Innovative Data Design, Inc.
Concord, CA   510-680-6818

MODACAD
Los Angeles, CA   310-312-6632

Mountain Software
Charleston, WV   304-346-9585

PRODUCTEC SA
Rossenaison, Switzerland
41-227-193

Sussex Informatics Limited
Ottawa, ON Canada   613-789-5444

Tanner Research, Inc.
Pasadena, CA   818-792-3000

Courseware Authoring

Acquired Knowledge Inc.
San Diego, CA   619-587-4668

Design Access, Inc.
Chicago, IL   312-465-0528

Hypermedia Solutions
Middleburg, VA   703-687-3390

Institute for the Study of Adult Literacy
University Park, PA   814-863-3777

Interactive Design Associates
Salem, OR   503-399-8327

Learning Associates International
Schiedam, The Netherlands
31-010-426-22-78

Learning Curve Ltd.
Mawson, Australia   616 290-1594

NEW MEDIA, INC.
503 E. 200th Street, Suite 202
Cleveland , OH 44119-1543
Contact: Leonard W. Pagon, Jr., President
Phone: 216-481-7900
Fax: 216-481-1570
AppleLink: NEWMEDIA
Projects: We offer a comprehensive technical curriculum geared to retaining organizations with emerging client/server and workgroup tools and design techniques. All of our courseware and instructors are certified by vendors such as Microsoft, and Powersoft. Our extensive practical development experience is leveraged in a formal instructional setting. We offer monthly public classes at daily rates, and customized training. Our current courses include Visual BASIC, PowerBuilder,, Visual C++, MS Access, FoxPro, C++, SQL, UI Techniques, Workflow Design, Lotus Notes, Windows NT, SQLServer, UI Design, Relational Analysis, and much more.
▣

DEVELOPMENT & PROGRAMMING

APPLICATIONS DEVELOPMENT

Accounting

Architecture

Business

CAD

Courseware Authoring

Education

Engineering

Entertainment

Financial

Government

Legal

Manufacturing

Medical

Publishing/ Graphics

Parson Consulting
Austin, TX   512-441-6932

Power Up Software Corporation
San Mateo, CA   415-345-5900

The Salisbury Research Group
Seattle, WA   206-364-7486

Warren-Forthought, Inc.
Angleton, TX   409-849-1239

Education

Albany Micro Solutions
Albany, NY   518-482-4824

Albathion Software Inc.
San Francisco, CA   415-824-5704

Alberta Education
Barrhead, AB Canada 403-674-5333

Bibliogem Inc.
Bloomington, IN   812-332-6549

Biomedical Teaching & Information
Parkville, Australia   613-344-5848

Brooks/Cole Publishing Company
Pacific Grove, CA   408-373-0728

Brownstone Research Group
Denver, CO   303-333-6974

Calico Publishing
Bridgeton, MO   314-298-0767

Career Publishing Incorporated
Orange, CA   800-854-4014

CEO Software Solutions
Matawan, NJ   908-566-4545

Chalk Butte
Boulder, WY   307-537-5261

Childs Consulting Associates Inc.
Southfield, MI   313-569-2355

COMPanion
Salt Lake City, UT   800-347-6439

Computer Solutions
Olympia, WA   206-456-1888

Cordova Research Associates
Cordova, TN   901-756-7481

Creative Software
Durham, NC   919-493-9503

DEMCO, INC.
Madison, WI   800-356-8394

Didatech Software Ltd.
Burnaby, Canada   800-665-0667

DxR Development Group, Inc.
Carbondale, IL   618-453-1140

Ed Tech Northwest
Kent, WA   206-432-6844

EMA Software
Los Altos, CA   415-969-4679

Exceller Software Corporation
Ithaca, NY   607-257-5634

From The Heart Software
Moscow, ID   208-883-4941

FSCreations, Inc.
Cincinnati, OH   513-241-3415

Imagination Technology
Derbyshire, England
                    0-298-872651

Intentional Educations
Watertown, MA   617-641-1405

Intermedia
Seattle, WA   206-284-2995

Jersey Cow Software Company, Inc.
Franklin Park, NJ   908-422-0101

KeyPeople Publishing, Inc.
Everett, WA   206-252-2002

Learning Tomorrow, Inc.
Bloomsburg, PA   800-722-1978

Libraries of the Mind
Vienna, Austria   431-278-7801

MacLaboratory Inc.
Devon, PA   215-688-3114

MAX STAX, et cetera
Phoenix, AZ   602-993-8415

Media In Motion
San Francisco, CA   415-621-0707

Medina Software Inc.
Longwood, FL   407-260-1676

MESS/DGEC
Montreal, QC Canada
                    514-873-2200

MetaTheory
Berkeley, CA   510-849-4478

MikroLogix Software Inc.
Tucson, AZ   602-325-8794

Mysterium Tremendum
Pittsburgh, PA   412-661-0285

Natural Interface Lab
Pasadena, CA   818-797-2157

New Media, Inc.
Cleveland, OH   216-481-7900
Please See Company Highlight Page 63.

Orcutt/Oeflein Software
Frankfort, MI 616-352-9071
Please See Company Highlight Page 67.

Quadrature
San Diego, CA 619-271-9224

Sandpiper Software, Inc.
St. Paul, MN 612-644-7395

Sea Studios
Monterey, CA 408-649-5152

Shopware, Inc.
Aberdeen, WA 206-532-3392

Sigmund Software
Hummelstown, PA 717-566-9255

Super School Software
Long Beach, CA 310-594-8580

Support Syndicate for Audiology
Pittsburgh, PA 412-481-2497

Taras Development Corporation
Provo, UT 801-225-0832

Technology & Learning Magazine
San Rafael, CA 415-457-4333

Techware Corporation
Altamonte Springs, FL
407-695-9000

**The Conroy Company/
Fulcrum Software**
Miami, FL 305-235-6479

Vernier Software
Portland, OR 503-297-5317

Vitale Software Group
Point Reyes Station, CA
415-663-9520

Wilkes University ITEC Center
Wilkes Barre, PA 717-824-4651

**William K. Bradford
Publishing Company, Inc.**
Acton, MA 508-263-6996

Woodbridge Information Solutions
Palo Alto, CA 415-424-9051

Engineering

A to Z Computers, Inc.
Voorhees, NJ 609-424-8517

Absoft Corporation
Rochester Hills, MI 313-853-0050

Accolade, Inc.
San Jose, CA 408-985-1700

Advanced System Technologies, Inc.
Englewood, CO 303-790-4242

Alternative Systems Concepts
Pelham, NH 603-635-3553

Andromeda Computer Systems Ltd.
Calgary, AB Canada 403-247-5300

Architrion Oregon
Beaverton, OR 503-626-7052

Aster
Chambéry, France 33 76-45-21-21

Aura CAD/CAM, Inc.
El Segundo, CA 310-536-9207

Automated Business Management
Cambridge, MA 617-621-0025

Bernstein Design Services
Livermore, CA 510-447-7654

Bimillennium Corporation
Los Gatos, CA 408-354-7511

Biometallics
Princeton, NJ 609-275-0133

BioTechnology Software
Philomath, OR 503-929-6405

Black & Ryan Engineering
Scottsdale, AZ 602-451-7137

BlackHawk Technology
Morgan Hill, CA 408-776-1106

Bureau of Economic Geology
Austin, TX 512-471-1534

. . . by Design, Inc.
Lake Mills, WI 414-648-3712

Camtronics
Camas Valley, OR 503-445-2824

Carlow International Incorporated
Falls Church, VA 703-698-6225

Company Seven Astro-Optics Division
Montpelier, MD 301-953-2000

Concord Consulting Group
Concord, MA 508-369-7696

Concurrent Engineering Tools Inc.
Mesa, AZ 602-464-8208

Craft Robot Company
New York, NY 212-619-3021

Critical Technologies Inc.
Utica, NY 315-793-0248

Dana Wood & Associates
Albuquerque, NM 505-822-1241

APPLICATIONS
DEVELOPMENT

Accounting
Architecture
Business
CAD
Courseware
Authoring
Education
Engineering
Entertainment
Financial
Government
Legal
Manufacturing
Medical
Publishing/
Graphics

Dapple Systems
Sunnyvale, CA   408-733-3283

Daystar Software Inc.
Kansas City, MO   816-741-4310

Dennis M. Nagel, Inc.
Delray Beach, FL   407-272-0700

Designed Data Company, Inc.
Bolingbrook, IL   708-739-3716

Digital Consultants
Lon Mott, CO   303-321-1119

Dover Technology Ltd.
Dartmouth, NS   902-461-9544

EBA Engineering Consultants Ltd.
Edmonton, AB Canada
403-451-2121

Electric Eye
Portland, OR   503-248-2265

EPIC Systems Group Inc.
Sierra Madre, CA   818-355-2988

GeoData Systems
Boulder City, NV   702-294-3065

Glenrose Systems
Austin, TX   512-448-1196

Grove Engineering-A BWNT Company
Palo Alto, CA   415-855-2305

Hoh Humm Ranch
Forks, WA   206-374-5337

IC Optometrology Inc.
Scottsdale, AZ   602-947-8833

InfoE
Sterling, VA   703-430-4502

Information and Mathematical Science Laboratory, Inc.
Tokyo, Japan   81-1-3590-5211

Information Systems Technology, Inc.
Hinsdale, IL   708-887-1911
Please See Company Highlight Page 67.
▣

Ingsoft Limited
North York, ON Canada
        416-730-9611

International TechnoGroup Incorporated
Milford, OH   800-783-9199

J. W. Havstad
Prospect, OR   503-560-3321

Klex Software
Farmington Hills, MI 313-473-0347

Komili Teknik Hiz. ve Sanayi AS.
Ankara, Turkey   4680588

KTAADN Inc.
Newton, MA   617-527-0054

LSB Technology
Clairton, PA   412-653-1082

McDonnell Douglas Aerospace
St. Louis, MO   314-234-4912

ORCUTT/OEFLEIN SOFTWARE
104 Fifth Street, P.O. Box 1573
Frankfort, MI 49635
Contact: Fred Oeflein, Partner
Phone: 616-352-9071
Fax: 616-352-7110
AppleLink: D3538
Skills: Multi-user, multiplatform applications, Macintosh and IBM porting, C, C++, Pascal.
Projects: University of Chicago School Mathematics Project, Quiz and Test Writer, HarperCollins QuizMaster, Interactive Tutorials and Test Generator/Editor for Mathematics, MacBible.
Clients: HarperCollins, Scott Foresman, Zondervan, Nelson-Hall Publishers.

INFORMATION SYSTEMS TECHNOLOGY, INC.
911 N. Elm Street, Suite 310
Hinsdale, IL 60521
Contact: Martin Volk
Phone: 708-887-1911
Fax: 708-654-1503
AppleLink: IST.INC
Skills: Software development: C++/C, DOS, Windows, Assembler, MPW, Labview, Mathlab, signal/image processing, PC/Macintosh hardware development (ISA, EISA, NuBus).
Clients: NASA, U.S. Army, and industry.   ▣

APPLICATIONS DEVELOPMENT

Accounting
Architecture
Business
CAD
Courseware Authoring
Education
Engineering
Entertainment
Financial
Government
Legal
Manufacturing
Medical
Publishing/ Graphics

Metric Systems
Round Rock, TX   512-388-4458

Micro Analysis & Design, Inc.
Boulder, CO   303-442-6947

Micro Specials Inc.
Roseville, MN   612-482-1546

MicroCode Engineering
Orem, UT   801-226-4470

Microspot
Cupertino, CA   408-253-2000

MicroStrategy Inc.
Wilmington, DE   302-427-8800

MK Consulting
Baltimore, MD   410-243-2216

Morton Associates Inc.
Santa Barbara, CA   805-966-3556

Nedrud Data Systems
Melbourne Beach, FL 407-984-1405

Noetic Systems Inc.
Baltimore, MD   410-889-4079

Northland Computer Services, Inc.
Parkville, MO   816-741-8089

Omicron Electronics Inc.
Warren, MI   313-757-8192

Oxford Molecular Ltd.
Oxford, England   44-865-784600

P.L. Kelly Engineering
Sunnyvale, CA   408-720-0790

Peter B. Holler
Pittsford, NY   716-586-5570

PMS Microdesign, Inc.
Pittsburgh, PA   412-731-4004

Potomac Software Engineering, Inc.
Rockville, MD   301-984-3982

Prescience Corporation
San Francisco, CA   415-543-2252

Problem Solving Tools
Livermore, CA   510-447-4969

Punos Electronic AB
Goteborg, Sweden   46-31-12-17-30

Qualisys Inc.
Glastonbury, CT   203-657-3585

RockWare, Inc.
Wheat Ridge, CO   303-423-5645

Sapia Mekatronik AB
Solna, Sweden   46-8-7647260

Seawell Microsystems Inc.
Seattle, WA   206-938-5420

Skoog Software & Consulting
San Jose, CA   408-265-7756

Softcraft AG
Untersiggenthal, Switzerland
    415-628-1116

SoftShell International Ltd.
Grand Junction, CO   303-242-7502

Software Development Group
Boulder, CO   303-444-8789

Spyglass, Inc.
Savoy, IL   217-355-6000

Summit Computer Systems Inc.
New York, NY   212-334-8087

Sunset Laboratory
Forest Grove, OR   503-357-5151

System Consultants Group
Kansas City, MO   816-842-2233

Texceed Corporation
Costa Mesa, CA   714-432-7083

The Epsilon Naught Company
Cambridge, MA   617-491-6428

Timberfield Systems
Framingham, MA   508-872-0796

Tripos Associates Inc.
St. Louis, MO   314-647-1099

ViviStar Consulting
Scottsdale, AZ   602-483-3123
Please See Company Highlight Page 69.
▣

WaveMetrics, Inc.
Lake Oswego, OR   503-620-3001

WFT
Denver, CO   303-321-1119

Williams Cadco
San Diego, CA   800-321-9193

Wintress Engineering
San Diego, CA   619-550-7300

Zumwalt Environmental Systems
Torrance, CA   310-375-7734

Entertainment

AcutAbove Software
Sun City, CA   909-672-7725

Baseline
New York, NY   212-254-8235

BOOKUP
Columbus, OH   800-949-5445

Brodie Lockard
Redwood City, CA   415-368-4967

Entertainment Solutions, Inc.
Los Angeles, CA   213-871-4481

Golden Empire Publications
Anaheim Hills, CA   714-283-3000

Green Dragon Creations, Inc.
Lake in the Hills, IL 708-854-1242

GSE Choice Ticketing Software
Toledo, OH   419-475-7755

International Computer Group Inc.
Bass River, NB Canada
                       506-785-4211

ISM, INC.
Owings Mills, MD   410-560-0973

Leviathan Media Corporation
Warren, MI   313-826-3560

Lieberman & Associates
Culver City, CA   310-337-7905

Lucida Corporation
New York, NY   212-765-6655

Maxis
Orinda, CA   510-254-9700

REBO Research
New York, NY   212-989-9466

VIVISTAR CONSULTING
7015 E. Aster Drive
Scottsdale, AZ 85254
Contact: Jon Hess
Project Manager
Phone: 602-483-3123
Fax: 602-483-3123
AppleLink: VIVISTAR
Skills: OOD/OOP, C++, Assembler, TCL, Macintosh Communications Toolbox, QuickTime, 3D animation, lex and yacc for parsing, and event languages for direct manipulation.
Projects: Qd3D—Commercial Macintosh 3D source code libraries including design, implementation, documentation, customer support, and maintenance. SVT—3D software visualization research tool for program understanding. Support software for industrial process monitoring and control. Two dimensional graphics output module for a UNIX database. AppleTalk network interface XCMDs for HyperCard.
▣

DEVELOPMENT & PROGRAMMING

APPLICATIONS DEVELOPMENT

Accounting
Architecture
Business
CAD
Courseware Authoring
Education
Engineering
Entertainment
Financial
Government
Legal
Manufacturing
Medical
Publishing/ Graphics

Schindler Imaging
West Hollywood, CA 310-652-5624

Sean Hill Software Development
Woodacre, CA   415-488-4510

Synth-Bank
Portland, OR   503-626-9084

Target Technologies, Inc.
Norwalk, CT   203-866-6010

The Dreamers Guild Inc.
Granada Hills, CA   818-349-7339

Words & Deeds
San Jose, CA   408-294-2974

Financial

Aatrix Software Inc.
Grand Forks, ND   800-426-0854

Absolute Advantage, Inc.
Chatsworth, CA   818-718-2027

Analytix Group, Inc.
Sun Valley, ID   208-726-4518

Automated Accounting Solutions Inc.
Silver Springs, MD   301-924-3502

Avalon Computer
Demarest, NJ   201-784-8470

Capitol Mac Consultants, Inc.
Ashland, VA   804-644-6800

Cito, Inc.
Scottsdale, AZ   602-443-4701

Clerk of the Works
Sandpoint, ID   208-263-3543

Computer Information XP, Inc.
Portland, OR   503-781-0164

Concept 2001
San Jose, CA   408-985-2001

Dargon Development
Anaheim, CA   714-974-3982

DCI Integrated Computer Systems
Evanston, IL   708-328-7362

Decision Graphics
Portland, OR   503-245-7865

Donald H. Kraft & Associates
Skokie, IL   708-673-0597

Ernst & Young
Kansas City, MO   816-474-5200

Fred Pittroff
Denver, CO   303-758-7538

Globalogic Inc.
Nepean, ON Canada
                     613-721-0240

Heidi C. Bowman, CPA
Menlo Park, CA   415-325-6416

Hil Bren Consulting Services
North Brunswick, NJ 908-545-7913

HMS Computer Company
Minnetonka, MN   612-934-2652

Integrated Accounting Systems
San Francisco, CA   415-550-7670

Investment Research Institute
Concord, CA   510-686-9067

Jack Irby Consulting
Huntington Beach, CA
    714-969-9494

Kula Corporation
Chicago, IL   312-341-4967

La Solution Douce
Roven, France   35881700

Lester Ingber Research
McLean, VA   800-L-INGBER

MarketSoft, Ltd.
Yokohama, Japan   81-45-903-1377

Micro Trading Software Inc.
Wilton, CT   203-762-7820

MicroComputer Technologies, Inc.
Irvine, CA   714-552-1193

Opal Computing
Bellerose, NY   718-343-4054

Paradigm Trading Systems
Los Gatos, CA   408-399-4385

Platinum Software Corporation
Irvine, CA   714-727-1250

Quire Inc.
Poughkeepsie, NY   914-471-8505

Relational Paradigms, Inc.
Brooklyn, NY   718-624-0546

Softek Design, Inc.
Telluride, CO   303-728-5252

Technology Research Limited
Essex, England   0279-433822

Tellan Software, Inc.
San Jose, CA   408-274-1110

The Decisionworks
Burlingame, CA   415-348-2257

The Oxbridge Group
Carbondale, CO   303-963-8933

Thomson Financial Services
Boston, MA   617-345-2556

Tresidder Ltd.
Brooklyn, NY   718-858-9407

Zuffoletto & Company
San Francisco, CA   415-543-8900

Government

Al Jen, Inc.
Fair Lawn, NJ   201-796-1128

Macintosh Accounting Consultants
Philadelphia, PA   215-745-4376

McGilly Information Systems Inc.
Montreal, QC Canada
    514-933-2323

Megalith Technologies Inc.
Ottawa, ON Canada 613-225-2300

Signal Science, Inc.
Santa Clara, CA   800-266-2020

Sisca
Sherbrooke, QC Canada
    819-564-4003

Software Systems and Products Corporation
Plymouth, MI   313-453-3370

STR CORPORATION
10700 Parkridge Blvd.
Reston, VA 22091
Contact: Bob Walters, Vice President
Phone: 703-758-1149
Fax: 703-758-1119
Skills: Manufacturing systems, Omnis 7 versions 1 and 2, Oracle, C, C++, Pascal, Macintosh, Windows, training, neural networks, expert systems, operations research.
Projects: Cross-platform manufacturing and shop floor management systems including production scheduling, loss tracking, performance feedback, reporting, barcoding, inventory, maintenance scheduling and tracking, logbooks, QA, instrument calibration histories. Scientific applications for flexible querying and reporting of chemical analyses and experiments. Personnel and time-keeping systems. Development with Omnis and Oracle engines.

APPLICATIONS DEVELOPMENT

Accounting
Architecture
Business
CAD
Courseware Authoring
Education
Engineering
Entertainment
Financial
Government
Legal
Manufacturing
Medical
Publishing/ Graphics

Legal

Array Technologies, Inc.
New York, NY   212-460-8169

Beacon Export Systems, Inc.
Brookline, MA   617-738-9300

Brumbaugh, Graves, Donohue & Raymond
New York, NY   212-408-2578

DeNovo Systems, Inc.
Vancouver, WA   206-695-9372

Desktop Information
Santa Barbara, CA   805-963-4095

DLA Technology Management Consultant
Woolloomooloo, Australia
          612 3574777

Legal Computer Solutions
Parker, CO   303-841-4545

Legal Computer Solutions, Inc.
Boston, MA   617-227-4469

Silva Systems
Brooklyn, NY   718-488-7702

Technology Management Consultants
Australia   612 3574777

Virginia Systems, Inc.
Midlothian, VA   804-739-3200

Manufacturing

1ST Desk Systems
Medway, MA   508-533-2203

Advanced Data Systems
Winter Park, FL   407-657-4805

AmeriChem Engineering Services Inc.
Phoenix, AZ   602-437-1188

Applied Statistics, Inc.
St. Paul, MN   612-481-0202

Automatix, Inc.
Billerica, MA   508-667-7900

Command Line Corporation
Edison, NJ   908-738-6500

Data Technologies International
Orange, CA   714-771-3605

Delta Catalytic Corporation
Mississauga, ON Canada
          905-821-3862

Gibbs And Associates
Moor Park, CA   805-523-0004

Green Tree Software
Irvine, CA   714-830-5682

GreenSpring Computers
Menlo Park, CA   415-327-1200

Imagine That, Inc.
San Jose, CA   408-365-0305

JBM Logic Inc.
Longueil, QC Canada
          514-646-6839

Kleinhans Systems
Cedar Grove, WI   414-668-6238

KPMG Peat Marwick Management Consultants
Boston, MA   617-723-7700

Maintenance Master Limited
Norwich, ON Canada 519-863-2551

Merion Software Associates, Inc.
Malvern, PA   215-648-3871

National Instruments
Austin, TX   800-433-3488

NuLogic® Inc.
Needham, MA   617-444-7680

OnBase Technology, Inc.
Irvine, CA   800-782-5682

Peter F. Wells
Rindge, NH   603-899-5460

Prime Prodata, Inc.
Canton, OH   216-456-8023

Qube Software, Inc.
Irvine, CA   714-559-5659

Raymond Software Inc.
Los Gatos, CA   408-395-6157

Remote Measurement Systems, Inc.
Seattle, WA   206-328-2255

SEG
Cambridge, MA   617-492-6664

SIB Consulting
Stoughton, MA   617-341-8516

Solustan, Inc.
Needham, MA   617-449-7666

Sterling Automation, Inc.
Minneapolis, MN   612-476-2700

STR Corporation
Reston, VA   703-758-1149
Please See Company Highlight Page 71.
▣

Strawberry Tree, Inc.
Sunnyvale, CA   408-736-8800

Strippit
Akron, NY   716-542-4511

Medical

A * A Data
Lubbock, TX   806-799-2323

Academic Software, Inc.
Lexington, KY   818-718-2027

Angiographic Devices Corporation
Littleton, MA   800-962-2617

Applied Informatics
Salt Lake City, UT   801-584-3060

Aries Systems Corporation
North Andover, MA   508-475-7200

Belmont Research
Cambridge, MA   617-868-6878

Bio-Logic, Inc.
San Bruno, CA   415-873-0406

BIOPAC Systems Inc.
Goleta, CA   805-967-6615

Body CT Imaging Lab
Baltimore, MD   410-955-5173

Capital Transactions
Greig, NY   315-348-8551

Class One Incorporated
Tempe, AZ   602-820-3696

Clinical Information Systems, Inc.
Seattle, WA   206-583-0338

Computing on Micro's
Bayaman, Puerto Rico
                     809-731-6275

Concepts In Healthcare, Inc.
Flower Mound, TX   214-539-3618

Delta Medical Shareware, Inc.
Somerset, KY   606-679-7745

Deltra P/L
Beecroft, Australia   484 1306

Digital Applications, Inc.
Darby, PA   215-534-8495
Please See Company Highlight Page 73.

Digital Voice Inc.
Jophin, MA   417-781-0717

Diversified Computer Corporation
Seattle, WA   206-233-0110
Please See Company Highlight Page 73.

Evergreen Technologics, Inc.
Castine, ME   207-326-8300

Ex Software, Inc.
St. Lambert, QC Canada
                     514-465-3871

Fast, Cheap, Reliable Inc.
Chicago, IL   312-774-6696

Gallaher & Associates, Inc.
Fort Smith, AR   501-452-8929

Harvard Psychiatric Consultants
Wenham, MA   508-468-2290

Health Data Sciences Corporation
San Bernardino, CA   714-888-3282

Homeopathic Bicycle Company
Northampton, England 4460428767

Icon Medical Systems, Inc.
Campbell, CA   408-879-1900

Info Dent
Area, HI   808-484-0234

Inpatients
Catasauqua, PA   215-264-2755

DIGITAL APPLICATIONS, INC.
207 S. 5th Street
Darby, PA 19023-2883
Contact: Mark Gavin, Vice
President
Phone: 215-534-8495
Fax: 215-284-4233
AppleLink: DIGAPP
Skills: MPW assembly, C, Pascal.
Macintosh Communications
Toolbox, MacApp, SCSI, NuBus,
XTND, XCMDs, and XCFNs.

**DIVERSIFIED COMPUTER
CORPORATION**
P.O. Box 2393
Seattle, WA 98111-2393
Contact: Liz Feeney
Phone: 206-233-0110
Fax: 206-233-0435
Projects: Outcomes tracking
software—customized PC software
for medical industry to meet the
exact needs of your practice.
Tracks patients, clinical information,
treatments, surgery, follow up,
results, and referrals. Featuring
tools for analysis, reports,
graphs, and correspondence.
Don't wait for health care reform!
Call Diversified Computer.

**APPLICATIONS
DEVELOPMENT**

Accounting

Architecture

Business

CAD

Courseware
Authoring

Education

Engineering

Entertainment

Financial

Government

Legal

Manufacturing

Medical

Publishing/
Graphics

AVALON ENGINEERING, INC.
45 Newbury Street, Suite 208
Boston, MA 02116
Contact: Michael Bonnette, Vice
President, Marketing
Phone: 617-247-7668
Fax: 617-247-7698
AppleLink: AVALON
CompuServe: 70541,2000
Skills: Newton, OOD/OOP,
imaging algorithms, color
calibration, QuickTime, Photoshop,
Quark, SCSI/Serial drivers.
Projects: PresenterPad for Newton,
PCS100 color workstation, KCMS
developer toolkit, QuickTime
digitizer, color photo-retouch
package, CD-ROM data retrieval
application, PIM database.
Clients: Kodak, Scitex/IRIS, ON
Technology, Pastel, Data
Translation, MicroRetrieval.
Publishing Graphics

Jonoke Software Development, Inc.
Edmonton, AB Canada
403-448-3647

KillerBytes Software
Birmingham, AL   205-995-4741

MacMedic Publications, Inc.
Houston, TX   713-960-1858

Marigold Database Systems Inc.
West Nyack, NY   800-524-0556

Maron Computer Services
Oxnard, CA   805-389-6606

MEDformatics, Inc.
Fayetteville, NC   910-323-1748

Neurodata Inc.
Pasadena, CA   818-564-9201

Ninth Wave Computing, Inc.
Chapel Hill, NC   919-929-8894

ORCA Software Company
Richmond, WA   206-868-7007

P & P Data Systems Inc.
Downsview, ON Canada
416-665-6450

Physicians' Educational Series
Atherton, CA   415-369-6897

Projects in Knowledge Inc.
Secaucus, NJ   201-617-9700

Richards Consulting Enterprises
Newport Beach, CA   714-261-2051

RTJ Corporation
Weston, MA   617-899-1266

SmileSystems Inc.
Elkins Park, PA   215-663-9155

SoftCare
Bainbridge Island, WA
206-780-1729

SoftEasy Software, Inc.
Conshohocken, PA   215-825-5510

Strategic Planning Systems, Inc.
Southport, CT   203-255-2916

Strichman Medical Equipment, Inc.
Medfield, MA   508-359-5312

Synapse Software Inc.
Rockingham, NC   919-895-6301

Systec Computer Services
San Jose, CA   408-723-2264

Technovation Training Inc.
Toledo, OH   419-537-1122

Teton Data Systems
Jackson, WY   307-733-5494

The Decision Support Group Inc.
Pasadena, CA   818-683-3801

The Garrison Group
Escondido, CA   619-731-5248

Universal Medsoft, Inc.
San Jose, CA   408-286-7880

Vision Chips
Costa Mesa, CA   714-831-1994

Wabash Medical Resources Inc.
Indianapolis, IN   317-579-5900

Windom Health Enterprises
Berkeley, CA   510-848-6980

World Company
Rockford, IL   815-633-9205

TURNING POINT SOFTWARE

Founded in 1983, Turning Point Software is a consulting firm specializing in the design and development of a wide variety of Macintosh, MS-Windows, and DOS software products. The company offers a full range of services including new product development, cross-platform development, multimedia development, conversions, and systems software. In addition to strong technical expertise, the company has a mature technical management and organizational structure. Turning Point is one of the largest, independent product development companies in the industry and employs a large, full-time staff of software engineers, technical managers, and quality assurance engineers. The company has a proven track record of success in commercial product development.
Skills: Product design/development, multimedia, cross platform, systems software, conversion, C, C++, Assembler, MS-Windows, MS-DOS.
Clients: Microsoft, Lotus, Broderbund.

TURNING POINT SOFTWARE, INC.
One Gateway Center
Newton, MA 02134
Phone: 617-332-0202
Fax: 617-332-1121
AppleLink: D0621

AVALON ENGINEERING, INC.
45 Newbury Street, Suite 208
Boston, MA 02116
Contact: Michael Bonnette, Vice President Marketing
Phone: 617-247-7668
Fax: 617-247-7698
AppleLink: AVALON
CompuServe: 70541,2000
Skills: Imaging algorithms, color calibration, QuickTime, Photoshop, Quark, SCSI/Serial Drivers, Newton, OOD/OOP.

HONEYBEE SOFTWARE INC.
5 East 47th Street
New York , NY 10017
Contact: James McBeath
Phone: 800-667-1233
Fax: 514-875-2940
AppleLink: CDA0270
Skills: 4th Dimension,FoxPro, C++, Pascal, Apple Media Language, AppleScript, Macromedia Lingo, HyperCard, multimedia publishing.

APPLICATIONS DEVELOPMENT

Accounting
Architecture
Business
CAD
Courseware Authoring
Education
Engineering
Entertainment
Financial
Government
Legal
Manufacturing
Medical
Publishing/ Graphics

Zayante Creek Productions
Felton, CA   408-335-7412

Publishing/Graphics
21st Century Graphics
Arvada, CO   303-420-4344

Adam Leffert
Boston, MA   617-254-7931

Adept Solutions
San Marcos, CA   619-727-8376

Affinity Software Corporation
Walpole, MA   508-668-7800

Avalon Engineering, Inc.
Boston, MA   617-247-7668
Please See Company Highlight Page 74, 75.

Azalea Software, Inc.
Seattle, WA   800-48-ASOFT

Balzer/Shopes Inc.
Brisbane, CA   415-468-6550

Baudville Inc.
Grand Rapids, MI   616-698-0888

Binders Computer Graphics
Atlanta, GA   404-252-2516

Bitstream Inc.
Cambridge, MA   617-497-6222

1-UP COMPUTING
1330 Deby Place
Colorado Springs, CO 80921
Contact: Chris Magnuson,
Project Manager
Phone: 719-488-0125
Fax: 719-488-0125
AppleLink: ONE.UP
Internet: oneup@oneup.com
Skills: Macintosh and PowerPC,
C/C++, MacApp,
THINK/Symantec, Apple MPW,
assembly, Microsoft Windows,
UNIX, X11, and Motif.
Projects: Digital audio filtering,
SCSI drivers, device drivers,
graphical user interfaces (GUI),
embedded systems design, custom
applications and control panels,
network applications, technical
writing.
Clients: Hewlett-Packard, Sonic
Foundry, Los Alamos National
Laboratories.

AVALON ENGINEERING, INC.
45 Newbury Street, Suite 208
Boston, MA 02116
Contact: Michael Bonnette, Vice
President Marketing
Phone: 617-247-7668
Fax: 617-247-7698
AppleLink: AVALON
CompuServe: 70541,2000
Skills: OOD/OOP, MacApp,
Newton, C++, imaging
algorithms, QuickTime, Windows
and UNIX to Macintosh
conversions.
Projects: PCS100 color
workstation, KCMS developer
toolkit, PresenterPad™,
QuickTime digitizer, color photo-
retouch package, CD-ROM data
retrieval application, PIM
database.
Clients: Kodak, Scitex/IRIS, ON
Technology, Pastel, Data
Translation, MicroRetrieval.

C4 Network, Inc.
Denver, CO   303-825-8183

Cart Systems
Rotterdam, Holland 31-10-4376628

Circle Noetic Services
Mount Vernon, NH   603-672-6151

Compumation Inc.
State College, PA   814-238-2120

Computer Graphics Group
Cincinnati, OH   513-241-8300

Crystal Graphics Inc.
Santa Clara, CA   408-496-6175

Datawindow Software
Eugene, OR   503-686-5771

Diehl.Volk Typographics
Los Angeles, CA   213-851-3111

Document Partners Nederland
AJ Oss, The Netherlands
                               31-4120-27272

EM Software, Inc.
Steubenville, OH   614-284-1010

Envent Group
Lexington, KY   606-273-9891

Euronix Computing
Cheltenham, England
                               44-242-250504

FCS, S.L.
Palma, Spain   3471-75 4831

Fine Artist's Color & Ink
Santa Monica, CA   310-397-9908

FSL Computer Services Division
Warrington, England   0925 34214

Full News Information Service
Ann Arbor, MI   313-761-1236

Hermes Systems S.A.
Angleur, Belgium
                               011-32-41-678-372

Honeybee Software Inc.
New York, NY   800-667-1233
Please See Company Highlight Page 75.

Image Systems
Stamford, CT   203-323-3396

In Software
Escondido, CA 619-743-7502

Integrated Software Inc.
New York, NY 212-545-0110

International Computer Systems
Greenville, SC 803-676-9292

JMT Technologies, Inc.
Niceville, FL 904-897-2380

Knowledge Software, Inc.
Ossining, NY 914-762-7667

KyTek, Inc.
Weare, NH 603-529-2512

Lara Consulting Group
Boston, MA 617-248-6999

Laserpoint
Sacramento, CA 916-847-5273

Linguist's Software, Inc.
Edmonds, WA 206-775-1130

Littauer Associates
Clifton Park, NY 518-371-5073

Macreations Publishing
Boulder, CO 303-665-7250

management graphics
Minneapolis, MN 612-854-1220

Maxwell Data Management, Inc.
Costa Mesa, CA 714-435-7703

Meadows Information Systems, Inc.
Schaumburg, IL 708-882-8202

Memory International
Aliso Viejo, CA 800-266-0488

Miles & Miles
Ellensburg, WA 509-925-5280

Modability Inc.
Los Angeles, CA 310-312-5358

Monarch Design Systems
Glendale, NY 718-894-8520

North Atlantic Publishing Systems, Inc.
Chelmsford, MA 508-250-8080

Pixel Perfect
Escondido, CA 619-480-1827

Plug-In Systems
Boulder, CO 303-530-9344

Ray Dream Inc.
Mountain View, CA 415-960-0768

Sackman Associates
Sudbury, MA 508-443-3354

Second Glance
Laguna Hills, CA 714-855-2331

Synaptic Micro. Solutions
Appleton, WI 800-526-6547

The VALIS Group
Richmond, CA 510-236-4124

Total Integration, Inc.
Palatine, IL 708-776-2377

Totem Graphics Inc.
Tumwater, WA 206-352-1851

Turning Point Software
Newton, MA 617-332-0202
Please See Ad Page 75.
▣

Visions Edge, Inc.
Tallahassee, FL 904-386-4573

Weingarten Gallery
Dayton, OH 513-435-0134

CONSULTING SOLUTIONS, INC.
100-25 Queens Blvd.
Forest Hills, NY 11375
Contact: Steven S. Gold, President
Phone: 718-275-8976
Fax: 718-275-8976
CompuServe: 71662,515
Projects: Network design and installation, hardware searches, software package searches and installation, database design, custom programming, systems requirements studies, system troubleshooting and fine tuning, training and seminars. Manufacturing and financial specialists.
Clients: Local 282 Trust Funds, Formal Fabrics Ltd., Deutsche Bank AG, Berger Industries Inc., American Bank Note Company.
▣

DIGITAL APPLICATIONS, INC.
207 S. 5th Street
Darby, PA 19023-2883
Contact: Mark Gavin, Vice President
Phone: 215-534-8495
Fax: 215-284-4233
AppleLink: DIGAPP
Skills: MPW assembly, C, Pascal. Macintosh Communications Toolbox, MacApp. SCSI, NuBus, XTND, XCMDs, and XCFNs.

DEVELOPMENT & PROGRAMMING

APPLICATIONS DEVELOPMENT

Accounting
Architecture
Business
CAD
Courseware Authoring
Education
Engineering
Entertainment
Financial
Government
Legal
Manufacturing
Medical
Publishing/ Graphics

CONTRACT PROGRAMMING

Assembler
C++, Object Oriented
C. Pascal
HyperTalk
THINK

MACXPERTS, INC.
3228 L. West Cary Street
Richmond, VA 23221
Contact: Karen Cauthen,
Director, Sales
Phone: 804-353-7122
Fax: 804-358-3847
AppleLink: XPERTS
Skills: C and C++ in THINK and
MPW environments, THINK Class
Library, MacApp, HyperCard, the
Newton Toolkit, XCMDs, XFCNs,
Maintosh Communications
Toolbox, and user interface design.
Projects: MacXperts, a certified Apple
Developer and Partner, has extensive
experience in all aspects of Macintosh
and Newton software engineering and
development. Our goal is to provide
quality software solutions that are
cost effective. We specialize in
developing intelligent front ends for
mainframe applications utilitzing
DAL, SQL, DB2, etc. Our
programmers are supported by
on-site graphic artists that design
custom graphics for our programs.
Clients: Philip Morris, General
Electric, Federal Reserve,
Northern Telecom.

MASTER SOFTWARE INC.
1725 Springbrook Road
Lafayette, CA 94549
Contact: Meryl Natchez
Phone: 510-975-0650
Fax: 510-930-7304
Skills: C, C++, THINK C,
SmallTalk, MitemView, HyperCard,
TAL, COBOL, SCOBOL, DAL, RSC,
ObjectPAL, Visual BASIC, Visual
C++, SQL, Oracle, IBM Utilities, etc.

X-Ray Scanner Corporation
Torrance, CA   310-214-1900

Xante Corporation
Mobile, AL   800-926-8839

XMAN
San Francisco, CA   415-626-3359

CONTRACT PROGRAMMING

1-Up Computing
Colorado Springs, CO
                    719-488-0125
Please See Company Highlight Page 76.

Access Technologies, Inc.
Englewood, CA   303-799-0640

ACK Software & Beratungs
Dortmund, Germany
                  0049-231-527604

ARC Electronics
Brighton, England   44 273 207739

Armo
St. Louis, MO   314-821-4094

AutoSoft
East Greenwich, RI   401-885-3631

Avalon Engineering, Inc.
Boston, MA   617-247-7668
Please See Company Highlight Page 76.

Barnes Computer, Inc.
Upper Marlboro, MD 301-350-4752

Bergmann Und Langer GmbH
Munchen, Germany
                    49 89 342476
Bobcat Systems
Ossining, NY   914-762-2374

Cedrus Corporation
Silver Spring, MD   301-589-1828

Charles E. Brault
Rockville, MD   301-279-7164

Cheshire Group
Sebastopol, CA   707-887-7510

Cider Mill Software
Ann Arbor, MI   313-347-2503

Circuit Research Corporation
Nashua, NH   603-880-4000

Class Software
San Carlos, CA   415-592-5513

Coconut Info
Honolulu, HI   808-947-6543

CompuMod Software
Orchard Lake, MI   313-360-0456

COMPUTER: Applications Inc.
Raleigh, NC   919-846-1411

Consulting Solutions, Inc.
Forest Hills, NY   718-275-8976
Please See Company Highlight Page 77.

Critical Path Software, Inc.
Lake Oswego, OR   503-635-9585

Daniels Associates Inc.
Indianapolis, IN   317-692-8830

Data, Design + Engineering
Denver, CO   303-321-1119

DataPak Software Inc.
Vancouver, WA   206-573-9155

David Spector Associates
Waltham, MA 617-894-9455

Debron Enterprises
Littleton, CO 303-972-1243

Déwí Development Corporation
Plano, TX 214-422-9903

Digital Applications, Inc.
Darby, PA 215-534-8495
Please See Company Highlight Page 77.

Digital Objectives
Boundbrook, NJ 908-302-9600

Doctor Mac
Vienna, VA 800-45D-RMAC

E & C Manufacturing/Computer Supply Company
Bohemia, NY 516-244-7390

Ed-Sci Development
Modesto, CA 209-545-3656

EDGE Environmental Development Group
Santa Barbara, CA 805-563-2684

Engineerium
San Diego, CA 619-292-1900

Exact Systems, Inc.
Roseville, MN 612-486-7501
Please See Ad Page 66.

Finnegan O'Malley & Company Inc.
San Francisco, CA 415-288-4400

Focal Point Systems, Inc.
Woodside, CA 415-851-0211

Gem City Software
Dayton, OH 513-435-8887

Geni Inc.
Chelmsford, MA 508-256-7992

Good Northwest
Bainbridge Island, WA
206-842-7164

Goodall Software Engineering
Rohnert Park, CA 707-795-2335

Green Arbor Software
Salt Lake City, UT 801-575-5369

Husk
Manhattan Beach, CA
310-372-1757

HV Consultants
Houston, TX 713-488-0808

Independent Consultant
Leawood, KS 913-451-2532

IronMike Software Inc.
Decatur, GA 404-687-9646

JGI
Playa del Rey, CA 800-423-0814

John Pane, Consultant
Pittsburgh, PA 412-363-8280

John Shockey
Cambridge, MA 617-547-7815

JP Imaging
Phoenix, AZ 602-992-4064

JTZ Engineering, Inc.
Torrance, CA 310-534-8559

Kanbay Resources Inc.
Chicago, IL 312-274-3890

MLT SOFTWARE, INC.
P.O. Box 19787
Portland, OR 97280
Contact: Michael Trigoboff, Ph.D., President
Phone: 503-452-0652
AppleLink: MLT.SOFTWARE
Skills: Prograph, HyperCard, THINK C/C++, TCL, MPW, Assembler, LISP.

NEW MEDIA, INC.
503 E. 200th Street, Suite 202
Cleveland , OH 44119-1543
Contact: Leonard W. Pagon, Jr., President
Phone: 216-481-7900
Fax: 216-481-1570
AppleLink: NEWMEDIA
Skills: PowerBuilder, Visual BASIC, 4th Dimension, FoxPro, Lotus Notes, Omnis 7, Visual C++, C, MacApp, SQL server, Oracle, Windows NT.
Projects: We offer a full range of application development and education services focusing on graphical, client/server, workflow, OOP, and cross-platform technology areas. We assist as organizations migrate toward emerging technologies such as client/server and workgroup computing, and provide planning, education, and development to facilitate knowledge transfer. Typical projects include: marketing support, financial reporting, decision support, EIS, sales automation, customer service, order entry, project tracking for Fortune 1000 companies.

APPLICATIONS DEVELOPMENT

Accounting
Architecture
Business
CAD
Courseware Authoring
Education
Engineering
Entertainment
Financial
Government
Legal
Manufacturing
Medical
Publishing/ Graphics

CONTRACT PROGRAMMING

Assembler
C++, Object Oriented
C, Pascal
HyperTalk
THINK

PROSOFT ENGINEERING INC.

942 Finovino Court
Pleasanton, CA 94566
Contact: Greg Brewer, President
Phone: 510-462-8935
AppleLink: PROSOFT
Skills: SCSI, Ethernet, Token
Ring, Assembler, C, C++, Pascal,
HyperCard, MPW, THINK, INIT,
CDEV, DA, XFCN, and XCMD.
Projects: Custom software for
graphics, databases, scheduling,
data backup, sound editing,
communications, printers,
plotters, fax modems, and
interapplication communications.

RWD TECHNOLOGIES, INC.

10480 Little Patuxent Parkway,
Parkview Bldg., Suite 1200
Columbia, MD 21044
Contact: Johnny Baker, Director,
Business Development
Phone: 404-551-8198
Fax: 404-551-8105
AppleLink: BAKER.RWD
Skills: C, C++, MPW, MacApp,
HyperCard, MitemView, Oracle,
Visual BASIC, Nexpert Object,
Omnis 7, MetroWerks Code
Warrior, AppleScript.
Projects: As an Apple Preferred
Integration Partner and Microsoft
Solutions Partner, RWD provides
custom solutions in the areas of
customer service and call centers,
sales force automation,
performance support systems,
client/server database design,
VITAL consulting, and cross-
platform software development.
Clients: Apple Computer Inc.;
Motorola; Steelcase; Holiday Inn;
Citicorp; Gannett; Federal
Express; General Electric.

Kinetic Software Inc.
Woodside, CA   415-851-4484

Knowledge Bank, Inc.
Blaine, MN   612-754-8140

Knowledge Factory
Burnsville, MN   612-890-8292

Landgrove Associates
Flemington, NJ   908-932-3685

Language Systems Corporation
Herndon, VA   800-252-6479

Lapin Systems Inc.
West Chester, PA   610-696-2179

Lawinger Consulting, Inc.
Maple Grove, MN   612-425-6164

LICA Systems Inc.
Fairfax, VA   703-359-0996

Lighthouse Technology
Mission Viejo, CA   714-457-1656

Logicat
New York, NY   212-529-1840

Logikal Solutions
Naperville, FL   708-420-0210

Los Angeles Software Inc.
Santa Monica, CA   310-450-8500

REUSABLE SOLUTIONS

Skills: Reusable Solutions offers a full spectrum of expert services in
the areas of distributed information systems and object-oriented
software. We are experts in SmallTalk, C++, MacApp, NextStep, and
VisualWorks.

Projects: RSI has two decades of experience in the design, development,
delivery, and deployment of object-oriented systems and applications.
RSI is expert in object-oriented technology, databases, communication
networks, vertical MIS applications, multimedia, and project
management. RSI services include mentoring, training, design and
integration, analysis, and custom-designed classes.

Clients: RSI has provided services to clients in the areas of finance,
health services, manufacturing, transportation, and more.

REUSABLE SOLUTIONS, INC.
1130 S.W. Morrison Street, Suite 318
Portland, OR 97205
Phone: 503-223-6892
Fax: 503-223-4498

VITAL
849 South Pine Court
Lynden, WA 98264-9775
Contact: Brad Kollmyer
Phone: 206-354-8120
Fax: 206-354-8622
AppleLink: KOLLMYER
Skills: C, C++, 680x0, Assembler, MPW, THINK C, TCL, TCP/IP, printer drivers, installer scripts, UNIX, Macintosh Communications Toolbox tools, networking, algorithm optimizations.
Projects: Custom development of applications, control panels, printer drivers, external code resources.
Clients: Microsoft, Adobe Systems, Sentient Software.

SHELL SYSTEMS LTD.

Jill Merriam-Knotts, Owner/Developer
471 Buckhurst Drive
Kernersville . North Carolina . 27284
tel 910-996-8485
fax 910-996-8611

SHELL SYSTEMS LTD. is a software development company specializing in solutions for small (and *very* small) businesses - especially niche market businesses with unique application needs. Services are offered in custom, desktop database development using *Omnis 7* (for Macintosh or Windows) and *PowerBuilder Desktop* (for Windows; Macintosh available soon). Please call, write, or fax to discuss a solution for *your* business.

Lou Harrison & Associates, Inc.
Princeton Junction, NJ
609-275-8318

Lynch's Computer Services, Inc.
Shalimar, FL   904-862-1831

Maconsult
Concord, CA   510-686-9067

MacSourcery
Escondido, CA   619-747-2980
▣

MacXperts, Inc.
Richmond, VA   804-353-7122
Please See Company Highlight Page 78.
▣

Master Software Inc.
Lafayette, CA   510-975-0650
Please See Company Highlight Page 78.
▣

Micro Solutions
Haysville, KS   316-522-1500

MindStorm, Inc.
Berkeley, CA   510-644-3902
▣

Minerva Technology, Inc.
Dallas, TX   214-871-7033

Mintaka Technologies
Stroudsburg, PA   717-421-1184

Miracle Concepts, Inc.
Lancaster, PA   717-299-7382

MLT Software, Inc.
Portland, OR   503-452-0652
Please See Company Highlight Page 79.

Morgenlender Associates
Newton Highlands, MA
617-965-7514

Morrison Consulting
Paia, HI   808-575-9160

Nadcomp Systems Inc.
Brooklyn, NY   718-336-3318

Netcetera
El Segundo, CA   310-414-9534

NeuWorld Services
San Diego, CA   619-485-1456

New Media, Inc.
Cleveland, OH   216-481-7900
Please See Company Highlight Page 79.
▣

Oakleaf Designs
Cupertino, CA   408-257-1547

APPLICATIONS DEVELOPMENT

Accounting

Architecture

Business

CAD

Courseware Authoring

Education

Engineering

Entertainment

Financial

Government

Legal

Manufacturing

Medical

Publishing/ Graphics

CONTRACT PROGRAMMING

Assembler

C++, Object Oriented

C, Pascal

HyperTalk

THINK

Oliver.Creation
Gernering, Germany
49 89 8401693

OmniVision
Highland, CA   909-886-1734

Open Designs, Inc.
San Francisco, CA   415-929-0924

P. A. Christenson
Fremont, CA   510-793-6766

PBM-Analys AB
Skarholmen, Sweden
468 710 4825

PowerHouse Programmers
Walnut Creek, CA   510-946-0904
Please See Ad Page 67.
▣

Prosoft Engineering Inc.
Pleasanton, CA   510-462-8935
Please See Company Highlight Page 80.

PSC Consultants
Redondo Beach, CA   310-372-5096

Quansa
Incline Village, NV   702-831-8829

Randal Jones & Associates
Mountlake Terrace, WA
206-774-9044

Re: Software
Tempe, AZ   602-897-9703

Recommended Test Labs, Inc.
San Francisco, CA   415-928-1192

Redwolf
Redwood City, CA   415-369-8741

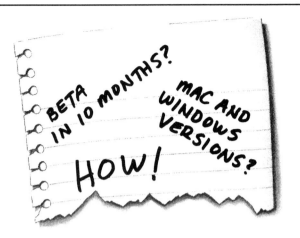

TURN TO TURNING POINT

For a very simple reason - We understand the business of software product development and we've been doing it successfully since 1983.

Our approach to project management insures proper controls, scheduling and budgeting. With a full time Quality Assurance and experienced Software Engineering staff, we have the technical excellence and proven track record to get your product done right. Plus, our experience in Macintosh®, MS-Windows® and DOS cross platform development is unparalleled.

Turning Point Software, the one to turn to for software product development services at its best.

Call or write for a free portfolio.

One Gateway Center
Newton, Massachusetts 02158
617-332-0202

VINTAGE CONSULTING GROUP

P.O. Box 1805
Sonoma, CA 95476
Contact: Jay Hall, President
Phone: 707-939-8387
Fax: 707-939-1102
Skills: Visual BASIC, Pascal, C, Crystal Reports, Windows application development, XBASE, Btrieve, SQL Windows, Quest, Dynamics, system analysis and design.

ART & LOGIC

P.O. Box 56465
Sherman Oaks, CA 91413
Contact: Justin Souter, Partner
Phone: 818-501-6990
Fax: 818-995-8669
AppleLink: J.SOUTER
Skills: C++, assembly, MacApp, MFC, and OWL.

WEST VALLEY ENGINEERING

Established in 1968, we have been providing technical contractors in the software realm to some of the Silicon Valley's most reputable companies. We pride ourselves in providing superior caliber contractors at a moment's notice. We have supported projects of every size and complexity, and offer a full range of services to assist you in your staffing needs.

Skills: Macintosh, MPW, C/C++, MacApp, Macintosh Communications Toolbox, QuickTime, THINK, A/UX, GUI development, UNIX, TCP/IP, Oracle, SCSI, Windows, Visual BASIC/C++.

Projects: SW development, technical support, QA/Testing, database design, network engineering, graphic design/illustration and publications.

WEST VALLEY ENGINEERING, INC.
1183 Bordeaux Drive
Sunnyvale, CA 94089
Phone: 408-744-1420
Fax: 408-734-4338

Reusable Solutions Inc.
Portland, OR   503-223-6892
Please See Ad Page 80.

Richardson Technical Services
St. Louis, MO   314-427-8142

Robert S. Lenoil
Mountain View, CA   415-968-0882

Robert T. Culmer Consulting Services
Dallas, TX   214-321-5191

Rock Ridge Enterprises
Ann Arbor, MI   313-663-0706

RTS Corporation
San Diego, CA   619-484-7509

RWD Technologies, Inc.
Columbia, MD   404-551-8198
Please See Company Highlight Page 80.

Scott Knudsen
Rapid City, SD   605-348-1782

Script Software International
Fairfield, IA   515-469-3916

Second Difference
Troy, MI   810-689-3051

SILC, Incorporated
Germantown, MD   301-428-1439

Software by Mann
Santa Cruz, CA   408-426-0846

DEVELOPMENT & PROGRAMMING

APPLICATIONS DEVELOPMENT

Accounting
Architecture
Business
CAD
Courseware Authoring
Education
Engineering
Entertainment
Financial
Government
Legal
Manufacturing
Medical
Publishing/ Graphics

CONTRACT PROGRAMMING

Assembler
C++, Object Oriented
C. Pascal
HyperTalk
THINK

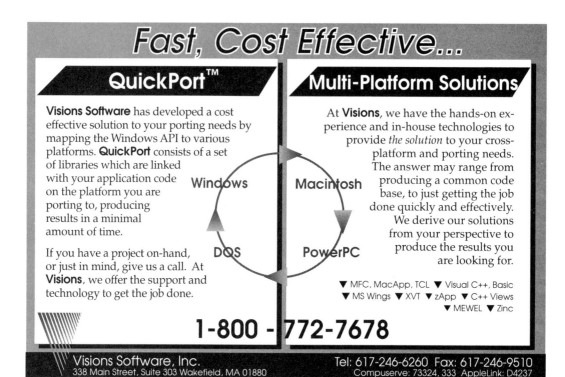
Software Designs Unlimited, Inc.
Chapel Hills, NC   919-968-4567

Sound Logic
New York, NY   212-533-0466

Spellbinder Systems Group
North Hollywood, CA
818-760-3956

Spring City Software
Spring City, PA   215-469-4600

Stage Research
Parma Heights, OH   216-888-8295

Starlight Software Solutions
Oakland, NJ   201-405-1208

Steven Fine
Cary, NC   419-481-2538

Sumbolon Corporation
Cambridge, MA   617-576-0758

Synergy Group
Los Angeles, CA   310-471-7897

Synthesis Design
Raleigh, NC   919-787 3571

Team Development Corporation
Austin, TX   512-892-1095

Techbridge, Inc.
San Diego, CA   619-224-4881

Technology Locator
San Diego, CA   800-275-4852

The Registry, Inc.
Newton, MA   800-248-9119

The Soft Programer
Oakland, CA   510-841-6500

Triad International Corporation
Minneapolis, MN   612-832-5574

Trillium Business Learning, Inc.
Campbell, CA   408-879-0111

TriLogic, Inc.
Seattle, WA   206-784-3117

Triple Point, Inc.
Beaverton, OR   503-531-2890

Turning Point Software
Newton, MA   617-332-0202
Please See Ad Page 68.
▣

Vector Systems
Fort Wayne, IN   219-478-8088

Vintage Consulting Group
Sonoma, CA   707-939-8387
Please See Company Highlight Page 83.
▣

Vital
Lynden, WA   206-354-8120
Please See Company Highlight Page 81.

West Side Electronics Inc.
Canoga Park, CA   818-884-4794

West Valley Engineering, Inc.
Sunnyvale, CA   408-744-1420
Please See Ad Page 83.

Zephron Corporation
Lynnwood, WA   206-778-8396

Assembler

Dynamic Engineering
Ben Lomond, CA   408-336-5531

Korody-Coleman, Inc.
Milpitas, CA   408-956-0322

C++, Object Oriented

Abraxas Software, Inc.
Portland, OR   503-244-5253

ADS Designs
Henderson, NC   919-438-6321

Air Land Systems
Fairfax, VA   703-573-1100

All Star Computer Services
San Francisco, CA   415-282-0540

Applied Technologies GmbH
Berlin, Germany   49-30-8592958

Arborworks, Inc.
Ann Arbor, MI   313-747-7087
▣

Art & Logic
Sherman Oaks, CA   818-501-6990
Please See Company Highlight Page 83.
▣

Asgard Consulting
Beltsville, MD   703-521-8403

AVALON ENGINEERING, INC.
45 Newbury Street, Suite 208
Boston, MA 02116
Contact: Michael Bonnette,
Vice President, Marketing
Phone: 617-247-7668
Fax: 617-247-7698
AppleLink: AVALON
CompuServe: 70541,2000
Skills: OOD/OOP, MacApp,
Newton, C++, imaging algorithms,
QuickTime, Windows and UNIX
to Macintosh conversions.
Projects: PCS100 color
workstation, KCMS developer
toolkit, PresenterPad™,
QuickTime digitizer, color photo-
retouch package, CD-ROM data
retrieval application, PIM
database.
Clients: Kodak, Scitex/IRIS, ON
Technology, Pastel, Data
Translation, MicroRetrieval.

**APPLICATIONS
DEVELOPMENT**

Accounting

Architecture

Business

CAD

Courseware
Authoring

Education

Engineering

Entertainment

Financial

Government

Legal

Manufacturing

Medical

Publishing/
Graphics

**CONTRACT
PROGRAMMING**

Assembler

C++, Object
Oriented

C, Pascal

HyperTalk

THINK

BEAR RIVER ASSOCIATES, INC.
P.O. Box 1900
Berkeley, CA 94701-1900
Contact: Rodney Smith
Phone: 510-644-9400
Fax: 510-644-9778
AppleLink: BEARRIVER
Internet: info@bearriver.com
Skills: Programming, systems integration, training, and consulting for Macintosh, Windows, and Newton platforms. Complete range of services, from product development to in-house systems. Curriculum includes Macintosh technology, OOP, AppleTalk, Newton, and VITAL.

COPIOUS SYSTEMS
P.O. Box 6703
Los Osos, CA 93412
Contact: Richard Leddy, Owner
Phone: 805-528-2685
AppleLink: COPIOUS.SYS
Skills: Languages (C, C++, HyperTalk), MPW, and MacApp. TCP/IP experience. Algorithm design research and development: AI, Numerics, etc.

Avalon Engineering, Inc.
Boston, MA   617-247-7668
Please See Company Highlight Page 85.

Bear River Associates, Inc.
Berkeley, CA   510-644-9400
Please See Company Highlight Page 86.

Biocomp
Carlsbad, CA   619-931-9148

Bitworks
Simi Valley, CA   805-583-2547

Bloom Software
Broomfield, CO   303-469-7348

Blue Tree Technology Inc.
Pacifica, CA   415-738-1754

Calliope Enterprises Inc.
Redlands, CA   909-793-5995

Canyonlands Software
Moab, UT   801-259-7680

Century Software
Berlin, Germany   030/6242420

CFJ R & D
Le Plessis, Bouchard, France
33-1-30-72-06-90

Chris Forden
Novato, CA   415-897-7284

Christophe Vanhecke
Pau, France   33-59-83-73-58

Computer Results
Moorpark, CA   805-529-3618

Copious Systems
Los Osos, CA   805-528-2685
Please See Company Highlight Page 86.

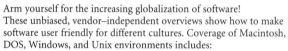
DIGITAL APPLICATIONS, INC.
207 S. 5th Street
Darby, PA 19023-2883
Contact: Mark Gavin, Vice President
Phone: 215-534-8495
Fax: 215-284-4233
AppleLink: DIGAPP
Skills: MPW assembly, C, Pascal. Macintosh Communications Toolbox, MacApp, SCSI, NuBus, XTND, XCMDs, and XCFNs.
Projects: Custom and commercial Macintosh applications. Socket-level DECnet, TCP/IP, and ADSP communications, serial communications, backup software for SCSI tape drives, network updating of Macintosh computers across wide area networks. APIs, drivers, and INITS.
Clients: SmithKline Beecham, E.I., DuPont, GE Aerospace, FMC.

INNOVA SYSTEMS
5775 8th Avenue
Montreal, QC H1Y 2L9 Canada
Contact: Martin Dufort, President
Phone: 514-374-2486
Fax: 514-374-2486
Internet: innova@cam.org
Skills: Object-oriented analysis, design, and development. Prograph CPX, Macintosh Communications ToolBox, C++ and application frameworks, UNIX, object-oriented database. Custom object-oriented solutions. Multiplatform development.
Projects: Geographical information systems (GIS), graphical client/server front end, communications software.
Clients: National Defense Canada (DREV), Confederation-Life Insurance, Bombardier Inc., YMCA, Hydro-Quebec.

DEVELOPMENT & PROGRAMMING

APPLICATIONS DEVELOPMENT

Accounting
Architecture
Business
CAD
Courseware Authoring
Education
Engineering
Entertainment
Financial
Government
Legal
Manufacturing
Medical
Publishing/ Graphics

CONTRACT PROGRAMMING

Assembler
C++, Object Oriented
C, Pascal
HyperTalk
THINK

Digital Applications, Inc.
Darby, PA   215-534-8495
Please See Company Highlight Page 87.

DNS, Inc.
San Francisco, CA   415-433-1077

Electronic Learning Systems Inc.
Gainesville, FL   800-443-7971

Emphasys Technologies, Inc.
Dallas, TX   214-380-4947

Entropy
Forest Knolls, CA   415-488-4143

Fundamental Software
Sandy, UT   801-944-0133

future tense
Mercer Island, WA   206-232-1475

FutureSoft System Designs Inc.
New York, NY   212-219-0599

Graffio, Inc.
New York, NY   212-366-1404

HDS Systems
Tucson, AZ   602-325-3004

Hutchings Software Development
Danville, CA   510-820-6413

HyperProject, Inc.
Granada Hills, CA   818-831-0404

Hypertek, Inc.
Derwood, MD   301-216-9836

**Icon EDV Informations-
Systeme GmbH**
Wien, Austria   43 (1) 545-5155

Imagine Better Software
Boulder, CO   303-499-1377

**Information Conversion
Services, Inc.**
Deerfield, IL   708-405-0501

INNOVA systems
Montreal,QC Canada 514-374-2486
Please See Company Highlight Page 87.

Instantiations Inc.
Portland, OR   503-242-0725

Interval Music Systems
Los Angeles, CA   310-478-3956

Janus Technologies
St. Paul, MN   612-293-0108

KASA
San Diego, CA   619-578-1831

Langley Autosystems
Sunnyvale, CA   408-252-4700

LC Resources
Amity, OR   503-835-4803

LinksWare
Monterey, CA   408-372-4155

Mark/Space Softworks
Santa Clara, CA   408-982-9781

Match Data Systems
Bellevue, WA   206-453-2951

Mentat Research Inc.
Kingston, ON Canada 613-544-3563

Micro Alliance Inc.
Wakefield, MA   617-245-8879

Molecular Solutions
Livermore, CA   510-447-5101

Multimedia Design Group, Inc.
Centreville, VA   703-266-9213

Navigation Technologies Inc.
Annapolis, MD   410-268-9701

Nelson Laffey Associates, Inc.
St. Louis, MO   314-436-9725
▣

NeoLogic Systems
San Francisco, CA   415-566-9207

New Media, Inc.
Cleveland, OH   216-481-7900
Please See Company Highlight Page 89.
▣

Object Factory Inc.
Maple Grove, MN   612-420-9876

Oxford & Associates Inc.
Cupertino, CA   408-996-9961

Pacific Systems, Inc.
Santa Cruz, CA   408-429-1814

PacPics
Telopea, Australia   61-2-684-2570

Paradigm Software
Concordia, MO   816-463-2217

Philmont Software Mill
Philmont, NY   518-672-4890

Polymorph
Suffolk, England   0374 651 740

Positive Logic
Fairfax, VA   703-591-4908

Pragma
Austin, TX   512-335-2311

Prodigy Technologies Corporation
Vancouver, BC Canada
                          604-687-4636

Quantic Corporation
St. Paul, MN   612-698-4268

QuesTech
Farmington, NY   716-924-5497

Ralph Krug, P.E.
Dexter, MI   313-426-3503

Richard D.Robbins,
Independent Consultant
Wilton, CT   203-761-0749

Seishin Creations
Cross City, FL   904-498-7325

Skamp Computer Services Inc.
Eden Prairie, MN   612-941-0696

STM Languages, Enterprises
Encinitas, CA   619-599-7922

Technical Programming Services Inc.
Dallas, TX   214-241-9920

Techway Solutions
Bruce, Australia   06-256-3444

The Philmont Software Mill
Philmont, NY   518-672-4890

The Thought Shop
Prior Lake, MN   612-447-8475

NEW MEDIA, INC.
503 E. 200th Street, Suite 202
Cleveland , OH 44119-1543
Contact: Leonard W. Pagon, Jr.,
President
Phone: 216-481-7900
Fax: 216-481-1570
AppleLink: NEWMEDIA
Skills: We offer a full range of
client/server and workflow
development and certified training
with tools such as PowerBuilder,
Visual BASIC, 4th Dimension,
Lotus Notes, Access, Windows NT,
SQL server, and more.
▣

WEST VALLEY ENGINEERING, INC.
1183 Bordeaux Drive
Sunnyvale, CA 94089
Contact: Chris Van Groningen
Phone: 408-744-1420
Fax: 408-734-4338
AppleLink: WVE.SFTWRENG
CompuServe: 72053,34
Skills: Macintosh, MPW,
C/C++, MacApp, Macintosh
Communications Toolbox,
QuickTime, THINK, A/UX, GUI
development, UNIX, TCP/IP,
Oracle, SCSI, Windows, Visual
BASIC/C++.
Projects: SW Development,
technical support, QA/Testing,
database design, network
engineering, graphic
design/illustration and publications.

DEVELOPMENT & PROGRAMMING

APPLICATIONS DEVELOPMENT

Accounting

Architecture

Business

CAD

Courseware Authoring

Education

Engineering

Entertainment

Financial

Government

Legal

Manufacturing

Medical

Publishing/ Graphics

CONTRACT PROGRAMMING

Assembler

C++, Object Oriented

C, Pascal

HyperTalk

THINK

The Visaeon Corporation
Port Chester, NY   914-939-2579
▣

Tranquility System Advisors
West Jordan, UT   801-967-0658

Turning Point Software
Newton, MA   617-332-0202
Please See Ad Page 70.
▣

Victor Consulting
Mt. View, CA   415-964-9870

Visions Software, Inc.
Wakefield, MA   617-246-6260
Please See Ads Pages 67, 84.
▣

Visual Programming, Inc.
Cupertino, CA   408-865-6690

Vital
Lynden, WA   206-354-8120

ViviStar Consulting
Scottsdale, AZ   602-483-3123
▣

West Valley Engineering, Inc.
Sunnyvale, CA   408-744-1420
Please See Company Highlight Page 89.

Yale University School of Medicine Biomedical Media Production
New Haven, CT   203-785-4088

Zihua
Pacific Grove, CA   408-372-0155

C, Pascal

Adventurer Software
Belmont, MA   617-926-6705

Archway Systems
Huntington Beach, CA
    714-374-0440

Arroyo Software
Milan, MI   313-439-3828

B. W. Software
Ann Arbor, MI   313-769-8587

Bear River Associates, Inc.
Berkeley, CA   510-644-9400
Please See Company Highlight Page 91.
▣

Catspaw Inc.
Salida, CO   719-539-3884

Douglas Corarito
Rowe, MA   413-339-0246

DPK Software
Ann Arbor, MI   313-996-0771

Engineered Software Solutions Corporation
Hot Springs, AR   501-262-2048

Enlightened Software Corporation
Anaheim, CA   714-998-4220

Ford Consulting
Orange, CA   714-771-7509

Gary J. Hardy, Inc.
Belmont, CA   415-595-5899

GEO Computing Systems
Tucson, AZ   602-743-0950

Grant Holland & Associates
Duluth, GA   404-447-5471

KKS Software Inc.
Exton, PA   215-594-0552

Kutoroff Development
Clearwater, FL   813-796-8725

Lion's Share
Salt Lake City, UT   801-268-3218

M/Mac
Arlington, VA   703-237-2498

Moonlighting Software Development
Clear Water, FL   813-796-8725

Orcutt/Oeflein Software
Frankfort, MI   616-352-9071

Pharos Technologies
Cincinnati, OH   513-573-7100

Pine Grove Software
Trenton, NJ   609-730-1430

Shireman Software
Sebastopol, CA   707-887-2809

Software Masters
Woodinville, WA   206-483-2564

Symbionics
Los Gatos, CA   408-353-2016

The Hybrid Group, Inc.
Rockaway, NJ   201-540-1505

HyperTalk

AI Consultants, Inc.
Cupertino, CA   408-253-7299

Architectronica
Redondo Beach, CA   310-376-7054

Berumen & Associates
Cupertino, CA   408-971-4401

Bliss Interactive Technologies
Comanche, OK   405-439-2247

Chrysalis Software, Inc.
Toronto, ON Canada 416-466-1915

Computer Help Services
Denver, CO   303-428-3609

Creative Computing
Columbus, OH   614-488-6930

EPSI Computer Systems, Inc.
Delta, Canada   604-589-4412

Exact Systems, Inc.
Roseville, MN   612-486-7501

Ganesa Designs Inc.
San Anselmo, CA   415-456-0348

Highlighted Data Inc.
Arlington, VA   703-516-9211

Hurn Computing
Collinsville, IL   618-345-3569

Hyper Active Software
Minneapolis, MN   612-724-1596
Please See Company Highlight Page 91.

Inter/Action
Sunnyvale, CA   408-749-9539

BEAR RIVER ASSOCIATES, INC.
P.O. Box 1900
Berkeley, CA 94701-1900
Contact: Rodney Smith
Phone: 510-644-9400
Fax: 510-644-9778
AppleLink: BEARRIVER
Internet: info@bearriver.com
Skills: Programming, systems integration, training, and consulting for Macintosh, Windows, and Newton platforms. Complete range of services, from product development to in-house systems. Curriculum includes Macintosh technology, OOP, AppleTalk, Newton, and VITAL.

HYPER ACTIVE SOFTWARE
5226 W. Nokomis Parkway
Minneapolis, MN 55417
Contact: Jacqueline Gay, President
Phone: 612-724-1596
AppleLink: HYP.ACT.SFTW
CompuServe: 72027,3225
AOL: HYPER1
Genie: J.GAY4
Skills: HyperCard, SuperCard, multimedia.
Projects: Wide variety of applications: business, education, scheduling, telecommunications. Programs include sending cueing tones to a television satellite, room and equipment scheduling and tracking, "stand-alone" Finder applications, special-needs teaching programs, business evaluation and education.
Clients: American Cancer Society, Minnesota State Department of Education, Hubbard Broadcasting Corporation.

MicroWorks

MicroWorks is a multiplatform database development company. We utilize s/w engineering principles to provide flexibility and timely product delivery. Our programmers are experienced in accounting and medical database systems, telecommunications and data transmission, touch-screen video, biofeedback, project management and scheduling.
Operating Systems: UNIX, Macintosh, MS/DOS, MS/Windows, XWindows, OS/VS2, DEC PathWorks, Novell NetWare, LAN Manager, Banyan VINES, AppleShare, OS/2, Solaris, OSF/Motif.
Software: C++, Pascal, Structured COBOL, COBOL II, CICS, IMS, Assembler, TSO, JES2/JES3 JCL, MVS/XA, Intertest, Comparex, VSAM, Xpeditor, Roscoe, Dylakor, Micro Focus Workbench, PCtools, Textra, Micro Focus COBOL, EDE.
Databases: 4th Dimension, Ingres, Informix, FoxBASE, DBase, Watcom/SQL, QNA, FileMaker Pro, Oracle, Gupta/SQL, Paradox.

MicroWorks
345 East 81st, Suite 3F
New York, NY 10028
Phone: 212-794-4466
Fax: 212-861-0588

APPLICATIONS DEVELOPMENT

Accounting
Architecture
Business
CAD
Courseware Authoring
Education
Engineering
Entertainment
Financial
Government
Legal
Manufacturing
Medical
Publishing/ Graphics

CONTRACT PROGRAMMING

Assembler
C++, Object Oriented
C, Pascal
HyperTalk
THINK

DEVELOPMENT & PROGRAMMING

THE SLEETER GROUP
952 San Jose Street
San Leandro, CA 94577-3833
Contact: Don Sleeter, Partner
Phone: 510-614-8148
CompuServe: 71101,2130
Skills: HyperTalk, WindowScript, XCMDs, C++, MacApp, Visual BASIC, database programming.
Projects: HAPPE Desktop Shopper, Employee Performance Review, FormsNAVIGATOR, Connections.
Clients: Apple Computer, Inc.; National Semiconductor; Microsoft; Danny Goodman; NOAH Software.

VOLDSTAD INTERACTIVE DESIGN
524 S. Castlerock Terrace
Sunnyvale, CA 94087
Contact: Karyn Voldstad, President
Phone: 408-733-4116
Fax: 408-773-8303
AppleLink: KARYN.V
AOL: KARYN.V
Skills: Information and interface design; HyperTalk and AppleScript; some Director scripting. Design and development of custom software and interactive training courses.

ALABANZA CONSULTING
1265 Beech Street
East Palo Alto, CA 94303
Contact: Shannon Pekary, Owner
Phone: 415-327-5433
Fax: 415-327-5433
AppleLink: ALABANZA
Skills: THINK C with Objects, Windows cross-platform development, HyperCard, CDEVs, INITs, Desk Accessories, System 7.
Projects: Complete product design services, including software, manuals, packaging, production, and marketing. Specialties also include high-speed text retrieval systems and object-oriented desk accessories.

Jennie's Code Boutique
San Francisco, CA   415-664-4010

KEA
Portland, OR   503-223-1149

Kentary, Inc.
Highlands Ranch, CO 303-791-2077

L & L Products, Inc.
Hanover, NH   603-643-4503

Second Nature
Sunnyvale, CA   408-737-8374

SoftMaven
Berkeley, CA   510-525-7532

Soothsong
San Francisco, CA   415-931-1614

StepUp Software
Dallas, TX   214-520-7717

Steve Blake Design
Stoughton, MA   617-341-8763

Symplex Systems
Burnaby, BC Canada 604-433-1795

The Sleeter Group
San Leandro, CA   510-614-8148
Please See Company Highlight Page 92.

The Turnaround Team, Inc.
Westfield, NJ   908-654-7117

Voldstad Interactive Design
Sunnyvale, CA   408-733-4116
Please See Company Highlight Page 92.

Wette Enterprises
Clayton, MO   314-863-1248

THINK

Alabanza Consulting
East Palo Alto, CA   415-327-5433
Please See Company Highlight Page 92.

Bartlett, Brandley & Lucky
Apopka, FL   407-869-9421

QuickSilver Software, Inc.
Costa Mesa, CA   714-241-0601

DATABASE PROGRAMMING

Adjuvare, Inc.
Virginia Beach, VA   804-481-1975

After Hours Software
Van Nuys, CA   818-780-2220

Ambit Informatic
Barcelona, Spain   34-3-419 3358

American Retail Consultants
La Jolla, CA   619-457-1087

ANEXTEK
Webster, NY   716-671-5190

Ariel Software Consultants, Inc.
Chicago, IL   312-764-3434

Ashmead Computers
Bryn Mawr, PA   215-527-9560

AwareTech Design
Palo Alto, CA   415-324-9240

Bannister Lake Software Incorporated
Cambridge, ON Canada
519-622-9535

92   AGORA DIGITAL MARKETPLACE

C & C Logic Engineering
Brighton, MA   617-782-4981

CINNABAR Macintosh
Gardiner, MT   406-848-7978

Click Click, Inc.
Chanhassen, MN   612-934-7926

Click Systems
Clinton, NJ   908-996-3773

Comptrol, Inc.
Redmond, WA   206-869-2700

Computer Dynamics
Denton, TX   817-566-5515

Computer Survival
Grand Prairie, TX   214-647-8239

Database Designs
Cambridge, MA   617-876-2727

DataCraft
Lakewood, CO   303-232-4321

DataMasters
Mt. Airy, MD   301-831-0183
▣

DATATAG
Bensalem, PA   215-245-5352

David Berman Developments Inc.
Ottawa, ON Canada 800-665-1809

Demometricka
Los Angeles, CA   310-390-6380
▣

Desktop Edit
Milano, Italy   39-2-2363931

Drextec Inc.
Mount Laurel, NJ   609-234-7969

Durrant Software Limited
York, England   44 904 44181

E. E. S. Companies, Inc.
Framingham, MA   508-653-6911
Please See Company Highlight Page 93.

Edu-Tech Associates, Inc.
Melbourne Beach, FL
▣   407-952-0745

Ernest De Gidio
Columbus, OH   614-447-1825

Fain & Co.
Atlanta, GA   404-876-4668
Please See Company Highlight Page 93.

Forty-Two Software
Hamburg, Germany   49 40381924

Fractal Solutions
Marietta, GA   404-955-5169

Herrel Business Systems
Orefield, PA   215-398-8280

**HJM Computer
Consulting Group, Inc.**
Toledo, OH   419-471-1223

Imagination Solutions Corporation
Morgan Hill, CA   408-779-3961

Info Serv Information Service Inc.
Potomac, MD   301-299-6404

InfoMaker Inc.
Chicago, IL   312-736-4059

Intramedia
Hyannis, MA   508-775-9033

E.E.S. COMPANIES, INC.
2 Vernon Street, Suite 404
Framingham, MA 01701
Contact: Hank Szretter
Phone: 508-653-6911
Fax: 508-650-1872
AppleLink: D2582
CompuServe: 72146,1214
Skills: 4th Dimension, HyperCard, Pascal, C, C++.
Projects: Design, develop, support client/server based database programs. Accounting, inventory control, bar-coding, order entry, point-of-sale, credit card processing, and network communications.
Clients: John Hopkins University, Nestle Beverage Company, Raytheon, Turner Broadcasting.

FAIN & CO.
957 Blue Ridge Avenue
Atlanta, GA 30306
Contact: David Fain, President
Phone: 404-876-4668
Fax: 404-876-4085
AppleLink: D6620
Skills: Specializing in database development in Omnis 7. Multimedia interfacing with Director and HyperCard.
Projects: Databases for inventory tracking, auction tool, and human resources tracking tool.
Clients: Business, medical.

DEVELOPMENT & PROGRAMMING

CONTRACT
PROGRAMMING

Assembler

C++, Object
Oriented

C, Pascal

HyperTalk

THINK

DATABASE
PROGRAMMING

4th Dimension

DAL

DBase

Filemaker Pro

FoxBASE

Helix

Omnis 7

Oracle

Paradox

SQL

Sybase

NEW MEDIA, INC.

503 E. 200th Street, Suite 202
Cleveland, OH 44119-1543
Contact: Leonard W. Pagon, Jr.,
President
Phone: 216-481-7900
Fax: 216-481-1570
AppleLink: NEWMEDIA
Skills: PowerBuilder, Visual BASIC,
4th Dimension, FoxPro, Lotus
Notes, Omnis 7, Visual C++, C,
MacApp, SQL server, Oracle,
Windows NT.
Projects: We offer a full range of
application development and
education services focusing on
graphical, client/server, workflow,
OOP, and cross-platform
technology areas. We assist as
organizations migrate toward
emerging technologies such as
client/server and workgroup
computing, and provide planning,
education, and development to
facilitate knowledge transfer.
Typical projects include: marketing
support, financial reporting,
decision support,
EIS, sales automation, customer
service, order entry, project
tracking for Fortune 1000
companies.

NANCY A. RIDENHOUR, CDP

801 Southland Road
Huntersville, NC 28078
704-875-0144
Projects: Handle responsibility for
any project tasks from definition
through post-evaluation and
support. Very strong analytical and
programming skills with related
abilities to organize, plan, and
direct. Expertise in banking and
textile industries using IBM
mainframes, COBOL, TSO, IMS,
VSAM, and Hogan. Knowledgeable
in CICS, Easyplus, AS400 RPG, and
PCs.

J. Schachter Enterprises
Skokie, IL   708-329-1111

JP Systems
Burke, VA   703-644-6644

Kracom Computer Services
Wheeling, IL   708-590-0250

Laser Solutions Inc.
Atlanta, GA   404-992-3914

MacTechnologies Consulting
New York, NY   212-807-5611

Maximum Software
Cherry Hill, NJ   609-795-2041
Please See Company Highlight Page 99.

MDG Computer Services
Arlington Heights, IL 708-818-9991

Medical Database Systems
San Diego, CA   619-558-2002

MegaBase Inc.
Mountain View, CA 415-960-3575

Michael J. Harper
Novato, CA   415-479-4034

Micromega Systems, Inc.
San Francisco, CA   415-346-4445

MicroWorks
New York, NY   212-794-4466
Please See Ad Page 91.

MTP Systems Consulting, Ltd.
Arlington Heights, IL 708-392-9908

Nancy A. Ridenhour, CDP
Huntersville, NC   704-875-0144
Please See Company Highlight Page 94.

New Media, Inc.
Cleveland, OH   216-481-7900
Please See Company Highlight Page 94.

Odin Technologies, Inc.
Wilton, CT   203-762-9628

Online Computer Systems Inc.
Germantown, MD   301-428-3700

Pepa Informatik
Winterthur, Switzerland
                          052-222-76-44

Personal Library Software
Rockville, MD   301-926-1402

PinPoint Solutions
Mountain View, CA 415-962-9857
Please See Company Highlight Page 95.

Practical Computer Solutions, Inc.
Anchorage, AK   907-561-3878

Rae Technology, Inc.
Cupertino, CA   408-725-2850
Please See Company Highlight Page 95.

Randy Schroeder
Portland, OR   503-228-4020

Robert F. Miller & Associates
Modesto, CA   209-545-2909

SelectStar, Inc.
New York, NY   212-243-8413

SFC Desktop Business Systems
San Francisco, CA   415-255-0200

Shell Systems, Ltd.
Kernersville, NC   910-996-1757

Soft Solutions, Inc.
Atlanta, GA   404-457-9400

Soft Way Computer Software
Mamaroneck, NY   914-381-4626

Software Design Technologies
New City, NY   914-634-2051

SpaceTime Systems
Cambridge, MA   617-354-4618

Stephanas & Company
Lake Jackson, TX   409-297-6647

Strata Systems
Austin, TX   512-327-8334

SYSTEM REENG Inc.
Camarillo, CA   805-388-0908

TaskMan Business Systems
Anaheim, CA   714-502-9051

TEC Computer Consultants
New York, NY   212-274-9441

The Automation Group
San Francisco, CA   415-777-9167

TM Computer Consulting, Inc.
Stamford, CT   203-359-3082

Unlimited Access
San Francisco, CA   415-255-8958
Please See Company Highlight Page 96.
▣

Unlimited Ink
New Braunfels, TX   210-629-7483

Valad Data Solutions, Inc.
Annandale, VA   703-820-4026

Vintage Consulting Group
Sonoma, CA   707-939-8387
▣

Way Cool Productions
Douglassville, PA   610-385-6080

White Creek Software
Buskirk, NY   518-686-1760
Please See Ad Page 107.

Wizdom Micro Systems, Inc.
Lake Montezuma, AZ
                    602-567-5011
Please See Company Highlight Page 96.
▣

4th Dimension

7 Star Computer Solutions
Sacramento, CA   916-925-2125

A la Carte Systems
New York, NY   212-779-8090

ACI US, Inc.
Cupertino, CA   408-252-4444

adINFINITUM Development
Brooklyn, NY   718-788-7092

Advanced Laser Graphics
Washington, DC   202-342-2100

Alto Stratus
Yachats, OR   503-547-3264

Amicus Software
Austin, TX   512-258-6373

Andante Systems
St. Paul, MN   612-699-2709

Another Dimension Ltd.
Hornchurch, Essex, England
                    44 708 701 511

PINPOINT SOLUTIONS
2095 Landings Drive
Mountain View, CA 94043
Contact: Charles Lloyd
Phone: 415-962-9857
Fax: 415-962-9858
Skills: Paradox (Windows/DOS),
FoxPro (Windows/DOS/Mac),
Clipper, Access, 4th Dimension,
FoxBase+, SQL server, Sybase,
Oracle, Informix, FileMaker Pro,
Visual BASIC, Visual C++, C, C++,
FORTRAN, LISP, COBOL, Pascal.
Projects: Custom database
design for business and research
applications. We specialize in
the needs of biotech and
multimedia firms.
Clients: Alcatel Comptech, Hewlett
Packard, MetraBio Systems,
LipoMatrix, Media Tech.
▣

RAE TECHNOLOGY, INC.
19672 Stevens Creek Blvd.
Cupertino, CA 95014
Contact: Norman Gilmore
Phone: 408-725-2850
Fax: 408-725-2855
AppleLink: RAE
Projects: Rae Technology is a leader
in building information
management solutions for
knowledge workers and
professionals. Our emphasis on
participatory design, prototyping,
and quality assurance ensures that
the product you get is the product
you want. Whether you need a
front end or a complete solution,
Rae has the Macintosh experience
you need.
▣

CONTRACT
PROGRAMMING

Assembler

C++, Object
Oriented

C, Pascal

HyperTalk

THINK

DATABASE
PROGRAMMING

4th Dimension

DAL

DBase

Filemaker Pro

FoxBASE

Helix

Omnis 7

Oracle

Paradox

SQL

Sybase

UNLIMITED ACCESS

529 Noe Street
San Francisco, CA 94114
Contact: Bren Besser, Consultant
Phone: 415-255-8958
CompuServe: 73057,3045
Skills: 4th Dimension, SQL,
HyperTalk, Visual BASIC,
Revelation, Word, Excel,
Windows, Macintosh.
Projects: Unlimited Access
provides the services for creating
business information systems. We
have developed custom solutions
for
a variety of companies from
different industries, ranging in
size from sole proprietors to those
in the Fortune 500.
Clients: Transamerica, University
of San Francisco, Kodak, Primo
Angel, Inc., ITT Financial.

WIZDOM MICRO SYSTEMS, INC.

P.O. Box 5444
Lake Montezuma, AZ 86342
Contact: James Trammel, President
Phone: 602-567-5011
Fax: 602-567-5011
CompuServe: 76416,1212
AOL: MACWIZDOM
Skills: 4th Dimension, C, BASIC,
SQL, DAL.
Projects: Personal, client/server,
SQL solutions, including: sales
representative automation for
world's largest biotech firm:
Amgen; billing system: A&M
Recording Studios; radio airplay
tracking: The Album Network;
experience in publishing, personal
injury, finance, marketing,
communications, human
resources, and more. Emphasis on
user interface, function, and speed.

Arlington Technology Group
Arlington, VA   703-553-3976

Armadillo Computer Services
Manchester, MO   314-256-0824

Beyond Technology
New York, NY   212-675-3764

Braided Matrix, Inc.
Shokan, NY   914-657-6411

Business Computer Solutions Inc.
Columbia, MD   301-596-5005

Business Software Applications
Inver Grove, MN   612-455-3000

Business Solutions
Hermosa Beach, CA   310-372-1583

C4SI, Inc.
Oak Park, IL   708-386-3060

Cargas Systems, Inc.
Lancaster, PA   717-560-9928

Charles Cooper Consulting
Pittsboro, IN   317-892-4588

Charles Rogers & Associates Inc.
Sunnyvale, CA   408-253-8215

Christensen Design
Southlake Drive, TX 817-424-3312

Coda
Stockholm, Sweden   46 86116972

Compas Technologies
Camarillo, CA   805-484-9205

COMPUTE-X
Unionville, NY   212-674-4158

CST Consulting
Cupertino, CA   408-257-1952

Custom Interfacing Solutions
Nashua, NH   603-889-1098

CustomWare Inc.
Toronto, ON Canada 416-932-9443

Dart Computing
Ventura, CA   805-658-9240

Data Dimensions, Inc.
Seattle, WA   206-783-7611

Database Techniques Pty, Ltd.
Marayong, Australia
                           61-2-837-2075

Desert Sky Software, Inc.
Phoenix, AZ   602-279-4600

Desjardin Consulting
Fremont, CA   510-659-1546

Digital Designs Corporation
Sioux Falls, SD   605-334-1588
Please See Company Highlight Page 97.

Digital Thought
Irvine, CA   714-282-0127

Eclipse Services
Upper Darby, PA   215-352-6800

Edo Communications
Canton, MA   617-821-6324

Efficiency & Software
Highlands Ranch, CO 303-791-4444

**Emerging Information
Technologies, Inc.**
Needham, MA   617-444-6185

Excalibur Technologies
Manchester, MO

Extra Computer Services, GmbH
Wiesbaden, Germany 49-611-39257

FMI Group, Ltd.
McLean, VA   703-905-0006

Footprints, Inc.
Salt Lake City, UT   800-635-5280

Footprints, Inc., NW Operations
Seattle, WA   800-635-5280

Frostbyte Software, Inc.
Brighton, MI   313-229-3110

Globus Systems, Inc.
San Francisco, CA   415-292-6744

Halley & Scott
Kirkland, WA   206-822-0970

Holder, Egan & Company, Inc.
Midland, MI   517-636-7373

Honeybee Software Inc.
New York, NY   800-667-1233
Please See Company Highlight Page 97.
▣

IM Strategies
Campbell, CA   408-378-4444

Impact Solutions Inc.
Pittsburgh, PA   412-367-8833

Informed Solutions Inc.
Brookline, MA   617-739-0306

JM Associates
Cambridge, MA   617-864-9806

John Pyra Consulting
Westford, MA   508-692-8070

Les Logiciels Macapa
St. Lambert, QC Canada
                     514-923-0887

LGH Informati Zurich
Zurich, Switzerland   411 4612571

MacDesigns
San Francisco, CA   415-863-1551

Macsys Inc.
Kanata, ON Canada   613-591-9200

Magenta Seven, Inc.
Raleigh, NC   919-787-2787

ManPower Corporation
Cortland, NY   607-756-4150

Meta-Solutions, Inc.
Gatineau, ON Canada
                     819-561-9173

Microtrade
Wien, Austria
                     43-1-435930

Montage Software Systems
Wilton, CT   203-834-1144
▣

Muirhead & Associates
Elgin, IL   708-888-1695

Natural Intelligence Inc.
Cambridge, MA   617-876-4876

New Line
Lille, France   33 20578218

New Media, Inc.
Cleveland, OH   216-481-7900
Please See Company Highlight Page 97.
▣

Newhoff & Associates
Woodinville, WA   206-481-8175

DIGITAL DESIGNS CORPORATION
2505 S. Jefferson Avenue
Sioux Falls, SD 57105
Contact: David Knoflicek
Phone: 605-334-1588
Fax: 605-335-4312
AppleLink: D4064
Skills: 4th Dimension single-user and client/server applications.
Projects: General accounting and retail management service systems; medical billing systems for clinics; wholesale, retail, manufacturing inventory control, multilevel automated pricing systems; development of integrated customized applications.

HONEYBEE SOFTWARE INC.
5 East 47th Street
New York , NY 10017
Contact: James McBeath
Phone: 800-667-1233
Fax: 514-875-2940
AppleLink: CDA0270
Skills: 4th Dimension, Pascal, C++ extensions, accounting, job management, contact management.
▣

NEW MEDIA, INC.
503 E. 200th Street, Suite 202
Cleveland, OH 44119-1543
Contact: Leonard W. Pagon, Jr., President
Phone: 216-481-7900
Fax: 216-481-1570
AppleLink: NEWMEDIA
Skills: We offer a full range of client/server and workflow development and certified training with tools such as PowerBuilder, Visual BASIC, 4th Dimension, Lotus Notes, Access, Windows NT, SQL server, and more.
▣

CONTRACT
PROGRAMMING

Assembler

C++, Object
Oriented

C. Pascal

HyperTalk

THINK

DATABASE
PROGRAMMING

4th Dimension

DAL

DBase

Filemaker Pro

FoxBASE

Helix

Omnis 7

Oracle

Paradox

SQL

Sybase

BEAR RIVER ASSOCIATES, INC.
P.O. Box 1900
Berkeley, CA 94701-1900
Contact: Rodney Smith
Phone: 510-644-9400
Fax: 510-644-9778
AppleLink: BEARRIVER
Internet: info@bearriver.com
Skills: Programming, systems
integration, training, and
consulting for Macintosh,
Windows, and Newton platforms.
Complete range of services, from
product development to in-house
systems. Curriculum includes
Macintosh technology, OOP,
AppleTalk, Newton, and VITAL.
▣

PINPOINT SOLUTIONS
2095 Landings Drive
Mountain View, CA 94043
Contact: Charles Lloyd
Phone: 415-962-9857
Fax: 415-962-9858
Skills: Paradox (Windows/DOS),
FoxPro (Windows/DOS/Mac),
Clipper, Access, 4th Dimension,
FoxBase+, SQL server, Sybase,
Oracle, Informix, FileMaker Pro,
Visual BASIC, Visual C++, C, C++,
FORTRAN, LISP, COBOL, Pascal.
▣

Nexial
Brewster, NY   914-279-7486

Off Key Microsystems
Pasadena, CA   818-794-8100

Options Computer Consulting
New York, NY   212-645-3577

Opus Systems
San Rafael, CA   510-525-5742

Oryx Associates
San Francisco, CA   415-563-9971

Ourtime Publishing
Columbia, MD   410-964-8062

Peripheral Visions Inc.
Hillsboro, OR   503-640-1317

Personal Consulting Services
Schaumburg, IL   708-310-0080

Philip Davis & Associates
Shawnee, KS   913-962-0389

Pickering & Associates
Columbus, OH   614-459-1670

Pindar Graphics Systems
Scarborough, England 0723 362222

PinPoint Solutions
Mountain View, CA 415-962-9857
▣

Preferred Technologies
Denver, CO   303-987-3411

Professional Systems
Brookfield, WI   414-783-5151

Relevant Technologies, Inc.
Cambridge, MA   617-864-9500

Revelar Software
Salt Lake City, UT   801-485-3291

Rubicon, Inc.
Ann Arbor, MI   313-677-2050

S2 Software
Cupertino, CA   408-257-7272
Please See Ad Page 76.

Sapphire Systems
Minneapolis, MN   612-944-0212

Sequoia Computing Solutions
Nashua, NH   603-888-5973

Seth Greenberg Computer Consulting
New York, NY   212-431-9132

Sigma 4, Inc.
Las Cruces, NM   505-382-8799

Small Business Computer Solutions
Novato, CA   415-897-4420

Sneakers Software, Inc.
Jersey City, NJ   201-798-3102

Software & Consulting
Wiesbaden, Germany 61-40-01-42

Spherix Software
San Francisco, CA   415-241-0101

Strong/Tyler Systems
Santa Rosa, CA   707-542-0545

Systems InterAction
Denver, CO   303-321-1119

**The Orlando Mac
Consulting Group Inc.**
Orlando, FL   407-678-4580

Unlimited Access
San Francisco, CA   415-255-8958
▣

Virtual Image Inc.
Ayer, MA   508-772-4225

WIS Computer Systems
Tukwila, WA   206-575-0965

Wizard Computers
Redwood City, CA   415-365-3818

Zicon Software Corporation
Lake Oswego, OR   503-635-9622

DAL

Bear River Associates, Inc.
Berkeley, CA   510-644-9400
Please See Company Highlight Page 98.
▣

Panergy Ltd.
Tel-Aviv, Israel   972-3-5612541

DBase

PinPoint Solutions
Mountain View, CA   415-962-9857
Please See Company Highlight Page 98.
▣

Filemaker Pro

A. E. Wood Consulting
Berkeley, CA   510-548-4920

Acrobyte Software
Mission Viejo, CA   714-768-8490

Apriori Inc.
Arlington Heights, IL 708-253-2856

Atkeison Consulting
Norristown, PA   215-275-7764

Baccus & Associates
Altadena, CA   818-398-1401

BlackMax
Laguna Niguel, CA   714-496-6669

Christine Maggio Consulting
Garfield, NJ   201-797-9272

Consulting Resources & Design
Pittsford, NY   716-586-6177

Crown Communications
W. St. Paul, MN   612-457-5008

Honeybee Software Inc.
New York, NY   800-667-1233
Please See Company Highlight Page 99.
▣

Joel M. Bowers & Associates
Hampton Falls, NH   603-778-7494

MacEmpowered
Portland, OR   503-284-8058

MacMinded Computer Specialists
Lincoln, NE   402-483-6937

MacTech
Basel, Switzerland   41-61-331-4081

Maximum Software
Cherry Hill, NJ   609-795-2041
Please See Company Highlight Page 99.

Michael Bodmer
Winkel, Switzerland 41-1-860-0110

Milesquare Associates
Hoboken, NJ   201-792-5415

HONEYBEE SOFTWARE INC.
5 East 47th Street
New York , NY 10017
Contact: James McBeath
Phone: 800-667-1233
Fax: 514-875-2940
AppleLink: CDA0270
Skills: Accounting, time tracking, job costing, Pascal, C++ database development.
▣

MAXIMUM SOFTWARE
121 Dumas Road
Cherry Hill, NJ 08003
Contact: Ralph Dratman, Owner
Phone: 609-795-2041
Fax: 609-354-2008
AppleLink: DRATMAN
Skills: FileMaker Pro, Omnis 7, Oracle, THINK C/Pascal, DOS, Windows, Excel, Retrospect, networking, and communications.
Projects: Clinical information systems, educational software, porting from DOS to Macintosh, graphical simulation, real-time instrument control, order-entry systems, engineering analysis.
Clients: McGraw-Hill, Campbell's Soup, Coronet Paper, Univeristy of Pennsylvania, medical and surgical practices.

CONTRACT PROGRAMMING
Assembler
C++, Object Oriented
C. Pascal
HyperTalk
THINK

DATABASE PROGRAMMING
4th Dimension
DAL
DBase
Filemaker Pro
FoxBASE
Helix
Omnis 7
Oracle
Paradox
SQL
Sybase

HONEYBEE SOFTWARE INC.

5 East 47th Street
New York , NY 10017
Contact: James McBeath
Phone: 800-667-1233
Fax: 514-875-2940
AppleLink: CDA0270
Skills: C++ extensions, AppleScripting, database applications, contact management.

▣

PINPOINT SOLUTIONS

2095 Landings Drive
Mountain View, CA 94043
Contact: Charles Lloyd
Phone: 415-962-9857
Fax: 415-962-9858
Skills: Paradox (Windows/DOS), FoxPro (Windows/DOS/Mac), Clipper, Access, 4th Dimension, FoxBase+, SQL server, Sybase, Oracle, Informix, FileMaker Pro, Visual BASIC, Visual C++, C, C++, FORTRAN, LISP, COBOL, Pascal.
Projects: Custom database design for business and research applications. We specialize in the needs of biotech and multimedia firms.
Clients: Alcatel Comptech, Hewlett Packard, MetraBio Systems, LipoMatrix,

▣

**Peat Marwick Thorne/
Strategic Solutions Inc.**
Toronto, ON Canada 416-777-3814

**Raymond Studer
Communication Publicitaire**
Bassilly, Belgium   32 68 55 28 35

SanSoft
Highlands Ranch, CO
                     303-947-6406

Sibony & Associates
Berkeley, CA   510-644-9322

SoftKare
Westport, CT   203-221-2881

Sonnet Technologies, Inc.
Irvine, CA   714-261-2800

SRS Integral, Inc.
San Francisco, CA   415-765-6705

Tokerud Consulting Group
Mill Valley, CA   415-388-8563

WegWeiser Macintosh Consulting
Allston, MA   617-945-3224

Xram Xpert Systems
New York, NY   212-989-8559

McGILLY INFORMATION SYSTEMS

McGilly Information Systems Inc. is a developer of corporate client/server applications, offering Omnis 7 consulting and development to Fortune 500 companies, government organizations, and small businesses.
Clients: Bombardier Inc., IST Group, Government of Canada, Government of Quebec, Canadian Center for Geomatic Research, Le Devoir (daily newspaper), American Apparel Inc.
Systems: Financial, project management, newspaper subscription, apparel, call management.
Skills: Multiplatform (Macintosh and Windows), client/server, Omnis 7, FoxPro, FileMaker Pro, SQL, Oracle, DAL, Ingres, TCP/IP, Novell.
Product: The Corporate Village is a client/server application with which a large organization can create an online directory of its people and services. Designed for internal use, it allows employees to look up other employees, departments, department mandates, organization charts, services, boardrooms, fax machines, etc.

BENEFITS:
• More economical than traditional printed directories

• Can be used to generate printed directory if one is needed

• Can be integrated with existing SQL databases, thus avoiding duplication of corporate data.

• Supports users in several languages

• Fully Macintosh and Windows compatible

• Customization available

CONTACT: RICHARD MCGILLY

McGILLY
INFORMATION SYSTEMS
4030 Saint-Ambroise, #440
Montreal, Canada H4C 2C7
Phone: 514-933-2323
Fax: 514-937-1052
AppleLink: MCGILLY
Internet:
70403.2611@compuserve.com

FoxBASE

Acolyte Software Corporation
Chesire, CT   203-250-8600

Applications Unlimited
Natick, MA   508-653-9300

ASD, Inc.
Pasadena, CA   818-584-6979

B-TEK
Phoenix, AZ   602-470-0705

Chertov & Associates
Sebastopol, CA   707-829-1213

Corporate Computing Services
Norfolk, VA   804-423-8503

D. Kevin Rowe
Plymouth, MI   313-420-2167

Data By Design
Olathe, KS   913-829-4975

DataLan
White Plains, NY   914-682-2022

DFC Enterprises Inc.
Laguna Beach, CA   714-497-0611

Fox & Mouse
New York, NY   212-662-0455

Foxtron Systems
Pittsburgh, PA   412-922-4844

Get Creative Technologies
Chicago, IL   312-327-8503

**Get Info Computer
Systems Incorporated**
Toronto, ON Canada 416-361-3400

HDA Technical Services
Plymouth, NH   603-536-3880

HJM Computer Consulting
Toledo, OH   419-535-8647

Honeybee Software Inc.
New York, NY   800-667-1233
Please See Company Highlight Page 100.

Information Systems Research, Inc.
Cincinnati, OH   513-772-4636

John Wong Systems Consultants
Boulder, CO   303-444-1252

MedComp Consultants
Redlands, CA   909-335-1837

Micro Management Associates
Longview, TX   903-757-6930

MicroAssist, Inc.
Northfield, MN   800-735-3457

Northwest Programming Inc.
Portland, OR   503-598-0200

Perseus Systems Corporation
Kennett Square, PA   215-388-6003

PinPoint Solutions
Mountain View, CA 415-962-9857
Please See Company Highlight Page 100.

Powers Hills, Inc.
Midwest City, OK   405-769-7695

PowerTraining
Redondo Beach, CA 310-370-4793

Richard Battin
Delray Beach, FL   407-496-1443

SFC DESKTOP BUSINESS SYSTEMS
190 Hubbell Street, Suite 201
San Francisco, CA 94107
Contact: Steve Fogel, President
Phone: 415-255-0200
Fax: 415-255-1936
AppleLink: SFC
AOL: 73057,1206
Skills: One of the largest and most experienced Omnis developers in the United States. Data modeling, CASE, SQL programming, distributed systems, multiplatform deployment.
Projects: Custom systems with emphasis on client/server technology and GUI front ends to database servers (such as Oracle and Sybase).
Clients: VISA; U.S. Airforce; Apple Computer, Inc.; McDonnell Douglas; University of California.

DEVELOPMENT & PROGRAMMING

DATABASE PROGRAMMING

4th Dimension
DAL
DBase
Filemaker Pro
FoxBASE
Helix
Omnis 7
Oracle
Paradox
SQL
Sybase

STR CORPORATION
10700 Parkridge Blvd.
Reston, VA 22091
 Contact: Bob Walters, Vice
President
Phone: 703-758-1119
Fax: 703-758-1119
Skills: Omnis 7 versions 1 and 2,
Oracle, C, C++, Pascal,
manufacturing systems,
Macintosh, Windows, training,
neural networks, expert systems,
operations research.
Projects: Cross-platform database
applications. Manufacturing
systems including production
scheduling, loss tracking,
maintenance scheduling/tracking,
logbooks, QA, performance
feedback, reporting, barcoding.
Scientific applications for flexible
querying and reporting of
chemical analyses/experiments.
Personnel and time-keeping
systems. Government databases
for document reviews, work
breakdown structures, mailing
lists, Omnis, or Oracle engines

Sanders & Sanders, Inc.
Raleigh, NC   919-782-4251

**Software Performance
Specialist, Inc.**
Palos Hills, IL   708-430-0290

Specialty Software
Evansville, IN   407-728-1199

SSTi
Mt. Laurel, NJ   609-231-7711

**System Oriented
Solutions Corporation**
Akron, OH   216-867-5881

System Solvers Ltd.
Madison Heights, MI 313-588-7400

Systems Imagineering
Naperville, IL   708-420-2044

Technique
Burbank, CA   818-718-9092

Wadsworth Data Systems AB
Helsingborg, Sweden 46-42 140201

Helix

Autograph Systems
Mansfield, PA   717-662-7718

HEARTLAND SOFTWARE CORPORATION

We specialize in Oracle support and development. Services offered include database tuning and troubleshooting, design consultation, on-site and remote support for clients with occasional need for Oracle skills, and new client/server development in Omnis 7^2.
We are most comfortable with Macintosh and UNIX as operating environments, but we also work with Windows, OS/2, VMS, and Novell. All new development is backed by CASE-based analysis.
Clients: Our clients include Fortune 500 companies as well as smaller organizations. International inquires are welcome. Recent assignments include DBA support for Oracle production applications, and development of a major new Sales Force Automation package.
See also listing under Development and Programming; Database Programming: Omnis 7.

HEARTLAND SOFTWARE CORPORATION
5917 Shandwick Place
Mississauga, ON Canada L5M 2M7
Phone: 905-858-1415
Fax: 905-826-6259
CompuServe: 70524,2346

Breakthrough Productions
Nevada City, CA   916-265-0911

DataBright Management Systems
Mill Valley, CA   415-381-9120

Datadyne Systems
Mamaroneck, NY   914-381-5704

Easy Computing
Seaside, OR   503-738-3521

Elefunt Software
Berkeley, CA   510-843-7725

POWER SERVICES of Ne Inc.
San Juan Capistrano, CA
714-496-7143

Richmond Software Corporation
Alpharettea, GA   404-623-4898

Rodus International Corporation
West Vancouver, BC Canada
604-925-9848

Roy Posner & Associates
Lafayette, CA   510-283-1146

Roy Sablosky Design
San Anselmo, CA   415-454-5771

Sandhill Systems
Acton, MA   508-635-9440

Viewpoint Consulting, Inc.
Beverly Hills, MI   313-647-9145

Wizard Software
Cleveland, OH   216-582-0582

Omnis 7

AccuWare Business Solutions Ltd.
Calgary, AB Canada   403-245-0477

Actoris Software Corporation
Richardson, TX   214-231-7588

AFTECH Corporation
Riverside, CT   203-637-4343

Chaparral Software
Beverly Hills, CA   310-273-4904

Command Systems Inc.
Natick, MA   508-651-0530

Core Business Systems
Wolfville, NS   902-542-7777

DATABEHEER
Dillbeek, Belgium   32-2-569-65-94

DirectLine Technologies, Inc.
Modesto, CA   209-545-2557

Double Click Systems, Inc.
Silver Spring, MD   202-342-5629

Essex Systems Inc.
Bloomfield, NJ   201-338-4336

Golden Avatar Software
Eugene, OR   503-343-9879

Graphic Data Designs
Mill Valley, CA   415-388-3806

GroundZero Software Solutions
Rancho Santa Marguerita, CA
714-858 1184

Heartland Software Corporation
Mississauga, ON Canada
905-858-1415

Houlberg Development
Tualatin, OR   503-692-4162

WORD MASTER, INC.
320 Earls Court
Deerfield, IL 60015
Contact: David M. Ferri, Vice President
Phone: 708-948-9600
Fax: 708-948-9617
Skills: Omnis 3.5, 7v1.x and 7v2.x.
Projects: Omnis 7 programming and design; large multi-user cross-platform client/server implementations using RdB, Sybase, Oracle, and SequeLink on VAX/IBM/UNIX platforms. Custom designed applications for small businesses.
Clients: Fortune 500 companies, e.g. Motorola, Harris Bank, FMC Corp., A.C. Nielsen; small businesses. See also listing under Development and Programming; Multiplatform Development.

BEAR RIVER ASSOCIATES, INC.
P.O. Box 1900
Berkeley, CA 94701-1900
Contact: Rodney Smith
Phone: 510-644-9400
Fax: 510-644-9778
AppleLink: BEARRIVER
Internet: info@bearriver.com
Skills: Programming, systems integration, training, and consulting for Macintosh, Windows, and Newton platforms. Complete range of services, from product development to in-house systems. Curriculum includes Macintosh technology, OOP, AppleTalk, Newton, and VITAL.

DATABASE PROGRAMMING

4th Dimension
DAL
DBase
Filemaker Pro
FoxBASE
Helix
Omnis 7
Oracle
Paradox
SQL
Sybase

EXACT SYSTEMS, INC.
2345 Rice Street, Suite 230
Roseville, MN 55113
Contact: Bryan Menell, President
Phone: 612-486-7501
Fax: 612-486-7505
AppleLink: MENELL
CompuServe: 72307,2100
AOL: EXACT
Skills: Oracle, Brio Products,
HyperCard, SuperCard,
AppleScript, 4th Dimension,
FileMaker Pro, C, VITAL,
FirstClass Servers, Newton.
Projects: Worked with Andersen
Windows personnel on the
Andersen Window of Knowledge
System; a quarter million row
database with a SuperCard
frontend now deployed at over
400 sites around the country.

NEW MEDIA, INC.
503 E. 200th Street, Suite 202
Cleveland, OH 44119-1543
Contact: Leonard W. Pagon, Jr.,
President
Phone: 216-481-7900
Fax: 216-481-1570
AppleLink: NEWMEDIA
Skills: We offer a full range of
client/server and workflow
development and certified
training with tools such as
PowerBuilder, Visual BASIC, 4th
Dimension, Lotus Notes, Access,
Windows NT, SQL server,
and more.

Information Management Systems Inc.
South Bend, IN   219-232-7372

James Pistrang Computer Resources
Amherst, MA   413-256-4569

JP Computer Resources
Amherst, MA   413-256-4569

L & B Software
N. Miami Beach, FL   305-653-3080

Logisoft Inc.
Lafayette, CA   510-939-3556

MacSolutions Inc.
Portland, OR   503-289-7174

Manufacturing And Computer Systems
Wayzata, MN   612-475-3402

McGilly Information Systems Inc.
Montreal, QC Canada 514-933-2323
Please See Ad Page 100.

Memphis Area Computer Services
Memphis, TN   901-681-0917

Microautomation Associates
Pittsburgh, PA   412-431-6148

Niche Solutions
Allentown, PA   215-435-0741

North Mountain Software
San Jose, CA   408-297-5824

Pathos One Inc.
La Plata, MD   301-932-1133

Plusware Inc.
Markham, ON Canada   905-477-0015

RDR Inc.
Portland, OR   503-643-2723

SFC Desktop Business Systems
San Francisco, CA   415-255-0200
Please See Company Highlight Page 101.

Shell Systems, Ltd.
Kernersville, NC   910-996-1757
Please See Ad Page 81.

Solutions Unlimited
Turlock, CA   209-668-0600

Stokes Electronic Enterprises P/L
Victoria, Australia   03 509 2200

STR Corporation
Reston, VA   703-758-1149
Please See Company Highlight Page 102.

Technologies Plus, Inc.
Belvidere, NJ   908-475-8883

Word Master, Inc.
Deerfield, IL   708-948-9600
Please See Company Highlight Page 103.

Worthington Software Engineering, Inc.
Minneapolis, MN   612-525-5901

Oracle

Bear River Associates, Inc.
Berkeley, CA   510-644-9400
Please See Company Highlight Page 103.

Databases, Inc.
Salt Lake City, UT   801-467-7111

Exact Systems, Inc.
Roseville, MN   612-486-7501
Please See Company Highlight Page 104.

Heartland Software Corporation
Mississauga, ON Canada
905-858-1415
Please See Ad Page 102.

**Information Management
Resources, Inc.**
Gaithersburg, MD   301-330-9022

Millstone River Systems, Inc.
Hightstown, NJ   609-443-1420

New Media, Inc.
Cleveland, OH   216-481-7900
Please See Company Highlight Page 104.
▣

PinPoint Solutions
Mountain View, CA   415-962-9857
Please See Company Highlight Page 105.
▣

STR Corporation
Reston, VA   703-758-1100
Please See Company Highlight Page 107.
▣

Paradox

Charles B. Olson & Associates
Palo Alto, CA   415-328-1708

**Comprehensive Business
Solutions Group, Inc.**
Stone Mountain, GA 404-261-4516

DataBase Designs, Inc.
Buffalo Grove, IL   708-634-9355

Datastream
Greenville, SC   803-297-6775

Diversified Computer Corporation
Seattle, WA   206-233-0110

E. J. SYSTEMS
Capitola, CA   408-462-2507

Guardianware
Dearborn, MI   313-562-9342

Montclair Data Services Corporation
Oakland, CA   510-339-8541

Mundo Corporation
Willoughby Hills, OH
216-943-4400

Puget Pastings
Roy, WA   206-843-2216

Rittenhouse & Associates
Evanston, IL   708-328-4033

**DEVELOPMENT &
PROGRAMMING**

**DATABASE
PROGRAMMING**

4th Dimension
DAL
DBase
Filemaker Pro
FoxBASE
Helix
Omnis 7
Oracle
Paradox
SQL
Sybase

STARBOARD

Starboard specializes in professional localization, translation, and consulting services for developers and distributors involved in Japanese Macintosh and Windows markets. Services range from simple localization reports and market analysis to complete package localization, printing, and production tailored to your needs and marketing plans. Starboard's strengths include: local project management, bilingual/native Japanese localization staff, expertise in Japanese Macintosh and Windows platforms, in-depth knowledge of the Japanese software market, complete layout, printing, and packaging capabilities.
Skills: MPW C/Pascal, THINK C, KanjiTalk, Text Services Manager, ResEdit, PageMaker Japanese, Quark Japanese.
Clients: ACI US, Aldus, Adobe Systems, Global Village, Light Source, Macromedia, and Transpac Software.

STARBOARD INC.
4300 Stevens Creek Blvd., Suite 245
San Jose, CA 95129
Phone: 408-261-7570
Fax: 408-984-6303
AppleLink: STAR007.DVJ

PINPOINT SOLUTIONS
2095 Landings Drive
Mountain View, CA 94043
Contact: Charles Lloyd
Phone: 415-962-9857
Fax: 415-962-9858
Skills: Paradox (Windows/DOS), FoxPro (Windows/DOS/Mac), Clipper, Access, 4th Dimension, FoxBase+, SQL server, Sybase, Oracle, Informix, FileMaker Pro, Visual BASIC, Visual C++, C, C++, FORTRAN, LISP, COBOL, Pascal.
▣

Southern Horizons Corporation
Alpharetta, GA   404-552-6875
▣

Strategic Micro Systems
Millersville, PA   717-871-9126
▣

The Systems Group
Des Moines, IA   515-278-9168

U. S. Computer
Saratoga, CA   408-446-0387

Wiltshire Computer Management
Kennebunkport, ME 207-967-2226

SQL

PinPoint Solutions
Mountain View, CA   415-962-9857
Please See Company Highlight Page 106.
▣

Shapiro & Company
Santa Barbara, CA   805-962-8109
▣

Sybase

Bear River Associates, Inc.
Berkeley, CA   510-644-9400
Please See Company Highlight Page 108.
▣

New Media, Inc.
Cleveland, OH   216-481-7900
Please See Company Highlight Page 108.
▣

Trivium Computer Systems Inc.
Montreal, QC Canada
                        514-335-9080

MULTIPLATFORM DEVELOPMENT

ADS Designs
Henderson, NC   919-438-6321
Please See Company Highlight Page 109.

Alabanza Consulting
East Palo Alto, CA   415-327-5433

Altura Software Inc.
Pacific Grove, CA   408-655-8005

Arbor Intelligent Systems, Inc.
Ann Arbor, MI   313-996-4238

Art & Logic
Sherman Oaks, CA   818-501-6990
Please See Company Highlight Page 109.

Avalon Engineering, Inc.
Boston, MA   617-247-7668
Please See Company Highlight Page 110.

BAL Associates Inc.
Los Altos, CA   415-941-6015

Bear River Associates, Inc.
Berkeley, CA   510-644-9400
Please See Ad Page 105.

Burton Computer Consulting
Hudson, WI   715-386-6114

Cheyenne Software Inc.
Roslyn Heights, NY   516-484-5110

CoDesign
Berkeley, CA   510-845-3170

ComputerCrafts
Nashua, NH   603-437-7973

CPSA
Livermore, CA   510-449-7744

Envisage Ltd.
Stamford, CA   203-965-0902

Image Builder Software
Portland, OR   503-684-5151

Impact Communication Group
Fountain Valley, CA 714-963-6760

INNOVA systems
Montreal, QC Canada
514-374-2486

InterOptica Publishing Limited
San Francisco, CA   415-788-8788

Jackson Enterprises
Boca Raton, FL   407-487-8336

KidWare
Oakland, CA   510-836-0965

Manley & Associates, Inc.
Issaquah, WA   206-392-0577

McKune Consulting Services
Rolla, MO   314-364-8487

MGlobal International Inc.
Houston, TX   713-960-0205

New Media, Inc.
Cleveland, OH   216-481-7900
Please See Company Highlight Page 111.

Perceptics Corporation
Knoxville, TN   615-966-9200

Printing Communications Associates, Inc.
Smyrna, GA   404-436-1714

PSS Systems Design, Ltd.
Oklahoma City, OK 405-528-7774

STR CORPORATION
10700 Parkridge Blvd.
Reston, VA 22091
Contact: Warren L. Capps
Phone: 703-758-1100
Fax: 703-758-1119
Skills: SQL*Forms v3.0, SQL*Reportwriter v1.1, Forms 4.0, Reports 2.0, database administration/tuning, data modeling, Oracle applications development, training, CASE.
Projects: Cross-platform Oracle applications including military hardware configuration management, data conversion, municipal bond data management, drug clinical test results, marketing systems documentation services, Oracle training for all levels of expertise, Oracle consulting in database administration and applications performance tuning, Omnis 7 front ends to Oracle engines.

Quorum Software Systems
Menlo Park, CA   415-323-3111

Rhyton Software
Carmel, CA   408-626-1250

Robert Gezelter Software Consultant
Flushing, NY   718-463-1079
Please See Company Highlight Page 111.

DATABASE PROGRAMMING

4th Dimension
DAL
DBase
Filemaker Pro
FoxBASE
Helix
Omnis 7
Oracle
Paradox
SQL
Sybase

MULTIPLATFORM DEVELOPMENT

PRODUCT LOCALIZATION

USER INTERFACE DESIGN

BEAR RIVER ASSOCIATES, INC.
P.O. Box 1900
Berkeley, CA 94701-1900
Contact: Rodney Smith
Phone: 510-644-9400
Fax: 510-644-9778
AppleLink: BEARRIVER
Internet: info@bearriver.com
Skills: Programming, systems integration, training, and consulting for Macintosh, Windows, and Newton platforms. Complete range of services, from product development to in-house systems. Curriculum includes Macintosh technology, OOP, AppleTalk, Newton, and VITAL.

NEW MEDIA, INC.
503 E. 200th Street, Suite 202
Cleveland , OH 44119-1543
Contact: Leonard W. Pagon, Jr., President
Phone: 216-481-7900
Fax: 216-481-1570
AppleLink: NEWMEDIA
Skills: We offer a full range of client/server and workflow development and certified training with tools such as PowerBuilder, Visual BASIC, 4th Dimension, Lotus Notes, Access, Windows NT, SQL server, and more.

Software Engineering Professionals, Inc.
Indianapolis, IN   317-843-1640

Software Transformation Inc.
Cupertino, CA   408-973-8081

SpectraLogic, Inc.
Atlanta, GA   404-874-4200

Turning Point Software
Newton, MA   617-332-0202
Please See Ad Page 82.

Tutorland
Cupertino, CA   408-973-0472

Visions Software, Inc.
Wakefield, MA   617-246-6260
Please See Ad Page 84.

Word Master, Inc.
Deerfield, IL   708-948-9600

Xerox Special Information Services
Pasadena, CA   818-351-2351

YARC Systems Corporation
Newbury Park, CA   805-499 -9444

PRODUCT LOCALIZATION

Alpha Inc.
Middleton, WI   608-836-7673

Alpnet Inc.
Salt Lake City, UT   801-265-3300

Arturo Droguett
Santa Cruz, CA   408-429-5212

Asia CD Ltd.
Wanchai, Hong Kong
852-824-0781

Athena Consult
Mortsel, Belgium   32-3-440-78-12

Baltic Consulting & Computer Services
Montclair, NJ   201-744-2497

Berlitz International
Woodland Hills, CA 818-340-5147

Berlitz Translation Services
New York, NY   212-777-7878

CAPCOM USA Inc.
Santa Clara, CA   408-727-0400

CCIC System Pacifica
Berkeley, CA   510-843-5626
Please See Company Highlight Page 111.

DDESIGN SA
Montreux, Switzerland
41-21-961-1362

Digi Media
Graz, Austria   43 0316-81-73-97

Digital Domain
Madrid, Spain   91 504-60-91

E.D.I.T.S.
Munich, Germany   49-89-772227

European Languages Plus
Portland, OR   800-878-8523
Please See Ad Page 88.

Font World Inc.
Rochester, NY   716-235-6861

German Localizations
Cary, NC   919-460-7191

Globalink, Inc.
Fairfax, VA   800-767-0035
Please See Ad Page 85.
Please See Company Highlight Page 111.

Greco and Associates
Mill Valley, CA   415-389-1307

IDOC/International
Documentation Company
Los Angeles, CA   800-336-9898

International Accessability
Corporation
Santa Cruz, CA   408-454-0200
Please See Company Highlight Page 111.
▣

International Software Products
Amstel, The Netherlands
                    31-2963-5271

Intersoft, Ltd.
Aoba-ku Sendai, Japan
                    022 268-6643

Jovian Systems Development, Inc.
Ithaca, NY   607-253-7997

Logi 27
Paris, France   33 1 42 74 7055

Med-I-Bit GmbH
Hamburg, Germany
                    49 40 25167125

Metafact Technology Inc.
Richmond, BC Canada
                    604-244-9662
Please See Ad Page 87.
▣

Multimedia Language Systems
Delmar, NY   518-439-7785

Nihongo Software
Stinson Beach, CA   408-446-2168

Promo Datentechnik +
Systemberatung GmbH
Hamburg, Germany
                    49-40-431360-0

Rocky Mountain Translators Inc.
Boulder, CO   800-365-3736

Softrade International
San Jose, CA   408-927-6866
Please See Ad Page 86.

Software Studio
Langenthal, Switzerland
                    416-323-0871

Starboard Inc.
San Jose, CA   408-261-7570
Please See Ad Page 106.

Van Nostrand Reinhold
New York, NY   800-544-0550
Please See Ad Page 87.

WORDSTATION GmbH
Neu-Isenburg, Germay
                    49-6102 31095
Please See Company Highlight Page 111.

World Ready Software
San Francisco, CA   415-957-1300

Yellow Shark Software
Stockholm, Sweden   46-8-333-593

Zytech Marketing Party Ltd.
Bunbury, Australia   619-791-3622

USER INTERFACE DESIGN

Human Interface

A O-K Services, Inc.
Pennsauken, NJ   609-488-1793

ADS DESIGNS
Route 9, P.O. Box 206
Henderson, NC 27536-9244
Contact: Michael Smith,
Owner/Consultant
Phone: 919-438-6321
Fax: 919-438-6321
Skills: Custom design of
analog/digital hardware,
ISA/MCA adapters,
DOS/Windows software,
embedded/real-time systems
hardware/software, product
development. See also listing
under Development and
Programming; Conract
Programming: C++, Object
Oriented.

ART & LOGIC
P.O. Box 56465
Sherman Oaks, CA 91413
Contact: Justin Souter, Partner
Phone: 818-501-6990
Fax: 818-995-8669
AppleLink: J.SOUTER
Skills: C++, assembly, MacApp,
MFC, and OWL.
▣

MULTIPLATFORM
DEVELOPMENT

PRODUCT
LOCALIZATION

USER INTERFACE
DESIGN

Human Interface

Screen Graphics

AVALON ENGINEERING, INC.
45 Newbury Street, Suite 208
Boston, MA 02116
Contact: Michael Bonnette,
Vice President, Marketing
Phone: 617-247-7668
Fax: 617-247-7698
AppleLink: AVALON
CompuServe: 70541,2000
Skills: OOD/OOP, MacApp,
Newton, C++, imaging
algorithms, QuickTime,
Windows and UNIX to
Macintosh conversions.
Projects: PCS100 color
workstation, KCMS developer
toolkit, PresenterPad™,
QuickTime digitizer, color photo-
retouch package, CD-ROM data
retrieval application, PIM
database.
Clients: Kodak, Scitex/IRIS, ON
Technology, Pastel, Data
Translation, MicroRetrieval.

Alamo Computer
Alamo, CA   510-820-1399
Please See Ad Page 86.

Apeiron
Dallas, TX   214-423-2276

Arcadia Designs
Palo Alto, CA   415-323-7604
Please See Company Highlight Page 112.

AXE Communication Entreprises
Nyon, Switzerland 41-22-361-90-41

Bayle Collaborations
Medford, MA   617-391-1934

Beta Research Inc.
Cupertino, CA   408-252-3172

Cyber Viz
Dedham, MA   617-326-1879

Deborah J. Mayhew & Associates
W. Tisbury, MA   508-693-7149

Drucker & Associates
Cambridge, MA   617-876-1505

Eclipse Multimedia
Waynesboro, VA   703-949-7262

Elisabeth Waymire
San Carlos, CA   415-598-2847

Elrick & Lavidge
San Francisco, CA   415-434-0536

General Systems
Copalis Beach, WA   206-289-0900

Human Media Limited
Chatswood, Australia
          61-2-331-2882

Human-Computer Systems Company
Edison, NJ   908-572-1594

Intuitive Design Engineering
Cardiff, CA   619-944-4575

Mentor Software Innovations, Inc.
Atlanta, GA   404-874-4833

Open Software Associates Limited
Victoria, Australia   6138711666

Pacific Science & Engineering Group
San Diego, CA   619-535-1661

**Penny Bauersfeld Human
Interface Design**
San Carlos, CA   415-637-0801

Productivity Through Technology
Union City, CA   510-471-2776
Please See Ad Page 51.

Stewart Carl Engineering
Palo Alto, CA   415-323-3022

TeleMac Visualization
Dallas, TX   214-423-2276

The Communication Studio
New York, NY   212-924-3729

The Hiser Consulting Group
Prahan, Australia   61 3 521 3311

ThinkThink
Santa Cruz, CA   408-427-0956

Vanguard Media
New York, NY   212-242-5317

Vent
Campbell, CA   408-559-4015

Visual Interface Design
Menlo Park, CA   415-327-5352

ROBERT GEZELTER
SOFTWARE CONSULTANT
35-20 167th Street, Suite 215
Flushing, NY 11358-1731
Contact: Robert Gezelter, Principal
Phone: 718-463-1079
Fax: 718-461-2872
Internet: gezelter@rlgsc.com
Skills: Systems programming,
technical support (in person and
over the telephone), PostScript,
DECnet, Pathworks, OpenVMS,
TCP/IP, Windows NT, computer
security, systems architecture, and
design.

CCIC SYSTEM PACIFICA
605 Addition Street, Suite A
Berkeley, CA 94710
Contact: Scot Campbell
Phone: 510-843-5626
Fax: 510-843-5173
AppleLink: CCIC.USA
CompuServe: 73054,455
Projects: Software and hardware
localization for Japan. Integrated
marketing, distribution, support,
product evaluation/support
assistance. Services include
feasibility studies,
document/software translation,
advertising, marketing support,
product testing. Focus on
interactive media and cross-
platform products. Japanese
business consultation service also
provided.
Clients: Lind Electronic Design,
Mitsubishi Kasei, MacPEAK
Research, Substance Interactive.

INTERNATIONAL ACCESSABILITY
CORPORATION
500 Chestnut Street, Suite 200
Santa Cruz, CA 95060-3602
Contact: Susan C. Paulsen,
President
Phone: 408-454-0200
Fax: 408-454-0300
AppleLink: IAC
CompuServe: 70534,2623
Internet: iac.com
Skills: Official Macintosh,
Microsoft, and UNIX developer,
ResEdit, MPW, AppleGlot, C++, all
major DTP software.
Projects: Complete localization
services, software development,
testing Q/A, compilation;
documentation, DTP; localization
guidelines, troubleshooting. All
languages. Multiplatform.
Clients: AT&T, Now Software,
Calera Recognition Systems, Caere
Corp., Hayes Microcomputers,
Light Source, Microsoft, Santa Cruz
Operation, WordPerfect, Wyse.

WORDSTATION GMBH
Freiherr-vom-Stein-Str. 18R
Neu-Isenburg, D-63263 Germany
Contact: Wolfram Endemann,
Managing Director
Phone: +49-6102 31095
Fax: +49-6102 31097
AppleLink: GER.XSE0172
Skills: Complete process of
software and documentation
localization, high-tech translation
tools, major publishing software,
CRC production.
Projects: Software localization,
compilation and testing,
documentation translation,
terminology work, electronic
publishing, consulting and support
for internationalization issues.
Clients: Dantz, DeltaPoint, Polaris,
Symantec, Informix, PRISMA.

NEW MEDIA, INC.
503 E. 200th Street, Suite 202
Cleveland , OH 44119-1543
Contact: Leonard W. Pagon, Jr.,
President
Phone: 216-481-7900
Fax: 216-481-1570
AppleLink: NEWMEDIA
Skills: PowerBuilder, Visual BASIC,
4th Dimension, FoxPro, Lotus
Notes, Omnis 7, Visual C++, C,
MacApp, SQL server, Oracle,
Windows NT.
Projects: We offer a full range of
application development and
education services focusing on
graphical, client/server, workflow,
OOP, and cross-platform
technology areas. We assist as
organizations migrate toward
emerging technologies such as
client/server and workgroup
computing and provide planning,
education, and development to
facilitate knowledge transfer.
Typical projects include: marketing
support, financial reporting,
decision support,
EIS, sales automation, customer
service, order entry, project
tracking for Fortune 1000
companies.

GLOBALINK, INC.
9302 Lee Highway, 12th Floor
Fairfax, VA 22031-1208
Contact: Jennifer Ting
Phone: 800-767-0035
Fax: 703-273-3866
Skills: Globalink, the leader and
marketer of foreign language
translation software, is also the
resource for software localization
and translation of manuals for
virtually all spoken and written
languages.

USER INTERFACE
DESIGN

Human Interface
Screen Graphics
VIRTUAL REALITY

DEVELOPMENT &
PROGRAMMING

ViviStar Consulting
Scottsdale, AZ   602-483-3123
Please See Company Highlight Page 112.

Screen Graphics

AMCI
Santa Cruz, CA   408-423-0112

Cantrell Design Group
Lancaster, PA   717-396-1134

Howard Goldstein Design
Van Nuys, CA   818-987-2837

Software Usability Seminars
Mendham, NJ   201-267-6007

VIRTUAL REALITY

3D TV Corporation/ StereoScopic Video
San Rafael, CA   415-488-1570

Cybernet Systems Corporation
Ann Arbor, MI   313-668-2567

Digital Media Reality Labs
San Francisco, CA   415-641-7092

High Techsplanations, Inc.
Rockville, MD   301-984-3706

Immersive Technologies
Oakland, CA   510-261-0128

Kinetic Sciences Inc.
Vancouver, BC Canada
604-822-2144

PMS Microdesign, Inc.
Pittsburgh, PA   412-731-4004
Please See Company Highlight Page 112.

SophisTech Research
Lakewood, CA   800-487-7687

Straylight Corporation
Warren, NJ   908-580-0086

Virtual Reality Labs
San Luis Obispo, CA 805-545-8515

ARCADIA DESIGNS
1431 Arcadia Place
Palo Alto, CA 94303
Contact: Mary Medoff
Phone: 415-323-7604
Fax: 415-325-1965
Skills: Prototype software, help determine functionality, create animation, design visuals: layout, typography, color, and icons. Director, Cinemation, Photoshop, Infini-D, Studio/8, Illustrator.

VIVISTAR CONSULTING
7015 E. Aster Drive
Scottsdale, AZ 85254
Contact: Jon Hess, Project Manager
Phone: 602-483-3123
Fax: 602-483-3123
AppleLink: VIVISTAR
Skills: OOD/OOP, C++, Assembler, TCL, Macintosh Communications Toolbox, QuickTime, 3D animation, lex and yacc for parsing, and event languages for direct manipulation.

PMS MICRODESIGN, INC.
1904 Brushcliff Road
Pittsburgh, PA 15221
Contact: Phillip Sauter, President
Phone: 412-731-4004
Fax: 412-731-6743
Skills: Integrate multimedia (Director, Authorware) with virtual reality (reality satellite, human gesture systems) to create dynamic presentations. Engineering, programming, authoring, consulting. See also listing under Multimedia; Multimedia: General.

USER INTERFACE
DESIGN

Human Interface

Screen Graphics

VIRTUAL REALITY

II5

Marketing & Distribution

In this section you will find expert help in marketing and distributing your product, from initial conception to final release. Each category contains service providers with specific areas of expertise.

Marketing   **116**
  Advertising   116
  Business Presentations   116
  Consulting   117
  Copywriting   118
  Demo Disks   118
  Direct Mail   118
  Graphic Design   119
  International   120
  Market Research   120
  Public Relations   120
  Sales   121
  Trade Show Services   121

Package Design   **121**
Product Testing   **122**
Software Distribution   **123**
  Catalog/Retail   123
  Value Added Resellers   123

MARKETING

Advertising

Ahrens Creative Group, Inc.
Chicago, IL   312-243-5550

Albert Frank-Guenther Law
San Francisco, CA   415-989-7010

Arete CA Incorporated
New York, NY   212-777-2012

BBDO
San Francisco, CA   415-274-6200

Calico Subscription Company
Milpitas, CA   408-262-4036

California Marketing Group
Garden Grove, CA   714-895-1447

Citadel Systems
Houston, TX   713-686-6400

Cogar, Melton & Associates
Cupertino, CA   408-253-9656

Common Sense Computing, Inc.
Huntington, MA   413-667-5797

Dennis Trager Associates
Fairfax, CA   415-456-5655

Fortune & Associates
Palo Alto, CA   415-494-9919
▣

Goodlove & Moon
Berkeley, CA   510-204-9120

Harper House Inc.
Dallas, TX   214-744-4646

Hertrich Graphics
Aurora, IL   708-851-6581

Holmes Agency Inc.
Silver Spring, MD   301-589-1251

Inbody Bruck & Company Advertising
Los Angeles, CA   213-939-2929

International Communications Inc.
Natick, MA   508-651-9232

Laser Set
Houston, TX   713-586-7556

Levy & Wurz Channel Marketing
Seattle, WA   206-621-8358

Novation Technology Inc.
Lake Oswego, OR   800-248-7988

Optima Design & Advertising
Trenton, NJ   609-392-7772

Pacifico Inc.
San Jose, CA   408-293-8600

PRX Inc.
San Jose, CA   408-287-1700

Shattinger Interactive
St. Louis, MO   314-621-2408

South Florida Wire Service
Ft. Lauderdale, FL   800-741-SFWS

Stone House Systems Inc.
Kenilworth, IL   708-256-5813

Success Stories by Kris Newby
Palo Alto, CA   415-329-8150

Tactical Marketing Group
Kensington, CA   510-524-1356

Technical Analysis, Inc.
Seattle, WA   206-938-0570

The Newsletter People
Brooklyn, NY   718-596-5225

Winston Advertising Inc.
Santa Clara, CA   408-982-3830

Wordwright Associates
San Antonio, TX   512-696-6868

Business Presentations

**Applied Business
Communications Inc.**
Walnut Creek, CA   510-938-4642

Boardwalk Designs
Atlanta, GA   408-892-7772

C & A Graphics
Houston, TX   713-974-3844

Cactus Computer Service
Phoenix, AZ   602-266-7312

Captured Images, Inc.
Westlake Village, CA 818-707-9491

Computer Mentors
New Orleans, LA   504-529-7248

Extron Electronics
Santa Fe Springs, CA 310-802-8804

Fain & Co.
Atlanta, GA   404-876-4668

General Parametrics
Berkeley, CA   510-524-3950

Howard M. Cutler Productions
Rowayton, CT   203-857-4332

**Image Architects
Computer Graphic Slides**
Los Altos, CA   415-968-1141

KB Communications
Vancouver, WA   206-256-9508

Live Marketing
Los Altos, CA   415-941-8188

Marriner Associates
San Rafael, CA   415-454-1300

Michael R. Mizen & Associates, Inc.
River Forest, IL   708-366-2060

Munday & Collins Rents
San Jose, CA   408-451-9155

Sales Systems Development Inc.
Mountain View, CA   415-691-9622

Technology Inc.
Foster City, CA   415-345-4018

William Rush Voice Consultants
Evanston, IL   708-328-1753

Consulting

Absolute Inc.
Dallas, TX   214-748-0184

Access Education
Santa Clara, CA   408-727-1096

Aviation Management Associates, Inc.
Springfield, VA   703-644-4465

Benchmark Publications, Inc.
New Canaan, CT   203-966-6653
Please See Company Highlight Page 118.

Cirrus Technology
Worcester, MA   508-755-5242

Clement Mok Designs, Inc.
San Francisco, CA   415-703-9900

Crossfield Marketing
Los Altos Hills, CA   415-949-3937

D'Agostini Organizzazione
Udine, Italy   39 432 507332

Delio Consulting
Millbrook, NY   914-877-9424

ELB Consulting
Tucson, AZ   602-886-2646

Elizabeth A. Strode
Hillsborough, CA   415-340-1377

Empire RBDMS
Cape Canaveral, FL   407-784-2116

Golden Gate Tax Service
Concord, CA   510-686-4864

Jack Fox Associates
San Diego, CA   619-599-3255

Kalb & Associates
Santa Monica, CA   310-829-9790

Local Knowledge
Durham, NH   603-868-2300

Machover Associates Corporation
White Plains, NY   914-949-3777

Macsultants
Farmington, CT   203-678-8622

Martin Goffman Associates
Edison, NJ   908-549-5433

Medialine International
Antwerpen, Belgium   132 33 66 20 92

Mendon & Associates
Kansas City, MO   816-421-4677

Multi-Impressions Corporation
Tulsa, OK   918-665-6633

Olson & Company Strategy & Marketing
Menlo Park, CA   415-326-0373

Other Company, Inc.
Milwaukee, WI   414-374-3747

RADX Corporation
Plano, TX   214-422-9903

Reardon & Wynn Associates
San Diego, CA   619-450-3131

Ring of Fire, Inc.
Shibuya-Ku,Tokyo   3-5485-5985

Robert T. Coolidge, AIA
Guilford, CT   203-458-9759

Scott Satovsky, Sat's Graphics
Southfield, MI   810-354-4333

SilverStar Enterprises
Powder Springs, GA   404-880-5794

SMG: Consulting
San Francisco, CA   415-928-2514

Software Company Legal Guide
New York, NY   212-421-6000

Spiral Communications
Merrimack, NH   603-424-0545

StrategicMedia
Oakland, CA   510-658-0105

The Idea Bank
Bainbridge Island, WA   206-842-5420

The Seroka Group, Inc.
Greenwich, CT   203-862-9700

Tilted Windmill Ltd.
Hinsdale, IL   708-887-5814

Tronca Associates Inc.
Cedar Grove, WI   414-785-5544

MARKETING

Advertising
Business Presentations
Consulting
Copywriting
Demo Disks
Direct Mail
Graphic Design
International
Market Research
Public Relations
Sales
Trade Show Services

BENCHMARK PUBLICATIONS, INC.
76 Elm Street
New Canaan, CT 06840
Contact: Alice Powers McElhone,
President
Phone: 203-966-6653
Fax: 203-972-7129
AppleLink: BENCHMARKPUB
Skills: Change management
support, systems/procedures
documentation, courseware
design/development, marketing
programs, technology transfer
measurement.
Projects: Marketing
communications; software tutorials,
references, and Help systems;
application- and job-specific
custom courseware, CBT; pilot
programs; employee skills
assessment.
Clients: Major corporations and
software developers nationwide.

BENT MEDIA, INC.
6630 Memphis Street
New Orleans, LA 70124
Contact: Brad Brewster, President
Phone: 504-482-8278
Fax: 504-482-8278
Internet: bentmedia@aol.com
Skills: Director, Authorware, 3D,
QuickTime, Photoshop, cross-
platform development, multilingual
(Spanish/French).

SMARTNET MARKETING CONNECTIONS
1235 Laurel Sreet, #9
Menlo Park, CA 94025
Contact: Karen Taggart
Phone: 415-321-3868
Fax: 415-321-3872
Skills: smartNET Marketing
Connections specializes in result-
oriented solutions for marketing
communications services including
direct mail for selected clients.
Turnkey solutions include strategic
planning, project management,
design, copywriting, list acquisition,
printing, labels, and mailing.

Turning Point Development, Inc.
West Augusta, SC   803-219-2552

Vermont Software
Groton, VT   802-584-4020

Copywriting

Betsy Strode
Hillsborough, CA   415-340-1377

Coalescence
Longmont, CO   303-776-9425

smartNET Marketing Connections
Menlo Park, CA   415-321-3868

Wolf, Greenfield & Sacks
Boston, MA   617-720-3500

Demo Disks

Bent Media, Inc.
New Orleans, LA   504-482-8278
Please see Company Highlight Page 118.

Block Communications
Los Altos, CA   415-254-7600

LaRan Technologies
Hamburg, Germany 040-536-60-20

McLaren Associates
Portland, OR   503-230-6939

Media Lab Inc.
Louisville, CO   303-499-5411

New Science InterActive
Emeryville, CA   510-653-6034

Pillar Corporation
Foster City, CA   415-349-6200

Robis, Inc. Software Marketing
Wheaton, IL   708-752-0220

Show & Tell Systems, Inc.
Mountain View, CA 415-691-1077

Tecval Memories SA
Renens, Lausanne 41-21-635-90-91

Videomation
Santa Clara, CA   408-988-6100

Direct Mail

21st Century Marketing
Farmingdale, NY   516-293-8550

Alexander & Lord
Monterey, CA   408-655-6000

American List Council Inc.
Princeton, NJ   800-822-LIST

Business Builders
Cupertino, CA   408-253-6679

CKS Partners
Campbell, CA   408-378-2444

Direct Mailing Systems
Rohnert Park, CA   707-584-4884

Direct Media
Greenwich, CT   203-532-1000

Hunter Mail
Oakland, CA   510-444-1767

Hunza Graphics
Berkeley, CA   800-992-2431

InfoBase
New York, NY   212-983-0154

JLH Direct Marketing
West Sacramento, CA
                       800-877-4554

Johnson Direct Advertising
Palo Alto, CA   415-321-3727

MacTimes
Santa Barbara, CA   805-966-3353

CLEMENT MOK DESIGNS, INC.
600 Townsend Street, Penthouse
San Francisco, CA 94103-4908
Contact: Shel Perkins, Vice
President, Operations
Phone: 415-703-9900
Fax: 415-703-9901
AppleLink: CMD
Skills: Multidisciplinary, cross
platform.
Projects: Design, marketing, and
communication services, including
consultation, identity, print
materials, animation, video,
packaging, exhibits, and computer
interface.
Clients: DEC; Apple Computer,
Inc.; Hewlett-Packard; Autodesk;
3Com; Walt Disney; Revo
Sunglasses; Expervision; Logitech;
Xircom.

JPD COMMUNICATIONS
2712 Ninth Street
Berkeley, CA 94710-2606
Contact: John Paul, Partner
Phone: 510-843-8048
Fax: 510-843-8050
AppleLink: JPD.COMM
Skills: Full-service versatile
studio. Print and multimedia
applications. Specializing in cost-
effective solutions that enhance
client's image.
Projects: Corporate identity,
brochures, catalogs, annual
reports, book covers, newsletters,
CD-ROM and software packaging.
Also, provide management and
coordination of special events.

MARKETING
Advertising
Business Presentations
Consulting
Copywriting
Demo Disks
Direct Mail
Graphic Design
International
Market Research
Public Relations
Sales
Trade Show Services

Miller/Kadanoff Promotional Marketing, Inc.
San Francisco, CA   415-554-0424

MUG News Service (MNS)
Schenectady, NY   518-374-1088

Pearson Communications Group
Santa Clara, CA   408-496-5885

PSE Network Distribution Systems
Hayward, CA   510-429-5002

RSVP Publications
San Rafael, CA   415-485-0996

smartNET Marketing Connections
Menlo Park, CA   415-321-3868
Please See Company Highlight Page 118.

The Pacific Marketing Group
San Francisco, CA   415-788-8764

User Group Connection
Scotts Valley, CA   408-461-5725

Worldata
Boca Raton, FL   407-393-8200

Graphic Design

Alben & Faris
Santa Cruz, CA   408-426-5526

Aster Services
Laguna Hills, CA   714-855-6554

Bay Graphics Design Inc.
Berkeley, CA   510-843-0701

Carew Design
Sausalito, CA   415-331-8222

Clement Mok Designs, Inc.
San Francisco, CA   415-703-9900
Please See Company Highlight Page 119.

Deborah Designs
Campbell, CA   408-378-7748

Denis Darby's Creative Data
Aurora, CO   303-680-6352

Earl Office
San Francisco, CA   415-252-0587

Grafica
Canoga Park, CA   818-712-0071

Harris Design Office
Hockessin, DE   302-234-5700

James Graca Design Group
Ventura, CA   805-339-9304

Jann Greenland Communications
Little Rock, AR   501-374-8297

USER GROUP Connection

Market Your Product to Apple User Groups

Since1985, User Group Connection has been Apples official liaison to its User Group community. Today, we offer you access to over 2,000 Apple Authorized User Groups in the U.S. and Canada hundreds of thousands of technology users, early adopters, and product evangelists. From our monthly mailing to a custom User Group program, we have a range of cost-effective services to market to User Groups.

Contact:
Sam Decker
(408) 461-5725
FAX (408) 461-5701
Alink: Decker.S
eWorld: UGC Sam

Clients: Adobe, Apple, APS, Citibank, Claris, Global Village, Intuit, Kensington, Momentum Software, Now Software, WordPerfect and many others!

NVISION3

875 Fourth Street
San Rafael, CA 94901
Contact: Jon Goodchild,
Phone: 415-459-5077
Fax: 415-457-8095
Skills: Design group with
extensive publication and
packaging experience; interactive
CD-ROM design.
Projects: Publications and
packaging designers, print and
multimedia.
Clients: William Morrow, Alfred
Knopf, Smithsonian Institution,
Macmillan, Penguin USA,
Chronicle Books, Noetics Institute,
WordStar, Bank of America,
TestDrive Corporation, Yosemite
Association, Sierra Club.

SOUTH FLORIDA WIRE SERVICE

1800 N. Andrews Avenue,
Suite 12-A
Ft. Lauderdale, FL 33311
Contact: Doug Bell, President
Phone: 800-741-SFWS
Fax: 305-763-2997
AppleLink: D5723
Projects: Free Macintosh
hardware and software reviews for
1,300 subscribing clients; free
distribution of product press
releases to all clients.
Clients: Nine hundred
newspapers, corporate and small
businesses, colleges, universities,
school boards, governmental
facilities, and specialized companies

JPD Communications
Berkeley, CA   510-843-8048
Please See Company Highlight Page 119.

Land Graphics
Pasadena, CA   310-588-9399

Michael Brandman Associates
Santa Ana, CA   714-250-5555

Modern Lines
Phoenix, AZ   602-251-2499

NVision3
San Rafael, CA   415-459-5077
Please See Company Highlight Page 120.

Our Designs, Inc.
New York, NY   212-505-8565

PageWorks + TriDesign
Denver, CO   303-337-7770

Propaganda
Virginia Beach, VA   804-640-7166

Rivanne Advertising
Brooklyn, NY   718-998-2903

The Morgan Agency
Salt Lake City, UT   801-539-1328

International

Softrade International
San Jose, CA   408-927-6866

Market Research

Addison Design
San Francisco, CA   415-391-3090

ADF Research
San Rafael, CA   415-459-1115

**Creative Strategies
Research International**
Santa Clara, CA   408-748-3400

Gallup Organization
Irvine, CA   714-474-7900

Griffin Dix Research Associates
Berkeley, CA   510-527-1451

Hybridge Inc.
Calgary, AB Canada   403-239-7778

Interconsult
North Hampton, NH 603-964-6464

Market Vision
Santa Cruz, CA   408-426-4400

**Neo Directions
Computer Support Ltd.**
Hanbassey Hills, NY 516-627-7518

Professional Business Assistance
Oxford, CT   203-888-6451

The Adams Company
Palo Alto, CA   415-325-9822

The Hartsook Letter
Alameda, CA   510-521-4988

Public Relations

AFM Associates
New York, NY   212-721-4826

**Business & Technical
Communications**
Walnut Creek, CA   510-945-6779

Computer Learning Foundation
Palo Alto, CA   415-327-3347

Consult Rosen Communication
Mandeville, LA   504-898-0904

Consultech Communications Inc.
Troy, NY   518-283-8444

Cunningham Communication, Inc.
Santa Clara, CA 408-982-0400

G. A. Bell & Associates
San Jose, CA 408-241-1997

Hewitt/Katona International
San Francisco, CA 415-957-1560

Hi-Tech Public Relations Inc.
San Francisco, CA 415-904-7000

Janal Communications
Sunnyvale, CA 510-831-0900

Kearney Rietmann
Half Moon Bay, CA 415-726-1135

Laden Relations
Colorado Springs, CO
719-260-8035

Lindsay Public Relations
Santa Clara, CA 408-984-7242

MacDaniels Henry & Sproul Inc.
San Francisco, CA 415-981-2250

Martin and Wichmann
Minneapolis, MN 612-724-2633

McLean Public Relations
San Mateo, CA 415-513-8800

Media Map/Cambridge Communications
Cambridge, MA 617-374-9300

Schweichler Associates, Inc.
Corte Madera, CA 415-924-7200

South Florida Wire Service
Ft. Lauderdale, FL 800-741-SFWS
Please See Company Highlight Page 120.

User Group Connection
Scotts Valley, CA 408-461-5725
Please See Ad Page 119.

White & Cromer Public Relations
Palo Alto, CA 415-354-8800

Sales

Ariel PSS Corporation
Mountain View, CA 415-694-7880

Atlantech, Inc.
Bradenton, FL 813-739-2554

Endpoint Marketing Information Systems
Sunnyvale, CA 408-737-3831

Engineering Software Concepts, Inc.
Palo Alto, CA 800-325-1289

Hawks Associates
Naples, NY 716-374-5397

Hecht & Associates
Sunnyvale, CA 408-730-2234

Infotec Training Institute
Santa Ana, CA 800-282-7990

MaxSacks International Professional Selling Clinic
El Segundo, CA 800-488-4629

Morgan Consulting Group
Santa Rosa, CA 707-571-8800

Motivation Consultants Inc.
San Carlos, CA 415-591-6621

Objectic Systems Inc.
Renton, WA 206-271-6864

Progressive Allied Marketing Inc.
San Diego, CA 619-571-5440

Sales Automation, Inc.
Northampton, PA 215-262-4555

The Vass Company
Boulder, CO 800-424-8277

Trade Show Services

Crimson Consulting Group
Menlo Park, CA 415-325-0677

Ferro Enterprises
Grinnell, IA 515-236-6148

Image Associates, Inc.
Raleigh, NC 919-876-6400

Marketing Research & Consultant Services
Oakland, CA 510-444-0585

Piic
Los Altos, CA 408-450-1511

Planning Showcase
Cupertino, CA 408-253-6679

Reprographic Technologies
New Berlin, WI 414-796-8162

Senecio Software, Inc.
Bowling Green, OH 419-352-4281

Wave Technologies Training, Inc.
St. Louis, MO 314-878-2050

PACKAGE DESIGN

Cornice Graphics
Upland, CA 714-985-8323

Maddocks & Company
Los Angeles, CA 310-477-4227

McHale Design
Long Beach, CA 310-420-2609

Package Express Inc.
Marshall, MO 816-886-4800

Software Packaging Associates
Cincinnati, OH 800-837-4399

MARKETING
Advertising
Business Presentations
Consulting
Copywriting
Demo Disks
Direct Mail
Graphic Design
International
Market Research
Public Relations
Sales
Trade Show Services
PACKAGE DESIGN
PRODUCT TESTING
SOFTWARE DISTRIBUTION

SOUTH FLORIDA WIRE SERVICE

1800 N. Andrews Avenue,
Suite 12-A
Ft. Lauderdale, FL 33311
Contact: Doug Bell, President
Phone: 800-741-SFWS
Fax: 305-763-2997
AppleLink: D5723
Projects: Free Macintosh hardware and software reviews for 1,300 subscribing clients; free distribution of product press releases to all clients.
Clients: Nine hundred newspapers, corporate and small businesses, colleges, universities, school boards, governmental facilities, and specialized companies.

INTERMEDIA

1300 Dexter N
Seattle, WA 98109
Contact: Susan Hoffman, President
Phone: 206-284-2995
Fax: 206-283-0778
Skills: Intermedia is a distributor of social interest video and multimedia programs. Our proven telemarketing approach ensures that your programs will successfully reach buyers.

ACKNOWLEDGE SOLUTIONS

Acknowledge Solutions provides a full range of developer services including testing, project planning, interface consulting, technical review of documentation, custom utility programming, and programming test tools. Provides complete quality-assurance services, or augments your staff during peak periods. Helps design testability into software to speed the product's time to market. Past projects include many premier Macintosh products. See also listing under Publishing; Technical Writing/Documentation: End User.
Skills: Pascal, C, HyperTalk, OOP, MacsBug, ResEdit.
Projects: DiskPaper, SoundEdit, Ofoto, Vision, Opcode MIDI System.
Clents: Farralon; Apple Computer, Inc.; Light Source; Opcode Systems; NeXT.

ACKNOWLEDGE SOLUTIONS
701 7th Avenue
Redwood City, CA 94063
Phone: 415-345-4639
Fax: 415-345-7568
AppleLink: ACKSOL

Univenture CD Packing and Storage	Jack Lewis & Associates
Dublin, OH 800-992-8262	Palm City, FL 407-336-3581

PRODUCT TESTING

Acknowledge Solutions
Redwood City, CA   415-345-4639
Please See Ad Page 122.

**Computer Product
Testing Services, Inc.**
Manasquan, NJ   908-223-5700

**International Language
Engineering Corporation**
Boulder, CO   303-447-2363

MWA Consulting
Palo Alto, CA   415-323-4780

Rivers Edge Corporation
San Antonio, TX   512-590-9528

Scott Hysmith
Edmonds, WA   206-742-0133

South Florida Wire Service
Ft. Lauderdale, FL   800-741-SFWS
Please See Company Highlight Page 122.

SOFTWARE DISTRIBUTION

Catalog/Retail

Baker and Taylor Software
Chatsworth, CA   800-641-1057

Bindco
Redwood City, CA   415-363-2200

Double Click AB
Goteborg, Sweden   46-31-14-59-10

inTouch Communications Ltd.
Singapore   296-9700

Nisus Software
Solana Beach, CA   619-481-1477

The Ambit Group/TAGs Channel Compass
San Francisco   415-957-9433

Value Added Resellers

Bradley Group
Hollywood, CA   213-465-7593

CCIC System Pacifica
Berkeley, CA   510-843-5626

Intermedia
Seattle, WA   206-284-2995
Please See Company Highlight Page 122.

Jam Software Limited
Meriden, CT   203-630-0055

Mac, S.A.
Miami, FL   809-542-6192

Multimedia Specialists
Fairfax , CA   415-459-3553

Peggi Sturm & Associates
Los Angeles, CA   310-470-9390

RenderTech
Houston, TX   713-524-2000

Simply Software, Inc.
Marshall, MO   800-774-1123

Summit Business Systems-Macromedia VAR
Long Beach, CA   310-498-8006

Video Images
Waukesha, WI   414-785-8998

PACKAGE DESIGN

PRODUCT TESTING

SOFTWARE DISTRIBUTION

Catalog/ Retail

Value Added Resellers

127

Multimedia

This section contains artists and producers who specialize in a broad spectrum of multimedia develpment services.

Multimedia **129**

  Animation 143

  Audio 144

  Content Development 146

  Database Development 147

  Graphics/Interface 147

  Legal Services 148

  Marketing & Sales 148

  Video 148

Multimedia Producers 149

  Education & Training 150

  Entertainment 151

  Information 152

CD ROM **152**

  Archiving Services 152

  Development 152

  Duplication 153

  Photo CD 153

ANIMATION
ILLUSTRATION
INTERACTIVE
PRESENTATION
SIMULATION
INTERFACE
INTEGRATED

LINGUA

SERVICE
ASSOCIATES

66 BELL STREET #101
SEATTLE, WA 98121-1600
PHONE 206-448-8404
FAX 206-728-4552

MULTIMEDIA

21st Century Media
Milwaukee, WI   414-771-8906
▣

A. Visual
Montreal, QC Canada
                      514-933-3657

A. W. Vidmer & Company
Brentwood, TN   615-373-1851

ad • hoc Technologies
San Diego, CA   619-551-0109

Adam Gewanter Consulting
New York, NY   212-674-3940

After Hours Computer Group
Irvine, CA   714-573-3800

AGS Information Services, Inc.
Clark, NJ   908-396-4321

All Night Media
Pittsburgh, PA   412-471-9590

Alphabets Design Group Inc.
Evanston, IL   708-328-2733

Amazing Media
San Anselmo, CA   415-453-0686

ART & LOGIC
P.O. Box 56465
Sherman Oaks, CA 91413
Contact: Justin Souter, Partner
Phone: 818-501-6990
Fax: 818-995-8669
AppleLink: J.SOUTER
Skills: C++, assembly, MacApp, MFC, and OWL.
▣

BENT MEDIA, INC.
6630 Memphis Street
New Orleans, LA 70124
Contact: Brad Brewster, President
Phone: 504-482-8278
Fax: 504-482-8278
Internet: bentmedia@aol.com
Skills: Director, Authorware, 3D, QuickTime, Photoshop, cross-platform development. Multilingual (Spanish/French).
Projects: Interactive multimedia production and design, 2D and 3D animation, and digital video production for demonstration disks, CD-ROMs, kiosks, presentations, CBT, and games. Recent projects include "Discover Tulane."
Clients: Apple Computer, Inc.; Tulane University; Louisiana Children's Museum; Stevens Inc.; Laitram Corporation.

MULTIMEDIA

MULTIMEDIA

Animation

Audio

Content
Development

Database
Development

Graphics/Interface

Legal Services

Marketing & Sales

Video

BLUE WATERS
1129 Folsom Street
San Francisco, CA 94103
Contact: Ming Lau
Phone: 415-431-1284
Fax: 415-861-0826
Skills: QuickTime and multimedia production facility in SF/SOMA. Capture, record, and convert: NTSC video <-> QuickTime digital formats. Image processed video -> highest-quality Cinepak movies. Cutting-edge digital effects, LaserColor storyboards, Mac paintbox, PPC nonlinear editing, 20 x 30 soundstage, ultimat bluescreen, giga storage, and CD-ROM one-offs.
Projects: Interactive commercials; trade show demos, video presentations; image creation for broadcast and CD-ROMs.
Clients: Adobe Systems; Apple Computer, Inc.; Aristos; Bank of America; Macromedia; MacWeek; MotionWorks USA; Prentice Hall; RasterOps; Sanctuary Woods; SUN Microsystems; SuperMac; Storage Dimensions; SF/MDG; Video Fusion.

CLEMENT MOK DESIGNS, INC.
600 Townsend Street, Penthouse
San Francisco, CA 94103-4908
Contact: Shel Perkins, Vice President, Operations
Phone: 415-703-9900
Fax: 415-703-9901
AppleLink: CMD
Skills: Multidisciplinary, cross-platform design, marketing, and communication services, including consultation, identity, print materials, animation, video, packaging, exhibits, and computer interface. See also listing under Marketing and Distribution; Marketing: Graphic Design.

Animatics
Ottawa, ON Canada   613-235-9000

AR Design
Stockton, CA   209-943-5231

Arborescence SF
San Francisco, CA   415-931-7415

Art & Logic
Sherman Oaks, CA   818-501-6990
Please See Company Highlight Page 129.

Artist House
Beula, MI   616-352-5060

Audio-Video Corporation
Menands, NY   518-449-7213

Autologic Inc.
Thousand Oaks, CA 805-498-9611

Avalon Integrated Services
Washington, DC   202-408-7039

AVCA
Austin, TX   512-472-4995

Bent Media, Inc.
New Orleans, LA   504-482-8278
Please See Company Highlight Page 129.

Blue Waters
San Francisco, CA   415-431-1284
Please See Company Highlight Page 130.

Bryten, Inc.
Norwich, VT   802-649-3252

Buechting:Pieroth
Berlin, Germany   49-30-874685

Burnette Multimedia Services
Hood River, OR   503-386-9369

Burns, Connacher & Waldron
Stamford, CT   203-323-1330

Butler Graphics, Inc.
Troy, MI   313-528-2808

C-Wave
San Francisco, CA   415-397-3722

Carousel Mediaworks, Inc.
Rochester, NY   716-777-4023

Centerline Productions
Denver, CO   303-698-1321

Chedd-Angier Production Company
Watertown, MA   617-926-8300

Ciphers
Los Gatos, CA   408-356-9983

Class One Software
Vancouver, BC Canada
                      604-261-1843

Clement Mok Designs, Inc.
San Francisco, CA   415-703-9900
Please See Company Highlight Page 130.

CommGraphics
Lincoln, NE   402-438-1919

Communication Design
Tempe, AZ   602-345-1770

Computer Based Enterprises, Inc.
Eau Claire, WI   715-835-3448

Computer Management International, Inc.
Marlborough, CT   203-295-8436

Computer Resource Sysems, Inc.
Knoxville, TN   615-558-6273

Computize
Houston, TX   713-771-6667

Creative Enterprises
Long Beach, CA   310-987-3450
Please See Ad Page 129.

FAIN & CO.
957 Blue Ridge Avenue
Atlanta, GA 30306
Contact: David Fain, President
Phone: 404-876-4668
Fax: 404-876-4085
AppleLink: D6620
Skills: Multimedia development
using a variety of PC/Macintosh
authoring, 3D, and animation
tools.
Projects: 2D and 3D animated
presentations, interactive
touchscreen, audio, video, kiosks,
data collection, demonstration
diskettes, onscreen graphics, and
training.
Clients: Educational software
publishers, healthcare clients,
post-production houses.

**HOWARD M. CUTLER
PRODUCTIONS**
10 Harstrom Place
Rowayton, CT 06853
Contact: Howard Cutler,
President
Phone: 203-857-4332
Fax: 203-857-4627
Skills: Concept, content, media,
and interface design; total project
management.
Projects: Large-scale electronic
media environments and
presentations integrating multiple
technologies, multimedia family
learning resources, interactive
training simulations, multimedia
support for live presentations.
Clients: Jimi Hendrix Museum,
D.E.C., Benetton SportSystem,
Nike, IBM, Phillips, Biosphere 2,
Dennis Earl Moore Productions,
Fusion Communications,
TransFiction, Mobius.

MULTIMEDIA

Animation
Audio
Content
Development
Database
Development
Graphics/Interface
Legal Services
Marketing & Sales
Video

Creative Perspectives
Charlottesville, VA   804-971-6795

Current Designs Corporation
New York, NY   212-463-0795

Dataway
Toronto, ON Canada 416-599-1200

Dave Saunders & Associates
Thousand Oaks, CA 805-379-0726

David H. Lawrence
San Francisco, CA   415-621-3283

David Rose Design
San Jose, CA   408-377-2770

DC Productions
San Francisco, CA   415-387-3649

Design Factory APS
Copenhagen, Denmark
45 33 93 91 10

Design Mirage, Inc.
Bellefonte, PA   814-353-9051

DigitalFacades Corporation
Los Angeles, CA   310-208-0776
Please See Ad Page 131.

Digital Media Solutionz
Birmingham, AL   205-323-5994

KAMEN AUDIO PRODUCTIONS/CD ARCHIVES

701 Seventh Avenue, 6th Floor
New York, NY 10036
Contact: James Berry
Phone: 212-575-4660
Fax: 212-575-4799
CompuServe: 73312,2621
Skills: Digital audio workstations with complete music and sound FX supply and creation. Voice-over talent and recording. Programming archive for CD-ROM. CD-ROM one-offs, computer graphic design. Video editing and production. Real-time MPEG encoding. CD-ROM duplication.
Projects: For 12 years we have been producing audio for radio and television spots for major advertising agencies. Also, music for films and records. Creating computer graphics for industrial and promotional tapes. Archiving radio, television spots, and print advertising to one CD-ROM. Pressing CD-ROM. Designing software for retrieval of CD-ROM archive files.
Clients: Major advertising agencies in the United States.

KMS SYSTEMS, INC.

P.O. Box 7857
The Woodlands, TX 77380
Contact: George P. Mallard, President
Phone: 713-363-9154
Fax: 713-298-1911
Skills: Developer of a 1993 WordPerfect Reader's Choice Award winner, several custom life safety systems, integrated voice-data systems, and multimedia kiosks.

N B E N G I N E E R I N G

NB Engineering (NBE) specializes in the design, development, integration, testing, and support of interactive multimedia applications using a wide variety of full-motion digital video compression techniques. Development under the DOS, Windows, and OS/2 environments using C, C++, Authorware, Iconauthor, Toolbook, and Visual BASIC. We specialize in turnkey multimedia applications requiring off-the-shelf hardware and software, custom software, system integration, and video compression services. NBE has over 500 corporate and government clients including: Arthur Andersen Consulting, CSX Transportation, Dow Jones & Company, IBM, Intel, Jostens Learning Corporation, SAIC, Toshiba, United States Holocaust Memorial Museum, and Wackenhut Services Inc.

N B E N G I N E E R I N G
2110 Priest Bridge Drive
Crofton, MD 21114
Phone: 410-721-5725
Fax: 410-721-5726

Digital Vistas
Del Mar, CA   619-431-3896

Diversified Music Design Inc.
East Chatham, NY   518-766-5940

Dori Friend Design
San Francisco, CA   415-863-8919

Dot Dash, Inc.
New York, NY   (212) 251-8670

Drochelman Meng & Associates
St. Louis, MO   314-991-0123

Duthie Associates, Inc.
Nashville, TN   615-386-3061

Easy Street Software
Monte Sereno, CA   408-395-1158

Edge Technologies
Queensland, Australia
                    619-878-2994

Emerging Technology Consultants Inc.
St. Paul, MN   612-639-3973

Engaging Media
Houston, TX   713-952-5475

Equilibrium
Sausalito, CA   415-332-4343

Evenview Corporation
Atlanta, GA   404-982-0600

Eyejam/Earwax
San Francisco, CA   415-775-5020

Fain & Co.
Atlanta, GA   404-876-4668
Please See Company Highlight Page 131.

Fearless Eye
Kansas City, MO   816-353-6177

Feldman Film Medien & Kommunikation
Nuernberg, Germany
                     49-911-533078

Form & Function
San Francisco, CA   415-664-4010

Forsight, Inc.
Rockville, MD   301-816-4900

Frame-by-Frame Media Services
Fremont, CA   510-651-6330

Fresh Cream Design Group
Nesconset, NY   212-446-8557

Galileo, Inc.
Atlanta, GA   404-425-4536

GIS plan
Aalborg, Denmark   45-9815-8522

Grafica Multimedia
Belmont, CA   415-595-5599

Grahame-Harding Productions
San Francisco, CA   415-626-7116

Graphics Edge
Austin, TX   512-454-1254

Grass Valley Multimedia
Grass Valley, CA   916-273-6349

GXStudios
Austin, TX   512-416-0558

Hahn Computer Institute
Downsview, ON Canada
                     416-633-8600

Haukom Associates
San Francisco, CA   415-922-0214

Hill Productions
Sacramento, CA   916-369-2353

Honeybee Software Inc.
New York , NY   800-667-1233
Please See Ad Page 134.

HOT-Tech Multimedia, Inc.
New York, NY   212-925-3010

Howard M. Cutler Productions
Rowayton, CT   203-857-4332
Please See Company Highlight Page 131.

i MEDIA Solutions, Inc.
Ventura, CA   805-339-4242

IBM
Atlanta, GA   404-238-2533

ICONOS
Minneapolis, MN   612-879-0504

IDEA sas
Reggio Emilia, Italy
                     0-522-45-22-25

Image Technologies, Inc.
St. Petersburg, FL   813-573-5268

Imagination Software Consultants
Houston, TX   713-467-2339

Imaginia Inc.
San Francisco, CA   415-788-6840

In Focus Systems
Portland, OR   503-628-3876

In-House Productions
San Ramon, CA   510-828-7056

Industrial Line Multimedia, Inc.
Toronto, ON Canada
                     416-539-0095

NB ENGINEERING
2110 Priest Bridge Drive
Crofton, MO 21114
Contact: Ralph LaBarge
Phone: 410-721-5725
Fax: 410-721-5726
Skills: Multimedia application development using DVI, Indeo, JPEG, MPEG, QuickTime, and TrueMotion compressed digital formats under DOS, Windows, and OS/2.

NEW MEDIA ENTERTAINMENT
1252 Mountain Quail Circle
San Jose, CA 95120
Contact: Rick Rickards, President
Phone: 408-927-6866
AppleLink: NME
Skills: Interactive presentation/kiosk design and development, desktop audio/video production, animation. Director, Photoshop, Illustrator, QuickTime, Infini-D, Video Fusion, Persuasion, and Premiere.

NVISION3
875 Fourth Street
San Rafael, CA 94901
Contact: Jon Goodchild
Phone: 415-459-5077
Fax: 415-457-8095
Skills: Design group with extensive publication experience; multimedia specialists, cross platform.
Projects: Project developers for multimedia programs of all types, including collateral materials.
Clients: William Morrow, Alfred Knopf, Smithsonian Institution. Macmillan, Penguin USA, Chronicle Books, Noetics Institute, WordStar, Bank of America, TestDrive Corporation, Marin Community Foundation.

MULTIMEDIA

MULTIMEDIA

Animation
Audio
Content
Development
Database
Development
Graphics/Interface
Legal Services
Marketing & Sales
Video

PERKINS/BOYER ADVERTISING & DIGITAL PRODUCTIONS

1377 Fulton Street, Suite 3
San Francisco, CA 94117
Phone: 415-346-8820
Fax: 415-346-8834
Projects: Creatives with advertising agency direct marketing project management, scriptwriting, design, and production experience offer complete content development and interactive production services for multimedia business/marketing presentations/titles on disk or CD-ROM. Director authoring experience, plus a variety of 2D/3D illustration, modeling, animation, and video editing software. Edutainment title development.

PMS MICRODESIGN, INC.

1904 Brushcliff Road
Pittsburgh, PA 15221
Contact: Phillip Sauter, President
Phone: 412-731-4004
Fax: 412-731-6743
Skills: Integrate multimedia (Director, Authorware) with virtual reality (reality satellite, human gesture systems) to create dynamic presentations. Engineering, programming, authoring, consulting. See also listing under Development and Programming; Virtual Reality.

Informania, Inc.
San Diego, CA   619-296-4662

InfoUse
Berkeley, CA   510-549-6520

Inkman & Associates
Novato, CA   415-898-2353

Integrated Media, Inc.
New York, NY   212-229-1200

Interactive Design, Inc.
Seattle, WA   206-523-7879

Interactive Engineering
Chicago, IL   312-986-0321

Interactive Factory
Cambridge, MA   617-494-9517

Interactive Multimedia Project
Austin, TX   512-326-8858

Interactive Presentation Technology, Inc.
San Diego, CA   800-326-6141

Interdimensional Arts
Oakland, CA   510-655-1872

InterMagic
Waitsfield, VT   802-496-9667

HONEYBEE SOFTWARE, INC.

Comprehensive programming and development services for multimedia. Database integration with leading multimedia tools for productions, trade show exhibits, employee training, interactive educational presentations, interactive catalogues, new product listings, or boardroom and fundraising demonstrations. Full turnkey development in AppleScript, Apple Media Tool Language, Macromind Lingo, HyperCard's HyperTalk and full programming with 4th Dimension, Pascal, C++, and FoxPro. See also listings under Development and Programming; Applications Development: Accounting, and Development and Programming; Database Programming.

Skills: Apple Media Tool (programming), Macromind (lingo programming), AppleScript, HyperCard.

HONEYBEE SOFTWARE INC.
5 East 47th Street
New York, NY 10017
Phone: 800-667-1233
Fax: 514-875-2940
AppleLink: CDA0270

International Interactive Communications Society (IICS)
503-579-IICS
Please See Ad Page 184.

International Software Products
Brattleboro, VT   802-258-2551

InVision b.v.
Nuenen, Holland   31-40-631260

J. L. Cooper Electronics
Los Angeles, CA   310-306-4131

James Robinson Design & Production
New York, NY   212-864-1415

Jane Sallis & Associates
Seattle, WA   206-522-5522

JAYCOR
Huntsville, AL   205-837-9100

Joe Czop Photography
San Francisco, CA   415-359-4579

JRA Interactive
Olympia, WA   206-866-0533

Kallisto Productions, Inc.
Oakland, CA   510-531-3288

THE WORD AND IMAGE
4470 18th Street
Bettendorf, IA 52722
Contact: Nancy Jacobs,
Phone: 319-332-6324
Fax: 319-332-6324
Projects: Communication specialists with expertise in multimedia and interactivity. We emphasize clear content and human-computer interface design. **Full service:** animation; photography; video taping; digitized video/audio; copyediting; appealing, comprehensible text and graphics layout. Medical, scientific, technical presentations. Textbook conversions/enhancements on CD-ROM for Macintosh and Windows.

UNLIMITED ACCESS
529 Noe Street
San Francisco, CA 94114
Contact: Bren Besser, Consultant
Phone: 415-255-8958
CompuServe: 73057,3045
Skills: Custom database access to media (network and single-user); 4th Dimension, SQL, HyperTalk, Visual BASIC, Revelation.

MULTIMEDIA

MULTIMEDIA

Animation

Audio

Content
Development

Database
Development

Graphics/Interface

Legal Services

Marketing & Sales

Video

Kamen Audio Productions/
CD Archives
New York, NY   212-575-4660
Please See Company Highlight Page 132.

KAR Enterprises, Inc.
Sunnyvale, CA   408-739-9517

Khalsa Productions
Phoenix, AZ   602-678-0743

KMS Systems, Inc.
The Woodlands, TX
                     713-363-9154
Please See Company Highlight Page 132.

KnoSys
Grass Valley, CA   916-274-7852

Komenar Production &
Marketing Group
Tiburon, CA   415-435-9470

KV Graphics
Chanhassen , MN   612-949-2902

Latent Image Productions
San Francisco, CA   415-824-7808

LeBlanc Design
Los Angeles, CA   213-651-5924

Leo Home Media
Los Angeles, CA   213-913-3038

Limburgs University Centre
Diepenbeek, Belgium
                     32 11 26 8166

Lindamood-Bell Learning Processes
San Luis Obispo, CA 805-541-3836

Lingua Service Associates
Seattle, WA   206-448-8404
Please See Ad Page 128.

Lumigenic Media
Felton, CA   408-335-4849

Mac Art Multimedia
Cupertino, CA   408-773-9614

Macsimum Creative Enterprises
Lakewood, CO   303-232-1336

WEST VALLEY ENGINEERING

Established in 1968, we have been providing technical contractors in the software realm to some of the Silicon Valley's most reputable companies. We pride ourselves in providing superior caliber contractors at a moment's notice. We have supported projects of every size and complexity, and offer a full range of services to assist you in your staffing needs.

Skills: Macintosh, MPW, C/C++, MacApp, Macintosh Communications Toolbox, QuickTime, THINK, A/UX, GUI development, UNIX, TCP/IP, Oracle, SCSI, Windows, Visual Basic/C++.

Projects: SW development, technical support, QA/Testing, database design, network engineering, graphic design/illustration and publications.

WEST VALLEY ENGINEERING, INC.
1183 Bordeaux Drive
Sunnyvale, CA 94089
Phone: 408-744-1420
Fax: 408-734-4338

WEST VALLEY ENGINEERING, INC.
1183 Bordeaux Drive
Sunnyvale, CA 94089
Contact: Chris Van Groningen,
Phone: 408-744-1420
Fax: 408-734-4338
westvalley@cup.portal.com
Skills: Macintosh, MPW, C/C++, MacApp, Macintosh Communications Toolbox, QuickTime, THINK, A/UX, GUI development, UNIX, TCP/IP, Oracle, SCSI, Windows, Visual BASIC/C++.
Projects: SW Development, technical support, QA/Testing, database design, network engineering, graphic design/illustration and publications.

RED SKY INTERACTIVE, INC.
50 Green Street
San Francisco, CA 94111
(415)421-7332
FAX (415) 421-0927
AppleLink: REDSKY
Compuserve: 724303144
Skills: Red Sky Interactive provides advertising and entertainment products. AVID MediaComposer, Premiere, CoSa video editing. Director and Authorware programming. Graphics, modeling, and animation using Photoshop, Painter, Illustrator, DeBabelizer, StudioPro. Extensions in C.
Projects: JC Penny (Dallas, TX): Custom image sequencer written in Director and FoxPro for satellite distribution of product information to buyers in 2,000+ stores nationwide. Wells Fargo Bank (San Francisco, CA): Series of interactive product "brochures" on floppy disks for Wells financial products. Direct mail and network distribution to consumers. US West (Denver, CO): Interactive multimedia presentations for internal executive-level strategic planning meetings.

MULTIMEDIA

Animation
Audio
Content Development
Database Development
Graphics/Interface
Legal Services
Marketing & Sales
Video

Magic Teleprompting Inc.
San Francisco, CA   415-626-5283

Magnet Interactive Studios, Inc.
Washington , DC   202-625-1111

Magneton Consulting
Corona, CA   714-724-5922

Media Concepts
San Jose, CA   408-288-8010

Media Designer
San Diego, CA   619-456-9153

Media Direct, Inc.
Tenafly, NJ   201-894-5548
Please See Ad Page 141.

Media Kinematics
Concord, CA   510-674-1282

Media Synergy
San Francisco, CA   415-241-9999

Medialab Information Design
Taufkirchen, Munich 089-6121068

Megafusion
Montreal, QC Canada
514-579-5721

MegaMedia Inc.
Philadelphia, PA   215-848-1377

Micro Visual Systems
Newton, MA   617-964-0640

Viridis is a full service production studio specializing in original design, development and production of high-quality interactive entertainment and games on CD-ROM, 3DO, CDI, Interactive Television and emerging platforms as they become available.

Founded in 1990, Viridis staffs some of the industry's most creative computer artists and programmers, who utilize proprietary software tools and state-of-the-art audio, video and computer hardware on behalf of our clients.

Electronic Arts, IVI Publishing, Philips Interactive Media, The 3DO Company, Thomson Consumer Electronics, GTE, The Los Angeles Times and Nintendo are among the companies who have benefited from Viridis' wide range of development capabilities.

VIRIDIS
11022 Santa Monica Blvd.
#450 Los Angeles, CA 90025

Phone: (310) 445-2055
Fax: (310) 445-2057
Internet: marketing@viridis.com

Microspace Communications Corporation
Raleigh, NC   919-850-4515

Mixed Media Works
Blue Bell, PA   215-832-5960

MontreuxMedia c/o DDESIGN SA
Montreux, Switzerland
                     41 21 9611362

Moov Design
Del Mar, CA   619-259-6300

Morgan Research Corporation
Huntsville, AL   205-533-3233

Morph's Outpost on the Digital Frontier
Orinda, CA   510-238-4550
Please See Ad Page 42.

Morphonix
San Anselmo , CA   415-456-2561

Motion Works International
Vancouver, BC Canada
                     604-732-0289

MultiMedia AB
Stockholm, Sweden   468-660-93-20

Multimedia Computing Corporation
Santa Clara, CA   408-369-1233

Nash Video + Interactive
Langhorne, PA   215-750-1926

NB Engineering
Crofton, MO   410-721-5725
Please See Ad Page 132.
Please See Company Highlight Page 133.
⊡

NDG Phoenix, Inc.
Bethesda, MD   301-718-8880

Neotech Interactive
Santa Monica, CA   310-392-2711

New Media Entertainment
San Jose, CA   408-927-6866
Please See Company Highlight Page 133.

New Visions Media Works
Encino, CA   818-905-7886

Nighthawk Productions, Inc.
Baltimore, MD   410-484-1656

NVision3
San Rafael, CA   415-459-5077
Please See Ad Page 136.
Please See Company Highlight Page 133.

Octavo Productions, Inc.
North Vancouver, BC Canada
                     604-987-5270

On-Line Design, Inc.
Decatur, GA   404-325-2977
Please See Ad Page 135.
⊡

Open Eyes Video
Arlington, MA   617-646-7708

Opticon Pictures Corporation
Mayerthorpe, AB Canada
                     403-439-5862

Optimal Sounds
Austin, TX   512-442-0400

Ottawa Researchers
Ottawa, ON Canada   613-828-5235

Pacific Coast Sound Works
West Hollywood, CA 213-655-4771

**Pacific Interactive
Design Corporation**
Santa Monica, CA   310-458-1898

Palamar Communications
Topanga, CA   310-455-1002

Paradigm Interactive, Inc.
Winston Salem, NC   919-768-7844
🔲

Parallel Media
Los Angeles, CA   310-470-3839

Parcway Software Inc.
Los Altos, CA   415-965-7873

**Perkins/Boyer Advertising & Digital
Productions**
San Francisco, CA   415-346-8820
Please See Company Highlight Page 134.
🔲

Philips Professional Products
Rahway, NJ   908-827-8648

**Pioneer New Media
Technologies, Inc.**
Upper Saddle River, NJ
                      201-327-6400

Planet X Productions
San Jose, CA   408-971-7215

Please Seek, Incorporated
Milwaukee, WI   414-771-3466

PMS Microdesign, Inc.
Pittsburgh, PA   412-731-4004
Please See Company Highlight Page 134.
🔲

Power R, Inc.
Seattle, WA   206-547-8000

Presage Software Development
San Rafael , CA   415-454-7007

Presentation Technologies, Inc.
Atlanta, GA   404-393-3820
🔲

Presentations Plus
San Diego, CA   619-283-5370

R & D Multimedia Productions
Glendora, CA   818-335-8498

THIRD COAST MULTIMEDIA GROUP
6322 Goliad Avenue
Dallas, TX 75214-3601
Contact: James M. Jordan,
Principal
Phone: 214-826-9810
Fax: 214-826-0314
CompuServe: 73114,3514
Skills: Creative Direction,
instructional design, interface/
graphic design, multiplatform
authoring, 3D animation.
Projects: Floppy, hard disk, CD-
ROM marketing presentations,
instruction, technical guides,
corporate communications, kiosk
development - marketing/
informational.
Clients: Big Hand Productions;
BODYBILT Seating; Corporate
Magic, McGahan Multimedia,
Oryx Energy, Powerhouse
Productions, PSM International,
Programmed Communications.

MULTIMEDIA

MULTIMEDIA

Animation

Audio

Content
Development

Database
Development

Graphics/Interface

Legal Services

Marketing & Sales

Video

*Multimedia Communications
for over 20 years*

DOLPHIN
MULTI·MEDIA
INC

Macintosh • DOS • Windows • UNIX • CD-ROM

2440 Embarcadero Way   Palo Alto, California 94303
tel.: 415.354.0800   fax.: 415.354.0808   AppleLink: Dolphin.M

Rall & Company
Columbia, MD   410-730-1706

Rampant Lyon
Tehachapi, CA   805-821-5108

ReadyToGo Presentations
San Francisco, CA   415-563-3674

Red Sky Interactive
San Francisco, CA   415-421-7332
Please See Ad Page 34.
Please See Company Highlight Page 137.

Redwood Software
Arcata, CA   707-822-6545

Results Training Group
Oxford, England   0993/811595

Rigel Engineering S.A.
Brussels, Belgium   32 2 7355571

RPM Productions
San Francisco, CA   415-474-3177

Rusch Design
San Francisco, CA   415-621-4740

Screen Media Software
Westlake Village, CA 818-991-8491

Screenplay Systems
Burbank, CA   818-843-6557

Shoestring Multimedia
San Francisco, CA   415-487-6930

Silk City Software Inc.
Hebron, CT   203-228-0091

Solar Systems Software
San Bruno, CA   415-952-2375

SSG/Skippack Systems Group
North Wales, PA   215-699-9658

Starboard Inc.
San Jose, CA   408-261-7570

Stat™ Media
Yorba Linda, CA   714-779-8176

Steinberg Media
Hamburg, Germany   49-40211594

StoryGame Software
Rowe, MA   413-339-0246

Studio Graphics
San Mateo, CA   415-344-3855

Susan Strumer
Brookfield, CT   203-791-4973

SWeDE Corporation
Newport Beach, CA 714-640-5584

Thank Evan For Desktop Video
San Diego, CA   619-222-3861

The Alan i Harris Group, Inc.
Pittsburgh, PA   412-338-8600

The American Multimedia Group
Auburn, CA   916-887-1216

The Computer Lab
Louisa, VA   703-894-0511

The Design Practice London Ltd.
London, England   071-493-3391

The Human Element, Inc.
Cincinatti, OH   513-745-9204

KAMEN AUDIO PRODUCTIONS/ CD ARCHIVES
701 Seventh Avenue, 6th Floor
New York, NY 10036
Contact: James Berry
Phone: 212-575-4660
Fax: 212-575-4799
CompuServe: 73312,2621
Skills: Digital audio workstations with complete music and sound FX supply and creation. Voice-over talent and recording. Programming archive for CD-ROM. CD-ROM one-offs, computer graphic design. Video editing and production. Real-time MPEG encoding. CD-ROM duplication.
Projects: For 12 years we have been producing audio for radio and television spots for major advertising agencies. Also, music for films and records. Creating computer graphics for industrial and promotional tapes. Archiving radio, television spots, and print advertising to one CD-ROM. Pressing CD-ROM. Designing software for retrieval of CD-ROM archive files.
Clients: Major advertising agencies in the United States.

THE VOICE EMPORIUM
505 Court Street, Suite 6J
Brooklyn, NY 11231
Phone: 718-522-7533
Fax: 718-522-7533
Skills: World-class, broadcast-quality voiceovers (straight, narrative, original characters) that will bring your interactive project to life!

MEDIA DIRECT, INC.

Skills: Authorized Macromedia Developer; Authorware Professional and Director for Windows and Macintosh; personalized consultation, development, and writing; strong corporate MIS background and experience; professional medical writer on staff; DeBabelizer.
Projects: Developer; new product training materials for pharmaceutical sales representatives. Developer; simulation of telecommunications device for consumer focus groups. Consultant; CD-ROM based books for major scientific publisher. Consultant; multimedia training center for the handicapped.
Clients: JMP/Jack Morton Productions, ECCO Designs (AT&T), Van Nostrand Reinhold, The Choices Center.

MEDIA DIRECT, INC.
P.O. Box 302
Tenafly, NJ 07670
Phone: 201-894-5548
Fax: 201-894-5586
Compuserve: 76657,2357

The Hypermedia Group, Inc.
Emeryville, CA   510-601-0900

The Masters Group
Chattanooga, TN   615-499-0706

The Whitley Group
Atlanta, GA   404-843-8550

The Word & Image Workshop, Inc.
Bettendorf, IA   319-332-6324
Please See Company Highlight Page 135.

Third Coast Multimedia Group
Dallas, TX   214-826-9810
Please See Company Highlight Page 139.

Tom Nicholson Associates, Inc.
New York, NY   212-274-0474

TouchMedia
Virginia Beach, VA   804-464-2191

Trailblazer Productions
Sebastopol, CA   707-795-3087

TRANS Pro Media
New York, NY   212-989-4909

Treehouse Computer Services
Houston, TX   713-356-7926

TW DESIGN
Atlanta, GA   404-237-3958

MULTIMEDIA
Animation
Audio
Content Development
Database Development
Graphics/Interface
Legal Services
Marketing & Sales
Video

BLOCK COMMUNICATIONS

5150 El Camino Real, B14
Los Altos, CA 94022-1527
Contact: Megan Gallagher,
Manager, Marketing
Phone: 415-254-7600
Fax: 415-254-1760
AppleLink: BLOCKCOMM
Skills: Director, Authorware,
Premiere, Illustrator, Photoshop,
AfterEffects.
Projects: Multimedia marketing
communications specialists—
demo disks, CD-ROMs, kiosks,
speaker support, direct mail,
electronic catalogs, and training
systems. Full-service packaging
and promotional literature.
Clients: Apple Computer, Inc.;
Cisco Systems; Hewlett-Packard;
Nikon; LucasArts Entertainment;
Sybase; SynOptics; 20th Century-
Fox; Walt Disney Imagineering.

TEKNOWLEDGY

7525 Market Place Drive
Eden Prairie, MN 55344
Contact: Richard Perry
Phone: 612-946-0106
Fax: 612-946-0105
Skills: Teknowledgy is skilled in
Authorware, QuickTime, Sound,
and most 3D and animation tools.
Projects: Teknowledgy is an
interactive multimedia developer
of custom corporate sales and
marketing productions designed
to automate the sales process (not
the sales person). These
productions play on PowerBooks
and future unannounced
products.
Clients: NCR, Zeos, Rosemount,
National Computer Systems.

SOFTGUIDE

■ Introducing SoftGuide. We are a high-energy, creative, enthusiastic, professional team with technical and artistic expertise and a solid background in interactive multimedia programming, instructional design, training, education, video production, music composition, theatrical sound design, audio engineering, computer art, animation, scriptwriting, copywriting, editing, and publishing.

■ Interactive SoftGuide Systems. We will design, storyboard, and create custom computer presentations or full-blown interactive multimedia programs on Macintosh or Amiga platforms for informational kiosks, trade shows, conferences, employee or customer training, or education.

■ SoftGuide Custom Music. We offer exciting original music and sounds on CDs for your multimedia productions. Write for our brochure.

SOFTGUIDE
P.O. Box 870531
Dallas, TX 75287-0531
Phone: 214-306-2029
Fax: 214-307-3023

Unlimited Access
San Francisco, CA   415-255-8958
Please See Company Highlight Page 135.

Viridis
Santa Monica, CA   310-445-2055
Please See Ad Page 138.

Virtual Beauty
New York, NY   212-675-0699

Visual Impact!
Royal Oak, MI   313-583-2080

Visual Logic
Hockessin, DE   302-234-5707

Voldstad Interactive Design
Sunnyvale, CA   408-733-4116

WaveForms
Berkeley, CA   510-848-2143

Way Cool Productions
Schenectady, NY   518-346-3590

West Valley Engineering, Inc.
Sunnyvale, CA   408-744-1420
Please See Ad Page 137.

Windhorse Productions
Halifax, NS   902-492-4523

Wonderplay Inc.
New York, NY   212-595-7894

MEDIA CONCEPTS

1052-B N. Fifth Street
San Jose, CA 95112
Contact: Kristell Mazzuco, Vice
President, Marketing
Phone: 408-288-8010
Fax: 408-288-8086
Skills: Award-winning media
design company. QuickTime
movies. Avid nonlinear random
"access" editing. Macintosh
graphics to videotape.
Projects: Multimedia video
communications, interactive
education programs, CD-ROM
titles, multilanguage programs,
and corporate productions. Stock
footage availabe or customized
for multimedia projects.
Clients: Apple Computer, Inc.;
Computer Curriculum
Corporation; Paramount
Communications Company;
country of Singapore; IBM; Intel;
PBS Great Performances; Sega;
Vanished Children's Alliance.

NB ENGINEERING

2110 Priest Bridge Drive
Crofton, MO 21114
Contact: Ralph LaBarge
Phone: 410-721-5725
Fax: 410-721-5726
Projects: NBE operates one of
the world's largest offline
professional video compression
service bureaus, offering
DVI/PLV, Indeo, JPEG, MPEG,
QuickTime, and TrueMotion
compressed digital video formats.
Analog input tapes accepted in 1"
BetaCam, BetaCam-SP, and D2
formats. NBE also provides
mobile multimedia solutions
using Toshiba portable and pen-
based computers.
回

MULTIMEDIA

Animation
Audio
Content
Development
Database
Development
Graphics/Interface
Legal Services
Marketing & Sales
Video

MULTIMEDIA

Animation

Aerie Animation
San Diego, CA   619-496-8550

Christopher L. Schneck
Chicago, IL   312-883-0146

**Computer Center of Hayward/
San Jose**
Hayward, CA   510-538-4480

Dan R. Sukiennik
Berkeley, CA   510-486-0245

Dolphin Multimedia
Palo Alto, CA   415-354-0800
Please See Ad Page 139.
回

Drumlin Interactive Design
Victoria, BC Canada 604-361-1903

Electric Image, Incorporated
Pasadena, CA   818-577-1627

Flying Rhino
Sausalito, CA   415-332-7868

Illuminati
Durham, NC   919-683-2424

Jesse Sugarman
New York, NY 212-925-5663

KnowledgeVision
Myrtle Beach, SC 803-272-4483

Live Wire Productions™
Rancho Palos Verdes, CA
310-831-6227

Maus Haus
Burlingame, CA 415-343-2996

Medior Inc.
El Granada, CA 415-728-5100

Minds Eye Graphics
Richmond, VA 804-643-0441

Moving Media
San Francisco, CA 415-861-1759

Multimedia Creation
Danville, CA 510-866-2968

Oxygen Farm
Eden, NC 910-635-1669

Rodney Vaughan Associates
Redwood City, CA 415-364-0129

Tree Frog Studio
Palo Alto, CA 415-856-3764

Viewpoint Animation Engineering
Orem, UT 801-224-2222

Valence, Inc.
Tiburon, CA 415-435-9252

Vividus Corporation
Palo Alto, CA 415-321-2221

Zona Corporation
Newburyport, MA 508-465-9632

Audio

850 Productions Inc.
Chicago, IL 312-642-8520
Please See Ad Page 140.

Adamsound
Petaluma, CA 707-763-5732

Advanced Audioworks
Plano, TX 214-517-9154

Aesthetic Engineering
New York, NY 212-925-7049

Ames & Associates
Redwood City, CA 415-366-5153

ASR Recording
Carson, CA 310-327-3180
Please See Ad Page 143.

Clarity
Garrison, NY 914-424-4071

Digital Hieroglyphics
San Francisco, CA   415-431-0611

Digital One
Portland, OR   503-226-7223

Filmsonix, Inc.
Los Angeles, CA   213-465-7697

**Freq Sound/Workman
Computer Services**
Columbia, MD   410-964-3548

Greytsounds Sound Development
Northridge, CA   503-347-4700

Hearing Voices
Oakland, CA   510-452-9274

Interactive Audio
San Francisco, CA   415-431-0778

Judy Munsen
Oakland, CA   510-763-4007

**Kamen Audio Productions/
CD Archives**
New York, NY   212-575-4660
Please See Company Highlight Page 141.

Music Annex, Inc.
San Francisco, CA   510-226-0800

Music & MIDI Sales
Overland Park, KS   913-648-8225

Passport Designs, Inc.
Half Moon Bay, CA   415-726-0280

Please Seer Systems, Inc.
Palo Alto, CA   415-856-0265

Polygram Special Markets
New York, NY   212-333-8549

Pulse Productions
Pacifica, CA   415-355-5252

Quintessence Audio
Tulsa, OK   918-582-1200

Raphael & De Jong
Utrecht, The Netherlands
    31-30-368367

SMARTALK
San Francisco, CA   415-821-7722

Sonic Byte
Cypress, CA   800-505-9160

Sound-Arts Company Inc.
Ocean, NJ   908-493-8666

Steinberg Jones
Northridge, CA   818-993-4091

Studer Dyaxis
Nashville, TN   615-391-3399

Synthesis, Inc
Conway, AR   501-327-2517

Symbolic Sound Corporation
Champagne, IL   217-335-6273

The Voice Emporium
Brooklyn, NY   718-522-7533
Please See Company Highlight Page 141.

Tree Media Digital Music Services
Watertown, MA   617-926-4502

V/March, Inc.
San Jose, CA   408-365-8601

Vandellos Studios
San Mateo, CA   415-574-8446

Warner Cable
Shorewood, WI   414-963-1716

Zola Technologies Inc.
Atlanta, GA   404-843-2972

VERIDIAN
268 9th Avenue
San Francisco, CA 94118
Contact: Nancy Martin,
Phone: 415-386-0429
Fax: 415-386-6924
Skills: Character animation,
content development, user
interface design, 3D animation,
and lingo programming for
promotions, presentations, and
games.

21ST CENTURY MEDIA
1224A Glenview Avenue
Milwaukee, WI 53213
Contact: Nancy Cavanaugh,
Phone: 414-771-8906
AOL: JPLAM
Skills: 21st Century Media offers
interactive multimedia design,
consultation, production. Projects
include: "Interactive Course
Builder" - AFI; "Salt of the Earth" -
Voyager.

**INSTRUCTIONAL DESIGN
GROUP, INC.**
144 Speedwell Avenue
Morristown, NJ 07960
Contact: Mark Didriksen,
Phone: 201-538-2226
Fax: 201-538-2219
Projects: The Instructional Design
Group integrates proven
instructional design principles
with today's digital technologies to
produce performance solutions
that get results. IDG has
established leadership in the
development of quality custom
courses for sales, financial,
technical, and management
training. If the success of your
training project is critical...talk to
IDG.

MULTIMEDIA

Animation
Audio
Content
Development
Database
Development
Graphics/Interface
Legal Services
Marketing & Sales
Video

MULTIMEDIA

WILDWARE
307 Grayson Court
Menlo Park, CA 94025
Contact: Tom Neuman, Owner
Phone: 415-367-3682
Fax: 415-367-2410
Skills: Affordable multimedia for small businesses. Floppy disk–based advertising, trade show kiosks, corporate presentations, training. Macintosh, Windows, and cross platform.

Content Development

Adams Consulting Group
Western Springs, IL   708-246-0766

Anne Dorfman
San Francisco, CA   415-928-2462

ASK International
Long Beach, CA   310-987-2071

Bulldog Studios
San Francisco, CA   415-641-5700

Cooper Communications
South Orange, NJ   908-723-6147

Eileen Mullinaux
San Francisco, CA   415-922-1236

Flying Pictures/Mercuria Interactive
New York, NY   212-861-9502

Fulcrum Media Services
San Anselmo, CA   415-459-4429

General Picture
Atlanta, GA   404-377-6161

Glass Eye Productions
Ocean City, NJ   609-399-6833

IME
Los Angeles, CA   213-461-4925

**Ken Braband
Business Communications**
Cedarburg, WI   414-375-9253

M2 Multimedia
San Jose, CA   408-432-3364

MZ Media Group
San Francisco, CA   415-543-8290
Please See Ad Page 13.

Orpheum Productions
Studio City, CA   818-985-9854

Panache Productions
Dallas, TX   214-363-3533

Parallax Technologies
Pleasanton, CA   510-416-8080

Peter Samis Art Services
Berkeley, CA   510-527-8759

Sam Adams
Brooklyn, NY   718-383-6437

Texas Learning Technology Group
Austin, TX   800-580-8584

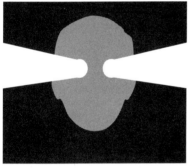

Z Z Y Z X
VISUAL SYSTEMS

Professional Photo CD Scanning, Image Archiving, CD ROM Publishing, Electronic Image Retouching and Transmission, Photoshop Classes

1011 N. Orange Drive, Los Angeles, CA 90038
800.995.1025 213.883.1060 Fax: 213.883.1064

The Katherine Company
Tucson, AZ 602-749-1560

Thomas M. Basista
Kittanning, PA 412-548-7425

Tony & Meryl Perutz
Santa Barbara, CA 805-565-0925

TT Productions
Oakland, CA 510-420-1630

Ventura College and La Vie
Ventura, CA 805-654-6400

Video Simulations
New York, NY 212-663-6812

Database Development

Adventures for Gifted & Talented, Inc.
Birmingham, AL 205-870-5948

ATI Advertising Technologies Inc.
New Westminster, BC
604-521-7179

Binary Designs
Portland, OR 503-232-2909

bopp productions inc.
Basel, Switzerland 41-61-681 8812

Film Works Software, Inc.
Santa Monica, CA 310-451-3756

HeyerTech-IICS
Palo Alto, CA 415-325-8522

MZ Media Group
San Francisco, CA 415-543-8290
Please See Ad Page 34.

Graphics/Interface

3D Perception
Chula Vista, CA 619-656-3865

Aaron Marcus and Associates, Inc.
Emeryville, CA 510-601-0994

Andree R. Oreck
Mt. Shasta, CA 916-926-4681

Arcadia Designs
Palo Alto, CA 415-323-7604

Beachware
San Diego, CA 619-492-9529

David Anderson Consulting
Mountain View, CA 415-969-9296

Design Teknekh
Decatur, GA 404-378-7900

E Ware
New York, NY 800-743-8645

Forman & Flack, Inc.
Watertown, MA 617-923-0124

Golden Branch Interactive Productions
New York, NY 212-595-4474

Graphic Directions
San Francisco, CA 415-239-7024

Imagetects
Saratoga, CA 408-252-5487

In Context
Cambridge, MA 617-497-5816

Interplay Artists
San Francisco, CA 415-564-2072

Kristi Wachter
San Francisco, CA 415-931-1614

Loch Moy
North Berwick, Scotland
0620-5411

Media Group
Santa Cruz, CA 408-457-9143

Mediacom, Inc.
Richmond, VA 804-794-0700

NewOrder Media, Inc.
Nashville, TN 615-386-3636

Newton Design Company
Surrey, England 0428-722155

Persuasive Presentations
Redmond, WA 206-868-5702

Pixel Translations Inc.
Cupertino, CA 408-865-6600

Premier Design
Pleasant Hil, CA 510-674-8440

ScreenDesign
Berlin, Germany 49-30-3938438

Stephanie Wong
San Francisco, CA 415-442-7915

Terry Brown
Santa Clara, CA 408-974-0936

Time Inc. Picture Collection
New York, NY 212-522-8800

Tumble Interactive Media, Inc.
New York, NY 212-316-0200

Two Twelve Associates, Inc.
New York, NY 212-925-6885

Valence, Inc.
Tiburon, CA 415-435-9252

Wayne Media Group
Germering, Germany
49-89-3595904

MULTIMEDIA

Animation
Audio
Content Development
Database Development
Graphics/Interface
Legal Services
Marketing & Sales
Video

West Valley Engineering, Inc.
Sunnyvale, CA   408-744-1420
Please See Company Highlight Page 137.

Wood River Gallery
Mill Valley, CA   415-388-6500

Legal Services

Branfman & Associates
San Diego, CA   619-481-5800

Cooley Godward
Palo Alto, CA   415-845-5163

Morrison & Foerster
San Francisco, CA   415-677-6210
Please See Ad Page 126.

Rosenfeld, Meyer & Susman
Beverly Hills , CA   310-246-3210

Silverberg, Katz, Thompson & Braun
Los Angeles, CA   310-445-5858

Marketing & Sales

Block Communications
Los Altos, CA   415-254-7600
Please See Company Highlight Page 142.

Chazz Communications Company
Lynbrook, NY   516-887-6675

Display Tech Multimedia, Inc.
Concord, CA   510-676-9362

LNS Communications
San Francisco, CA   415-552-6462

MEDIUS IV
San Francisco, CA   415-905-6959

Minerva Interactive
San Francisco, CA   415-863-9484

Multimedia Business Presentations
San Francisco, CA   415-863-6270

Multimedia Research Group
Sunnyvale, CA   408-524-9767

R. Seide & Associates International
Los Angeles, CA   213-938-9408

SoftGuide
Dallas, TX   214-306-2029
Please See Ad Page 142.

Teknowledgy
Eden Prairie, MN   612-946-0106
Please See Company Highlight Page 142.

The Resource
Fairfax, CA   415-485-1447

Wisdom Ware
Foster City , CA   415-574-2683

Video

Abbate Video, Inc.
Millis, MA   508-376-3712

Adair & Armstrong
San Francisco, CA   415-826-6500

Advanced Digital Imaging
Anaheim , CA   714-779-7772

Avid Corporation
Cambridge, MA   508-640-6789

Communication Bridges
Sausalito, CA   415-331-3133

Communications Concepts Inc.
Cape Canaveral, FL   407-783-5232

Complete Solutions/QTFX
Amesbury, MA   508-388-3736

Compression Labs, Inc.
San Jose, CA   408-435-3000

Cremer & Associates
San Francisco, CA   415-821-7023

Digital Post & Graphics
Seattle, WA   206-623-3444

Display Research Laboratory
Tsuen Wan,   852-4121121

Film Rite Entertainment Group, Inc.
White Plains, NY   914-946-5262

Four Media Company
Burbank, CA   818-840-7156

Frank Scales Productions
San Francisco, CA   415-621-1649

Gerin Productions, Inc.
Bedford Hills, NY   914-666-0542

Guillermo Pulido
Oakland, CA   510-839-7708

Harappa Films
San Francisco, CA   415-642-1620

**Howard Metzenberg
Multimedia Consultant**
San Francisco, CA   415-695-7952

I-Per Media
Milan, Italy   2- 66800996

IMAGIC
London, England   44-71-589-1708

Insync Productions
Rochester, NY   716-422-2100

Interactive Solutions, Inc.
San Mateo, CA   415-377-0136

**Interface International
Communications**
Redondo Beach, CA   310-316-5822
Please See Ad Page 140.

John Gammon Video Service
Castro Valley, CA   510-886-5588

Koala Acquisitions, Inc.
Morgan Hill, CA   408-776-8181

Lynx System Developers, Inc.
Woburn, MA   617-935-6959

Magnagraphics, Inc.
Cincinnati, OH   513-221-2230

Media Concepts
San Jose, CA   408-288-8010
Please See Company Highlight Page 143.

Mediaware Development Group Inc.
Tucson, AZ   602-298-5355

Michael Cowey
Houston, TX   713-220-7872

Michael Feerer & Associates
Bellingham, WA   206-647-0112

MSI
Indianapolis, IN   317-842-5097

NB Engineering
Crofton, MO   410-721-5725
Please See Ad Page 144.
Please See Company Highlight Page 143.
回

NFL Films
Mt. Laurel, NJ   609-778-1600

Prelinger Associates, Inc.
New York, NY   212-633-2020

Preview Media
San Francisco, CA   415-397-2494

QuickSoft
Ra'anana, Israel   972-52-444249

RETINA
Munich, Germany   0-89-144286

Sheahan Productions, Inc.
Princeton, NJ   609-497-1112

Silicon Valley Bus Company
San Juan Bautista, CA 408-623-2300

Sinard Productions
Minneapolis, MN   612-338-7771

Taft Development Group
Boulder, CO   303-494-4575

The Graphic Resource Center
Oklahoma City, OK   405-840-4723

Video Arts Inc.
San Francisco, CA   415-546-0331

Video-It Post
Culver City, CA   310-280-0505

Visual Solutions
Atlanta, GA   404-365-0839

Workstation Technologies, Inc.
Irvine, CA   714-250-8983

MULTIMEDIA PRODUCERS

Advance Reality Systems
San Francisco, CA   415-974-1044

Allied Film and Video
San Francisco, CA   415-777-1700

AlterNet Television, Inc
Sausalito, CA   415- 331-8835

American Institute for Learning
Austin, TX   512-472-3251

Andersen Consulting
San Diego, CA   619-578-1700

Animated Systems & Design
Palo Alto, CA   415-424-8586

Art & Logic
Sherman Oaks, CA   818-501-6990

Broderbund Software
Novato, CA   415-382-4591

Buffalo Brothers Marketing
Port St. Lucie, FL   800-709-7909

Busch Creative Services Corporation
St. Louis, MO   314-289-7711

Calypso Interactive
San Francisco, CA   415-824-7651

Collosal Pictures
San Francisco, CA   415-550-8772

Digital Development Corporation
Los Angeles, CA   310-279-1202

Digital United
Cornwall-on-the-Hudson, NY
914-271-4959

DoremiLabs, Inc.
Los Angeles, CA   818-966-2454

Dreamworks
Newtown, PA   215-860-0888

e Motion Technologies
Sausalito, CA   415-331-4030

EAR Professional Audio/Video
Phoenix, AZ   602-267-0600

EdgeWriter Film/Video Systems Inc.
Fairfax, CA   415-459-3926

EDR Media
Beachwood, OH   216-292-7300

Ellen Bari
New York, NY   212-662-6099

Frontier Media Group, Inc.
Malvern, PA   610-641-5535

Harris Consulting
Woodacre, CA   415-488-1137

MULTIMEDIA
Animation
Audio
Content
Development
Database
Development
Graphics/Interface
Legal Services
Marketing & Sales
Video
**MULTIMEDIA
PRODUCERS**
Education &
Training
Entertainment
Information

MULTIMEDIA

Human Code, Inc.
Austin, TX   512-477-5455

Long and Company
San Francisco, CA   415-922-4016

MasterPiece Video
Fairfield, NJ   201-808-4546

McGraw Advertising/Design
Troy, NY   518-272-3030

Minerva Systems, Inc.
Santa Clara, CA   408-970-1782

Multimedia Magic
New York, NY   212-289-7119

Multimedia Scientific
San Diego, CA   619-549-4600

Quartet
San Francisco, CA   415-647-1777

Red Sky Interactive
San Francisco, CA   415-421-7332
Please See Ad Page 34.
Please See Company Highlight Page 151.

Scott Mize Productions
Woodside, CA   415-851-4126

The Digital Artist, Inc.
Seattle, WA   206-935-4606

The Glyph Media Group Inc.
New York, NY   212-989-7026

The Lerro Corporation
Philadelphia, PA   215-223-8200

Veridian
San Francisco, CA   415-386-0429
Please See Company Highlight Page 145.

Xenon Communications Corporation
Arlington Heights, IL 708-577-7057

Education & Training

21st Century Media
Milwaukee, WI   414-771-8906
Please See Company Highlight Page 145.
▣

Adrienne Schure
New York, NY   212-580-2246

**Amuse Interactive
Learning Environment**
Tiburon, CA   415- 435-7791

Anderson Soft Teach
Los Gatos, CA   408-399-0100

Ariel PSS Coporation
Portland, OR   503-232-0221

Avatar Numedia
Palo Alto, CA   415-322-3838

Center for Multimedia
Bellevue, WA   206-643-9039

Cheryl L. Blundell
Fremont, CA   510-713-1039

Claire Moore Instructional Design
Lincoln, CA   916-645-2085
▣

CLE Group
Menlo Park, CA   415-324-1827

Dale Komai
Fremont, CA   510-656-6387

DDLabs
Palo Alto, CA   415-856-9067

Einstein's Bicycle
Los Angeles, CA   310-397-7209

Elmo Productions
Oakland, CA   510-482-8756

Excel Instruction
Minneapolis, MN   612-379-3883

EXEGI
Pleasant Hill, CA   510-827-3681

Frax Incorporated
San Jose, CA   408-279-3059

Hartley Metzner, Huenink
New Berlin, WI   414-784-1010

**Health & Education Communication
Consultants**
Redwood City, CA   415-368-0418

Individual Software
Pleasanton, CA   510-734-6767

Instructional Design Group, Inc.
Morristown, NJ   201-538-2226
Please See Company Highlight Page 145.

Integrated Strategies, Inc.
Minnetonka , MN   612-544-3080

Intra-Active Designs
Minnetonka, MN   612-938-1473

Kasdin Productions
Malibu, CA   310-454-6760

Learning Systems Sciences
North Hollywood, CA
                     818-505-6222

Management Advisory Services
Bloomfield Hills, MI 313-606-7596

MED.I.A. Inc.
Milwaukee, WI   414-352-9336

Morgan Interactive
San Francisco, CA   415-693-9596

**Multi Lingual Media
Presentations & Training**
San Diego, CA   619-578-1357

MultiTrain International
Long Beach, CA   310-494-4091

MW Productions
San Francisco, CA   415-641-8844

New Renaissance
San Diego, CA   619-287-0093

Oracle Multimedia
Wilmette, IL   708-256-2290

Paoletti Technologies
San Francisco, CA   415-391-7610

Peter C. Reynolds & Associates
Palo Alto, CA   415-589-6939

Planet Productions
Portland, OR   503-241-1644

Presentation Media
South Amboy, NJ   908-525-1700

Printz-Electronic Design
San Francisco, CA   415-543-5673

Richard L. Bergman
New York, NY   212-677-8195

Scholastic Software
New York, NY   212-505-6006

Schubert Media Design
Redwood City, CA   415-365-6878

Soft One Corporation
Orem, UT   801-226-8611

Sussman Media
Santa Cruz, CA   408-427-9579

Tech Museum of Innovation
San Jose, CA   408-279-7174

Teknowledgey Design Corporation
Honolulu, HI   808-539-3667

The Choices Center
Port Chester, NY   914-937-3454

The Write Thing
Paradise, CA   916-872-7279

Toby L. Sanders
New York, NY   212-956-0678

User Active Media
Moscow, ID   208-883-5548

Ventura Community College
Ventura, CA   805-648-8906

Wildware
Menlo Park, CA   415-367-3682
Please See Company Highlight Page 146.

Wisconsin Technical College System Foundation Incorporated
Waunakee, WI   608-849-2400

Entertainment

21st Century Media
Burbank, CA   818-848-4543
Please See Company Highlight Page 151.

Alan i Harris Group, Inc.
Pittsburgh, PA   412-338-8600

DK Digital Media
San Francisco, CA   415-441-7659

Horizons Technology, Inc.
Spring Valley, CA   619-292-8860

Image Smith
Torrance, CA   310-325-5999

Incline Productions
Santa Monica, CA   310-314-7519

Leland Interactive Media
San Diego, CA   619-284-9458

RED SKY INTERACTIVE,INC.
50 Green Street
San Francisco, CA 94111
(415)421-7332
FAX (415) 421-0927
AppleLink: REDSKY
Compuserve
Skills: Red Sky Interactive provides advertising and entertainment products. AVID MediaComposer, Premiere, CoSa video editing. Director and Authorware programming. Graphics, modeling, and animation using Photoshop, Painter, Illustrator, DeBabelizer, StudioPro. Extensions in C.
Projects: JC Penny (Dallas, TX): Cusotm image sequencer written in Director and FoxPro for satellite distribution of product information to buyers in 2,000 stores nationwide. Wells Fargo Bank (San Francisco, CA): Series of interactive product "brochures" on floppy disks for Wells financial products. Direct mail and netwrok distribution to consumers. US West (Denver, CO): Interactive multimedia presentations for internal executive-level strategic planning meetings.

21ST CENTURY MEDIA
1066 Clybourn Avenue
Burbank, CA 91505
Contact: James Lambert, Partner
Phone: 818-848-4543
Fax: 818-848-4543
AOL: JPLAM
Skills: 21st Century Media offers interactive multimedia design, consultation, production. Projects include: "Salt of the Earth" - Voyager; "Interactive Course Builder" - AFI.

MULTIMEDIA

MULTIMEDIA
Animation
Audio
Content Development
Database Development
Graphics/Interface
Legal Services
Marketing & Sales
Video
MULTIMEDIA PRODUCERS
Education & Training
Entertainment
Information

Luminaria
San Francisco, CA   415-821-0536

Main Street Multimedia
Santa Monica, CA   310-396-4084

Rittenhouse Communications
Yardley, PA   215-321-6860

Sligo Video
Los Angeles, CA   310-837-5422

Information

Bussard & Associates
Pasadena, CA   818-794-2991

D S Simon Productions
New York, NY   212-727-7770

Design Mirage, Inc.
State College, PA   814-234-2616

Dynacom, Inc.
Chicago, IL   312-951-5510

**GTE Hotel Interactive
Television Services**
Needham, MA   617-449-7676

Kirk Mahoney
Houston, TX   713-952-5475

LJR Communications, Inc.
New York, NY   212-744-9140

MarCole Enterprises
Walnut Creek, CA   510-933-9792

Media in Content
San Francisco, CA   415-621-0707

Mercury Multi Media
Brooklyn, NY   718-330-1159

Novette Incorporated
Pittsburgh, PA   412-521-2758

Reflections Publishing, Inc.
Morgan Hill, CA   408-779-6616

U.S. Media Group
San Francisco, CA   415-274-8555

Virtual Company Visits, Inc.
San Francisco, CA   415-777-3438

CD-ROM

Archiving Services

CD-Press
Elgin, IL   800-505-3344

Digital Designs
Dallas, TX   214-407-9303

Graphic Detail, Inc.
Raleigh, NC   919-833-3366

Mac Software Registry
Bronxville, NY   914-961-8743

Photo Library Management Services
Ventura, CA   805-641-2400

ZZYZX Visual Systems
Los Angeles, CA   800-995-1025
Please See Ad Page 146.

Development

Bent Media, Inc.
New Orleans, LA   504-482-8278

Bogner Entertainment Inc.
Los Angeles, CA   310-473-0139

BOLDer MultiMedia
Golden, CO   303-642-3087

CD Technology Inc.
Sunnyvale, CA   408-752-8500

Computer Modules Inc.
Santa Clara, CA   408-496-1881

Ebook, Inc.
Union City, CA   510-429-1331

Folkstone Design Inc.
Grantham's Landing, BC Canada
604-886-4502

Glaser Media Group
San Carlos, CA   415-593-6607

Grid Media Limited
Causeway Bay, Hong Kong
852-591-0730

Ikonic
San Francisco, CA   415-864-3200

ink
Toronto, ON Canada
416-360-3894

M3 Dimensions, Inc.
Whittier, CA   310-907-6590

Metatec Corporation
Dublin, OH   614-761-2000

Multimedia Asia Ltd.
Hong Kong   852-824-0781

Reactor Inc.
Chicago, IL   312-573-0800

S.I.A. - Advanced Information Systems
Verlaine, Belgium   32-19-567-135

Shardonnay Audio Visual, Inc.
Los Angeles, CA   213-913-1238

Software Mart Incorporated
Austin, TX   512-346-7887

Spatial Data Architects
San Francisco, CA   415-397-6431

TBP, Inc.
Westlake Village, CA 818-889-2870

Timebox Inc.
Flemington , NJ   908-782-5643

Wayzata Technology
Grand Rapids, MN   218-326-0597

Duplication

Catalogic
Mountain View, CA   415-961-4649
Please See Company Highlight Page 153

Optical Media International
Los Gatos, CA   408-376-3511

Software Services Group
Omaha, NE   800-622-3873,
Please See Ad Page 152.

Photo CD

Mega Media
Ventura, CA   805-659-0252

Procom Technology
Irvine, CA   800-800-8600

ZZYZX Visual Systems
Los Angeles, CA   800-995-1025

MULTIMEDIA

MULTIMEDIA PRODUCERS
Education & Training
Entertainment
Information

CD ROM
Archiving Services
Development
Duplication
Photo CD

157

Networking

Client server network experts, both solution providers and systems integration vendors, can be found here under specific categories which define their area of expertise.

Client/Server   **159**

Network & Systems
  Integration   **159**

  Design 163

  Enterprise Network
    Solutions 165

  Installations 165

  System Integration 166

  Training 167

Network Systems &
  Protocols   **167**

Network Services   **168**

Networks   **168**

BEFORE YOU PURCHASE NETWORK COMPUTING PRODUCTS, LOOK IN HERE.

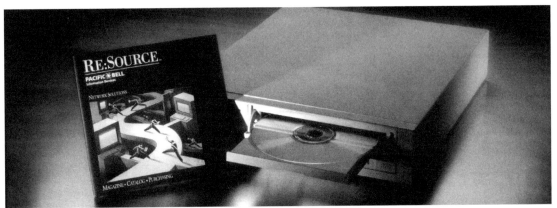

NETWORK SOLUTIONS ON DEMAND.

From trade journals and data sheets to white papers and seminars, today's IS professional is faced with a dizzying array of information sources. In fact, it's all but impossible for today's network professional to keep abreast of the explosive developments surrounding networking hardware, software, and services. Until now.

MAKE YOUR TIME MORE PRODUCTIVE

Introducing Re:Source Network Solutions. It's a multimedia CD-ROM publication that gives you, one easy-to-use, comprehensive source of information. With text, audio, interactive graphics and QuickTime™ video, Re:Source gives you a complete knowledge base, in a powerful easily-accessed format.

THREE GREAT TOOLS

Re:Source Magazine. The latest news, the newest products, in-depth articles, and industry leaders looking to the future. The Magazine is an invaluable source of what's going on in the world of network computing.

Re:Source Network Solution Catalog. An electronic source that catalogs hundreds of the latest Macintosh networking products with detailed specifications. Everything in one easy-to-use place.

Re:Source Easy Ordering. Tag products as you browse, and you can create an ordering list, an RFQ for competitive pricing, or export the list (with or without specs) at the touch of a button.

Re:Source Network Solutions. It's the solution for today's busy IS professional.

RE:SOURCE™
NETWORK SOLUTIONS

PACIFIC BELL.
Information Services

FOR MORE INFORMATION CALL 1(800)303-7247.

CLIENT/SERVER

Bear River Associates, Inc.
Berkeley, CA   510-644-9400
Please See Company Highlight Page 159.

Bruce, Bruce, & Bruce
Glynoon, MD   410-526-3791

Francis Tanner Inc.
DeLanson, NY   518-872-2756

Gateway Group Inc.
Lafayette, CA   510-283-7900

**Innovative Information
Concepts, Inc.**
Bohemia, NY   516-981-1990

Integral Information Systems
Berkeley, CA   510-524-5200

Moose Systems, Inc.
Jackson Hole, WY   307-789-9758

New Media, Inc.
Cleveland , OH   216-481-7900
Please See Company Highlight Page 160.

Oak Enterprises
Glen Ellyn, IL   708-858-4443

Personal Systems Services, Inc.
Atlanta, GA   404-432-8179

RWD Technologies, Inc.
Columbia, MD   404-551-8198
Please See Company Highlight Page 161.

ShowCase Corporation
Rochester, MN   507-288-5922

Software Complement
Matamoras, PA   717-491-2492

Software Development Factory
Hunt Valley, MD   410-666-8129

Stanford Business Systems, Inc.
Culver City, CA   310-215-8444
Please See Company Highlight Page 161.

The Planet Group, Inc.
Chicago, IL   312-772-8333

United Data Corporation
San Francisco, CA   415-750-8068

NETWORK & SYSTEMS INTEGRATION

A. L. Freeman, Jr. & Associates, Inc.
Falkland, NC   919-758-7040

Advanced Integrated Technology
Columbia, TN   615-381-4388

Alexander LAN, Inc.
Nashua, NH   603-880-8800

Arcom Electronics, Inc.
San Jose, CA   408-452-0678

BEAR RIVER ASSOCIATES, INC.
P.O. Box 1900
Berkeley, CA 94701-1900
Contact: Rodney Smith, Anthony Meadow.
Phone: 510-644-9400
Fax: 510-644-9778
Internet: info@bearriver.com
Skills: Macintosh, Newton, Windows, A/UX, UNIX, DAL, Oracle, Sybase.
Projects: Database applications, sales force automation, information retrieval, text processing, image processing, object-oriented graphics. Services include software development and consulting for systems and applications design across a wide range of computing environments; system architecture and design analysis; object-oriented analysis, design, and development; client/server and distributed computing; user interface and internal design consulting.

NETWORKING

CLIENT/SERVER

NETWORK & SYSTEMS INTEGRATION

Design

Enterprise Network Solutions

Installations

System Integration

Training

NEW MEDIA, INC.

503 E. 200th Street, Suite 202
Cleveland, OH 44119-1543
Contact: Leonard W. Pagon, Jr.,
President
Phone: 216-481-7900
Fax: 216-481-1570
AppleLink: NEWMEDIA
Skills: PowerBuilder, Visual
BASIC, FoxPro, Lotus Notes,
Visual C++, C, SQL server, Oracle,
Windows NT, 4th Dimension,
MacApp, Omnis 7.
Projects: We offer a full range of
application development and
education services focusing on
graphical, client/server, workflow,
OOP, and cross-platform
technology areas. We assist as
organizations migrate toward
emerging technologies such as
client/server and workgroup
computing and provide planning,
education, and development to
facilitate knowledge transfer.
Typical projects include:
marketing support, financial
reporting, decision support, EIS,
sales automation, customer
service, order entry, project
tracking for Fortune 1000
companies.

Beyond Consulting, Inc.
Weehawken, NJ   201-223-0723

Business Solutions For The Mac
Fairfax, CA   415-453-6324

Catalyst Computer Services
Los Angeles, CA   310-836-5755

CCIC System Pacifica
Berkeley, CA   510-843-5626
Please See Company Highlight Page 162.

Celan Technology
San Jose, CA   408-434-6888

Centurion Software Associates, Inc.
Brooklyn, NY   718-373-4588

ComNet
St. Peters, MO   314-926-8456

**Computer Services and
Consulting, Inc.**
Chicago, IL   312-360-1100

Computer Solutions & Innovations
Sunnyvale, CA   408-629-4374

Computer Support
Lawrence, KS   913-842-1009

Comsul Ltd.
Pasadena, CA   818-449-3200

ComTek
Memphis, TN

Corporate Systems Group
Miami, FL   305-266-1188

Cross International Corporation
Boulder, CO   303-440-7313

Crossroad Systems
Rhinebeck, NY   914-876-2222
Please See Ad Page 164.

Cyberresources Corporation
Mountainside, NJ   908-789-3000

DataSoft Corporation
Minneapolis, MN   612-893-9680

DaVinci Systems Corporation
Raleigh, NC   919-881-4320

DeskTop Consulting, Inc.
Florissant, MO   314-831-9000

Diversified Computer Systems
Boulder , CO   303-447-9251

Dulles Networking Associates, Inc.
Sterling, VA   703-450-6909

Eicon Technology Corporation
Montreal, QC Canada
514-631-2592

Enabling Technologies Corporation
Greenbelt, MD   301-498-2820

Evergreen Consulting, Inc.
Laguna Hills, CA   714-643-8760

Robert Gezelter
SOFTWARE CONSULTANT

Reputation

The source for solutions to all sizes & varieties of problems
Internationally respected author and speaker
OpenVMS, DECnet, TCP/IP, PostScript, OS/2, PATHWORKS, WindowsNT,
MS-DOS, RSX-11, and related areas
Realtime, Process Control, Simulation, and Online Systems
System Management, Security, & Systems Programming
On the phone, or in-person

35 – 20 167th Street, Suite 215
Flushing, New York 11358
Internet: sales@rlgsc.com
800 – 688 – 2990
In NY State: 718 – 463 – 1079

Gordian
Santa Ana Heights, CA
714-850-0205
Please See Company Highlight Page 162.
▣

Granite Graphics
West Orange, NJ   201-325-1881

Greenline Electronics
Boston, MA   617-422-8644
▣

GXR Systems Services
Vancouver, BC Canada
604-433-3001

Holmstead Partners
Provo, UT   801-375-8890

Informant Communications Group
Elk Grove, CA   916-686-6610
Please See Ad Page 162.

Information Resources
New York, NY   212-691-1435

Jack Daley and Company
Palo Alto, CA   415-493-0947

Jasnic Consulting Services
Landsdale, PA   215-361-8929

JEDtech Consulting
Farmington Hills, MI 313-661-4832

JPH Consultant Services
Silver Spring, MD   301-495-4812

KMS Systems, Inc.
The Woodlands, TX 713-363-9154
▣

KPMG • ExIS
Palo Alto, CA   415-473-3310

Kustom Automated Technologies Inc.
Naperville, IL   708-355-3585

Ky Housing Corporation
Frankfort, KY   502-223-3010

LanSharks
Irvine, CA   714-556-9912
Please See Company Highlight Page 163.

LDR, Litho Development & Research
Portland, OR   503-255-5800

Logic Plus Inc.
Chicago, IL   312-663-5682

Mac Solutions
Hilliard, OH   614-529-1969

MacInstitute
Hollywood, FL   305-920-3899

MacSpecialists Inc.
Philadelphia, PA   215-387-8237

Mactivity, Inc.
Los Gatos, CA   408-354-2500

Magic Solutions, Inc.
Mahwah, NJ   201-529-5533

McComb Research
Cupertino, CA   408-725-1448

Metamor Technologies
Chicago, IL   312-943-8266

MPACT IMMEDIA
Montreal, QC Canada
514-397-9747

N:Deavor Group, Inc.
Farmington, CT   203-677-4321

Naval Air Warfare Center
Indianapolis, IN   317-353-7886

Nelson Laffey Associates, Inc.
St. Louis, MO   314-436-9725
Please See Company Highlight Page 163.
▣

RWD TECHNOLOGIES, INC.
10480 Little Patuxent Parkway,
Parkview Bldg., Suite 1200
Columbia, MD 21044
Contact: Johnny Baker, Director,
Business Development
Phone: 404-551-8198
Fax: 404-551-8105
AppleLink: BAKER.RWD
Skills: C, C++, MPW, MacApp,
HyperCard, MitemView, Oracle,
Visual BASIC, Nexpert Object,
Omnis 7, MetroWerks Code
Warrior, AppleScript.
Projects: As an Apple Preferred
Integration Partner and Microsoft
Solutions Partner, RWD provides
custom solutions in the areas of
customer service and call centers,
sales force automation,
performance support systems,
client/server database design,
VITAL consulting, and cross-
platform software development.
Clients: Apple Computer, Inc.;
Motorola; Steelcase; Holiday Inn;
Citicorp; Gannett; Federal Express;
General Electric.

**STANFORD BUSINESS
SYSTEMS, INC.**
400 Corporate Pointe, Suite 415
Culver City, CA 90230
Contact: Mohsen Moazami,
President
Phone: 310-215-8444
Fax: 310-417-5364
AppleLink: SBSI
Skills: Client/server and graphical
user interface database
development.
Projects: Marketing systems
automation, client/server using
Sybase, SQL server, and Macintosh
and Windows front ends.
Enterprise-wide client/server
contact management. 4th
Dimension and Sybase.
Clients: Hughes Aircraft, Northrop
Corporation, Harvard University.

NETWORKING

**NETWORK &
SYSTEMS
INTEGRATION**

Design

Enterprise Network
Solutions

Installations

System Integration

Training

CCIC SYSTEM PACIFICA
605 Addition Street, Suite A
Berkeley, CA 94710
Contact: Scot Campbell,
Phone: 510-843-5626
Fax: 510-843-5173
CompuServe: 73054,455
Skills: Macintosh, DOS:
AppleTalk, LocalTalk, EtherTalk.
Service-oriented technical VAR.
Design, training, and
troubleshooting for multilingual,
multicultural networks.
Implement and support
internetworking, AOCE, MAPI, e-
mail, telecommuting, cross-
platform connectivity.

GORDIAN
20361 Irvine Avenue
Santa Ana Heights, CA 92707
Contact: John Kalucki
Phone: 714-850-0205
Fax: 714-850-0533
AppleLink: GORDIAN
Projects: Terminal servers, printer
servers, wide area networking,
local area networking, routers,
bridges, Ethernet tranceivers,
Ethernet repeaters, Macintosh and
UNIX networking software,
terminals, laser printers,
Ethertalk, LocalTalk, TCP/IP,
NetWare, DECnet, and LAT.
Clients: Lantronix, Citoh, Talaris.

INFORMANT COMMUNICATIONS GROUP

Informant Consulting offers an extensive family of professional services, ranging from user training to system planning. We work with Fortune 1000 clients from all industries. We specialize in LAN-based database application development using a variety of front-end tools and RDBMs running on many operating systems, including Paradox, DBase, PowerBuilder, Access, WordPerfect Informs, InterBase, SQL server, Oracle, Informix, NetWare, Windows NT, OS/2, and UNIX.

Informant Consulting is the systems integration division for Informant Communications Group. ICG started publishing Paradox Informant magazine in 1990 and also includes Informant Press and Informant Labs, a comprehensive client/server, proof of concept, application development, and training facility.

INFORMANT COMMUNICATIONS GROUP
10519 E. Stockton Blvd., Suite 142
Elk Grove, CA 95624-9704
Phone: 916-686-6610
Fax: 916-686-8497
CompuServe: 70461,76

Network International
Cerritos, CA   310-402-5095

P.S.C. Consultants
Redondo Beach, CA   310-372-5096

Pacific Telesis Electronic Publishing Services/Re:Source Network Solutions
San Francisco, CA   800-303-7247
Please See Ad Page 158.

Passport Communications
Austin, TX   512-328-9830

PF Consulting
Marlton, NJ   609-988-1756

Relational Systems, Inc.
Lakewood, OH   216-226-4546

Robert Gezelter Software Consultant
Flushing, NY   718-463-1079
Please See Ad Page 160.

RWD Technologies, Inc.
Columbia, MD   404-551-8198

South Sound Software
Olympia, WA   206-456-4103

Stellar Solutions
San Luis Obispo, CA 805-543-3744

Strategic Support Systems, Inc.
Richardson, TX   214-690-8411

Sylvan Software
Norwich, VT   802-649-2231

Systems Contracting
Denver, CO   303-321-1119

TechSys Corporation
Miami, FL   305-854-5146

Telluride
Newton, MA   617-332-7177

The EDI Connection
Torrance, CA   310-373-6675

The Systems Expert, Inc.
Woodbury, CT   203-263-0216

Tronvision
Budapest, Hungary   361-1358291

Warever Computing, Inc.
Los Angeles, CA   800-WAREVER
Please See Company Highlight Page 163.
▣

West Valley Engineering, Inc.
Sunnyvale, CA   408-744-1420
Please See Company Highlight Page 164.

Design

**Abernathy Business
Consultants, Inc.**
Gaithersburg, MD   301-831-1055

Advantage Memory Corporation
Aliso Viejo, CA   800-245-5299

Alliance Consulting
Warrenville, IL   708-393-0330

Altura Systems Integration Inc.
New York, NY   212-832-1730

BCG, Inc.
Deerfield Beach, FL   305-688-9253

Blue Waters
San Francisco, CA   415-431-1284

Chris Hurley
Cambridge, MA   617-864-8961

Compusoft, Inc.
Hazlet, NJ   908-615-4484

Computer Answer Line
Lyon, France   33-782-40948

Connexus
Brookfield, CT   203-775-5155

Corporate Advisory Group
Carefree, AZ   602-488-1026

CSI, Inc.
Melbourne, FL   407-676-2923

Designed Information Systems
Burnaby, BC Canada   604-294-4357

DILAN
Hickory, NC   704-328-8551

Doradus Corporation
Minneapolis, MN   612-572-1000

Education Catalysts Inc.
Boston, MA   617-482-8982

Engage Communication, Inc.
Aptos, CA   408-688-1021

Essential Systems Consulting
Seattle, WA   206-399-3707

Focus Enhancements
Woburn, MA   617-938-8088

Innovative System Design Ltd.
Tucson, AZ   602-791-3323

JHAMCON Company
Los Gatos, CA   408-354-5022

LANSHARKS
3972 Barranca Parkway, Suite 650
Irvine, CA 92714
Contact: Henry N. Manney
Phone: 714-556-9912
Fax: 714-556-9915
Skills: LanSharks is Apple
authorized (VAR) and a
client/server consulting house.
Novell network specialists and
Microsoft software developers.

NELSON LAFFEY ASSOCIATES, INC.
1919 Park Avenue
St. Louis, MO 63104
Contact: Linda Laffey, General
Manager
Phone: 314-436-9725
Fax: 314-436-1629
Skills: C, C++, LISP, OOP, Major
Networks, Paradox, FileMaker Pro,
OS/2, Windows, A/UX, Excel, S/l.
Projects: Networking computers
and data communications projects:
factory floor automation; electronic
transmittal and receipt of data;
quality control and status software;
subscription control system.
Clients: Ralston Purina, Edward D.
Jones & Co., Optec Sales of
America, CBIS Federal, Pulsar Data
Systems, Saddle and Bridle
magazines.
▣

WAREVER COMPUTING, INC.
10961 Palms Blvd.
Los Angeles, CA 90034-6130
Contact: Jeff Sherman, President
Phone: 800-WAREVER
Fax: 310-280-0502
Internet: warever@kbbs.com
Projects: We are your one stop for
all your needs, providing hardware
and software sales, installation,
training, networking, service and
repair, maintenance, consulting,
and custom programming.
▣

NETWORKING

NETWORK &
SYSTEMS
INTEGRATION

Design
Enterprise Network
Solutions
Installations
System Integration
Training

WEST VALLEY ENGINEERING, INC.

1183 Bordeaux Drive
Sunnyvale, CA 94089
Contact: Chris Van Groningen
Phone: 408-744-1420
Fax: 408-734-4338
Internet:
westvalley@cup.portal.com
Skills: Macintosh, MPW, C/C++,
MacApp, Macintosh
Communications Toolbox,
QuickTime, THINK, A/UX, GUI
development, UNIX, TCP/IP,
Oracle, SCSI, Windows, Visual
BASIC/C++.
Projects: SW Development,
technical support, QA/Testing,
database design, network
engineering, graphic
design/illustration and
publications.

BEAR RIVER ASSOCIATES, INC.

P.O. Box 1900
Berkeley, CA 94701-1900
Contact: Rodney Smith, Anthony
Meadow
Phone: 510-644-9400
Fax: 510-644-9778
Internet: info@bearriver.com
Skills: Programming, systems
integration, training, and
consulting for Macintosh,
Windows, and Newton platforms.
Complete range of services, from
product development to in-house
systems. Curriculum includes
Macintosh technology, OOP,
AppleTalk, Newton, and VITAL.

Johnathon Freeman Technologies
San Francisco, CA   415-822-8451

MacWizards
Gilbert, AZ   602-553-8966

Mallin Consulting
Minneapolis, MN   612-733-5867

Mark One Computer Networks, Inc.
Cincinnati, OH   513-421-5267

Micro Computer Networks
Spring Valley, NY   914-356-4000

MicroAge Solutions, Inc.
Chicago, IL   312-715-3100

Networkers
Southaven, MS   601-349-2243

Open Network Solutions Inc.
Sterling, VA   703-430-2668

Protec Microsystems Inc.
Pointe-Claire, QC Canada
514-630-5832

QCC Communications Corporation
Saskatoon, SKCanada
306-665-6488

Richard Vallens Consulting
Irvine, CA   714-651-8337

Rossnick Consulting
New York, NY   212-671-0584

Telecom Planning
Melbourne Beach, FL 407-725-9100

The Acacia Group
Long Beach, CA   714-995-0606

The AG Group Inc.
Walnut Creek, CA   510-937-7900

ThinkNet Inc.
Toronto, ON Canada 416-585-9678

Total Solutions
Cupertino, CA   408-996-7850

UniPress Software
Edison, NJ   908-287-2100

Up & Running Systems Ltd.
Ottawa, ON Canada 613-232-6050

Zantos Control Systems
Huntington Beach, CA
714-960-9530

Ziegler Ross, Inc.
San Francisco, CA   415-386-0501

Zocalo Engineering
Berkeley, CA   510-540-8000

Enterprise Network Solutions

Ansan Industries, Ltd.
Rockford, IL   815-874-6881

API Engineering
San Jose, CA   408-262-6962

Asanté Technologies, Inc.
San Jose, CA   408-435-8401

CMI (Corporate Microsystems, Inc.)
Lebanon, NH   603-448-5193

Custom Cable Industries
Tampa, FL   813-623-2232

Dana Shultz & Associates
Oakland, CA   510-420-8414

Entrepreneurial Technologies, Inc.
Fort Worth, TX   817-924-1215

Farallon Computing, Inc.
Alameda, CA   510-814-5000

General Information Services, Inc.
Wilmington, DE   302-478-1000

Information Presentation Technologies, Inc.
San Luis Obispo, CA 805-541-3000

MultiAccess Computing Corporation
Santa Barbara, CA   805-964-2332

Scovell Communications
Calgary, AB Canada   403-252-7152

Sproul Consulting
N. Brunswick, NJ   908-246-3749

Stafford Associates, Inc.
Selden, NY   516-698-2827

Stony Brook Services Inc.
Bohemia, NY   516-567-6060

Technology Works, Inc.
Austin, TX   512-794-8533

World Benders, Inc.
Nashua, NH   603-881-5432

Installations

AdvanTel, Inc.
San Jose, CA   408-435-5436

Alan M. Gordon Consulting
North Woodmere, NY 516-374-6414

Cimarron International Inc.
Aurora, CO   303-368-0988

BROCKMAN CONSULTING
29757 Strawberry Hill Drive
Agoura Hills, CA 91301
Contact: Wayne Brockman, Founder
Phone: 818-889-6035
Fax: 818-889-4788
AppleLink: BC.WAYNE
Skills: Macintosh, IBM, UNIX, and Newton multiplatform installation, integration, and support. Networking, documentation, training. See The Alternate Approach for programming services. See also listing under Publishing; Desktop Publishing: Design and Layout.

CCIC SYSTEM PACIFICA
605 Addition Street, Suite A
Berkeley, CA 94710
Contact: Scot Campbell,
Phone: 510-843-5626
Fax: 510-843-5173
CompuServe: 73054,455
Skills: Macintosh, DOS support. Service-oriented technical VAR. Multilingual, multicultural systems integration. Cross-platform Japanese systems support. Systems design, implementation, training.

COLOR SYSTEM SUPPORT GROUP (CSS GROUP)
11865 IH 10 West, Suite 611
San Antonio, TX 78230
Contact: Steve Cooper
Phone: 800-448-8432
Fax: 210-561-9788
AppleLink: CSSGROUP
Projects: Color System Support Group provides consultation/system integration for Macintosh-based electronic publishing and prepress. Now available from CSS is a new high-speed networking and graphics file cataloging system, d'ARTNet (Databased Art Rapid Transfer Network). Based on new FDDI and CDDI technology, d'ARTNet revolutionizes the graphics production environment. CSS also offers graphics training and training videotapes.

NETWORKING

NETWORK & SYSTEMS INTEGRATION

Design
Enterprise Network Solutions
Installations
System Integration
Training

DCA
Cincinnati, OH   513-745-0500

Entertainment Solutions, Inc.
Los Angeles, CA   213-656-5500

Featherstone Communications Network, Inc.
Los Alamitos, CA   310-799-9494

Lan Data Voice Technologies Inc.
Glenview, IL   708-729-0168

LanMinds
Berkeley, CA   510-843-6389

Mac Systems
Lawrence, KS   913-832-2121

MacMinn & Associates
Los Angeles, CA   213-874-1793

Sargent Electric Company
Pittsburgh, PA   412-394-7580

System Integration

Art Machines Inc.
New York, NY   212-431-4400

Aztec Systems
Dalias, TX   214-484-3060

Bailey Bailey & Bailey Ltd.
Wollonbean, NSW   042 265 579

Bear River Associates, Inc.
Berkeley, CA   510-644-9400
Please See Company Highlight Page 164.
▣

Brockman Consulting
Agoura Hills, CA   818-889-6035
Please See Company Highlight Page 165.

CalComp Digitizer Products Group
Scottsdale, AZ   602-948-6540

Calumet Professional Imaging
Bensenville, IL   708-860-0966

CCIC System Pacifica
Berkeley, CA   510-843-5626
Please See Company Highlight Page 165.

Century Technologies, Inc.
Dayton, OH   513-426-9220

Christopher Wesselman
Irving, TX   214-401-3007

Color System Support Group (CSS Group)
San Antonio, TX   800-448-8432
Please See Company Highlight Page 165.

Computer Advantage
Phoenix, AZ   602-263-0509

Computer Methods Corporation
Marlton, NJ   609-596-4360

Creative Technologies
St. Louis, MO   314-994-9773

D & L Enterprises
Richardson, TX   214-386-4500

Dataman Services Inc.
Fairport, NY   716-381-8590

Dome Software Corporation
Carmel, IN   317-573-8100

Electro Plasma Inc.
Millbury, OH   419-255-5197

EPIC Consulting Services
Seattle, WA   206-243-3251

Excalibur Technologies
Fairport, NY   716-377-9154

Federal Software Inc.
Buffalo, NY   716-836-7998

Frye Computer Systems, Inc.
Boston, MA   617-451-5400

Futurity Systems
Waukesha, WI   414-547-8687

Global Investment Technology
Allendale, NJ   201-818-0455

Group 20/20 Ltd.
Almont, MI   313-798-8171

HeyerTech Inc.
Palo Alto, CA   415-325-8522

Image Control Systems Inc.
Seattle, WA   206-624-2646

Imagination Solutions Corporation
Morgan Hill, CA   408-779-3961
Please See Ad Page 159.

Infomax Corporation
New York, NY   212-730-7930

InfoTech
Naperville, IL   708-355-5779

InfoTech Plus, Inc.
Berwyn, PA   215-651-0390

Integrated Management Resources
Stow, MA   508-897-7064
▣

Interconnect Networking Consulting Group Inc.
Santa Monica, CA   310-392-2800

ITI SA Intégration texte et images
Féchy, Switzerland   021-808-71-75

Jim Sharp & Associates
Manhattan, KS   913-539-5837

Mariette Systems International
San Mateo, CA   415-344-1519

McHenry Consulting and Development
Albert Lea, MN 507-377-9651

Media Systems
Clackamas, OR 503-698-5842

MicroMac Technology
Aliso Viejo, CA 714-362-1000

New Technology Consulting Associates
Spring, TX 713-251-3443

Passport Communications
Austin, TX 512-328-9830

R. A. Meyers & Associates
Chicago, IL 312-666-2032

Real Time Enterprises Inc.
Pittsford, NY 716-383-1290

Rikei Corporation
Cupertino, CA 408-257-7943

Robert A. Frankel Management Consultants
Croton-on-Hudson, NY
914-271-2233

RWD Technologies, Inc.
Columbia, MD 404-551-8198
Please See Company Highlight Page 167.

Sassafras Software, Inc.
Hanover, NH 603-643-3351

Second Wave, Inc.
Austin, TX 512-343-9661

Studio 4
Freehold, NJ 908-303-0962

Texas PrePress Systems Inc.
Spicewood, TX 512-264-1690

The Mac Consultants
Dayton, OH 513-294-7447

TPS Electronics
Palo Alto, CA 415-856-6833

VGC Corporation
Orange, CA 714-639-1101

W. M. Treadway & Associates, Inc.
Houston, TX 713-840-8921

Training

Bear River Associates, Inc.
Berkeley, CA 510-644-9400
Please See Company Highlight Page 167.

DeNetwork Group, Inc.
Seattle, WA 206-789-3111

Next Age
Norwalk, CT 203-849-3388

RB Graphic Supply Company
Orange, CA 714-921-8600

Winehouse Computer Company
Los Gatos, CA 408-354-2500

NETWORK SYSTEMS & PROTOCOLS

Bear River Associates, Inc.
Berkeley, CA 510-644-9400
Please See Company Highlight Page 168.

Creative Media Software Solutions Inc.
St. Louis, MO 314-961-9124

Digilog
Horsham, PA 215-956-9570

RWD TECHNOLOGIES, INC.
10480 Little Patuxent Parkway,
Parkview Bldg., Suite 1200
Columbia, MD 21044
Contact: Johnny Baker, Director, Business Development
Phone: 404-551-8198
Fax: 404-551-8105
AppleLink: BAKER.RWD
Skills: C, C++, MPW, MacApp, HyperCard, MitemView, Oracle, Visual BASIC, Nexpert Object, Omnis 7, MetroWerks Code Warrior, AppleScript.
Projects: As an Apple Preferred Integration Partner and Microsoft Solutions Partner, RWD provides custom solutions in the areas of customer service and call centers, sales force automation, performance support systems, client/server database design, VITAL consulting, and cross-platform software development.
Clients: Apple Computer, Inc.; Motorola; Steelcase; Holiday Inn; Citicorp; Gannett; Federal Express; General Electric.

BEAR RIVER ASSOCIATES, INC.
P.O. Box 1900
Berkeley, CA 94701-1900
Contact: Rodney Smith, Anthony Meadow
Phone: 510-644-9400
Fax: 510-644-9778
Internet: info@bearriver.com
Skills: Programming, systems integration, training, and consulting for Macintosh, Windows, and Newton platforms. Complete range of services, from product development to in-house systems. Curriculum includes Macintosh technology, OOP, AppleTalk, Newton, and VITAL.

NETWORKING

NETWORK & SYSTEMS INTEGRATION

Design
Enterprise Network Solutions
Installations
System Integration
Training
NETWORK SYSTEMS & PROTOCOLS

BEAR RIVER ASSOCIATES, INC.
P.O. Box 1900
Berkeley, CA 94701-1900
Contact: Rodney Smith, Anthony
Meadow
Phone: 510-644-9400
Fax: 510-644-9778
Internet: info@bearriver.com
Skills: Programming, systems
integration, training, and
consulting for Macintosh,
Windows, and Newton
platforms. Complete range of
services, from product
development to in-house
systems. Curriculum includes
Macintosh technology, OOP,
AppleTalk, Newton, and VITAL.

MPI Engineering
San Jose, CA   408-262-6962

NetSpec
New Orleans, LA   504-286-0107

Ridgewood Software
Cromwell, CT   203-635-9942

RWRAD
Aptos, CA   408-685-9431

Trio Systems Europe
Amsterdam, Holland 020-638-6507

Micro Systems Internet Services
Salt Lake City, UT   801-532-0316

Miramar Systems, Inc.
Santa Barbara, CA   805-966-2432

Network Express, Inc.
Ann Arbor, MI   313-761-5005

Raindrop Software Corporation
Richardson, TX   214-234-2611

Tri Com Computer Systems
Warwick, RI   401-739-9347

NETWORK SERVICES

Ablon Associates
New York, NY   212-564-5430

B & L Parentheses
Aix les Orchies,   33-20-71-00-71

Better Way Computing
Bolingbrook, IL   708-378-1755

eMedia
San Francisco, CA   415- 648-1704

Entertainment Digital Network (EDNET)
San Francisco, CA   415- 274-8800

First Floor Software
Mountain View, CA 415-968-1101

Information Access Technologies Inc.
Berkeley, CA   510-704-0160

InterConnections, Inc.
Bellevue, WA   206-881-5773

Mark Pappas Development
Pensacola, FL   904-457-6800

MH Software
Northglenn, CO   303-438-9585

NETWORKS

Lancvation
Minneapolis, MN   612-379-3805

Laravela Associates, Inc.
Wilmington, DE   302-762-7758

NetSpan Corporation
Richardson, TX   214-690-8844

Triticom
Eden Prairie, MN   612-937-0772

NETWORKING

NETWORK SYSTEMS
& PROTOCOLS

NETWORK SERVICES

NETWORKS

ResNova
SOFTWARE INC.

Your one-stop information shop

Are you looking to set up your own information service/BBS?

With NovaLink Professional, you can:
- *Enhance customer support channels*
- *Streamline in-house communications*
- *Overcome insurmountable geographic boundaries*
- *Increase productivity*
- *Generate revenues*
- *Offer a custom graphic interface for Mac and PC users*
- *Connect to the internet*

Provide remote access to:
- *E-mail*
- *Message Forums*
- *File Libraries*
- *Conferencing and chats*
- *High Speed Test Searches*

ResNova can provide affordable custom solutions for your information processing needs

ResNova
SOFTWARE INC.

5011 Argosy Drive, Suite #13
Huntington Beach, CA 92649
Voice: (714) 379-9000
Fax: (714) 379-9014
Info Server (BBS): (714) 379-9004
Internet: sales@resnova.com

171
Publishing

For publishing and production needs, from computer publishers to technical writers, look under these specific categories.

Desktop Publishing　**172**
　Design & Layout　172
　Training　174

Disk Duplication　**175**

Imaging　**175**

Information & Online Services　**175**

Publishing　**175**
　CD ROM Publishers　175
　Computer Book Publishers　176
　Editors/Proofreaders　176
　Electronic Publishing　176
　Prepress　177
　Software Publishing　177

Technical Writing/ Documentation　**178**
　End User　178
　Technical　179

WHITE CREEK SOFTWARE
Stage Road, P.O. Box 15
Buskirk, NY 12028
Contact: Jeffrey Perry, President
Phone: 518-686-1760
Fax: 518-686-1761
CompuServe: 72567,3610
Skills: Macintosh consulting and
software development. Object-
oriented design, programming.
C/C++, SmallTalk, relational
databases, and Apple Events.
Apple, 4th Dimension,
QuarkXtension developer.
Projects: Billing, scheduling
systems; database publishing;
commercial QuarkXtension.

DIGITAL DESIGNS
17440 Dallas Parkway, Suite 245
Dallas, TX 75287
Contact: Patti Schulze, President
Phone: 214-407-9303
Fax: 214-733-1130
AppleLink: PSCHULZE
Projects: We are an Apple Partner
specializing in Macintosh services
for the graphic arts community.
We provide consulting and
training as well as graphic design
and creative services. Classes in:
Photoshop, Illustrator, Quark,
FreeHand, FileMaker Pro, Word,
Persuasion, and PageMaker.
Clients: EDS; Texas Instruments;
Apple Computer, Inc.; JC Penney;
advertising agencies;
small/medium businesses.

DESKTOP PUBLISHING

Design & Layout

Advanced Capabilities Design Group Inc.
New York, NY   212-921-0919

Arcade Fonts
San Diego, CA   619-698-8627

Architext Inc.
San Antonio, TX   512-490-2240

Benainous Communications
Berkeley, CA   510-548-2027

Bildrummet/MacHelp
Enskede, Sweden   46-8-796088

Binary Magic
Singapore   65-339 2925

Blue World Graphics
Hoboken, NJ   201-653-0222

Brockman Consulting
Agoura Hills, CA   818-889-6035

Brunner Professional Services
Buena Park, CA   714-521-1284

Cindy Hamner Graphic Designer
Fairfield, CA   707-425-1235

Cinema Desktop Publishing
Santa Monica, CA   310-829-7848

CODESCO GmbH
Oststewbek, Germany
          0049-140171300130

Communicating Ways™
Tukwila, WA   206-246-8759

Computrend
Anaheim, CA   714-758-0807

Continental Press, Inc.
Elizabethtown, PA   800-233-0759

CPS Technologies Inc.
Rockaway, NJ   201-625-7900

Curves
Oakland, CA   510-601-1032

Custom Typographic Solutions
Los Angeles, CA   213-851-3111

Desktop Dynamics
Dallas, TX   214-826-3080

DeskTop Production Services
Redwood City, CA   415-364-4092

Desktop Technologies Inc.
Ann Arbor, MI   313-663-3320

Devonian International Software Company
Montclair, CA   714-621-0973

Dream Maker Software
Englewood, CO   303-762-1001

Duggal Color Projects Inc.
New York, NY   800-382-9000

Duo Conseil
Puteaux, France   33- 1-677454 88

Dynamic Graphics Inc.
Peoria, IL   309-688-8800

Electronic Tablet Publishing Company, Ltd.
Brooklyn, NY   718-965-9622
Please See Ad Page 176.

Encryption Technology Corporation/Prism Packaging
Marietta, GA   404-952-0153

Eric Hook Graphic Design
Boston, MA   617-424-8894

Exact Art Design
Reno, NV   702-829-8422

Fog Press
Half Moon Bay, CA   415-726-2522

Free-lance Communications
Edmond, OK   405-340-6912

Gazlay Marketing Group
Kansas City, KS   913-371-4333

Grafik Solutions
Littleton, CO   303-933-9148

Graphic Arts Technology
Belmont, MA   617-484-9005

Graphic Connexions, Inc.
Cranbury, NJ   609-655-8970

Graphics Universal Inc.
Tulsa, OK   918-665-6633

H. K. Stewart Creative Services
Little Rock, AR   501-661-9389

Hal Chorpenning Communications
Boulder, CO   303-541-0155

Haywood & Sullivan
Cambridge, MA   617-576-3344

Help!
Pasadena, CA   818-577-5270

I.M.A.G.E. Inc.
New York, NY   212-714-2700

Image Club Graphics, Inc.
Calgary, AB Canada   403-262-8008

Images Design Group Inc.
New York, NY   212-645-6100

Imagesetter Inc.
Madison, WI   608-244-6243

In • Color Graphics
Santa Barbara, CA   800-676-1611

Jacque Consulting, Inc.
Dearborn, MI   313-561-6280

Jowaisas Design
Cazenovia, NY   315-655-3800

Landry Design Associates
Andover, MA   508-474-0456

Letter Perfect
Gig Harbor, WA   206-851-5158

Live Oak Press
Palo Alto, CA   415-853-0197

London Computing
Voorhees, NJ   609-795-4281

M/E Design
El Cerito, CA   510-527-5700

Mac Solutions of Memphis
Memphis, TN   901-367-0553

Mac-nificent Services
Los Angeles, CA   213-931-7013

MacCreations— Layout & Design
Ft. Lauderdale, FL   305-566-0109

MacD Enterprises
Temple, TX   817-773-8392

Mainstay Business Services Inc.
Pembroke, MA   617-294-0867

Mark Siegel Creative Graphics
Watertown, MA   617-923-9021

Martin L. Deutsch, Inc.
Monroe, NY   914-783-9548

Michael Diehl Design
Los Angeles, CA   213-851-3111

MindCraft Publishing Corporation
Lincoln, MA   617-259-0448

Monotype Typography, Inc.
Chicago, IL   312-939-0125

New Media Entertainment
San Jose, CA   408-927-6866

Pacific Digital Image
San Francisco, CA   415-274-7234

Page Creations
Modesto, CA   209-527-1348

Pagecrafters
North Chelmsford, MA
   508-251-8180

DESKTOP
PUBLISHING

Design & Layout
Training

PUBLISHING

LINDA JAY BRANDT
963A La Mesa Terrace
Sunnyvale, CA 94086
Contact: Linda Brandt,
Writer/Editor
Phone: 408-737-1470
Fax: 408-737-1470
Skills: Seasoned writer/text editor
brings professional polish to
multimedia content. Copyedit
scripts and screens, proofread
storyboards, write promotions.

AL LUONGO
333 West 88th Street, #10
New York, NY 10024
Contact: Al Luongo
Phone: 212-877-3638
AOL: Aluongo
Skills: Certified Doc-to-Help
consultant. Online help, manuals,
presentations, training,
performance support systems,
CBT.

THE SOFTWARE RESOURCE PUBLICATIONS INC.
4513 Vernon Blvd., #17
Madison, WI 53705
Contact: Jeff Gilpin, President
Phone: 608-238-6644
Fax: 608-238-1344
Skills: Scientific, business, design,
and consumer software
documentation.
Projects: User guides, reference
manuals, online help.
Clients: Domestic and
international software developers
and publishers.

PMC/Mac Seps
Bellevue, WA — 206-861-9609

Power Graphics
Salt Lake City, UT — 801-363-7410

PROmote Communications
Minneapolis, MN — 612-825-2292

Rachel Richards
Placentia, CA — 714-528-5424

Rapid Design Services
San Francisco, CA — 415-398-3556

Re:Design
New York, NY — 212-627-3321

STG Graphic Communications, Inc.
San Francisco, CA — 415-864-4567

Subiacorp
Albuquerque, NM — 505-345-2636

TASCA
San Marino, CA — 818-577-1092

The Graphics Production Center
Norcross, GA — 404-903-0472

Translitera Media AB
Uppsala, Sweden — 4618-12-56-30

Valence, Inc.
Tiburon, CA — 415-435-9252

Vivid Publishing
Los Altos, CA — 415-949-4933

White Creek Software
Buskirk, NY — 518-686-1760
Please See Company Highlight Page 172.

Training

Ad Design Consulting
New York, NY — 212-431-9132

AppleTree Technologies Inc.
Atlanta, GA — 404-457-4500

Bersearch Information Services
Evergreen, CO — 800-851-0289

Bertram Gader
Los Angeles, CA — 213-856-9201

Binary Graphics
Seattle, WA — 206-447-0636

Boardman & Associates
Berkeley, CA — 510-649-5866

Concepts & Keystrokes
Fair Lawn, NJ — 201-797-9084

Courseware Design Services
San Jose, CA — 408-258-7795

Digital Designs
Dallas, TX — 214-407-9303
Please See Company Highlight Page 172.

Electronic Directions
New York, NY — 212-213-6500

Electronic Edge
Yellow Springs, OH — 513-767-7174

Foxglove Communications
Baltimore, MD — 410-426-7733

Graphic Traffic
Ventura, CA — 805-650-9807

Hoff Consulting
Guerneville, CA — 707-887-7778

I.D.E.A.S.
Naples, FL — 813-566-3091

Image Management
Honolulu, HI — 808-833-8978

Jeff Tanner Artistic Concepts
Dunedin, FL — 813-734-9863

Joseph Greco
New York, NY   212-867-7079

KB Design
Lantana, FL   407-439-6554

Keith Gilbert Consulting
St. Paul, MN   612-487-6081

Mac In Design
Westport, CT   203-221-1545

Macaroni
Oakland, CA   510-444-6463

Maharishi International University
Fairfier, IA   515-472-5031

New Edge Technologies
Peterborough, NH   603-547-2263

Presentation Graphics
High Point, NC   919-886-2309

Rasmusson Graphics
Monroeville, PA   412-373-6636

Stephen Chinn Consulting
Chicago, IL   312-871-4060

STUDIOTECH
Dallas, TX   214-979-9400

Synaptica:
Boulder, CO   303-499-8120

Technical Support Services, Inc.
Wauwatosa, WI   414-276-4165

The Computer Workshop, Inc.
Columbus, Ohio   614-487-9505

The Macintosh Learning Center
New York, NY   212-213-4960

DISK DUPLICATION

Allenbach Industries, Inc.
Carlsbad, CA   619-438-2258

Certified Media Corporation
San Jose, CA   408-456-9090

HLS Duplication, Inc.
Sunnyvale, CA   408-773-1500

International Datawares, Inc.
San Jose, CA   408-262-6660

Omni Resources Corporation
Millbury, MA   508-865-4451

Software Services Group
Omaha, NE   800-622-3873
Please See Ad Page 173. 402-453-1699

Star-Byte, Inc.
Hatfield, PA   800-243-1515

The Software Factory
Norcross, GA   800-955-3475

IMAGING

AWARE TECH
El Paso, TX   915-778-8391

Decision Images Inc.
Skillman, NJ   609-683-0234

Gal Computer Imaging
Jersey City, NJ   201-433-3553

InnovaTech Corporation
San Diego, CA   619-793-8789

Management Graphics Inc.
Downsview, ON Canada
                      416-667-8877

MDF Associates, Inc.
Carrollton, TX   214-416-6427

Systems Consulting, Inc.
Grand Forks, ND   701-795-9270

Third Wave Technologies, Inc.
Huntsville, AL   205-880-1622

Visual Business Systems Inc.
Atlanta, GA   404-956-0325

INFORMATION & ONLINE SERVICES

Caduceus
Portland, OR   503-228-6851

Infonautics
Wayne, PA   215-293-4770

Insight Systems, Inc.
Monroe, WA   206-788-9800

MZ Media Group
San Francisco, CA   415-543-8290
Please See Ad Page 13.

PEMD Education Group
Cloverdale, CA   707-894-3662

ResNova Software, Inc.
Huntington Beach, CA
                      714-379-9000
Please See Ad Page 170.

PUBLISHING

CD-ROM Publishers

Eduself Multimedia Publishing Ltd.
Holon, Israel   972-3-5562570

Grid Media Ltd.
Causeway Bay, Hong Kong
                      852 591 0730

DESKTOP PUBLISHING
Design & Layout
Training
DISK DUPLICATION
IMAGING
INFORMATION & ONLINE SERVICES
PUBLISHING
CD ROM Publishers
Computer Book Publishers
Editors/ Proofreaders
Electronic Publishing
Prepress
Software Publishing

TECH PROSE
1725 Springbrook Road
Lafayette, CA 94549
Contact: Meryl Natchez, President
Phone: 510-975-0660
Fax: 510-930-7304
AppleLink: TECH.PROSE
Skills: Windows, UNIX, Tandem, HyperCard, MitemView, C, C++.
Projects: Provides solutions for corporate end users' technical training and documentation needs. Specializes in online training for mainframes and microcomputers. Services include HyperText systems, online help, user manuals, and tutorials.
Clients: Charles Schwab, Pacific Bell, Westinghouse, Kaiser, and Apple Computer, Inc.

WRIGHT INFORMATION INDEXING SERVICES
6549 22nd NW
Seattle, WA 98117
Contact: Jan Wright, Owner
Phone: 206-784-2895
Fax: 206-782-7837
Skills: Provides print indexes as Windows or Macintosh text files, as embedded entries in client files, or for CD-ROM interactive projects.

MultiCom Publishing
Seattle, WA   206-622-5530

SUMERIA, Inc.
San Francisco, CA   415-904-0800

The Multimedia Library
New York, NY   212-674-1958

WPA Film Library
Oak Forest, IL   708-535-1540

Computer Book Publishers

Knowledge Industry Publications, Inc.
White Plains, NY   914-328-9157

Peachpit Press
Berkeley, CA   800-283-9444

Soft • Letter
Watertown, MA   617-924-3944

TBF Publications
St. Louis, MO   314-351-1729

Editors/Proofreaders

Linda Jay Brandt
Sunnyvale, CA   408-737-1470
Please See Company Highlight Page 174.

Logical Solutions
St. Paul, MN   612-659-2495

Morris Communications
El Sobrante, CA   510-222-6672

Update and More
Austin, TX   512-328-4621

Electronic Publishing

Addison-Wesley Publishing
Menlo Park, CA   415-853-2584

Bureau of Electronic Publishing
Parsippany , NJ   201-808-2700

Digital Libraries
Provo, UT   801-377-8062

Graphix Zone, Inc.
Irvine, CA   714-833-3838

Kingdom Graphics
Austin , TX   512-476-2276

Magnetic Press
New York, NY   212-219-2831

Network Publications, Inc.
Lawrenceville, GA   404-962-7220

Software Production Alexander Fushs
Barsinghausen, Germany
49-515003

Tim Duncklee-Consultant
Vero Beach, FL   407-562-3621

Wadsworth Publishing Company
Belmont, CA   415-637-7528

Prepress

C. V. Rao Consultants
Houston, TX   713-796-2512

Compuserve Consultants Limited
Hong Kong   852-544-7151

Cyberchrome
Branford , CN   203-488-9594

Digiflex®
Los Angeles, CA   213-933-7203

Grande Vitesse Systems
San Francisco, CA   415-777-0320

ITI SA
Rolle, Switzerland 41-21-826-03-71

Number One Graphics
E. Lansing, MI   517-332-6231

Skapa Publishing AB
Stockholm, Sweden   46 8 140760

Software Solutions, Inc.
Pleasanton, CA   510-426-6751
▣

Valence, Inc.
Tiburon, CA   415-435-9252

Software Publishing

Abacus Concepts, Inc.
Berkeley, CA   510-540-1949

**Age of Invention Computing
Resources Company**
Mt. Vernon, WA   206-856-1776

Atticus Software Corporation
Stamford, CT   203-348-6100

Daniels & Mara Inc.
Austin, TX   512-288-2511

Emigre Fonts
Sacramento, CA   916-451-4344

Falcon Software, Inc.
Warren, NH   603-764-5788

Great Ware Software
Scotts Valley, CA   408-438-1990

Iowa Market Systems
Iowa City, IA   319-354-7286

MacVONK • International B.V.
Zeist, The Netherlands
31 3404-21944

MADA
Cupertino, CA   408-253-2765

Merit Software
Dallas, TX   214-385-2353

Multi-Image Systems
Chico, CA   916-345-4211

Paragon Publishing Systems
Bedford, NH   603-471-0077

Pearl Computer Systems, Inc.
Moorestown, NJ   609-983-9265

Production First Software
San Francisco, CA   415-695-0881

Que Software
Carmel, IN   317-573-2500

Redrock Software Corporation
Phoenix, AZ   602-993-8914

Seven Hills Software Corporation
Tallahassee, FL   904-575-0566

Software Export Corporation
Cambridge, MA   617-354-9600

Topstack AG
Räfizweg, Switzerland   052-382243

Word Associates, Inc.
Northbrook, IL   708-291-1101

Wys System Ltd.
Wanchai, Hong Kong 852-529-1831

Xpand
San Jose, CA   408-279-8655

INFORMATION &
ONLINE SERVICES

PUBLISHING

CD ROM
Publishers

Computer Book
Publishers

Editors/
Proofreaders

Electronic
Publishing

Prepress

Software
Publishing

PUBLISHING

TECHNICAL WRITING/DOCUMENTATION

End User

Ace Communications
Portland, OR   503-274-2543

Acknowledge Solutions
Redwood City, CA   415-345-4639

Al Luongo
New York, NY   212-877-3638
Please See Company Highlight Page 174.

ANDROS SoftWear
San Mateo, CA   415-340-1040

Big Badge Productions
Woodland Hills, CA 818-888-2364

Black Gryphon Ltd.
Salt Point, NY   914-266-3527

Bottomline Communications
Pacific Grove, CA   408-375-2026

Caryl International
San Francisco, CA   415-981-3900

Centre Grafik Inc.
Wayne, PA   215-688-2949

Charles Rubin
Sedona, AZ   602-204-1057

Cultural Technology
Boynton Beach, FL   407-364-7830

Dart Products, Inc.
Miami, FL   305-232-5428

Dave Meyers
Cupertino, CA   408-255-2964

DocuClear
New York, NY   212-691-4926

Douglas Pundick Technical Writing
Berkeley, CA   510-559-9377

Drucker Documents
Cambridge, MA   617-876-6410

Electronic Pencil
West Hartford, CT   203-233-0370

Electronic Tablet Publishing Company, Ltd.
Brooklyn, NY   718-965-9622

EnerAnalytics
San Ramon, CA   510-867-0681

Erica Kerwien
Lexington, MA   617-674-2718

Full Circle Media
San Rafael, CA   415-453-9989

Godar & Hossenlopp Printing Company
South San Francisco, CA
                      415-593-5900

Heliotrope Inc.
Landenberg, PA   215-274-2145

In Writing
Mountain View, CA 415-968-9184

Information Engineering Company
Longmont, CO   303-530-5393

Information Surfers
Rueschlikon, Switzerland
                      411-724-2901

Khera Communications, Inc.
Rockville, MD   301-309-0969

Klouda Communications
Chalfont, PA   215-997-9383

Lasselle-Ramsay Inc.
Mountain View, CA 415-968-1220

Maria L. Langer
Harrington Park, NJ 201-767-7001

Marlene C. Semple Communication Services
Tampa, FL   813-286-6550

Merex Corporation
Tempe, AZ   602-921-7077

Miller Technical Publishing
Santa Cruz, CA   408-427-0173

Nadson & Terrill Communications
Torrance, CA   310-787-9054

New Heights
Sandy, UT   801-572-4320

P. Heidi Beeler
Berkeley, CA   510-841-5060

Pacifitech Corporation
Kamakura, Japan   81-467-25-4010

Paul Hoffman
Santa Cruz, CA   408-426-6222

Q1 Communicators
Columbus, OH   614-899-0060

Sandra Pakin & Associates, Inc.
Chicago, IL   312-271-2848

Semantic Imaging
San Francisco, CA   415-334-8109

Software Publishing Manuals
Montigny-le-Tilleul, Belgium
                      3271519024

Susan B. Morison Writer
Grosse Pointe Park, MI
                      313-824-7429

TalCo. Systems Services
San Diego, CA   619-549-4025

Te Corporation
Campton, NH   603-726-7177

Tech Prose
Lafayette, CA   510-975-0660
Please See Ad Page 177.
◻

Technical Writing PLUS
Dallas, TX   214-306-8387
Please See Ad Page 169.

Technical Writing Services
West Linn, OR   503-656-8062

TechWriters Ink
Laguna Niguel, CA   714-661-8861

Textware Corporation
Toronto, ON Canada
                                416-345-8487

The Cobb Group
Louisville, KY   502-491-1900

The Computer Learning Company
Westport, CT   203-222-7747

**The Software Resource
Publications Inc.**
Madison, WI   608-238-6644
Please See Company Highlight Page 174.

Thornhill Data Systems
Roswell, GA   404-998-0802

Using It buba
Brussels, Belgium   32 2 230 02 21

WordPlay Communications
Albuquerque, NM   505-243-6001

WordPlay Communications
Berkeley, CA   510-841-5858

Wordswork
San Francisco, CA   415-826-4716

Wright Information Indexing Services
Seattle, WA   206-784-2895

Write Design
Hillsboro, OR   503-648-7431

Zeta Data
Hanover, NH   603-643-6103

Technical

Al Luongo
New York, NY   212-877-3638

Blue Sky Research
Portland, OR   800-622-8398

Bridget Burke
Pacifica, CA   415-738-0560

Business and Automation Consulting
Forest Hills, NY   718-997-1460

Comtech Services Inc.
San Jose, CA   408-432-8243

Insight Communications Group
Miami, FL   305-861-8950

Island Resources
El Granada, CA   415-726-6448

LINK srl
Milano, Italy   392-583-10607

Page Studio Graphics
Chandler, AZ   602-839-2763

PUBLISHING

CD ROM
Publishers

Computer Book
Publishers

Editors/
Proofreaders

Electronic
Publishing

Prepress

Software
Publishing

**TECHNICAL
WRITING/
DOCUMENTATION**

End User

Technical

PUBLISHING

Tech Prose
Lafayette, CA   510-975-0660
Please See Company Highlight Page 176.
▣

Textware Canada
Toronto, ON, Canada416-777-0400

The Carl Group Inc.
Cupertino, CA   408-255-9171

**The Software Resource
Publications Inc.**
Madison, WI   608-238-6644

The Write Tech
Spokane, WA   509-927-0202

Ventana Studio
Valley Center, CA   619-751-2632

Warner-Cotter
San Francisco, CA   415-441-4011

Wright Information Indexing Services
Seattle, WA   206-784-2895
Please See Company Highlight Page 176.

**TECHNICAL
WRITING/
DOCUMENTATION**

End User

Technical

INFO CENTER

Call

1.800.388.5136

or use the tear-off

mailer, or the fax

order form on the

following page

to place your

order for the

Top100 Guide.

M E D I A

To better serve the growing needs of our readers, we've created the Top100 InfoCenter. You can use the Top100 InfoCenter to obtain data on companies, industries, as well as special rankings and studies done by MZ Media Group, Inc. and its affiliated companies. We can deliver this information to you in print, by fax, or on a computer disk. Contact one of our customer service representatives for assistance, or write or fax us with your order or inquiry. We'll respond quickly to ensure that you receive the critical information you need without delay.

Top100 Guide

REGIONAL DIRECTORIES OF MAJOR BUSINESS DEMOGRAPHICS:

Essential for sales people, job seekers, fund raisers and entrepreneurs.

A compact, easy to carry, bound book featuring:

- Executive names
- Company description
- Address, phone and fax numbers
- Revenues, profits and employers
- Rankings on various financial measurements

Call for your region of interest. $14.95 each plus tax, shipping and handling.

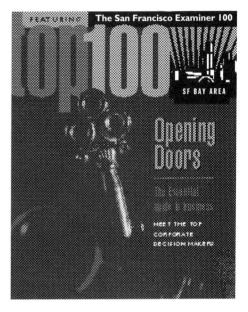

Houston Chronicle 100
Houston Area $14.95

Rocky Mountain News 100
Colorado $14.95

The Plain Dealer 100
Ohio $14.95

San Francisco Examiner 100
San Francisco Bay Area $14.95

All Four Guides
.....................................$49.95

SUPPORT

183

Support

Look here for technical service providers, as well as associations, user-groups and training experts, each within their pertinent category.

**Associations/User Groups
185**

**Data Conversion/
Recovery/Security   186**
Data Conversion 186

Data Recovery 186
Data Security 186

**Equipment Rental/
Leasing/Repair   187**
Technical Support   187
Training   188
Developer 188
User 189

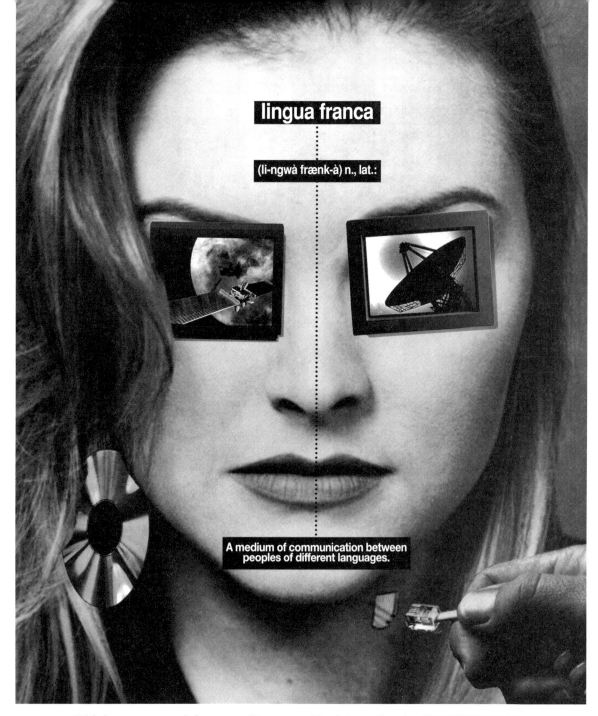

lingua franca

(li-ngwà frænk-à) n., lat.:

A medium of communication between peoples of different languages.

IICS (eye•eye•see•yès) *non-profit, assoc.:* The International Interactive Communications Society. A global knowledge network. A decade of professional experience in interactive arts and technologies. Call now. 503.579.IICS   mltimedia@aol.com

ASSOCIATIONS/ USER GROUPS

Alexander Technology
Norman, OK   405-360-5554

AT&T Computer Users Group
San Francisco, CA   415-885-6631

BMUG
Berkeley, CA   510-549-2684

Consortium for Laboratory & Industrial Applications of the Macintosh
Worcester, MA   508-755-5242

Crawford & Associates, Inc.
Rosemont, IL   708-698-6670

Independent Computer Consultants Association (ICCA)
St. Louis, MO   800-774-4222
Please See Ad Page 185.

International Association of Business Communications
Palo Alto, CA   408-746-3545

International Interactive Communications Society (IICS)
Beaverton, OR   503-579-IICS
Please See Ad Page 184.

ELAN TECHNOLOGIES INC.
970 Montee de Liesse, Suite 203
Montreal, QC H4T 1W7 Canada
Contact: Reed Bodwell, President
Phone: 514-332-3526
Fax: 514-332-2854
Projects: Postscript or PCL5 conversion software produces either TIFF or PCX fax-ready output. An API enables quick integration into fax and imaging applications. Available either as a software library for UNIX- or DOS-based PCs or with its own RISC coprocessor card (installed in the PC) for high-performance applications.

DRIVESAVERS, INC.
400 Bel Marin Keys Blvd.
Novato, CA 94949-6220
Contact: Scott Gaidano, President
Phone: 415-883-4232
Fax: 415-883-0780
AppleLink: DRIVESAVERS
Skills: Data recovery repair of hard drives, opticals, and removables.
Projects: DriveSavers is the most experienced and progressive Macintosh-only data recovery/drive repair service in the country. We have extensive Macintosh hard drive experience working with major drive manufacturers enabling data recovery from PowerBooks, hard drives, the Power Macintosh, removable/optical cartridges, and floppy disks.
Clients: Apple Computer, Inc.; Broderbund; Walt Disney; Yale; U.S. Army; SuperMac; Kodak; Computerland; Xerox; Ernst & Young; LucasFilm; Harvard; Barbara Mandrell; Muppets; Pacific Bell; Fed Ex; Arthur Andersen; Clarence Clemons; Smithsonian; MIT; Time-Life; Cornell.

ASSOCIATIONS/
USER GROUPS

Data Conversion/
Recovery/ Security

Data Conversion

Data Recovery

Data Security

EQUIPMENT
RENTAL/LEASING/
REPAIR

TECHNICAL
SUPPORT

SUPPORT

League for Engineering Automation Productivity (LEAP)
Virginia Beach, VA   804-495-8547

MacAcademy
Ormond Beach, FL   904-677-1918

Macintosh Movie Makers Guild
El Dorado, CA   916-622-5288

Macintosh Scientific & Technical Users Association
Worcester, MA   508-755-5242

National Association of Desktop Publishers
Topsfield, MA   508-887-7900

National Association of Macintosh Trainers
Newport News, VA   800-827-9719

Orca Software Solutions
Gilroy, CA   408-848-3046

Southwestern Pennsylvania Industrial Resource Centers
Duquesne, PA   412-469-3530

The Federation of International Distributors
Boston, MA   617-742-5599

DATA CONVERSION/ RECOVERY/SECURITY

Data Conversion

élan technologies inc.
Montreal, QC Canada
514-332-3526
Please See Company Highlight Page 185.

KANDU Software Corporation
Arlington, VA   703-532-0213

Simone (C.) and Associates
Washington, DC   301-369-1990

SYS TECH
Munchen, Germany   089-425649

Data Recovery

Computer Conversions, Inc.
San Diego, CA   619-693-1697

DriveSavers, Inc.
Novato, CA   415-883-4232
Please See Company Highlight Page 185.

DT Software
Arlington, VA   703-521-9427
Please See Ad Page 186.

Ontrack Data Recovery
Eden Prairie, MN   612-949-4021

Data Security

ASD Software, Inc.
Montclair, CA   909-624-2594

Baseline Software
Sausalito, CA   415-332-7763

Dolphin Software
Berkeley, CA   510-464-3000

Magna
San Jose, CA   408-282-0900
Please See Company Highlight Page 187.

Mircro Security Systems, Inc.
Salt Lake City, UT   800-456-2587

PC Dynamics
Westlake Village, CA 818-889-1741

RSA Data Security, Inc.
Redwood City, CA   415-595-8782

RSH Consulting, Inc.
Newton, MA   617-969-9050

EQUIPMENT RENTAL/LEASING/REPAIR

800-WE-FIX-MACS
Santa Clara, CA   800-933-4962

Arete
New York, NY   212-334-0334

DriveSavers, Inc.
Novato, CA   415-883-4232

DT & T Macintosh Services
Sunnyvale, CA   800-622-7977

GE Rental/Lease
Norcross, GA   800-GE-RENTS

M2 Ltd.
Gaithersburg, MD   301-977-4281

Mac Upgrade Specialists
Aliso Viejo, CA   714-362-5429

MacHardware Ind.
Kansas City, MO   816-842-9000

TTJ Data Processing Services, Inc.
Salem, OR   503-363-2693

TECHNICAL SUPPORT

24-Hour Macintosh Service
Walnut Creek, CA   510-945-1073

Abacus, Inc.
San Francisco, CA   415-974-7000

Aim High
Arvada, CO   303-423-1488

Alan M. Gordon Consulting
North Woodmere, NY
516-374-6414
Please See Company Highlight Page 187.

Cadre Systems
Norwalk, CT   203-838-1191

Communications Software, Inc.
Anchorage, AL   907-243-7800

Customer Service Solutions
Palo Alto, CA   415-321-2403

Digital Prepress Integration
Irvine, TX   713-896-0800

Elron Consulting Inc.
Cooper City, FL   305-680-9842

EMC2 Computer Solutions
Barre, VT   802-476-5800

Growing Minds Software
Ontario, CA   910-391-2252

Jessica M. Morris
Memphis, TN   901-382-8459

Kramer Group
Palo Alto, CA   415-856-3565

Laser Publishing
Westford, MA   508-692-8389

MAGNA
332 Commercial Street
San Jose, CA 95112
Contact: Cindy Johnson,
Marketing Coordinator
Phone: 408-282-0900
Fax: 408-275-9147
AppleLink: MAGNA
Projects: Magna develops and
markets a family of Macintosh
security software: Empower I
prevents unauthorized use of
PowerBooks; Empower II protects
data and programs stored on
shared Macintosh computers;
Empower Remote remotely
administers security options across
Macintosh networks.
Clients: Apple Computer, Inc.; Eli
Lilly; Bank of America; Bell
Atlantic; Motorola; and Northern
Telecom.

ALAN M. GORDON CONSULTING
51 Valley Lane East
North Woodmere, NY 11581
Contact: Alan Gordon
Phone: 516-374-6414
Fax: 516-374-3375
AppleLink: GORDON.ALAN
Skills: All forms of Macintosh
hardware and software
troubleshooting and repair; design
and installation of LocalTalk and
10Base-T Ethernet networks;
system administration; upgrades.
Projects: Network design and
installation, system software
upgrades, commercial software
installation, virus eradication,
network backup, FileMaker Pro
programming, configuration and
optimization, crash recovery,
remote computing.
Clients: Christies, Siegel & Gale-
New York, New York Hall of
Science Museum, Rugby-Darby
Group, Wachouia International
Banking Corporation.

ASSOCIATIONS/
USER GROUPS

**DATA CONVERSION/
RECOVERY/
SECURITY**

Data Conversion

Data Recovery

Data Security

**EQUIPMENT
RENTAL/LEASING/
REPAIR**

**TECHNICAL
SUPPORT**

TRAINING

Developer

User

SUPPORT

LOG-N-COMPUTING
Newtonville, NY   518-782-1132

Mac Help Canada
Toronto, ON Canada 416-979-7754

Mac Systems Consultants
Austin, TX   512-326-3458

Mark Prewitt Consulting
Aloha, OR   503-223-3976

Marketech Inc.
St. Petersburg, FL   813-823-0099

Martha S. Scheer, CPA: PC
Boulder, CO   303-447-9711

McLaughlin Consulting
Chicago, IL   312-878-4120

Michael Zolen Macintosh Consulting
Sacramento, CA   916-488-0923

MISCA
Boca Raton, FL   800-741-9956

OneOnOne™ Computer Training
Addison, IL   800-424-8668

Optimum Technology Consultants
Wichita, KS   316-262-4455

Parrothead Computercations
Moodus, CT   203-873-1196

Photon Inc.
Cambridge, MA   617-661-9046

Ron Allen Consulting Services
Stansbury Park, UT   801-882-3535

Sampson & Associates
Lawrence, KS   913-842-7764

Shaffstall Corporation
Indianapolis, IN   317-842-2077

Solutions..., Inc. of Racine
Racine, WI   414-791-2237

Staging Techniques
Hollywood, CA   213-874-5106

Support Central
Cincinnati, OH   513-984-0015

SupportNet
Highlands Ranch, CO
303-654-4100

Synergetics
Thatcher, AZ   602-428-4073

Systems Management Consulting
Oakland, CA   510-547-2425

Teknosys Inc.
Tampa, FL   813-620-3494

TRAINING

Developer

Application Developers Training Company
Minneapolis, MN   612-943-1363

Bear River Associates, Inc.
Berkeley, CA   510-644-9400
Please See Ads Pages 188, 190.

Benchmark Publications, Inc.
New Canaan, CT   203-966-6653

BEAR RIVER ASSOCIATES, INC.

Skills: Macintosh Communications Toolbox, MPW, AppleTalk, C, C++, MacApp, OOP, VITAL, Newton.

Projects: Technical training courses in four areas: Macintosh programming, Newton programming, object-oriented technology, and enterprise solutions. Bear River's curriculum transitions mainframe programmers over to the world of object-oriented client/server systems development.

Clients: Apple Computer, Inc.; Boeing; Kodak.

BEAR RIVER ASSOCIATES, INC.
P.O. Box 1900
Berkeley, CA 94701-1900
Contact: Rodney Smith, Anthony Meadow
Phone: 510-644-9400
Fax: 510-644-9778
Internet: info@bearriver.com

PORTER & PORTER
1069 Bryn Mawr Avenue
Bensenville, IL 60106
Contact: Vivienne Porter
Phone: 708-350-9090
Fax: 708-595-9071
Skills: Specialized, tailored on-site software training. Clients design their own courses by picking the features on which they want to be trained.

**WONG, PAMELA L.,
MACINTOSH CONSULTING SERVICES**
116 Carlotta Circle, #9
Mill Valley, CA 94941
Contact: Pamela Wong, Training Consultant
Phone: 415-388-9668
Fax: 415-388-1522
AppleLink: PAMWONG
Skills: Word, Excel, Quark, PageMaker, FileMaker Pro, PowerPoint, Persuasion, MacDraw, SuperPaint. Apple Training Alliance, Apple Solutions Provider, Microsoft Certified Professional.
Projects: On-site software training and technical support, using interactive instruction tailored to individual user projects. Cross-platform training in Macintosh/Windows programs.
Clients: Visa, Kaiser, Chevron, Bechtel, ADP, Pacific Bell, Aviation Methods, Computer Time, Training Alternative, Productivity Point, MTC.

CLH Wares
Bellaire, TX   713-245-1539

Data Vision Technologies
San Francisco, CA   415-543-7903

Empower Trainers & Consultants, Inc.
Kansas City, MO   816-753-8880

Flashpoint
Berkeley, CA   510-524-0852

Flip Track OneOnOne Computer Training
Addison, IL   708-628-0500

Lightship Software
Beaverton, OR   503-292-8765

Mac Generation Inc.
Coral Springs, FL   305-970-8950

MacMentor
San Jose, CA   408-433-0990

Media Res
Fullerton, CA

MTC New Horizons
Walnut Creek, CA   510-933-9955

PCES Inc.- Express Train
Pennington, NJ   609-737-8098

Personal Computers, Personal Solutions Inc.
Somerset, NJ   908-249-4044

Personal Training Systems
San Jose, CA   800-832-2499

Porter & Porter
Bensenville, IL   708-350-9090
Please See Company Highlight Page 189.

Pro Train
Cincinnati, OH   513-772-0367

Professional Computer Training
Reno, NV   702-829-9300

Quick Start Technologies
Huntington Beach, CA
                      714-894-1448

Richey Software Training
Guerneville, CA   707-869-2836

Schulco Training Corporation
West Conshohocken, PA
                      215-940-0100

STR Corporation
Reston, VA   703-758-1100
                      703-758-1119

Tech Prose
Lafayette, CA   510-975-0660

Terry Tufts & Associates
Arlington Heights, IL 708-577-7381

Wizard Works
Louisville, CO   303-665-7085

User

1st Step Computers/MicroAge
Richmond, VA   804-358-5881

8th Day Consulting, Training, and Software
Oak Forest, IL   708-535-1324

A Little Computing, Inc.
Littleton, CO   303-770-1286

Aaron's Computer Relief
Carlsbad, CA   619-943-7925

Alpine PC
Breckenridge, CO   303-543-2249

AM Computer Products
Southington, CT   203-621-8945

EQUIPMENT RENTAL/LEASING/REPAIR

TECHNICAL SUPPORT

TRAINING

Developer

User

SUPPORT

**Berkeley Education
and Training Center**
Bala-Cynwyd, PA   800-452-4033

C. Olson and Company
Santa Cruz, CA   408-458-3365

CAST, Inc.
Peabody, MA   508-531-8555

ColorExpert Inc.
Toronto, ON Canada
    416-360-3894

Computer Aided Results
Brookline, MA   617-730-5411

Computer Custom Services
Huntington, NY   516-673-8738

Computing Solutions
Chicago, IL   312-902-9900

Corporate Solutions
San Francisco, CA   415-392-1021

David Spound Associates
Northampton, MA   413-586-5652

DDP Training Center
Freehold, NJ   908-577-8969

Don Barth Consulting
Oshkosh, WI   414-235-0294

Easy
Kailua-Kona, HI   808-326-2025

Future Enterprises, Inc.
Washington, DC   202-662-7610

Gibson Computer Associates
Denver, CO   303-745-7960

Gorman Consulting
Arlington, VA   703-528-4405

Hagen MicroAge
Richfield, MN   612-866-3441

HFSI Education Services
Reston, VA   703-478-2000

Jane Mason, Computer Consultant
Washington, DC   202-986-2100

Kagi Engineering Inc.
Berkeley, CA   510-843-6140

Kolnick Consulting Services
San Francisco, CA   415-239-5922

Learnsoft, Inc.
San Diego, CA   619-546-1400

Logtec
Fairborn, OH   513-429-2928

Mac Info-To-Go
Arlington, TX   817-468-8871

Mac Resource
Amherst, MA   413-253-7223

Mac To School
Phoenix, AZ   602-279-5506

MacCounting
Minneapolis, MN   612-722-2564

MacGraphics
Aurora, CO   303-751-1012

MacSpec
Oklahoma City, OK   405-720-9622

MacTraining & Design, Inc.
Southfield, MI   313-557-0750

MacTraining House
Belmont, CA   415-306-0463

Master Trainers' Consortium
Fountain Valley, CA 714-968-8902

MBA Seminars, Inc.
Dallas, TX   214-746-5350

Media Design & Images
Roanoke, VA   703-772-3190

Mertens BDV-Beratung
Hamburg, Germany 49 40 3508549

Microage of San Diego
San Diego, CA   619-566-1900

MicroServ
New Haven, CT   203-776-6800

Motioneering
Redondo Beach, CA 310-316-7738

Mountain Data Works
Camino, CA   916-644-4500

New Ledger
San Diego, CA   619-558-0222
回

Next Actions
Wilton, CT   203-761-1255

Notti & Company, CPAs
Larkspur, CA   415-461-8301

Online Press Inc.
Bellevue, WA   206-641-3434

Paw Computers, Inc.
Bountiful, UT   801-295-2299

PCLC
New York, NY   212-953-9800

Pepperdine & Company, CPAs
Dallas, TX   214-241-4170

Peter David Lauwers Macintosh Support
Ann Arbor, MI   313-995-1130

Platt College
San Diego, CA   619-265-0107

Pratt & Chew
Seattle, WA   206-441-1998

Productivity Plus, Inc.
St. Louis, MO   314-569-2901

Productivity Point/MicroTrek
New York, NY   212-398-6410

Professional Support Services
New Canaan, CT   203-966-5818

Psychologi Logiciel Software
Embrun, ON Canada 613-443-2435

Randamax Inc.
Rochester, NY   716-546-5550

Santa Monica MicroAge
Santa Monica, CA   310-828-4911

Softeach
Newton, MA   617-244-0037

Solution Development Services, Inc.
Houston, TX   713-772-2128

SSE
St. Louis, MO   314-997-4700

The Computer Evolution
Venice, CA   310-821-6184

The Dublin Group, Inc.
San Francisco, CA   415-227-4777

The Learning Center/ Computer Land
Boise, ID   208-345-8024

The Oasis Group
Seattle, WA   206-524-5903

The Taylor Group
Manchester, NH   603-644-2141

Training Access
Denver, CO   303-745-9600

Tulane University
New Orleans, LA   504-862-8555

University of Oregon
Portland, OR   503-725-3058

Wong, Pamela L., Macintosh Consulting Services
Mill Valley, CA   415-388-9668
Please See Company Highlight Page 189.

EQUIPMENT
RENTAL/LEASING/
REPAIR

TECHNICAL
SUPPORT

TRAINING

Developer

User

SUPPORT

1-Up Computing, 16, **43**, **76**, 78   719-488-0125 ▣

1ST Desk Systems, 72   508-533-2203

1st Step Computers/MicroAge, 189   804-358-5881

21st Century Graphics, 75   303-420-4344

21st Century Marketing, 118   516-293-8550

21st Century Media, 25, **151**   818-848-4543 ▣

21st Century Media, 25, 129, **145**, 150   414-771-8906 ▣

24-Hour Macintosh Service, 187   510-945-1073

3D Perception, 147   619-656-3865

3D TV Corporation/StereoScopic Video, 112

   415-488-1570

7 Star Computer Solutions, 95   916-925-2125

800-WE-FIX-MACS, 187   800-933-4962

850 Productions Inc., 25, **140**, 144   312-642-8520 ▣

8th Day Consulting, Training, & Software, 189

   708-535-1324

A

A * A Data, 73   806-799-2323

A. A. Gole, Consulting, 60   201-612-1070

A. E. Wood Consulting, 99   510-548-4920

A. L. Freeman, Jr. & Associates, Inc., 159   919-758-7040

A la Carte Systems, 95   212-779-8090

A Little Computing, Inc., 189   303-770-1286

A O-K Services, Inc., 109   609-488-1793

A to Z Computers, Inc., 65   609-424-8517

A. Visual, 129   514-933-3657

A W A R E T E C H, 175   915-778-8391

A. W. Vidmer & Company, 129   615-373-1851

Aardvark Research Group, 60   802-658-2030

Aaron Marcus & Associates, Inc., 26, 147

   510-601-0994 ▣

Aaron's Computer Relief, 189   619-943-7925

Aatrix Software Inc., 70   800-426-0854

Abacot Information Systems, 43   602-795-6817

Abacus Concepts, Inc., 177   510-540-1949

Abacus, Inc., 187   415-974-7000

Abbate Video, Inc., 148   508-376-3712

Abernathy Business Consultants, Inc., 163   301-831-1055

Ablon Associates, 168   212-564-5430

Abraxas Software, Inc., 85   503-244-5253

Absoft Corporation, 65   313-853-0050

Absolute Advantage, Inc., 70   818-718-2027

Absolute Inc., 117   214-748-0184

Academic Software, Inc., 73   818-718-2027

Access Education, 117   408-727-1096

Access Technologies, Inc., 78   303-799-0640

Accolade, Inc., 65   408-985-1700

Account Ware Distributors, 36   905-738-4508

Accountasystems Ltd., 60   313-737-0031

AccuWare Business Solutions Ltd., 103   403-245-0477

Ace Communications, 178   503-274-2543

AceNet, 17, 43   818-405-0087 ▣

ACI US, Inc., 95   408-252-4444

ACK Software & Beratungs, 78   0049-231-527604

Acknowledge Solutions, **122**, 178   415-345-4639

Acolyte Software Corporation, 101   203-250-8600

Acquired Knowledge Inc., 63   619-587-4668

Acrobyte Software, 99   714-768-8490

Actoris Software Corporation, 103   214-231-7588

Acumen, Inc., 58   505-983-6463

AcutAbove Software, 69   909-672-7725

Ad Design Consulting, 174   212-431-9132

ad•hoc Technologies, 129   619-551-0109

Adair & Armstrong, 148   415-826-6500

Adam Gewanter Consulting, 129   212-674-3940

Adam Leffert, 75   617-254-7931

Adams Consulting Group, 145   708-246-0766

Adamsound, 144   707-763-5732

Adaptive Machine Technologies, Inc., 43   614-486-7741

Addison Design, 120   415-391-3090

Addison-Wesley Publishing, 176   415-853-2584

Adept Solutions, 75   619-727-8376

ADF Research, 120   415-459-1115

adINFINITUM Development, 95   718-788-7092

Adjuvare, Inc., 92   804-481-1975

Admiral, 43   212-744-1101

Adrienne Schure, 150   212-580-2246

ADS Designs, 85, 106, **109**   919-438-6321

Advance Reality Systems, 149   415-974-1044

Advanced Audioworks, 144   214-517-9154

Advanced Capabilities Design Group Inc., 172

   212-921-0919

Advanced Data Systems, 72   407-657-4805

Advanced Decisions Inc., 43   203-795-6255

Advanced Digital Imaging, 148   714-779-7772

Advanced Integrated Technology, 159   615-381-4388

Advanced Laser Graphics, 95 — 202-342-2100

Advanced System Technologies, Inc., 65 — 303-790-4242

Advantage Memory Corporation, 163 — 800-245-5299

Advantage Software Inc., 60 — 416-891-2901

AdvanTel, Inc., 165 — 408-435-5436

Adventurer Software, 90 — 617-926-6705

Adventures for Gifted & Talented, Inc., 147 — 205-870-5948

Aerie Animation, 143 — 619-496-8550

Aesthetic Engineering, 144 — 212-925-7049

Affinity Software Corporation, 75 — 508-668-7800

AFM Associates, 120 — 212-721-4826

AFTECH Corporation, 103 — 203-637-4343

After Hours Computer Group, 129 — 714-573-3800

After Hours Software, 92 — 818-780-2220

Age of Invention Computing Resources Company, 177 — 206-856-1776

Agie Seife Associates, Inc., 38 — 914-358-5707

AGS Information Services, Inc., 129 — 908-396-4321

Ahmac Associates, Inc., 60 — 516-922-4145

Ahrens Creative Group, Inc., 116 — 312-243-5550

AI Consultants, Inc., 90 — 408-253-7299

Aim High, 187 — 303-423-1488

Air Land Systems, 85 — 703-573-1100

Al Jen, Inc., 71 — 201-796-1128

Al Luongo, **174**, 178, 179 — 212-877-3638

Alabanza Consulting, **92**, 106 — 415-327-5433

Alamo Computer, 17, **86**, 110 — 510-820-1399

Alan George & Associates, Inc., 43 — 312-909-2509

Alan i Harris Group, Inc., 140, 151 — 412-338-8600

Alan M. Gordon Consulting, 28, 165, **187** — 516-374-6414

Albany Micro Solutions, 64 — 518-482-4824

Albathion Software Inc., 64 — 415-824-5704

Alben & Faris, 119 — 408-426-5526

Albert Frank-Guenther Law, 116 — 415-989-7010

Alberta Education, 64 — 403-674-5333

Alexander LAN, Inc., 159 — 603-880-8800

Alexander & Lord, 118 — 408-655-6000

Alexander Technology, 185 — 405-360-5554

Alexus Group Limited, 43 — 612-832-9930

All Night Media, 129 — 412-471-9590

All Star Computer Services, 85 — 415-282-0540

Allenbach Industries, Inc., 175 — 619-438-2258

Alliance Consulting, 163 — 708-393-0330

Allied Film & Video, 149 — 415-777-1700

Allied Support, 60 — 415-386-2242

Alpha Inc., 108 — 608-836-7673

Alpha Omega Systems Corporation, 43 — 714-939-7777

Alphabets Design Group Inc., 129 — 708-328-2733

Alpine PC, 189 — 303-543-2249

Alpnet Inc., 108 — 801-265-3300

Alternative Systems Concepts, 65 — 603-635-3553

AlterNet Television, Inc, 149 — 415-331-8835

Alto Stratus, 95 — 503-547-3264

Altura Software Inc., 106 — 408-655-8005

Altura Systems Integration Inc., 163 — 212-832-1730

AM Computer Products, 189 — 203-621-8945

Amazing Media, 129 — 415-453-0686

Ambit Informatic, 92 — 34-3-419 3358

AMCI, 112 — 408-423-0112

American Institute for Learning, 149 — 512-472-3251

American List Council Inc., 118 — 800-822-LIST

American Retail Consultants, 92 — 619-457-1087

American Software, 36 — 602-834-1579

AmeriChem Engineering Services Inc., 72 — 602-437-1188

Ames & Associates, 144 — 415-366-5153

Amicus Software, 95 — 512-258-6373

Amuse Interactive Learning Environment, 150 — 415-435-7791

Analytix Group, Inc., 70 — 208-726-4518

Andante Systems, 95 — 612-699-2709

Andersen Consulting, 149 — 619-578-1700

Anderson Soft Teach, 150 — 408-399-0100

Andree R. Oreck, 147 — 916-926-4681

Andromeda Computer Systems Ltd., 65 — 403-247-5300

ANDROS SoftWear, 178 — 415-340-1040

ANEXTEK, 92 — 716-671-5190

Angiographic Devices Corporation, 73 — 800-962-2617

Animated Systems & Design, 149 — 415-424-8586

Animatics, 130 — 613-235-9000

Anne Dorfman, 146 — 415-928-2462

Another Dimension Ltd., 95 — 44 708 701 511

Ansan Industries, Ltd., 165 — 815-874-6881

Antley Business Systems, Inc., 17, 58 — 612-542-9651

Anzus, 43 — 215-321-0249

Apeiron, 110 — 214-423-2276

API Engineering, 165 — 408-262-6962

Apple Computer Development Group, 43 408-862-6649

AppleTree Technologies Inc., 174 — 404-457-4500

Application Developers Training Company, 188 — 612-943-1363

Applications Unlimited, 101 — 508-653-9300

Applied Business Communications Inc., 116 — 510-938-4642

Applied Computer Solutions, Inc., 43 — 301-490-5575

Applied Imagination Inc., 43 — 212-645-7199

Applied Informatics, 73 — 801-584-3060

Applied Statistics, Inc., 72 — 612-481-0202

Applied Technologies GmbH, 85 — 49-30-8592958

Applied Technology Associates, Inc., 17, 43 — 713-981-4747 🔲

Appropriate Solutions, Inc., 37 — 603-924-6079

Apriori Inc., 99 — 708-253-2856

AR Design, 130 — 209-943-5231

Arabic Information Systems, 60 — 202-711-684

Arbor Intelligent Systems, Inc., 106 — 313-996-4238

Arborescence SF, 130 — 415-931-7415

Arborworks, Inc., 17, 85 — 313-747-7087 🔲

ARC Electronics, 78 — 44 273 207739

Arcade Fonts, 172 — 619-698-8627

Arcadia Designs, 110, **112**, 147 — 415-323-7604

Architectronica, 90 — 310-376-7054

Architext Inc., 172 — 512-490-2240

Architrion Oregon, 65 — 503-626-7052

Archway Systems, 90 — 714-374-0440

Arcom Electronics, Inc., 28, 159 — 408-452-0678 🔲

Arete, 187 — 212-334-0334

Arete CA Incorporated, 116 — 212-777-2012

Ariel PSS Coporation, 150 — 503-232-0221

Ariel PSS Corporation, 121 — 415-694-7880

Ariel Publishing, Inc., 43 — 509-923-2249

Ariel Software Consultants, Inc., 17, 92 — 312-764-3434 🔲

Aries Systems Corporation, 73 — 508-475-7200

Arlington Technology Group, 96 — 703-553-3976

Armadillo Computer Services, 96 — 314-256-0824

Armo, 78 — 314-821-4094

Array Technologies, Inc., 72 — 212-460-8169

Arroyo Software, 90 — 313-439-3828

Art & Logic,16, 17, 26, **38, 43, 44, 83,** 85, 107, **109, 129,** 130, 149 — 818-501-6990 🔲

Art Machines Inc., 166 — 212-431-4400

Artist House, 130 — 616-352-5060

Arturo Droguett, 108 — 408-429-5212

Asanté Technologies, Inc., 165 — 408-435-8401

ASD, Inc., 101 — 818-584-6979

ASD Software, Inc., 186 — 909-624-2594

Asgard Consulting, 85 — 703-521-8403

Ashmead Computers, 92 — 215-527-9560

Asia CD Ltd., 108 — 852-824-0781

ASK International, 146 — 310-987-2071

ASR Recording, **143**, 144 — 310-327-3180

Assembled Solutions, Inc., 43 — 319-363-1030

Aster, 65 — 33 76.45.21.21

Aster Services, 119 — 714-855-6554

AT&T Computer Users Group, 185 — 415-885-6631

Athena Consult, 108 — 32-3-440-78-12

ATI Advertising Technologies Inc., 147 — 604-521-7179

Atkeison Consulting, 99 — 215-275-7764

Atlantech, Inc., 121 — 813-739-2554

Atticus Software Corporation, 177 — 203-348-6100

Audio-Video Corporation, 130 — 518-449-7213

Augment, Inc., 60 — 919-489-9041

Aura CAD/CAM, Inc., 65 — 310-536-9207

Autograph Systems, 102 — 717-662-7718

Autologic Inc., 130 — 805-498-9611

Automated Accounting Solutions Inc., 70 — 301-924-3502

Automated Analysis Corporation, 63 — 919-876-1450

Automated Business Management, 65 — 617-621-0025

Automatix, Inc., 72 — 508-667-7900

AutoSoft, 78 — 401-885-3631

Avalon Computer, 70 — 201-784-8470

Avalon Engineering, Inc., **37**, 38, 43, **44, 74,** 75, **76**, 78, **85**, 86, 107, **110** — 617-247-7668

Avalon Integrated Services, 130 — 202-408-7039

Avatar Numedia, 150 — 415-322-3838

AVCA, 130 — 512-472-4995

Aviation Management Associates, Inc., 117 — 703-644-4465

Avid Corporation, 148 — 508-640-6789

AwareTech Design, 92 — 415-324-9240

AXE Communication Entreprises, 110 — 41-22-361-90-41

Azalea Software, Inc., 75 — 800-48-ASOFT

Aztec Systems, 166 — 214-484-3060

B

B & L Associates, Inc., 17, 43, **45**   609-397-8410 🔲

B & L Parentheses, 168   33-20-71-00-71

B. W. Software, 90   313-769-8587

B-TEK, 101   602-470-0705

Baccus & Associates, 99   818-398-1401

Bailey Bailey & Bailey Pty. Ltd., 166   042 265 579

Baker & Taylor Software, 123   800-641-1057

BAL Associates Inc., 107   415-941-6015

Baltic Consulting & Computer Services, 108   201-744-2497

Balzer/Shopes Inc., 75   415-468-6550

Bannister Lake Software Incorporated, 92   519-622-9535

Barnes Computer, Inc., 78   301-350-4752

Bartlett, Brandley & Lucky, 92   407-869-9421

Baseline, 69   212-254-8235

Baseline Software, 186   415-332-7763

Baudville Inc., 75   616-698-0888

Bay Graphics Design Inc., 119   510-843-0701

Bayle Collaborations, 110   617-391-1934

BBDO, 116   415-274-6200

BCG, Inc., 163   305-688-9253

Beachware, 147   619-492-9529

Beacon Export Systems, Inc., 72   617-738-9300

Bear River Associates, Inc., 16, 17, **36**, **38**, 43, **44**, **59**, 60, **86**, 90, **91**, **98**, 99, **103**, 104, **105**, 106, 107, **108**, **159**, **164**, 166, **167**, **168**, **188**, **190**

          510-644-9400 🔲

Belmont Research, 73   617-868-6878

Benainous Communications, 172   510-548-2027

Benchmark Publications, Inc., 117, **118**, 188

          203-966-6653

Bent Media, Inc., **118**, **129**, 130, 152   504-482-8278

Bergmann Und Langer GmbH, 78   4989342476

Berkeley Education & Training Center, 190   800-452-4033

Berlitz International, 108   818-340-5147

Berlitz Translation Services, 108   212-777-7878

Bernstein Design Services, 65   510-447-7654

Bersearch Information Services, 174   800-851-0289

Bertram Gader, 174   213-856-9201

Berumen & Associates, 90   408-971-4401

Beta Research Inc., 110   408-252-3172

Betsy Strode, 118   415-340-1377

Better Way Computing, 168   708-378-1755

Beyond Consulting, Inc., 160   201-223-0723

Beyond Technology, 96   212-675-3764

Bibliogem Inc., 64   812-332-6549

Big Badge Productions, 178   818-888-2364

Bildrummet/MacHelp, 172   46-8-796088

Bimillennium Corporation, 65   408-354-7511

Binary Designs, 147   503-232-2909

Binary Graphics, 174   206-447-0636

Binary Magic, 172   65-339 2925

Binary Techniques Inc., 60   617-628-7200

Bindco, 123   415-363-2200

Binders Computer Graphics, 75   404-252-2516

Bio-Logic, Inc., 73   415-873-0406

Biocomp, 86   619-931-9148

Biomedical Teaching & Information, 64   613-344-5848

Biometallics, 65   609-275-0133

BIOPAC Systems Inc., 73   805-967-6615

BioTechnology Software, 65   503-929-6405

Bishop Development, 44   714-857-6618

Bitstream Inc., 75   617-497-6222

Bitworks, 86   805-583-2547

Bizware Corporation, 16, 36   201-816-9271 🔲

Black Gryphon Ltd., 178   914-266-3527

Black & Ryan Engineering, 65   602-451-7137

BlackHawk Technology, 65   408-776-1106

BlackMax, 99   714-496-6669

Blank-Hitchcock Associates, 44   503-385-8998

Blankenship Systems Consulting, Inc., 60   708-530-2399

Blemks International, 37   31-41-13 3333

Bliss Interactive Technologies, 91   405-439-2247

Block Communications, 118, **142**, 148   415-254-7600

Bloom Software, 86   303-469-7348

Blue Sky Research, 179   800-622-8398

Blue Tree Technology Inc., 86   415-738-1754

Blue Waters, **130**, 163   415-431-1284

Blue World Graphics, 172   201-653-0222

Blueridge Technologies, Inc., 60   703-675-3015

BMUG, 185   510-549-2684

Boardman & Associates, 174   510-649-5866

Boardwalk Designs, 116   408-892-7772

Bob Harris Consulting, 59   415-669-7702

Bobcat Systems, 78   914-762-2374

Boca On-Line Systems, Inc., 44   407-395-0242

Body CT Imaging Lab, 73   410-955-5173

Bogner Entertainment Inc., 153   310-473-0139

BOLDer MultiMedia, 153   303-642-3087

BOOKUP, 69   800-949-5445

Bootstrap Enterprises Inc., 44   704-521-9167

bopp productions inc., 147   41-61-681 8812

Boston Systems Group Inc., 60   617-423-1670

Bottom Line Consulting, 34   203-454-1727

Bottomline Communications, 36, 178   408-375-2026

Boxes & Arrows Inc., 17, 60   904-446-4908 ▣

Bradley Group, 123   213-465-7593

Braided Matrix, Inc., 17, **56**, 59, 96   914-657-6411 ▣

Brainchild Corporation, 44   513-831-8451

Branfman & Associates, 148   619-481-5800

Breakthrough Productions, 103   916-265-0911

Bridget Burke, 179   415-738-0560

Brinkmann Consultants, 44   410-287-6743

Brio Technology Inc., 61   415-961-4110

Brockman Consulting, **165**, 166, 172   818-889-6035

Broderbund Software, 149   415-382-4591

Brodie Lockard, 69   415-368-4967

Brooks/Cole Publishing Company, 64   408-373-0728

Broughton Systems Inc., 44   804-672-1122

Brownstone Research Group, 64   303-333-6974

Bruce, Bruce, & Bruce, 18, 159   410-526-3791 ▣

Brumbaugh, Graves, Donohue & Raymond, 72

  212-408-2578

Brunner Professional Services, 172   714-521-1284

Bryten, Inc., 130   802-649-3252

BSO Management Support, 61   0031-70-3245555

Buechting:Pieroth, 130   49-30-874685

Buffalo Brothers Marketing, 149   800-709-7909

Bulldog Studios, 146   415-641-5700

Bunder Computer Services, 61   803-268-7063

Bureau of Economic Geology, 65   512-471-1534

Bureau of Electronic Publishing, 176   201-808-2700

Burnette Multimedia Services, 130   503-386-9369

Burns, Connacher & Waldron, 130   203-323-1330

Burton Computer Consulting, 107   715-386-6114

Busch Creative Services Corporation, 149   314-289-7711

Business & Automation Consulting, 179   718-997-1460

Business Brothers, Inc., 18, 44, **45**   612-853-3024 ▣

Business Builders, 118   408-253-6679A

Business Computer Solutions Inc., 96   301-596-5005

Business Software Applications, 96   612-455-3000

Business Solutions, 96   310-372-1583

Business Solutions For The Mac, 160   415-453-6324

Business & Technical Communications, 120   510-945-6779

Business Tools, Inc., 44   919-932-3068

Bussard & Associates, 152   818-794-2991

Butler Graphics, Inc., 130   313-528-2808

... by Design, Inc., 65   414-648-3712

C

C & A Graphics, 116   713-974-3844

C & C Logic Engineering, 93   617-782-4981

C. Olson & Company, 190   408-458-3365

C.T.A. Inc., 61   203-786-5828

C. V. Rao Consultants, 177   713-796-2512

C-Wave, 130   415-397-3722

C4 Network, Inc., 76   303-825-8183

C4SI, Inc., 96   708-386-3060

Cactus Computer Service, 116   602-266-7312

Cadre Systems, 187   203-838-1191

Caduceus, 175   503-228-6851

CalComp Digitizer Products Group, 166   602-948-6540

Calico Publishing, 64   314-298-0767

Calico Subscription Company, 116   408-262-4036

California Marketing Group, 116   714-895-1447

Calliope Enterprises Inc., 86   909-793-5995

Calumet Professional Imaging, 166   708-860-0966

Calypso Interactive, 149   415-824-7651

Campagne Associates Ltd., 61   800-582-3489

Camsoft Data Systems, Inc., 44   504-752-4391

Camtronics, 65   503-445-2824

Candes Systems Inc., 44   215-256-4130

Cantrell Design Group, 112   717-396-1134

Canyonlands Software, 86   801-259-7680

CAPCOM USA Inc., 108   408-727-0400

Capital Transactions, 73   315-348-8551

Capitol Mac Consultants, Inc., 70   804-644-6800

Captured Images, Inc., 116   818-707-9491

Career Publishing Incorporated, 64   800-854-4014

Carew Design, 119   415-331-8222

Cargas Systems, Inc., 96   717-560-9928

Carlow International Incorporated, 65   703-698-6225

Carousel Mediaworks, Inc., 130   716-777-4023

Cart Systems, 76 — 31-10-4376628
Caryl International, 178 — 415-981-3900
CAST, Inc., 190 — 508-531-8555
Castle Rock Software Development, 45 — 415-488-1563
Catalogic, 153 — 415-961-4649, 800-255-4020
Catalyst Computer Services, 160 — 310-836-5755
Catalyst Computer Systems, 61 — 708-289-0797
Catspaw Inc., 90 — 719-539-3884
CCIC System Pacifica, 108, **111**, 123, 160, **162**, **165**, 166 — 510-843-5626
CCS Enterprises, Inc., 37 — 410-820-4670
CD Technology Inc., 153 — 408-752-8500
CD-Press, 152 — 800-505-3344
CDBS-The Software Wizards, 45 — 818-441-4045
Cederblom & Associates, 61 — 206-772-0371
Cedrus Corporation, 78 — 301-589-1828
CEI Systems, Inc., 61 — 612-425-1167
Celan Technology, 160 — 408-434-6888
Cellular Hotline, 45 — 314-993-0050
Center for Multimedia, 150 — 206-643-9039
Centerline Productions, 130 — 303-698-1321
Central Coast Software, 45 — 408-458-0272
Centre Grafik Inc., 178 — 215-688-2949
Centurion Software Associates, Inc., 160 — 718-373-4588
Century Software, 86 — 030/6242420
Century Technologies, Inc., 166 — 513-426-9220
CEO Software Solutions, 64 — 908-566-4545
Certified Media Corporation, 175 — 408-456-9090
CF Software, 18, 45 — 708-824-7180
CFJ R & D, 86 — 33-1-30-72-06-90
Chalk Butte, 64 — 307-537-5261
Chaparral Software, 103 — 310-273-4904
Charles B. Olson & Associates, 105 — 415-328-1708
Charles Cooper Consulting, 18, 96 — 317-892-4588
Charles E. Brault, 78 — 301-279-7164
Charles Rogers & Associates Inc., 96 — 408-253-8215
Charles Rubin, 178 — 602-204-1057
Chazz Communications Company, 148 — 516-887-6675
Chedd-Angier Production Company, 130 — 617-926-8300
Chertov & Associates, 101 — 707-829-1213
Cheryl L. Blundell, 150 — 510-713-1039
Cheshire Group, 18, 78 — 707-887-7510
Cheyenne Software Inc., 107 — 516-484-5110
Childs Consulting Associates Inc., 64 — 313-569-2355

Chris Forden, 86 — 415-897-7284
Chris Hurley, 163 — 617-864-8961
Christensen Design, 96 — 817-424-3312
Christine Maggio Consulting, 99 — 201-797-9272
Christophe Vanhecke, 87 — 33-59-83-73-58
Christopher Gross, 18, 45 — 813-572-1149
Christopher L. Schneck, 143 — 312-883-0146
Christopher Wesselman, 166 — 214-401-3007
Chrones Software, Inc., 45 — 415-920-6900
Chrysalis Software, Inc., 91 — 416-466-1915
Cider Mill Software, 78 — 313-347-2503
Cimarron International Inc., 165 — 303-368-0988
Cindy Hamner Graphic Designer, 172 — 707-425-1235
Cinema Desktop Publishing, 172 — 310-829-7848
CINNABAR Macintosh, 93 — 406-848-7978
Ciphers, 130 — 408-356-9983
Circle Noetic Services, 76 — 603-672-6151
Circuit Research Corporation, 78 — 603-880-4000
Cirrus Technology, 117 — 508-755-5242
CIS Communication & Information Services, 37 — 704-264-5643
Citadel Systems, 116 — 713-686-6400
Cito, Inc., 70 — 602-443-4701
CKS Partners, 118 — 408-378-2444
Claire Moore Instructional Design, 26, 150 — 916-645-2085
Clarity, 144 — 914-424-4071
Class One Incorporated, 73 — 602-820-3696
Class One Software, 130 — 604-261-1843
Class Software, 78 — 415-592-5513
Claude J. Pany, 45, **46** — 408-922-0207
CLE Group, 150 — 415-324-1827
Clear Access-Fairfield Software, 45 — 515-472-7077
Clement Mok Designs, Inc., 117, **119**, **130** — 415-703-9900
Clerk of the Works, 70 — 208-263-3543
CLH Wares, 189 — 713-245-1539
Click Click, Inc., 93 — 612-934-7926
Click Systems, 93 — 908-996-3773
Clinical Information Systems, Inc., 73 — 206-583-0338
CMI (Corporate Microsystems, Inc.), 165 — 603-448-5193
CMJ Computers Inc., 61 — 406-378-2302
Coalescence, 118 — 303-776-9425
Coconut Info, 78 — 808-947-6543
Coda, 96 — 46 86116972

CODESCO GmbH, 172	0049/140171300130
CoDesign, 107	510-845-3170
Cogar, Melton & Associates, 116	408-253-9656
Cognitive Systems Inc., 61	617-742-7227
Colin-Data, 45	32 9 355 75 07
Colleague Business Software Inc., 61	800-926-9965
Collosal Pictures, 149	415-550-8772
Color System Support Group (CSS Group), **165**, 166	
	800-448-8432
ColorExpert Inc., 190	416-360-3894
Comacon, Inc., 38	302-764-1984
Command Line Corporation, 72	908-738-6500
Command Systems Inc., 103	508-651-0530
CommGraphics, 130	402-438-1919
Common Sense Computing, Inc., 116	413-667-5797
Commstalk, 38	0727-827146
Communicating Ways™, 172	206-246-8759
Communication Bridges, 148	415-331-3133
Communication Design, 130	602-345-1770
Communications Concepts Inc., 148	407-783-5232
Communications Software, Inc., 187	907-243-7800
ComNet, 160	314-926-8456
COMPanion, 64	800-347-6439
Company Seven Astro-Optics Division, 65	301-953-2000
Compare Technologies, Inc., 46	800-482-8824
Compas Technologies, 96	805-484-9205
Complete Data Solutions, 18, 46	512-329-6161 ▣
Complete Solutions/ QTFX, 148	508-388-3736
Comprehensive Business Solutions Group, Inc., 65	
	404-261-4516
Compression Labs, Inc., 148	408-435-3000
Comptrol, Inc., 93	206-869-2700
Compumation Inc., 76	814-238-2120
CompuMod Software, 78	313-360-0456
Compuserve Consultants Limited, 177	852-544-7151
Compusoft, Inc., 163	908-615-4484
COMPUTE-X, 96	212-674-4158
Computed Designs, 61	812-876-6923
Computer Advantage, 166	602-263-0509
Computer Aided Results, 190	617-730-5411
Computer Answer Line, 163	33-782-40948
Computer Applications Corporation, 46	901-458-8630
COMPUTER: Applications Inc., 18, 78	
	919-846-1411 ▣
Computer Associates International, Inc., 46	800-Call-CAI
Computer Based Enterprises, Inc., 130	715-835-3448
Computer Center of Hayward/San Jose, 143	510-538-4480
Computer Consultants & Service Center, Inc, 61	
.	314-647-8891
Computer Conversions, Inc., 186	619-693-1697
Computer Custom Services, 190	516-673-8738
Computer Dynamics, 93	817-566-5515
Computer Graphics Group, 76	513-241-8300
Computer Help Services, 90	303-428-3609
Computer Hyphenation Ltd., 46	44 0 274 733317
Computer Information XP, Inc., 70	503-781-0164
Computer Learning Foundation, 120	415-327-3347
Computer Management International, Inc., 130	
	203-295-8436
Computer Mentors, 116	504-529-7248
Computer Methods Corporation, 166	609-596-4360
Computer Modules Inc., 153	408-496-1881
Computer Presentations, Inc., 46	513-281-3222
Computer Product Testing Services, Inc., 121	
	908-223-5700
Computer Resource Sysems, Inc., 130	615-558-6273
Computer Results, 87	805-529-3618
Computer Science Innovations, 18, 46	407-676-2923 ▣
Computer Services & Consulting, Inc., 160	312-360-1100
Computer Solutions, 64	206-456-1888
Computer Solutions!, 46	413-534-2420
Computer Solutions & Innovations, 160	408-629-4374
Computer Solutions, Ltd., 46	319-351-7549
Computer Support, 160	913-842-1009
Computer Survival, 93	214-647-8239
ComputerCrafts, 107	603-437-7973
Computing on Micro's, 73	809-731-6275
Computing Solutions, 190	312-902-9900
Computize, 130	713-771-6667
Computrend, 172	714-758-0807
Comshare, 46	809-922-797 9
Comsul Ltd., 160	818-449-3200
Comtech Services Inc., 179	408-432-8243
ComTek, 160	
Concept 2001, 70	408-985-2001
Concept Information Systems, 46	203-363-2060
Concepts In Healthcare, Inc., 73	214-539-3618
Concepts & Keystrokes, 174	201-797-9084

Concord Consulting Group, 65 — 508-369-7696
Concurrent Engineering Tools Inc., 19, 65
— 602-464-8208 🔳
Connexus, 163 — 203-775-5155
Consensus, 37 — 44-0625-537777
Consortium for Laboratory & Industrial
  Applications of the Macintosh, 185 — 508-755-5242
CONSTAR, 61 — 619-581-0459
Consult Rosen Communication, 120 — 504-898-0904
Consultech Communications Inc., 120 — 518-283-8444
Consulting Resources & Design, 99 — 716-586-6177
Consulting Solutions, Inc., 19, **77**, 78 — 718-275-8976 🔳
Continental Press, Inc., 172 — 800-233-0759
Conure Software, 46 — 215-277-9071
Cooley Godward, 148 — 415-845-5163
Cooper Communications, 146 — 908-723-6147
Copious Systems, 19, **46**, 47, **86**, 87 — 805-528-2685 🔳
Coral Research, 47 — 702-831-9346
Cordant Imaging Systems, 36 — 508-352-5500
corder associates, inc., 38 — 602-993-8914
Cordova Research Associates, 64 — 901-756-7481
Core Business Systems, 103 — 902-542-7777
CORGROUP, 19, 61 — 203-458-9363 🔳
Cornerstone Data Systems, 47 — 714-772-5527
Cornice Graphics, 121 — 714-985-8323
Corporate Advisory Group, 163 — 602-488-1026
Corporate Computing Services, 101 — 804-423-8503
Corporate Solutions, 190 — 415-392-1021
Corporate Systems Group, 160 — 305-266-1188
Costanza & Associates, 47 — 215-752-5115
Cottage Micro Services, 47 — 214-435-2446
Courseware Design Services, 174 — 408-258-7795
Coyne Company, 61 — 714-855-4689
CPS Technologies Inc., 172 — 201-625-7900
CPSA, 107 — 510-449-7744
Craft Robot Company, 65 — 212-619-3021
Crawford & Associates, Inc., 185 — 708-698-6670
Creative Computing, 91 — 614-488-6930
Creative Consulting Associates, Inc., 47 — 908-273-8607
Creative Enterprises, 16, 19, **38**, 47, **129**, 130
— 310-987-3450 🔳
Creative Media Software Solutions Inc., 167
— 314-961-9124
Creative Perspectives, 131 — 804-971-6795

Creative Software, 64 — 919-493-9503
Creative Strategies Research International, 120
— 408-748-3400
Creative Technologies, 166 — 314-994-9773
Cremer & Associates, 148 — 415-821-7023
Cressey Consulting & SW, 47 — 413-648-9936
Crimson Consulting Group, 121 — 415-325-0677
Crisp Computer Corporation, 47 — 516-922-4056
Critical Path Software, Inc., 78 — 503-635-9585
Critical Technologies Inc., 65 — 315-793-0248
Cross International Corporation, 160 — 303-440-7313
Crossfield Marketing, 117 — 415-949-3937
Crossroad Systems, 28, 160, **164** — 914-876-2222 🔳
Crown Communications, 99 — 612-457-5008
Crystal Graphics Inc., 76 — 408-496-6175
CSI, Inc., 163 — 407-676-2923
CST Consulting, 96 — 408-257-1952
Cultural Technology, 178 — 407-364-7830
Cunningham Communication, Inc., 121 — 408-982-0400
Current Designs Corporation, 131 — 212-463-0795
Current Music Technology, 47 — 215-647-9426
Curves, 29, 172 — 510-601-1032 🔳
Custom Cable Industries, 165 — 813-623-2232
Custom Interfacing Solutions, 96 — 603-889-1098
Custom Software Inc., 47 — 714-261-1188
Custom Typographic Solutions, 172 — 213-851-3111
Customer Service Solutions, 187 — 415-321-2403
CustomWare Inc., 96 — 416-932-9443
Cutting Edge Computer Consulting, 47 — 914-631-2322
CVSI, 47 — 903-938-7776
Cyber Viz, 110 — 617-326-1879
Cyberchrome, 177 — 203-488-9594
Cybernet Systems Corporation, 112 — 313-668-2567
Cyberresources Corporation, 160 — 908-789-3000
Cyborg Systems, Inc., 36 — 312-454-1865

D

D & A Infosystems Inc., 47 — 516-538-1240
D. Kevin Rowe, 101 — 313-420-2167
D & L Enterprises, 166 — 214-386-4500
D S Simon Productions, 152 — 212-727-7770
D'Agostini Organizzazione, 117 — 39 432 507332
d-Log, 47 — 33-1-30 40 04 04

Dale Komai, 150	510-656-6387	David H. Lawrence, 131	415-621-3283
Dan R. Sukiennik, 143	510-486-0245	David Rose Design, 131	408-377-2770
Dana Shultz & Associates, 165	510-420-8414	David Spector Associates, 79	617-894-9455
Dana Wood & Associates, 65	505-822-1241	David Spound Associates, 190	413-586-5652
Daniel L. Roudelbush, 61	808-326-2025	DaVinci Systems Corporation, 160	919-881-4320
Daniels Associates Inc., 78	317-692-8830	Daystar Software Inc., 66	816-741-4310
Daniels & Mara Inc., 177	512-288-2511	DC Productions, 131	415-387-3649
Dapple Systems, 66	408-733-3283	DCA, 166	513-745-0500
Dargon Development, 70	714-974-3982	DCI Integrated Computer Systems, 70	708-328-7362
Darmstadter Designs, 36	409-632-3549	DDESIGN SA, 108	41-21-961-1362
Dart Computing, 96	805-658-9240	DDLabs, 150	415-856-9067
Dart Products, Inc., 178	305-232-5428	DDP Training Center, 190	908-577-8969
Data By Design, 101	913-829-4975	Deborah Designs, 119	408-378-7748
Data, Design + Engineering, 78	303-321-1119	Deborah J. Mayhew & Associates, 110	508-693-7149
Data Dimensions, Inc., 96	206-783-7611	Debron Enterprises, 79	303-972-1243
Data Flow Systems, 36	214-746-4882	Decision Graphics, 70	503-245-7865
Data Solutions, Inc., 19, **46**, 47	303-444-7969 ▣	Decision Images Inc., 175	609-683-0234
Data Technologies International, 72	714-771-3605	Decision Software Systems, 47	215-657-1448
Data Vision Technologies, 189	415-543-7903	Decision Technologies, 61	913-681-6640
Database Associates, 61	617-449-8387	Delio Consulting, 117	914-877-9424
Database Designs, 93	617-876-2727	Delta Catalytic Corporation, 72	905-821-3862
DataBase Designs, Inc., 105	708-634-9355	Delta Medical Shareware, Inc., 73	606-679-7745
Database International Inc., 61	617-859-8579	Deltam Systems, Incorporated, 47	415-571-0551
Database Techniques Pty, Ltd., 96	61-2-837-2075	Deltra P/L, 73	484 1306
Databases, Inc., 104	801-467-7111	DEMCO, INC., 64	800-356-8394
Databasics, Inc., 47	404-873-0064	Demometricka, 19, 93	310-390-6380 ▣
DATABEHEER, 103	32-2-569-65-94	Denis Darby's Creative Data, 119	303-680-6352
DataBright Management Systems, 103	415-381-9120	Dennis M. Nagel, Inc., 66	407-272-0700
DataCraft, 93	303-232-4321	Dennis Trager Associates, 116	415-456-5655
Datadesigns, 59	210-697-0780	DeNovo Systems, Inc., 72	206-695-9372
Datadyne Systems, 103	914-381-5704	Desert Sky Software, Inc., 96	602-279-4600
DataLan, 101	914-682-2022	Design Access, Inc., 63	312-465-0528
Dataman Services Inc., 166	716-381-8590	Design Factory APS, 131	45 33 93 91 10
DataMasters, 19, 93	301-831-0183 ▣	Design Mirage, Inc., 131	814-353-9051
DataPak Software Inc., 78	206-573-9155	Design Mirage, Inc., 152	814-234-2616
DataSoft Corporation, 160	612-893-9680	Design Teknekh, 147	404-378-7900
Datastream, 105	803-297-6775	Designed Data Company, Inc., 66	708-739-3716
DATATAG, 93	215-245-5352	Designed Information Systems, 163	604-294-4357
Dataway, 131	416-599-1200	Desjardin Consulting, 19, 96	510-659-1546 ▣
Datawindow Software, 76	503-686-5771	DeskTop Consulting, Inc., 160	314-831-9000
Dave Meyers, 178	408-255-2964	Desktop Dynamics, 172	214-826-3080
Dave Saunders & Associates, 131	805-379-0726	Desktop Edit, 93	39-2-2363931
David Anderson Consulting, 147	415-969-9296	Desktop Information, 72	805-963-4095
David Berman Developments Inc., 93	800-665-1809	Desktop Paging Software, Inc., 47	716-634-9010

DeskTop Production Services, 172   415-364-4092
Desktop Technologies Inc., 172   313-663-3320
Devonian International Software Company, 172
                                         714-621-0973
Déwí Development Corporation, 79   214-422-9903
DFC Enterprises Inc., 20, 101   714-497-0611 ▣
Didatech Software Ltd., 64   800-665-0667
Diehl.Volk Typographics, 76   213-851-3111
Digi Media, 108   43 0316-81-73-97
Digiflex®, 177   213-933-7203
Digilog, 167   215-956-9570
Digital Applications, Inc., **47**, 48, **73**, **77**, 79, **87**, 88
                                         215-534-8495
Digital Consultants, 66   303-321-1119
Digital Designs, 152, **172**, 174   214-407-9303
Digital Designs Corporation, **59**, 61, 96, **97**   605-334-1588
Digital Development Corporation, 149   310-279-1202
Digital Domain, 108   91 504-60-91
DigitalFacades Corporation, 26, **131** 310-208-0776 ▣
Digital Hieroglyphics, 145   415-431-0611
Digital Information Gallery, 20, 48
                                         716-832-2861 ▣
Digital Libraries, 176   801-377-8062
Digital Media Reality Labs, 112   415-641-7092
Digital Media Solutionz, 131   205-323-5994
Digital Objectives, 79   908-302-9600
D⁀ ⁀al One, 145   503-226-7223
Digital Post & Graphics, 148   206-623-3444
Digital Prepress Integration, 187   713-896-0800
Digital Science Corporation, 48   619-792-8833
Digital Systems Consulting, Inc., 48   516-435-3959
Digital Thought, 96   714-282-0127
Digital United, 149   914-271-4959
Digital Vision Design & Automation, 63   714-852-8660
Digital Vistas, 132   619-431-3396
Digital Voice Inc., 73   417-781-0717
DILAN, 163   704-328-8551
Dimension Consulting, Inc., 61   305-341-7077
Dimensional Insight, Inc., 61   617-229-9111
Dipl.-Ing. Thomas Gamisch, 38   49-8024-7380
Direct Mailing Systems, 118   707-584-4884
Direct Media, 118   203-532-1000
DirectLine Technologies, Inc., 103   209-545-2557
Display Research Laboratory, 148   852-4121121

Display Tech Multimedia, Inc., 148   510-676-9362
Diversified Computer Corporation, **73**, 105   206-233-0110
Diversified Computer Systems, 160   303-447-9251
Diversified Music Design Inc., 132   518-766-5940
DK Digital Media, 151   415-441-7659
DMP Associates, 48   508-476-7014
DNS, Inc., 88   415-433-1077
Doblin Group, 61   312-443-0800
Doctor Mac, 79   800-45D-RMAC
DocuClear, 178   212-691-4926
Document Partners Nederland, 76   31-4120-27272
Doktor Einrik's Software, 48   503-757-8499
Dolphin Multimedia, 26, **139**, 143   415-354-0800 ▣
Dolphin Software, 186   510-464-3000
Dome Software Corporation, 166   317-573-8100
Don Barth Consulting, 190   414-235-0294
Donald H. Kraft & Associates, 70   708-673-0597
Doradus Corporation, 163   612-572-1000
DoremiLabs, Inc., 149   818-966-2454
Dori Friend Design, 132   415-863-8919
Dot Dash, Inc., 132   212- 251-8670
Double Click ab, 123   46-31-14-59-10
Double Click Systems, Inc., 163   202-342-5629
Douglas Corarito, 90   413-339-0246
Douglas Pundick Technical Writing, 178   510-559-9377
Dover Technology Ltd, 66   902-461-9544
DPK Software, 90   313-996-0771
DRAC'S Technologies, 48   32-41-772 444
Dream Maker Software, 172   303-762-1001
DreamTime™, 48   619-236-1341
Dreamworks, 149   215-860-0888
Drextec Inc., 93   609-234-7969
DriveSavers, Inc., 30, **185**, 186, 187   415-883-4232 ⌐
Drochelman Meng & Associates, 132   314-991-0123
Drucker & Associates, 110   617-876-1505
Drucker Documents, 172   617-876-6410
Drumlir ⁀nteractive Design, 143   604-361-1903
DRW, Inc., 48   609-581-1425
DT Software, 186   703-521-9427
DT & T Macintosh Services, 30, 187   800-622-7977 ▣
Dubl-Click Software Corporation, 48   818-8ᴕᴕ-2068
Duggal Color Projects Inc., 172   800-382-9000
Dulles Networking Associates, Inc., 160 703-450-6909
Duo Conseil, 172   33-1-677454 88

Durrant Software Limited, 93 — 44 904 44181
Duthie Associates, Inc., 132 — 615-386-3061
DxR Development Group, Inc., 64 — 618-453-1140
Dynacom, Inc., 152 — 312-951-5510
Dynamic Engineering, 85 — 408-336-5531
Dynamic Graphics Inc., 172 — 309-688-8800

E

E.D.I.T.S., 108 — 49-89-772227
E. E. S. Companies, Inc., 93 — 508-653-6911
E. J. Systems, 105 — 408-462-2507
e Motion Technologies, 149 — 415-331-4030
E Ware, 147 — 800-743-8645
E & C Manufacturing/Computer Supply Company, 79 — 516-244-7390
EAR Professional Audio/Video, 149 — 602-267-0600
Earl Office, 119 — 415-252-0587
Easy, 190 — 808-326-2025
Easy Computing, 103 — 503-738-3521
Easy Street Software, 132 — 408-395-1158
EBA Engineering Consultants Ltd., 66 — 403-451-2121
Ebook, Inc., 153 — 510-429-1331
Eclipse Multimedia, 110 — 703-949-7262
Eclipse Services, 96 — 215-352-6800
Ecosophon®, 48 — 6-272-5038
Ed Tech Northwest, 64 — 206-432-6844
Ed-Sci Development, 79 — 209-545-3656
EDGE Environmental Development Group, 79 — 805-563-2684
Edge Technologies, 149 — 619-878-2994
EdgeWriter Film/Video Systems Inc., 149 — 415-459-3926
Edo Communications, 96 — 617-821-6324
EDP Consulting, Inc., 48 — 510-530-6314
EDR Consulting Services, Inc., 20, 48 — 201-797-7318
EDR Media, 149 — 216-292-7300
Edu-Tech Associates, Inc., 20, 93 — 407-952-0745
Education Catalysts Inc., 163 — 617-482-8982
Eduself Multimedia Publishing Ltd., 175 — 972-3-5562570
Efficiency & Software, 96 — 303-791-4444
Eicon Technology Corporation, 160 — 514-631-2592
Eileen Mullinaux, 146 — 415-922-1236
Einstein's Bicycle, 150 — 310-397-7209
elan technologies inc., **185**, 186 — 514-332-3526

ELB Consulting, **36**, 117 — 602-886-2646
Electric Eye, 66 — 503-248-2265
Electric Image, Incorporated, 143 — 818-577-1627
Electro Plasma Inc., 166 — 419-255-5197
Electronic Catalog Corporation, 61 — 800-777-7770
Electronic Directions, 174 — 212-213-6500
Electronic Edge, 174 — 513-767-7174
Electronic Learning Systems Inc., 88 — 800-443-7971
Electronic Pencil, 178 — 203-233-0370
Electronic Tablet Publishing Company, Ltd., 172, **176**, 178 — 718-965-9622
Elefunt Software, 103 — 510-843-7725
ELEX Computer, Inc., 48 — 82-2-780-4545
Elisabeth Waymire, 110 — 415-598-2847
Elizabeth A. Strode, 117 — 415-340-1377
Ellen Bari, 149 — 212-662-6099
Elmo Productions, 150 — 510-482-8756
Elrick & Lavidge, 110 — 415-434-0536
Elron Consulting Inc., 187 — 305-680-9842
EM Software, Inc., 76 — 614-284-1010
EMA Software, 64 — 415-969-4679
Emanuele Corso & Associates, Inc., 59 — 505-587-1022
EMC2 Computer Solutions, 187 — 802-476-5800
eMedia, 168 — 415- 648-1704
Emergent Behavior, **47**, 49 — 415-494-6763
Emerging Information Technologies, Inc., 96 — 617-444-6185
Emerging Technology Consultants Inc., 132 — 612-639-3973
Emigre Fonts, 177 — 916-451-4344
Emphasys Technologies, Inc., 88 — 214-380-4947
Empire RBDMS, 117 — 407-784-2116
Empower Trainers & Consultants, Inc., 189 — 816-753-8880
Enabling Technologies Corporation, 160 — 301-498-2820
Encryption Technology Corporation/Prism Packaging, 172 — 404-952-0153
Endpoint Marketing Information Systems, 121 — 408-737-3831
EnerAnalytics, 178 — 510-867-0681
Engage Communication, Inc., 163 — 408-688-1021
Engaging Media, 132 — 713-952-5475
Engineered Software Solutions Corporation, 90 — 501-262-2048
Engineering Resources, Inc., 49 — 201-875-7916
Engineering Software Concepts, Inc., 121 — 800-325-1289

Engineerium, 79 — 619-292-1900
Enlightened Software Corporation, 90 — 714-998-4220
Entertainment Digital Network (EDNET), 168 — 415- 274-8800
Entertainment Solutions, Inc., 166 — 213-656-5500
Entertainment Solutions, Inc., 69 — 213-871-4481
Entrepreneurial Technologies, Inc., 165 — 817-924-1215
Entropy, 88 — 415-488-4143
Envent Group, 76 — 606-273-9891
Envisage Ltd., 107 — 203-965-0902
EPIC Consulting Services, 166 — 206-243-3251
EPIC Systems Group Inc., 66 — 818-355-2988
EPSI Computer Systems, Inc., 90 — 604-589-4412
Equilibrium, 132 — 415-332-4343
Eric Hook Graphic Design, 172 — 617-424-8894
Erica Kerwien, 178 — 617-674-2718
Ernest De Gidio, 93 — 614-447-1825
Ernst & Young, 70 — 816-474-5200
ESOFT, 49 — 310-865-4078
ESS Development Company, 49 — 714-528-8958
Essential Systems Consulting, 163 — 206-399-3707
Essex Systems Inc., 103 — 201-338-4336
Eureka Software, 49 — 412-521-6303
Euronix Computing, 76 — 44 242 250504
European Languages Plus, 88,108 — 800-878-8523
Evenview Corporation, 132 — 404-982-0600
Evergreen Consulting, Inc., 160 — 714-643-8760
Evergreen Technologics, Inc., 73 — 207-326-8300
Evolution Computing, 49 — 602-967-8633
Ex Software, Inc., 73 — 514-465-3871
Exact Art Design, 173 — 702-829-8422
Exact Systems, Inc. 66, 79, 90, 104 — 612-486-7501
Excalibur Technologies, 97
Excalibur Technologies, 166 — 716-377-9154
Excel Instruction, 150 — 612-379-3883
Excel Software, 49 — 515-752-5359
Exceller Software Corporation, 64 — 607-257-5634
EXEGI, 150 — 510-827-3681
Exodus Software, 20, 49 — 513-522-0011 ▣
Extra Computer Services, GmbH, 90 — 49-611-39257
Extron Electronics, 116 — 310-802-8804
Eyejam/Earwax, 132 — 415-775-5020

F

F1 Consulting Services, 49 — 705-524-4357
Fain & Co., **47**, 49, **93**, 116, **131**, 133 — 404-876-4668
Falcon Software, Inc., 177 — 603-764-5788
Farallon Computing, Inc., 165 — 510-814-5000
Fashoro Langhill Inc., 61 — 510-736-7634
Fast, Cheap, Reliable Inc., 73 — 312-774-6696
FCS, S.L., 76 — 3471-75 4831
Fearless Eye, 133 — 816-353-6177
FeatherstoneCommunications Network, Inc., 166 — 310-799-9494
Federal Software Inc., 166 — 716-836-7998
Feldman Film Medien & Kommunikation, 133 — 49-911-533078
Ferro Enterprises, 121 — 515-236-6148
Fifth Generation Systems, 49 — 504-291-7221
Film Rite Entertainment Group, Inc., 148 — 914-946-5262
Film Works Software, Inc., 147 — 310-451-3756
Filmsonix, Inc., 145 — 213-465-7697
Fine Artist's Color & Ink, 76 — 310-397-9908
Finnegan O'Malley & Company Inc., 79 — 415-288-4400
First Floor Software, 168 — 415-968-1101
FIT Software, 61 — 408-562-5990
Flashpoint, 189 — 510-524-0852
Flashpoint, Inc., 61 — 617-625-3100
Flip Track OneOnOne Computer Training, 189 — 708-628-0500
Flying Pictures/Mercuria Interactive, 146 — 212-861-9502
Flying Rhino, 143 — 415-332-7868
FMI Group, Ltd., 97 — 703-905-0006
Focal Point Systems, Inc., 79 — 415-851-0211
Focus Enhancements, 163 — 617-938-8088
Fog Press, 173 — 415-726-2522
Folkstone Design Inc., 153 — 604-886-4502
Font World Inc., 108 — 716-235-6861
FoodStar Inc., 61 — 813-281-2705
Footprints, Inc., 97 — 800-635-5280
Footprints, Inc., NW Operations, 61 — 800-635-5280
Ford Consulting, 90 — 714-771-7509
ForeFront Long Island, 50 — 516-225-0179
Form & Function, 133 — 415-664-4010
Forman & Flack, Inc., 147 — 617-923-0124

Forsight, Inc., 133 — 301-816-4900
Fortune & Associates, 25, 116 — 415-494-9919 ▣
Forty-Two Software, 93 — 49 40381924
Four Media Company, 148 — 818-840-7156
Fox & Mouse, 101 — 212-662-0455
Foxglove Communications, 74 — 410-426-7733
Foxtron Systems, 101 — 412-922-4844
Fractal Solutions, 93 — 404-955-5169
Frame-by-Frame Media Services, 133 — 510-651-6330
Francis Tanner Inc., 159 — 518-872-2756
Frank Scales Productions, 148 — 415-621-1649
Franklin Estimating Systems, 61 — 801-355-5954
Frax Incorporated, 150 — 408-279-3059
Freagra, 59 — 0473 230202
Fred Pittroff, 70 — 303-758-7538
Frederic M. Fowler & Assoc., Inc., 50 — 408-720-9456
Free-lance Communications, 173 — 405-340-6912
Freewood Computer Services Inc., 50 — 908-255-8241
Freq Sound/Workman Computer Services, 145
— 410-964-3548
Fresh Cream Design Group, 133 — 212-446-8557
Fresh Software & Instructional, 20, 50 — 510-524-0852 ▣
From The Heart Software, 64 — 208-883-4941
Frontier Media Group, Inc., 149 — 610-641-5535
Frostbyte Software, Inc., 97 — 313-229-3110
Frye Computer Systems, Inc., 166 — 617-451-5400
FSCreations, Inc., 64 — 513-241-3415
FSL Computer Services Division, 76 — 0925 34214
Fulcrum Media Services, 146 — 415-459-4429
Full Circle Media, 178 — 415-453-9989
Full News Information Service, 76 — 313-761-1236
Fundamental Software, 88 — 801-944-0133
Future Enterprises, Inc., 190 — 202-662-7610
future tense, 88 — 206-232-1475
FutureSoft System Designs Inc., 88 — 212-219-0599
Futurity Systems, 166 — 414-547-8687

G

G. A. Bell & Associates, 121 — 408-241-1997
G'Day Software, Inc., 50 — 214-424-6164
G141J Systems Inc., 50 — 214-424-5038
Gal Computer Imaging, 175 — 201-433-3553
Galileo Inc., 133 — 404-425-4536

Gallaher & Associates, Inc., 73 — 501-452-8929
Gallup Organization, 120 — 714-474-7900
Ganesa Designs Inc., 90 — 415-456-0348
Gary J. Hardy, Inc., 90 — 415-595-5899
Gateway Group Inc., 159 — 510-283-7900
Gazlay Marketing Group, 173 — 913-371-4333
GE Rental/Lease, 187 — 800-GE-RENTS
Gem City Software, 79 — 513-435-8887
General Information Services, Inc., 165 — 302-478-1000
General Parametrics, 116 — 510-524-3950
General Picture, 146 — 404-377-6161
General Systems, 110 — 206-289-0900
Geni Inc., 79 — 508-256-7992
GenText, Inc., 36 — 214-691-0300
GEO Computing Systems, 90 — 602-743-0950
GeoData Systems, 66 — 702-294-3065
GEOPOINT Software, 50 — 415-957-1560
Gerin Productions, Inc., 148 — 914-666-0542
German Localizations, 108 — 919-460-7191
Get Creative Technologies, 101 — 312-327-8503
Get Info Computer Systems Incorporated, 101
— 416-361-3400
Gibbs & Associates, 72 — 805-523-0004
Gibson Computer Associates, 190 — 303-745-7960
GIS plan, 133 — 45-9815-8522
Glaser Media Group, 153 — 415-593-6607
Glass Eye Productions, 146 — 609-399-6833
Glenrose Systems, 66 — 512-448-1196
Global Investment Technology, 166 — 201-818-0455
Globalink, Inc., **85**, 109, **111** — 800-767-0035
Globalogic Inc., 70 — 613-721-0240
Globus Systems, Inc., 97 — 415-292-6744
Go Technology, Inc., 36 — 818-281-9409
Godar & Hossenlopp Printing Company, 178
— 415-593-5900
Golden Avatar Software, 103 — 503-343-9879
Golden Branch Interactive Productions, 147 — 212-595-4474
Golden Empire Publications, 69 — 714-283-3000
Golden Gate Tax Service, 117 — 510-686-4864
Goldsoft Corporation, 62 — 818-501-2837
Good News Marketing Inc., 62 — 617-643-7131
Good Northwest, 20, 79 — 206-842-7164 ▣
Goodall Software Engineering, 79 — 707-795-2335
Goodlove & Moon, 116 — 510-204-9120

Gordian, 28, 161, **162** — 714-850-0205 ▣
Gorman Consulting, 190 — 703-528-4405
Graffio, Inc., 88 — 212-366-1404
Grafica, 119 — 818-712-0071
Grafica Multimedia, 133 — 415-595-5599
Grafik Solutions, 173 — 303-933-9148
Grahame-Harding Productions, 133 — 415-626-7116
Grande Vitesse Systems, 133 — 415-777-0320
Granite Graphics, 161 — 201-325-1881
Grant Holland & Associates, 90 — 404-447-5471
Graphic Arts Technology, 173 — 617-484-9005
Graphic Connexions, Inc., 173 — 609-655-8970
Graphic Data Designs, 103 — 415-388-3806
Graphic Detail, Inc., 152 — 919-833-3366
Graphic Directions, 147 — 415-239-7024
Graphic Traffic, 174 — 805-650-9807
Graphics Edge, 133 — 512-454-1254
Graphics Universal Inc., 173 — 918-665-6633A
Graphix Zone, Inc., 176 — 714-833-3838
Grass Valley Multimedia, 133 — 916-273-6349
Great Ware Software, 177 — 408-438-1990
Greco & Associates, 109 — 415-389-1307
Green Arbor Software, 79 — 801-575-5369
Green Dragon Creations, Inc., 69 — 708-854-1242
Green Shades Software, Inc., 62 — 904-260-7766
Green Tree Software, 72 — 714-830-5682
Greenline Electronics, 28, 161 — 617-422-8644 ▣
GreenSpring Computers, 72 — 415-327-1200
Greystone Computer Management, Inc., 50 — 816-471-5550
Greytsounds Sound Development, 145 — 503-347-4700
Grid Media Limited, 153, 175 — 852-591-0730
Griffin Dix Research Associates, 120 — 510-527-1451
GroundZero Software Solutions, 103 — 714-858 1184
Group 20/20 Ltd., 166 — 313-798-8171
Grove Engineering-A BWNT Company, 66 — 415-855-2305
Growing Minds Software, 187 — 910-391-2252
GSE Choice Ticketing Software, 69 — 419-475-7755
GTE Hotel Interactive Television Services, 152 — 617-449-7676
Guardianware, 105 — 313-562-9342
Guillermo Pulido, 148 — 510-839-7708
GXR Systems Services, 161 — 604-433-3001
GXStudios, 133 — 512-416-0558

H

H. K. Stewart Creative Services, 173 — 501-661-9389
Hagen MicroAge, 190 — 612-866-3441
Hahn Computer Institute, 133 — 416-633-8600
Hal Chorpenning Communications, 173 — 303-541-0155
Halley & Scott, 97 — 206-822-0970
Harappa Films, 148 — 415-642-1620
Harper House Inc., 116 — 214-744-4646
Harris Consulting, 149 — 415-488-1137
Harris Design Office, 119 — 302-234-5700
Hartley Metzner, Huenink, 150 — 414-784-1010
Harvard Psychiatric Consultants, 73 — 508-468-2290
Haukom Associates, 133 — 415-922-0214
Hawks Associates, 121 — 716-374-5397
Haywood & Sullivan, 173 — 617-576-3344
HDA Technical Services, 101 — 603-536-3880
HDS Systems, 88 — 602-325-3004
Health Data Sciences Corporation, 73 — 714-888-3282
Health & Education Communication Consultants, 150 — 415-368-0418
Hearing Voices, 145 — 510-452-9274
Heartland Software Corporation, **102,** 103, 105 — 905-858-1415
Hecht & Associates, 121 — 408-730-2234
Hechtsoft, 62 — 089/884248
Heidi C. Bowman, CPA, 70 — 415-325-6416
Heliotrope Inc., 178 — 215-274-2145
Help!, 173 — 818-577-5270
Heritage Computer Consulting & Services, 20, 50 — 913-268-1469 ▣
Hermes Systems S.A., 76 — 011-32-41-678-372
Herrel Business Systems, 93 — 215-398-8280
Hertrich Graphics, 116 — 708-851-6581
Hewitt/Katona International, 121 — 415-957-1560
HeyerTech Inc., 166 — 415-325-8522
HeyerTech-IICS, 147 — 415-325-8522
HFSI Education Services, 190 — 703-478-2000
Hi-Tech Public Relations Inc., 121 — 415-904-7000
High Techsplanations, Inc., 112 — 301-984-3706
Highlighted Data Inc., 91 — 703-516-9211
Hil Bren Consulting Services, 70 — 908-545-7913
Hill Productions, 133 — 916-369-2353

HJM Computer Consulting Group, Inc., 93, 101
419-471-1223
HLS Duplication, Inc., 175   408-773-1500
HMS Computer Company, 70   612-934-2652
Hoff Consulting, 174   707-887-7778
Hoh Humm Ranch, 66   206-374-5337
Holder, Egan & Company, Inc., 97   517-636-7373
Holmes Agency Inc., 116   301-589-1251
Holmstead Partners, 161   801-375-8890
Homeopathic Bicycle Company, 73   4460428767
Honeybee Software Inc., 20, 50, **56, 57**, 59, 60,
    75, 76, **97, 99, 100**, 101, 133, **134**   800-667-1233 🔲
Horizons Technology, Inc., 151   619-292-8860
HOT-Tech Multimedia, Inc., 133   212-925-3010
HotCode Ltd., 50   617-259-8520
Houlberg Development, 103   503-692-4162
Howard Goldstein Design, 112   818-987-2837
Howard M. Cutler Productions, 116, **131,** 133
203-857-4332
Howard Metzenberg Multimedia Consultant, 148
415-695-7952
HR Hi-Tech Inc., 60   416-829-2290
HRF Associates, Inc., 50   203-961-1199
Human Code, Inc., 150   512-477-5455
Human Line Inc., 59   32-41-210238
Human Media Limited, 110   61-2-331-2882
Human Resource Microsystems, 62   800-972-8470
Human-Computer Systems, Company, 110   908-572-1594
Hunter Mail, 118   510-444-1767
Hunza Graphics, 118   800-992-2431
Hurn Computing, 91   618-345-3569
Husk, 79   310-372-1757
Hutchings Software Development, 88   510-820-6413
HV Consultants, 79   713-488-0808
Hybridge Inc., 120   403-239-7778
Hyper Active Software, 21, 50, **91**   612-724-1596 🔲
HyperDEX, 62   206-738-0541
Hypermedia Solutions, 63   703-687-3390
HyperProject, Inc., 88   818-831-0404
Hypertek, Inc., 88   301-216-9836

I

I.D.E.A.S., 174   813-566-3091
I.M.A.G.E. Inc., 173   212-714-2700
i MEDIA Solutions, Inc., 133   805-339-4242
I-Per Media, 148   2- 66800996
IBM, 133   404-238-2533
IC Optometrology Inc., 66   602-947-8833
Icon EDV Informations-Systeme GmbH, 88
43 1 545-5155
Icon Medical Systems, Inc., 73   408-879-1900
ICONOS, 133   612-879-0504
IDEA sas, 133   0-522-45-22-25
IDOC, an International Documentation Company, 109
800-336-9898
IDR UniCom, Inc., 50   610-825-6500
Ikonic, 153   415-864-3200
Illuminati, 143   919-683-2424
IM Strategies, 97   408-378-4444
Image Architects Computer Graphic Slides, 116
415-968-1141
Image Associates, Inc., 121   919-876-6400
Image Builder Software, 107   503-684-5151
Image Club Graphics, Inc., 173   403-262-8008
Image Control Systems Inc., 166   206-624-2646
Image Management, 174   808-833-8978
Image Smith, 151   310-325-5999
Image Systems, 76   203-323-3396
Image Technologies, Inc., 133   813-573-5268
Images Design Group Inc., 173   212-645-6100
Imagesetter Inc., 173   608-244-6243
Imagetects, 147   408-252-5487
IMAGIC, 148   44-71-589-1708
Imagination Software Consultants, 133   713-467-2339
Imagination Solutions Corporation, 93, **159**, 166
408-779-3961
Imagination Technology, 64   (0) 298-872651
Imagine Better Software, 88   303-499-1377
Imagine That, Inc., 72   408-365-0305
Imaginia Inc., 133   415-788-6840
IME, 146   213-461-4925
Immersive Technologies, 112   510-261-0128
Impact Communication Group, 107   714-963-6760

Impact Solutions Inc., 97   412-367-8833
IMS Information Management Solutions, Inc, 50
                                                   314-432-0997
In•Color Graphics, 173   800-676-1611
In Context, 147   617-497-5816
In Focus Systems, 133   503-628-3876
In Phase Consulting, **49**, 50   818-502-1424
In Software, 77   619-743-7502
In Writing, 178   415-968-9184
In-House Productions, 133   510-828-7056
Inbody Bruck & Company Advertising, 116 213-939-2929
Incline Productions, 151   310-314-7519
Independent Computer Consultants
     Association (ICCA), **185**   800-774-4222
Independent Consultant, 79   913-451-2532
Individual Software, 150   510-734-6767
Industrial Line Multimedia, Inc., 133   416-539-0095
Infinity Digital, Inc., 50   303-232-6906
Infinity Systems, 50   301-596-7741
Info Dent, 73   808-484-0234
INFO grafix, Inc., 38   404-607-1970
Info Serv Information Service Inc., 93   301-299-6404
Info Systems, 51   416-665-7638
Info Systems, Inc., 51   204-264-1948
InfoBase, 118   212-983-0154
InfoE, 66   703-430-4502
InfoMaker Inc., 93   312-736-4059
Infomax Corporation, 166   212-730-7930
Infonautics, 175   215-293-4770
Informania, Inc., 134   619-296-4662
Informant Communications Group, **45**, 51, 161, **162**
                                                   916-686-6610
Information Access Technologies Inc., 168 510-704-0160
Information & Mathematical Science Laboratory, Inc., 67
                                                   81-1-3590-5211
Information Conversion Services, Inc., 88 708-405-0501
Information Engineering Company, 178   303-530-5393
Information Management Resources, Inc., 105
                                                   301-330-9022
Information Management Systems Inc., 104 219-232-7372
Information Presentation Technologies, Inc., 165
                                                   805-541-3000
Information Resources, 161   212-691-1435
Information Surfers, 178   411-724-2901

Information Systems Research, Inc., 101   513-772-4636
Information Systems Technology, Inc., 21, 51, **67**
                                                   708-887-1911 🔲
Informed Solutions Inc., 97   617-739-0306
InfoServices, Inc., 38   616-530-2767
Infotec Training Institute, 121   800-282-7990
InfoTech, 166   708-355-5779
Infotech Information Services, 51   708-381-3837
InfoTech Plus, Inc., 166   215-651-0390
InfoUse, 26, 134   510-549-6520 🔲
Infrastructures for Information Inc., 36   416-920-6489
Ingsoft Limited, 67   416-730-9611
ink, 153   416-360-3894
Inkman & Associates, 134   415-898-2353
INNOVA systems, **87**, 88, 107   514-374-2486
InnovaTech Corporation, 175   619-793-8789
Innovative Data Design, Inc., 63   510-680-6818
Innovative Information Concepts, Inc., 159 516-981-1990
Innovative System Design Ltd., 163   602-791-3323
Innovative Systems & Solutions, 51   201-256-9036
Inpatients, 73   215-264-2755
Insight Communications Group, 179   305-861-8950
Insight Systems, Inc., 175   206-788-9800
Inspiration Software, Inc., 62   503-245-9011
Instant Information Inc., 51   503-692-9711
Instantiations Inc., 88   503-242-0725
Institute for the Study of Adult Literacy, 63 814-863-3777
Instructional Design Group, Inc., **145**, 150 201-538-2226
Insync Productions, 148   716-422-2100
INTE-GREAT Corporation, 51   301-654-9100
Integra Technologies Inc., 51   408-980-1371
Integral Information Systems, 159   510-524-5200
Integrated Accounting Systems, 71   415-550-7670
Integrated Management Resources, 29, 166
                                                   508-897-7064 🔲
Integrated Media, Inc., 134   212-229-1200
Integrated Software Inc., 77   212-545-0110
Integrated Strategies, Inc., 150   612-544-3080
Integration, 51   514-284-2284
Intentional Educations, 64   617-641-1405
Inter/Action, 91   408-749-9539
Interactive Audio, 145   415-431-0778
Interactive Design Associates, 63   503-399-8327
Interactive Design, Inc., 134   206-523-7879

Interactive Engineering, 134 — 312-986-0321

Interactive Factory, 134 — 617-494-9517

Interactive Multimedia Project, 134 — 512-326-8858

Interactive Presentation Technology, Inc., 134 — 800-326-6141

Interactive Software Engineering, 51 — 805-685-1006

Interactive Solutions, Inc., 148 — 415-377-0136

Interconnect Networking Consulting Group Inc., 166 — 310-392-2800

InterConnections, Inc., 168 — 206-881-5773

Interconsult, 120 — 603-964-6464

Interdimensional Arts, 134 — 510-655-1872

Interface International Communications, **140,** 148 — 310-316-5822

Interlinear Technology, Inc., 36 — 510-748-6850

InterMagic, 134 — 802-496-9667

Intermedia, 64, **122,** 123 — 206-284-2995

International Accessability Corporation, 21, 109, **111** — 408-454-0200 ▣

International Association of Business Communications, 185 — 408-746-3545

International Communications Inc., 116 — 508-651-9232

International Computer Group Inc., 69 — 506-785-4211

International Computer Systems, 77 — 803-676-9292

International Datawares, Inc., 175 — 408-262-6660

International Interactive Communications Society (IICS), 135, **184,** 185 — 503-579-IICS

International Language Engineering Corporation, 122 — 303-447-2363

International Software Consultants Inc., 51 — 405-924-6888

International Software Products, 109 — 31-2963-5271

International Software Products, 135 — 802-258-2551

International TechnoGroup Incorporated, 67 — 800-783-9199

InterOptica Publishing Limited, 21, 107 — 415-788-8788 ▣

Interplay Artists, 147 — 415-564-2072

Intersoft, Ltd., 109 — 022 268-6643

Interval Music Systems, 88 — 310-478-3956

inTouch Communications Pte. Ltd., 123 — 296-9700

Intra-Active Designs, 150 — 612-938-1473

Intramedia, 93 — 508-775-9033

Intuitive Design Engineering, 110 — 619-944-4575

Inventure Inc., 51 — 415-282-0280

Investment Research Institute, 71 — 510-686-9067

InVision b.v., 135 — 31-40-631260

Iowa Market Systems, 177 — 319-354-7286

IronMike Software Inc., 21, 79 — 404-687-9646 ▣

ISIS International, Inc., 62 — 818-788-4747

Island Micro Solutions, Inc., 59 — 808-833-6048

Island Resources, 179 — 415-726-6448

ISM, INC., 69 — 410-560-0973

ITech, Inc., 51 — 703-709-1244

ITI SA, 177 — 41-21-826-03-71

ITI SA Intégration texte et images, 166 — 021-808-71-75

J

J. L. Cooper Electronics, 135 — 310-306-4131

J. Schachter Enterprises, 94 — 708-329-1111

J.W.G. Enterprises, Inc.,51 — 919-286-9859

J. W. Havstad, 67 — 503-560-3321

Jack Daley & Company, 161 — 415-493-0947

Jack Fox Associates, 117 — 619-599-3255

Jack Irby Consulting, 71 — 714-969-9494

Jack Lewis & Associates, 122 — 407-336-3581

Jackson Enterprises, 107 — 407-487-8336

Jacque Consulting, Inc., 173 — 313-561-6280

JAG Enterprises, 59 — 212-627-0058

Jam Software Limited, 123 — 203-630-0055

James Graca Design Group, 119 — 805-339-9304

James Hays, 51 — 206-328-8188

James Pistrang Computer Resources, 104 — 413-256-4569

James Robinson Design & Production, 135 — 212-864-1415

Janal Communications, 121 — 510-831-0900

Jane Mason, Computer Consultant, 190 — 202-986-2100

Jane Sallis & Associates, 135 — 206-522-5522

Jann Greenland Communications, 119 — 501-374-8297

Janus Technologies, 88 — 612-293-0108

Jasnic Consulting Services, 161 — 715-361-8929

JAYCOR, 135 — 205-837-9100

JBM Logic Inc., 72 — 514-646-6839

Jeddak, 62 — 800-982-6900

JEDtech Consulting, 161 — 313-661-4832

Jeff Tanner Artistic Concepts, 174 — 813-734-9863

Jennie's Code Boutique, 92 — 415-664-4010

Jersey Cow Software Company, Inc., 64 — 908-422-0101

Jesse Sugarman, 144 — 212-925-5663

Jessica M. Morris, 187   901-382-8459
JGI, 79   800-423-0814
JHAMCON Company, 163   408-354-5022
Jim Sharp & Associates, 166   913-539-5837
Jirokichi & Company, Ltd., 51   81-467-32-2237
JLH Direct Marketing, 118   800-877-4554
JM Associates, 97   617-864-9806
JMT Technologies, Inc., 77   904-897-2380
Joe Czop Photography, 135   415-359-4579
Joel M. Bowers & Associates, 99   603-778-7494
John Gammon Video Service, 148   510-886-5588
John Pane, Consultant, 79   412-363-8280
John Pyra Consulting, 97   508-692-8070
John Shockey, 79   617-547-7815
John Wong Systems Consultants, 101   303-444-1252
Johnathon Freeman Technologies, 164   415-822-8451
Johnson Direct Advertising, 118   415-321-3727
Jonoke Software Development, Inc., 74   403-448-3647 ▣
Joseph Greco, 175   212-867-7079
Jovian Systems Development, Inc., 109   607-253-7997
Jowaisas Design, 173   315-655-3800
JP Computer Resources, 104   413-256-4569
JP Imaging, 79   602-992-4064
JP Systems, 94   703-644-6644
JPD Communications, **119**, 120   510-843-8048
JPH Consultant Services, 161   301-495-4812
JRA Interactive, 135   206-866-0533
JTZ Engineering, Inc., 79   310-534-8559
Judy Munsen, 145   510-763-4007

K

Kagi Engineering Inc., 190   510-843-6140
Kalb & Associates, 117   310-829-9790
Kallisto Productions, Inc., 135   510-531-3288
Kamen Audio Productions/CD Archives,
26, **132**, 136, **141**, 145   212-575-4660 ▣
Kanbay Resources Inc., 79   312-274-3890
KANDU Software Corporation, 186   703-532-0213
Kansas Bay Systems, Inc., 62   510-339-7300
KAR Enterprises, Inc., 136   408-739-9517
Karow Associates, Inc., 21, 51   410-276-4016 ▣
KASA, 88   619-578-1831
Kasdin Productions, 150   310-454-6760

KB Communications, 116   206-256-9508
KB Design, 175   407-439-6554
KEA, 92   503-223-1149
Kearney Rietmann, 121   415-726-1135
Keep It Simple Software, 62   406-442-3559
Keith Gilbert Consulting, 175   612-487-6081
Ken Braband Business Communications, 146
                                                414-375-9253
Kentary, Inc., 92   303-791-2077
KeyPeople Publishing, Inc. 64   206-252-2002
Khalsa Productionsm 136   602-678-0743
Khera Communications, Inc. 178   301-309-0969
KidWare, 107   510-836-0965
KillerBytes Software, 74   205-995-4741
Kinetic Sciences Inc., 112   604-822-2144
Kinetic Software Inc., 180   415-851-4484
Kingdom Graphics, 176   512-476-2276
Kirk Mahoney, 152   713-952-5475
Kjell Ingvarsson Konsult hb, 62   46-411 40184
KKS Software Inc., 90   215-594-0552
Kleinhans Systems, 72   414-668-6238
Klex Software, 67   313-473-0347
Klouda Communications, 178   215-997-9383
KMS Systems, Inc., 26, 29, **132**, 136, 161
                                                713-363-9154 ▣
KnoSys, 136   916-274-7852
Knowledge Bank, Inc., 80   612-754-8140
Knowledge Based Systems Inc., 51   409-696-7979
Knowledge Factory, 21, 80   612-890-8292 ▣
Knowledge Industry Publications, Inc., 176   914-328-9157
Knowledge Software, Inc, 77   914-762-7667
KnowledgeVision, 144   803-272-4483
Koala Acquisitions, Inc., 149   408-776-8181
Kolnick Consulting Services, 190   415-239-5922
Komenar Production & Marketing Group, 136
                                                415-435-9470
Komili Teknik Hiz. ve Sanayi AS., 67   4680588
Korody-Coleman, Inc., 85   408-956-0322
KPMG • ExIS, 161   415-473-3310
KPMG Peat Marwick Management Consultants, 72
                                                617-723-7700
Kracom Computer Services, 94   708-590-0250
Kramer Group, 187   415-856-3565
Kristi Wachter, 147   415-931-1614

KTAADN Inc., 67   617-527-0054
Kula Corporation, 71   312-341-4967
Kustom Automated Technologies Inc., 161 708-355-3585
Kutoroff Development, 90   813-796-8725
KV Graphics, 136   612-949-2902
Ky Housing Corporation, 161   502-223-3010
KyTek, Inc., 77   603-529-2512

L

L & B Software, 104   305-653-3080
L & L Products, Inc., 92   603-643-4503
La Solution Douce, 71   35881700
Laden Relations, 121   719-260-8035
Lan Data Voice Technologies Inc., 166   708-729-0168
Land Graphics, 120   310-588-9399
Land Lord Software Inc., 51   301-695-1544
Landgrove Associates, 80   908-932-3685
Landry Design Associates, 173   508-474-0456
Langley Autosystems, 88   408-252-4700
Language Engineering Corporation, 52   617-489-4000
Language Systems Corporation, 80   800-252-6479
LanMinds, 166   510-843-6389
Lanovation, 168   612-379-3805
LanSharks, 161, **163**   714-556-9912
Lapin Systems Inc., 80   610-696-2179
Lara Consulting Group, 77   617-248-6999
LaRan Technologies, 118   040-536-60-20
Laravela Associates, Inc., 168   302-762-7758
Larry Wisch Associates, 37   415-495-4959
Laser Publishing, 187   508-692-8389
Laser Set, 116   713-586-7556
Laser Solutions Inc., 94   404-992-3914
Laserpoint, 77   916-847-5273
Lasselle-Ramsay Inc., 178   415-968-1220
Latent Image Productions, 136   415-824-7808
Lawinger Consulting, Inc., 80   612-425-6164
LC Resources, 88   503-835-4803
LCS-Lawrence Computer Systems, 59   201-379-1547
LDR, Litho Development & Research, 161   503-255-5800
Le Blanc Consulting Group, Inc., 21, **49**, 52
                                         203-849-7737 ▣
Le Groupe Micro-Intel Inc., 52   514-528-1905
LeadingWay Corporation, 38   714-453-1112

League for Engineering Automation
Productivity (LEAP), 185   804-495-8547
Learning Associates International, 63   31-010-426-22-78
Learning Curve Ltd., 63   616 290-1594
Learning Systems Sciences, 150   818-505-6222
Learning Tomorrow, Inc., 64   800-722-1978
Learnsoft, Inc., 190   619-546-1400
LeBlanc Design, 136   213-651-5924
Legal Computer Solutions, 72   303-841-4545
Legal Computer Solutions, Inc., 72   617-227-4469
Leland Interactive Media, 151   619-284-9458
Leo Home Media, 136   213-913-3038
Les Logiciels Macapa, 97   514-923-0887
Les Logiciels SYSTAMEX Inc., 62   514-932-4431
Lester Ingber Research, 71   800-L-INGBER
Letter Perfect, 173   206-851-5158
Leviathan Media Corporation, 69   313-826-3560
Levy & Wurz Channel Marketing, 116   206-621-8358
LGH Informati Zurich, 97   411 4612571
Liberty Computer, 52   612-755-0351
Libraries of the Mind, 64   431-278-7801
LICA Systems Inc., 80   703-359-0996
Lieberman & Associates, 69   310-337-7905
Lighthouse Technology, 80   714-457-1656
Lightship Software, 189   503-292-8765
Limburgs University Centre, 136   32 11 26 8166
Lincoln Software, Inc., 60   617-259-4135
Linda Jay Brandt, **174**, 176   408-737-1470
Lindamood-Bell Learning Processes, 136   805-541-3836
Lindsay Public Relations, 121   408-984-7242
Lingua Service Associates, 26, **128**, 136 206-448-8404▣
Linguist's Software, Inc., 77   206-775-1130
LINK srl, 179   392-583-10607
LinksWare, 88   408-372-4155
Lion's Share, 90   801-268-3218
Lipschultz Brothers, Levin & Gray, 60   708-272-5300
Littauer Associates, 77   518-371-5073
Live Marketing, 117   415-941-8188
Live Oak Press, 173   415-853-0197
Live Wire Productions™, 144   310-831-6227
LJR Communications, Inc., 152   212-744-9140
LNS Communications, 148   415-552-6462
Local Knowledge, 117   603-868-2300
Loch Moy, 147   0620-5411

LOG-N-COMPUTING, 188   518-782-1132

Logi 27, 109   33 1 42 74 7055

Logic Plus Inc., 161   312-663-5682

Logical Solutions, 176   612-659-2495

Logicat, 80   212-529-1840

Logikal Solutions, 80   708-420-0210

Logisoft Inc., 104   510-939-3556

Logtec, 190   513-429-2928

London Computing, 173   609-795-4281

Long & Company, 150   415-922-4016

Los Angeles Software Inc., 80   310-450-8500

Los-Lawrence Computer Systems, 38   201-379-1547

Lou Harrison & Associates, Inc., 81   609-275-8318

LRM Consultants International, LC, 37

LSB Technology, 67   412-653-1082

Lucida Corporation, 69   212-765-6655

Lumigenic Media, 136   408-335-4849

Luminaria, 152   415-821-0536

Lynch's Computer Services, Inc., 81   904-862-1831

Lynx System Developers, Inc., 149   617-935-6959

M

(M)agreeable software, inc., 52   612-559-1108

M.I.B. Chock, 52   310-828-4788

M/E Design, 173   510-527-5700

M/Mac, 90   703-237-2498

M2 Ltd., 187   301-977-4281

M2 Multimedia, 146   408-432-3364

M3 Dimensions, Inc., 153   310-907-6590

Mac Art Multimedia, 136   408-773-9614

Mac Generation Inc., 189   305-970-8950

Mac Help Canada, 188   416-979-7754

Mac In Design, 175   203-221-1545

Mac Info-To-Go, 190   817-468-8871

Mac Resource, 190   413-253-7223

Mac, S.A., 123   809-542-6192

Mac Software Registry, 152   914-961-8743

Mac Solutions, 161   614-529-1969

Mac Solutions of Memphis, 173   901-367-0553

Mac Systems, 166   913-832-2121

Mac Systems Consultants, 188   512-326-3458

Mac To School, 190   602-279-5506

Mac Upgrade Specialists, 187   714-362-5429

Mac-nificent Services, 173   213-931-7013

MacAcademy, 186   904-677-1918

Macaroni, 175   510-444-6463

MacCounting, 190   612-722-2564

MacCreations– Layout & Design, 173   305-566-0109

MacD Enterprises, 173   817-773-8392

MacDaniels Henry & Sproul Inc., 121   415-981-2250

MacDesigns, 97   415-863-1551

MacEmpowered, 99   503-284-8058

MacGraphics, 190   303-751-1012

MacHardware Ind., 187   816-842-9000

MacHelp Associates, Inc., 62   302-734-7491

Machover Associates Corporation, 117   914-949-3777

MacInstitute, 161   305-920-3899

Macintosh Accounting Consultants, 71   215-745-4376

Macintosh Applications Consultants, 62   305-776-6777

Macintosh Movie Makers Guild, 185   916-622-5288

Macintosh Scientific & Technical Users Association, 185   508-755-5242

MacLaboratory Inc., 64   215-688-3114

MacMedic Publications, Inc., 74   713-960-1858

MacMentor, 189   408-433-0990

MacMinded Computer Specialists, 99   402-483-6937

MacMinn & Associates, 166   213-874-1793

Maconsult, 81   510-686-9067

MacPeak, 52   512-327-3211

Macreations Publishing, 77   303-665-7250

Macsimum Creative Enterprises, 136   303-232-1336

MacSolutions Inc., 104   503-289-7174

MacSourcery, 21, 81   619-747-2980 ▣

MacSpec, 190   405-720-9622

MacSpecialists Inc., 161   215-387-8237

Macsultants, 117   203-678-8622

Macsys Inc., 97   613-591-9200

MacTech, 99   41-61-331-4081

MacTechnologies Consulting, 94   212-807-5611

MacTimes, 118   805-966-3353

Mactivity, Inc., 161   408-354-2500

MacTraining & Design, Inc., 191   313-557-0750

MacTraining House, 191   415-306-0463

MacVONK•International B.V., 177   31 3404-21944

MacWizards, 164   602-553-8966

MacXperts, Inc., 21, **78**, 81   804-353-7122 ▣

MADA, 177   408-253-2765

Maddocks & Company, 121   310-477-4227

Magenta Seven, Inc., 97   919-787-2787

Magic Solutions, Inc., 161   201-529-5533

Magic Teleprompting Inc., 136   415-626-5283

Magna, 38, **50**, 52, 186, **187**   408-282-0900

Magnagraphics, Inc., 149   513-221-2230

Magnet Interactive Studios, Inc., 137   202-625-1111

Magnetic Press, 176   212-219-2831

Magneton Consulting, 137   714-724-5922

Maharishi International University, 175   515-472-5031

Main Street Multimedia, 152   310-396-4084

Mainstay, 62   818-991-6540

Mainstay Business Services Inc., 173   617-294-0867

Maintenance Master Limited, 72   519-863-2551

Mallin Consulting, 164   612-733-5867

Management Advisory Services, 150   313-606-7596

management graphics, 77   612-854-1220

Management Graphics Inc., 175   416-667-8877

Manex SPRL, 37   32 41 380 368

Manley & Associates, Inc., 107   206-392-0577

ManPower Corporation, 97   607-756-4150

Manufacturing & Computer Systems, 104   612-475-3402

MarCole Enterprises, 152   510-933-9792

Maria L. Langer, 178   201-767-7001

Mariette Systems International, 166   415-344-1519

Marigold Database Systems Inc., 74   800-524-0556

Marisys Inc., 52   407-272-3490

Mark One Computer Networks, Inc., 164   513-421-5267

Mark Pappas Development, 168   904-457-6800

Mark Prewitt Consulting, 188   503-223-3976

Mark Siegel Creative Graphics, 173   617-923-9021

Mark/Space Softworks, 88   408-982-9781

Market Vision, 120   408-426-4400

Marketech Inc., 188   813-823-0099

Marketing Research & Consultant Services, 121
        510-444-0585

MarketSoft, Ltd., 71   81-45-903-1377

Marlene C. Semple Communication Services, 178
        813-286-6550

Maron Computer Services, 74   805-389-6606

Marriner Associates, 117   415-454-1300

Martha S. Scheer, CPA: PC, 188   303-447-9711

Martin & Wichmann, 121   612-724-2633

Martin Goffman Associates, 117   908-549-5433

Martin L. Deutsch, Inc., 173   914-783-9548

Marubeni America Corporation, 52   212-599-3750

Master Software Inc., 22, **50**, 52, **78**, 81   510-975-0650 ▣

Master Trainers' Consortium, 191   714-968-8902

MasterPiece Video, 150   201-808-4546

Masterplans, 60   415-459-7574

Mastersoft Inc., 52   800-624-6107

Match Data Systems, 88   206-453-2951

Maui Software, 52   808-572-0673

Maus Haus, 144   415-343-2996

MAX STAX, et cetera, 64   602-993-8415

Maxim Software SA, 62   54-1-325-9281

Maximum Software, 94, **99**   609-795-2041

Maxis, 69   510-254-9700

MaxSacks International Professional Selling Clinic, 121
        800-488-4629

Maxwell Data Management, Inc., 77   714-435-7703

Mayfield Information Services, 52   405-765-5330

MBA Seminars, Inc., 191   214-746-5350

McClure Consultants Ltd., 52   708-382-6233

McComb Research, 161   408-725-1448

McDonnell Douglas Aerospace, 67   314-234-4912

McGilly Information Systems Inc., 22, 71, **100**, 104
        514-933-2323 ▣

McGraw Advertising/Design, 150   518-272-3030

McHale Design, 121   310-420-2609

McHenry Consulting & Development, 167   507-377-9651

McKune Consulting Services, 107   314-364-8487

McLaren Associates, 118   503-230-6939

McLaughlin Consulting, 188   312-878-4120

McLean Public Relations, 121   415-513-8800

MData Inc., 62   800-426-4963

MDF Associates, Inc., 175   214-416-6427

MDG Computer Services, 94   708-818-9991

Meadows Information Systems, Inc., 77   708-882-8202

MED.I.A. Inc., 150   414-352-9336

Med-I-Bit GmbH, 109   49 40 25167125

MedComp Consultants, 101   909-335-1837

MEDformatics, Inc., 74   910-323-1748

Media Concepts, 137, **143**, 149   408-288-8010

Media Design & Images, 191   703-772-3190

Media Designer, 137   619-456-9153

Media Direct, Inc., 27, 137, **141**   201-894-5548 ▣

Media Group, 147   408-457-9143

Media in Content, 152   415-621-0707
Media In Motion, 64   415-621-0707
Media Kinematics, 27, 137   510-674-1282 ▣
Media Lab Inc., 118   303-499-5411
Media Map/Cambridge Communications, 121
                                         617-374-9300

Media Res, 189
Media Synergy, 137   415-241-9999
Media Systems, 167   503-698-5842
Mediacom, Inc., 147   804-794-0700
Medialab Information Design, 137   089-6121068
Medialine International, 117   00 132 33 66 20 92
Mediaware Development Group Inc., 149   602-298-5355
Medical Database Systems, 22, 94   619-558-2002 ▣
Medina Software Inc., 64   407-260-1676
Medior Inc., 144   415-728-5100
MEDIUS IV, 148   415-905-6959
Mega Media, 153   805-659-0252
MegaBase Inc., 94   415-960-3575
Megafusion, 137   514-579-5721
Megalith Technologies Inc., 71   613-225-2300
MegaMedia Inc., 137   215-848-1377
Memory International, 77   800-266-0488
Memphis Area Computer Services, 104   901-681-0917
Mendon & Associates, 117   816-421-4677
Menlo Business Systems, Inc., 62   415-948-7920
Mentat Research Inc., 88   613-544-3563
Mentor Software Innovations, Inc., 110   404-874-4833
Mercury Multi Media, 152   718-330-1159
Merex Corporation, 178   602-921-7077
Merion Software Assoc., Inc., 72   215-648-3871
Merit Software, 177   214-385-2353
Mertens BDV-Beratung, 191   49 40 3508549
Mesa Graphics, Inc., 52   505-672-1998
MESS/DGEC, 64   514-873-2200
Meta-Solutions, Inc., 97   819-561-9173
Metafact Technology Inc., 22, **87**, 109 604-244-9662 ▣
Metamor Technologies, 161   312-943-8266
Metatec Corporation, 153   614-761-2000
MetaTheory, 64   510-849-4478
Metric Systems, 68   512-388-4458
Meyer Software, 52   215-675-3890
MG Management Group, 62   610-644-2833
MGlobal International Inc., 107   713-960-0205

MH Software, 168   303-438-9585
Michael Bodmer, 99   41-1-860-0110
Michael Brandman Associates, 120   714-250-5555
Michael Cowey, 149   713-220-7872
Michael Diehl Design, 173   213-851-3111
Michael Ericksen PC, 52   708-330-6328
Michael Feerer & Associates, 149   206-647-0112
Michael J. Harper, 94   415-479-4034
Michael R. Mizen & Associates, Inc., 117 708-366-2060
Michael Zolen Macintosh Consulting, 188 916-488-0923
Micro Alliance Inc., 89   617-245-8879
Micro Analysis & Design Inc., 68   303-442-6947
Micro Business Software, 36   800-354-MICR
Micro Computer Networks, 164   914-356-4000
Micro Consulting S.A., 52   21 653 2400
Micro Dynamics Ltd., 62   301-589-6300
Micro Management Associates, 101   903-757-6930
Micro Planning International Ltd., 62   272 509 417
Micro Solutions, 81   316-522-1500
Micro Specials Inc., 68   612-482-1546
Micro Systems Internet Services, 168   801-532-0316
Micro Trading Software Inc., 71   203-762-7820
Micro Visual Systems, 137   617-964-0640
MicroAge Computer Center, 52   509-946-4230
Microage of San Diego, 191   619-566-1900
MicroAge Solutions, Inc., 164   312-715-3100
MicroAssist, Inc., 101   800-735-3457
Microautomation Associates, 104   412-431-6148
MicroCode Engineering, 68   801-226-4470
MicroComputer Technologies, Inc., 71   714-552-1193
Microlytics Inc., 52   716-248-9150
MicroMac Technology, 167   714-362-1000
Micromega Systems, Inc., 94   415-346-4445
MicroServ, 191   203-776-6800
Microspace Communications Corporation, 138
                                         919-850-4515
Microspot, 68   408-253-2000
Microstar, 52   603-425-2553
MicroStrategy Inc., 68   302-427-8800
Microtrade, 97   43-1-435930
MicroWorks , 52, **91**, 94   212-794-4466
MicroWorks Businessworld, Inc., 22, **59**, 60, 62
                                         212-932-0001 ▣

Miller/Kadanoff Promotional Marketing, Inc., 119
415-554-0424
MikroLogix Software Inc., 64 602-325-8794
Miles & Miles, 77 509-925-5280
Milesquare Associates, 99 201-792-5415
Millennium Computer Corporation, 51, 52 716-248-0510
Millennium Software Company, 52 214-314-2688
Miller Technical Publishing, 178 408-427-0173
Miller/Burns Associates, Inc., 62 217-789-4430
Millstone River Systems, Inc., 105 609-443-1420
Mind & Motion, 52 503-388-9114
MindCraft Publishing Corporation, 173 617-259-0448
Minder Technologies, Inc., 62 414-789-7433
Minds Eye Graphics, 144 804-643-0441
MindStorm, Inc., 22, 81 510-644-3902 回
Minerva Interactive, 148 415-863-9484
Minerva Systems, Inc., 150 408-970-1782
Minerva Technology, Inc., 81 214-871-7033
Mintaka Technologies, 81 717-421-1184
Minuti Software Consulting, Inc., 52 603-483-5819
Miracle Concepts, Inc., 81 717-299-7382
Miramar Systems, Inc., 168 805-966-2432
Mircro Security Systems, Inc., 187 800-456-2587
MISCA, 188 800-741-9956
Mixed Media Works, 138 215-832-5960
MK Consulting, 68 410-243-2216
MLC Computer Services, 52 305-424-9514
MLT Software, Inc., 51, 52, 79, 81 503-452-0652
Modability Inc., 77 310-312-5358
MODACAD, 63 310-312-6632
Modern Lines, 120 602-251-2499
Molecular Arts Corporation, 52, 53 714-634-8100
Molecular Solutions, 89 510-447-5101
Monarch Design Systems, 77 718-894-8520
MonkWorks, 53 205-879-9867
Monotype Typography, Inc., 173 312-939-0125
Montage Software Systems, 22, 97 203-834-1144 回
Montclair Data Services Corporation, 105 510-339-8541
Montgomery Consulting Group, Inc., 36 816-224-4100
MontreuxMedia c/o DDESIGN SA, 138 41 21 9611362
Moonlighting Software Development, 90 813-796-8725
Moose Systems, Inc., 159 307-789-9758
Moov Design, 138 619-259-6300
Morgan Consulting Group, 121 707-571-8800

Morgan Interactive, 150 415-693-9596
Morgan Research Corporation, 138 205-533-3233
Morgenlender Associates, 81 617-965-7514
Morphonix, 138 415-456-2561
Morph's Outpost on the Digital Frontier, 42, 138
510-238-4550
Morris Communications, 176 510-222-6672
Morrison & Foerster, **126**, 148 415-677-6210
Morrison Consulting, 81 808-575-9160
Morton Associates Inc., 68 805-966-3556
Motion Works International, 138 604-732-0289
Motioneering, 191 310-316-7738
Motivation Consultants Inc., 121 415-591-6621
Mountain Data Works, 191 916-644-4500
Mountain Software, 63 304-346-9585
Moving Media, 144 415-861-1759
MPACT IMMEDIA, 161 514-397-9747
MPI Engineering, 168 408-262-6962
MSI, 149 317-842-5097
MTC New Horizons, 189 510-933-9955
MTEC, 53 618-997-6461
MTP Systems Consulting, Ltd., 94 708-392-9908
MUG News Service (MNS), 119 518-374-1088
Muirhead & Associates, 97 708-888-1695
Multi Lingual Media Presentations & Training, 150
619-578-1357
Multi-Image Systems, 177 916-345-4211
Multi-Impressions Corporation, 117 918-665-6633
MultiAccess Computing Corporation, 165 805-964-2332
MultiCom Publishing, 176 206-622-5530
MultiMedia AB, 138 468-660-93-20
Multimedia Asia Ltd., 153 852-824-0781
Multimedia Business Presentations, 148 415-863-6270
Multimedia Computing Corporation, 138 408-369-1233
Multimedia Creation, 144 510-866-2968
Multimedia Design Group, Inc., 89 703-266-9213
Multimedia Magic, 150 212-289-7119
Multimedia Research Group, 148 408-524-9767
Multimedia Scientific, 150 619-549-4600
Multimedia Specialists, 123 415-459-3553
MultiTrain International, 151 310-494-4091
Munday & Collins Rents, 117 408-451-9155
Mundo Corporation, 105 216-943-4400
Music Annex, Inc., 145 510-226-0800

Music & MIDI Sales, 145   913-648-8225

MW Productions, 151   415-641-8844

MWA Consulting,122   415-323-4780

Mysterium Tremendum, 64   412-661-0285

MZ Media Group, **13**, 145, 146, **147**, 175   415-543-8290

N

N:Deavor Group, Inc., 161   203-677-4321

n Dimensions Software House, 53   408-662-9703

Nadcomp Systems Inc., 81   718-336-3318

Nadson & Terrill Communications, 178   310-787-9054

Nancy A. Ridenhour, CDP, **94**   704-875-0144

Napa Valley Computing Company, 53   707-259-1349

Nash Video Interactive, 138   215-750-1926

National Association of Desktop Publishers, 186

    508-887-7900

National Association of Macintosh Trainers, 186

    800-827-9719

National Instruments, 72   800-433-3488

National Management Systems, 38   703-827-0797

Natural Intelligence Inc., 97   617-876-4876

Natural Interface Lab, 64   818-797-2157

Navaco, 62   814-833-2592

Naval Air Warfare Center, 161   317-353-7886

Navigation Technologies Inc., 89   410-268-9701

NB Engineering, 27, **132**, **133**, 138, **143**, **144**, 149

    410-721-5725

NDG Phoenix, Inc., 138   301-718-8880

Nedrud Data Systems, 68   702-221-6331

Nelson Laffey Associates, Inc., 16, 22, 29, **37**, 89, 161, **163**

    314-436-9725

Neo Directions Computer Support Ltd., 120   516-627-7518

NeoLogic Systems, 89   415-566-9207

Neotech Interactive, 138   310-392-2711

Netcetera, 81   310-414-9534

NetSpan Corporation, 168   214-690-8844

NetSpec, 168   504-286-0107

Network Express, Inc., 168   313-761-5005

Network International, 162   310-402-5095

Network Publications, Inc., 176   404-962-7220

Networkers, 164   601-349-2243

Neurodata Inc., 74   818-564-9201

NeuWorld Services, 81   619-485-1456

New Edge Technologies, 175   603-547-2263

New Heights, 178   801-572-4320

New Ledger, 30, 191   619-558-0222

New Line, 97   33 20578218

New Media Entertainment, **133**, 138, 173   408-927-6866

New Media, Inc., 16, 22, 29, **37**, 38, 53, **63**, 64, **79**, 81, **89**, **94**, **97**, **104**, 105, 106, 107, **108**, **111**, 159, **160**

    216-481-7900

New Renaissance, 151   619-287-0093

New Science InterActive, 118   510-653-6034

New Technology Consulting Associates, 167

    713-251-3443

New Visions, 53   405-239-6411

New Visions Media Works, 138   818-905-7886

Newhoff & Associates, 97   206-481-8175

NewOrder Media, Inc., 147   615-386-3636

Newton Design Company, 147   0428-722155

Nexial, 98   914-279-7486

Next Actions, 191   203-761-1255

NextAge, 167   203-849-3388

NFL Films, 149   609-778-1600

NHG Inc., 53   704-531-7654

Niche Solutions, 104   215-435-0741

Nighthawk Productions, Inc., 138   410-484-1656

Ninth Wave Computing, Inc., 74   919-929-8894

Nisus Software, 123   619-481-1477

Noetic Systems Inc., 68   410-889-4079

North Atlantic Publishing Systems, Inc., 77   508-250-8080

North Communications, 62   310-828-7000

North Mountain Software, 104   408-297-5824

Northland Computer Services, Inc., 68   816-741-8089

Northstar Systems, Inc., 53   603-673-5040

Northwest Data Services, Inc., 22, 53   206-252-7287

Northwest Programming Inc., 101   503-598-0200

NoteTaker Software, 62   916-587-7450

Notti & Company, CPAs, 191   415-461-8301

NOVA Electronics & Software, 53   714-781-7332

Novation Technology Inc., 116   800-248-7988

Novette Incorporated, 152   412-521-2758

NuLogic® Inc., 72   617-444-7680

Number One Graphics, 177   517-332-6231

NVision3, **120**, **133**, **136**, 138   415-459-5077

O

Oak Enterprises, 159	708-858-4443
Oakleaf Designs, 81	408-257-1547
OakTree Software Specialists, 53	407-339-5855
Object Factory Inc., 89	612-420-9876
Objectic Systems Inc., 121	206-271-6864
Ocean Beach Communications, 53	619-523-1182
Octavo Productions, Inc., 138	604-987-5270
Odin Technologies, Inc., 94	203-762-9628
Off Key Microsystems, 98	818-794-8100
Ogden Bio Services, 53	301-309-8280
OITC, Inc., 53	407-984-3714
Oliver. Creation, 82	49 89 8401693
Olson & Company Strategy & Marketing, 117	
	415-326-0373
Omicron Electronics Inc., 68	313-757-8192
Omni Resources Corporation, 175	508-865-4451
OmniVision, 82	909-886-1734
On-Line Design, Inc., 27, **135**, 138	404-325-2977 🔲
OnBase Technology, Inc., 72	800782-5682
OneOnOne™ Computer Training, 188	800-424-8668
Online Computer Systems Inc., 94	301-428-3700
Online Press Inc., 191	206-641-3434
Ontrack Data Recovery, 186	612-949-4021
Opal Computing, 71	718-343-4054
Open Designs, Inc., 82	415-929-0924
Open Eyes Video, 138	617-646-7708
Open Network Solutions Inc., 164	703-430-2668
Open Software Associates Limited, 110	6138711666
Open Systems Associates, Inc., 53	703-758-6708
Optical Media International, 153	408-376-3511
Opticon Pictures Corporation, 138	403-439-5862
Optima Design & Advertising, 116	609-392-7772
Optimal Sounds, 138	512-442-0400
Optimization Alternatives, 62	512-479-4140
Optimum Technology Consultants, 188	316-262-4455
Options Computer Consulting, 98	212-645-3577
Opus Systems, 98	510-525-5742
Oracle Multimedia, 151	708-256-2290
ORCA Software Company, 74	206-868-7007
Orca Software Solutions, 186	408-848-3046
Orcutt/Oeflein Software, 65, **67**, 90	616-352-9071

Orpheum Productions, 146	818-985-9854
Oryx Associates, 98	415-563-9971
OS Systems Group, 53	203-452-9043
Other Company, Inc., 117	414-374-3747
Ottawa Researchers, 139	613-828-5235
Our Designs, Inc., 120	212-505-8565
Ourtime Publishing, 98	410-964-8062
Oxford & Associates Inc., 89	408-996-9961
Oxford Molecular Ltd., 68	44-865-784600
Oxygen Farm, 144	910-635-1669

P

P. A. Christenson, 82	510-793-6766
P. Heidi Beeler, 178	510-841-5060
P.L. Kelly Engineering, 68	408-720-0790
P & P Data Systems Inc., 74	416-665-6450
P.S.C. Consultants, 162	310-372-5096
Pacific Telesis Electronic Publishing Services/	
Re:Source Network Solutions, 158, 162	
	800-303-7247
Pacific Coast Sound Works, 139	213-655-4771
Pacific Digital Image, 173	415-274-7234
Pacific Interactive Design Corporation, 139	310-458-1898
Pacific Science & Engineering Group, 110	619-535-1661
Pacific Systems, Inc., 89	408-429-1814
Pacifico Inc., 116	408-293-8600
Pacifitech Corporation, 178	81-467-25-4010
Package Express Inc., 121	816-886-4800
PacPics, 89	61-2-684-2570
Page Creations, 173	209-527-1348
Page Studio Graphics, 179	602-839-2763
Pagecrafters, 173	508-251-8180
PageWorks TriDesign, 120	303-337-7770
Palamar Communications, 139	310-455-1002
Panache Productions, 146	214-363-3533
Panergy Ltd., 99	972-3-5612541
Paoletti Technologies, 151	415-391-7610
PaperClip Products, 23, 53	800-497-5508 🔲
Paradigm Interactive, Inc., 27, 139	919-768-7844 🔲
Paradigm Software, 89	816-463-2217
Paradigm Trading Systems, 71	408-399-4385
Paradise Software Corporation, 53	602-759-0335
Paragon Publishing Systems, 177	603-471-0077

Parallax Technologies, 146 — 510-416-8080
Parallel Media, 139 — 310-470-3839
Parcway Software Inc., 139 — 415-965-7873
Parrothead Computercations, 188 — 203-873-1196
Parson Consulting, 64 — 512-441-6932
Passport Communications, 162, 167 — 512-328-9830
Passport Designs Inc., 145 — 415-726-0280
Pathos One Inc., 104 — 301-932-1133
Paul Hoffman, 178 — 408-426-6222
Paw Computers, Inc., 191 — 801-295-2299
PBM-Analys AB, 82 — 468 710 4825
PC Consulting Services, Inc., 53 — 206-670-1570
PC Dynamics, 187 — 818-889-1741
PCES Inc.- Express Train, 189 — 609-737-8098
PCLC, 191 — 212-953-9800
PCX Consulting, 62 — 412-471-7500
Peachpit Press, 176 — 800-283-9444
Peachtree Software, 62 — 800-247-3224
Pearl Computer Systems, Inc., 177 — 609-983-9265
Pearson Communications Group, 119 — 408-496-5885
Peat Marwick Thorne/Strategic Solutions Inc., 100 — 416-777-3814
Peggi Sturm & Associates, 123 — 310-470-9390
PEMD Education Group, 29, 175 — 707-894-3662 回
Penny Bauersfeld Human Interface Design, 110 — 415-637-0801
Pensee Corporation, 62 — 602-494-7075
Pepa Informatik, 94 — 052-222-76-44
Pepperdine & Company, CPAs, 191 — 214-241-4170
Perceptics Corporation, 107 — 615-966-9200
Peripheral Visions Inc., 98 — 503-640-1317
Perkins/Boyer Advertising & Digital Production, 27, 134, 139 — 415-346-8820 回
Perseus Systems Corporation, 101 — 215-388-6003
Personal Computers, Personal Solutions Inc., 189 — 908-249-4044
Personal Consulting Services, 98 — 708-310-0080
Personal Library Software, 94 — 301-926-1402
Personal Systems Services, Inc., 159 — 404-432-8179
Personal Training Systems, 189 — 800-832-2499
Persuasive Presentations, 147 — 206-868-5702
Peter B. Holler, 68 — 716-586-5570
Peter C. Reynolds & Associates, 151 — 415-589-6939
Peter David Lauwers Macintosh Support, 191

— 313-995-1130
Peter F. Wells, 72 — 603-899-5460
Peter Samis Art Services, 146 — 510-527-8759
PF Consulting, 162 — 609-988-1756
Pharos Technologies, 90 — 513-573-7100
Phase II Consulting Inc., 60 — 401-333-4536
Philip Davis & Associates, 98 — 913-962-0389
Philips Professional Products, 139 — 908-827-8648
Phillips Associates, 62 — 206-881-2856
Philmont Software Mill, 89 — 518-672-4890
Phoenix Management, Inc., 38 — 503-297-8720
Photo Library Management Services, 152 — 805-641-2400
Photon Inc., 188 — 617-661-9046
Physicians' Educational Series, 74 — 415-369-6897
Pickering & Associates, 98 — 614-459-1670
Pierian Spring Software, 37 — 503-222-2044
Piic, 121 — 408-450-1511
Pillar Corporation, 118 — 415-349-6200
Pindar Graphics Systems, 98 — 0723 362222
Pine Grove Software, 90 — 609-730-1430
Pinehill Software Corporation, 60 — 508-548-4470
PinPoint Solutions, 23, 94, 95, 98, 99, 100, 101, 105, 106 — 415-962-9857 回
Pioneer New Media Technologies, Inc., 139 — 201-327-6400
Pixel Perfect, 77 — 619-480-1827
Pixel Translations Inc., 147 — 408-865-6600
Planet Productions, 151 — 503-241-1644
Planet X Productions, 139 — 408-971-7215
Planning Showcase, 121 — 408-253-6679
Platinum Software Corporation, 71 — 714-727-1250
Platt College, 191 — 619-265-0107
Please Seer Systems, Inc., 145 — 415-856-0265
Please Seek, Incorporated, 139 — 414-771-3466
Plug-In Systems, 77 — 303-530-9344
Plusware Inc., 104 — 905-477-0015
PMC/Mac Seps, 174 — 206-861-9609
PMS Microdesign, Inc., 23, 27, 68, 112, 134, 139 — 412-731-4004 回
Polygram Special Markets, 145 — 212-333-8549
Polymorph, 89 — 0374 651 740
Porter & Porter, 30, 189 — 708-350-9090 回
Positive Logic, 89 — 703-591-4908
Potomac Software Engineering, Inc., 68 — 301-984-3982
Power Graphics, 174 — 801-363-7410

Power R, Inc., 139 — 206-547-8000
POWER SERVICES of Ne INC., 103 — 714-496-7143
Power Up Software Corporation, 63 — 415-345-5900
PowerHouse Programmers, 23, **67**, 82 — 510-946-0904 ▣
Powers Hills, Inc., 101 — 405-769-7695
PowerTraining, 101 — 310-370-4793
Practical Computer Solutions, Inc., 94 — 907-561-3878
Pragma, 89 — 512-335-2311
Prana Computing Inc., 53 — 310-826-4687
Pratt & Chew, 191 — 206-441-1998
Precision Computer Systems, 53 — 602-829-3131
Precision Data Corporation, 53 — 901-682-0732
Preferred Technologies, 98 — 303-987-3411
Prelinger Associates, Inc., 149 — 212-633-2020
Premier Design, 147 — 510-674-8440
Presage Software Development, 139 — 415-454-7007
Prescience Corporation, 68 — 415-543-2252
Presentation Graphics, 175 — 919-886-2309
Presentation Media, 151 — 908-525-1700
Presentation Technologies, Inc., 27, 139 — 404-393-3820 ▣
Presentations Plus, 139 — 619-283-5370
Preview Media, 149 — 415-397-2494
Prime Prodata, Inc., 72 — 216-456-8023
Printing Communications Associates, Inc., 107 — 404-436-1714
Printz-Electronic Design, 151 — 415-543-5673
Pro Train, 189 — 513-772-0367
Problem Solving Tools, 68 — 510-447-4969
Procom Technology, 153 — 800-800-8600
Prodigy Technologies Corporation, 89 — 604-687-4636
PRODUCTEC SA, 63 — 41-227-193
Production First Software, 177 — 415-695-0881
Productive Systems, Inc., 53 — 614-777-1748
Productivity Plus, Inc., 191 — 314-569-2901
Productivity Point, 53 — 404-816-5833
Productivity Point/MicroTrek, 191 — 212-398-6410
Productivity Through Technology, 51, 53 — 510-471-2776
Professional Business Assistance, 120 — 203-888-6451
Professional Computer Training, 189 — 702-829-9300
Professional Support Services, 191 — 203-966-5818
Professional Systems, 98 — 414-783-5151
Professional Systems International, 53 — 510-659-8144
Progressive Allied Marketing Inc., 121 — 619-571-5440

Progressive Computing, Inc., 53 — 817-572-6567
Projects in Knowledge Inc., 74 — 201-617-9700
Promo Datentechnik Systemberatung GmbH, 109 — 49-40-431360-0
PROmote Communications, 174 — 612-825-2292
Prompt, Inc., 53 — 203-651-8710
Propaganda, 120 — 804-640-7166
Prosoft Engineering Inc., **53**, 54, **80**, 82 — 510-462-8935
Protec Microsystems Inc., 162 — 514-630-5832
Prototype Systems, Inc., 23, 47, 54, **55** — 201-998-5850 ▣
PRX Inc., 116 — 408-287-1700
PSC Consultants, 82 — 310-372-5096
PSE Network Distribution Systems, 119 — 510-429-5002
PSS Systems Design, Ltd., 107 — 405-528-7774
Psychologi Logiciel Software, 191 — 613-443-2435
Puget Pastings, 105 — 206-843-2216
Pulse Productions, 145 — 415-355-5252
Punos Electronic AB, 68 — 46-31-12-17-30

Q

Q Technologies, Inc., 54 — 708-864-8505
Q1 Communicators, 178 — 614-899-0060
QCC Communications Corporation, 168 — 306-665-6488
QLS (Int.) Inc., 54 — 604-364-1921
Quadrature, 65 — 619-271-9224
Qualisys Inc., 68 — 203-657-3585
Quansa, 82 — 702-831-8829
Quantic Corporation, 89 — 612-698-4268
Quantum Solutions, Inc., 54 — 614-855-0265
Quartet, 150 — 415-647-1777
Qube Software, Inc., 72 — 714-559-5659
Que Software, 177 — 317-573-2500
QuesTech, 89 — 716-924-5497
Quick Start Technologies, 189 — 714-894-1448
QuickSilver Software, Inc., 92 — 714-241-0601
QuickSoft, 149 — 972-52-444249
Quintessence Audio, 145 — 918-582-1200
Quire Inc., 71 — 914-471-8505
Quorum Software Systems, 107 — 415-323-3111

R

R. A. Meyers & Associates, 167 — 312-666-2032
R & D Multimedia Productions, 139 — 818-335-8498
R & L Office Systems, 62 — 412-856-8707
R. Seide & Associates International, 148 — 213-938-9408
Ra Data A.S, 38 — 47 33317707
Rachel Richards, 174 — 714-528-5424
RADX Corporation, 117 — 214-422-9903
Rae Technology, Inc., 23, 94, **95** — 408-725-2850 ▣
Raindrop Software Corporation, 168 — 214-234-2611
Rajni Malik, 54 — 203-931-7722
Rall & Company, 140 — 410-730-1706
Ralph Krug, P.E., 89 — 313-426-3503
Rampant Lyon, 140 — 805-821-5108
Randal Jones & Associates, 82 — 206-774-9044
Randamax Inc., 191 — 716-546-5550
Randy Schroeder, 94 — 503-228-4020
Raphael & De Jong, 145 — 31-30-368367
Rapid Design Services, 174 — 415-398-3556
Rasmusson Graphics, 175 — 412-373-6636
Ray Dream Inc., 77 — 415-960-0768
Raymond Software Inc., 72 — 408-395-6157
Raymond Studer Communication Publicitaire, 100 — 32 68 55 28 35
RB Graphic Supply Company, 167 — 714-921-8600
RDR Inc., 104 — 503-643-2723
Re:Design, 174 — 212-627-3321
Re: Software, 82 — 602-897-9703
Reactor Inc., 153 — 312-573-0800
Read Technologies, Inc., 54 — 714-551-2049
ReadyToGo Presentations, 140 — 415-563-3674
Real Time Enterprises Inc., 167 — 716-383-1290
Reardon & Wynn Associates, 117 — 619-450-3131
REBO Research, 69 — 212-989-9466
Recommended Test Labs, Inc., 82 — 415-928-1192
Redrock Software Corporation, 177 — 602-993-8914
Red Sky Interactive, **34**, **137**, 140, 150, **151** — 415-421-7332
Redwolf, 82 — 415-369-8741
Redwood Software, 140 — 707-822-6545
Reflections Publishing, Inc., 152 — 408-779-6616
Reiter Consulting Services, 60 — 301-261-4505
Relational Paradigms, Inc., 71 — 718-624-0546

Relational Systems, Inc., 162 — 216-226-4546
Relevant Technologies, Inc., 98 — 617-864-9500
Remote Measurement Systems, Inc., 72 — 206-328-2255
RenderTech, 123 — 713-524-2000
Reprographic Technologies, 121 — 414-796-8162
ResNova Software, Inc., 170, 175 — **714-379-9000**
Results Training Group, 140 — 0993/811595
RETINA, 149 — 0-89-144286
Reusable Solutions Inc., 23, **80**, 83 — 503-223-6892 ▣
Revelar Software, 54, 98 — 801-485-3291
Revision, 54 — 206-382-6607
Rhythm Technology, 54 — 415-574-8312
Rhyton Software, 23, 107 — 408-626-1250 ▣
Richard Battin, 101 — 407-496-1443
Richard D.Robbins, Independent Consultant, 89 — 203-761-0749
Richard L. Bergman, 151 — 212-677-8195
Richard Soohoo Associates, Inc., 54 — 516-531-1953
Richard Vallens Consulting, 164 — 714-651-8337
Richards Consulting Enterprises, 74 — 714-261-2051
Richardson Technical Services, 83 — 314-427-8142
Richey Software Training, 189 — 707-869-2836
Richmond Software Corporation, 103 — 404-623-4898
Ridgewood Software, 168 — 203-635-9942
Rigel Engineering S.A., 140 — 32 2 7355571
Right Click!, 54 — 312-248-6072
Rikei Corporation, 167 — 408-257-7943
Ring of Fire, Inc., 117 — 3-5485-5985
RISM, 54 — 913-642-5600
Rittenhouse & Associates, 105 — 708-328-4033
Rittenhouse Communications, 152 — 215-321-6860
Rivanne Advertising, 120 — 718-998-2903
Rivers Edge Corporation, 122 — 512-590-9528
RJM Systems, Inc., 54 — 415-731-2884
Robert A. Frankel Management Consultants, 167 — 914-271-2233
Robert E. Nolan Company, 38 — 214-248-3727
Robert F. Miller & Associates, 94 — 209-545-2909
Robert Gezelter Software Consultant, 107, **111**, **160**, 162 — 718-463-1079
Robert S. Lenoil, 83 — 415-968-0882
Robert T. Coolidge, AIA, 117 — 203-458-9759
Robert T. Culmer Consulting Services, 83 — 214-321-5191
Robertson Associates, 54 — 415-322-5335

Robis, Inc. Software Marketing, 118	708-752-0220
Rock Ridge Enterprises, 83	313-663-0706
RockWare, Inc., 68	303-423-5645
Rocky Mountain Translators Inc., 109	800-365-3736
Rod Williams Resource Group, 38	408-685-9431
Rodney Vaughan Associates, 144	415-364-0129
Rodus International Corporation, 103	604-925-9848
Ron Allen Consulting Services, 188	801-882-3535
Ron Wallace Enterprises Inc., 62	309-685-4843
Rosenfeld, Meyer & Susman, 148	310-246-3210
Rossnick Consulting, 164	212-671-0584
Roy Posner & Associates, 103	510-283-1146
Roy Sablosky Design, 103	415-454-5771
RPM Productions, 140	415-474-3177
RSA Data Security, Inc., 187	415-595-8782
RSG International, 37	619-259-6890
RSH Consulting, Inc., 187	617-969-9050
RSVP Publications, 119	415-485-0996
RTJ Corporation, 74	617-899-1266
RTS Corporation, 83	619-484-7509
Rubicon, Inc., 98	313-677-2050
Ruigrok Innovations Inc., 62	604-683-5599
Rusch Design, 140	415-621-4740
RWD Technologies, Inc., 54, **80**, 83, 159, **161**, 162	
	404-551-8198
RWRAD, 168	408-685-9431

S

S.I.A. - Advanced Information Systems, 153	
	32-19-567-135
S2 Software, **76**, 98	408-257-7272
Sackman Associates, 77	508-443-3354
SaleMaker Corporation, 38	603-893-2422
Sales Automation, Inc., 121	215-262-4555
Sales Dominator Ltd., 62	612-544-1800
Sales Systems Development Inc., 117	415-691-9622
Sam Adams, 146	718-383-6437
Sampson & Associates, 188	913-842-7764
San Francisco Canyon Company Inc., 54	415-398-9957
Sanders & Sanders, Inc., 102	919-782-4251
Sandhill Systems, 103	508-635-9440
Sandpiper Software, Inc., 65	612-644-7395
Sandra Pakin & Associates, Inc., 178	312-271-2848
SanSoft, 100	303-947-6406
Santa Monica MicroAge, 191	310-828-4911
Sapia Mekatronik AB, 68	46-8-7647260
Sapphire Systems, 98	612-944-0212
Sargent Electric Company, 166	412-394-7580
Sassafras Software, Inc., 167	603-643-3351
Schindler Imaging, 70	310-652-5624
Scholastic Software, 151	212-505-6006
Schubert Media Design, 151	415-365-6878
Schulco Training Corporation, 189	215-940-0100
Schweichler Associates, Inc., 121	415-924-7200
Scientific Placement Inc., 54	713-496-6100
Scott Hysmith, 122	206-742-0133
Scott Knudsen, 83	605-348-1782
Scott Mize Productions, 150	415-851-4126
Scott Satovsky, Sat's Graphics, 25, 117	810-354-4333 ▣
Scovell Communications, 165	403-252-7152
Screen Media Software, 140	818-991-8491
ScreenDesign, 147	49-30-3938438
Screenplay Systems, 140	818-843-6557
Script Software International, 83	515-469-3916
SCV Consulting, Inc., 54	612-572-2425
Sea Studios, 65	408-649-5152
Seaborne Woodworking, 60	707-778-3474
Sean Hill Software Development, 70	415-488-4510
Seawell Microsystems Inc., 68	206-938-5420
Second Difference, 83	810-689-3051
Second Glance, 77	714-855-2331
Second Nature, 92	408-737-8374
Second Wave, Inc., 167	512-343-9661
SEG, 72	617-492-6664
Seishin Creations, 89	904-498-7325
SelectStar, Inc., 94	212-243-8413
Selfware, 54	703-506-0400
Semantic Imaging, 178	415-334-8109
Senecio Software, Inc., 121	419-352-4281
Sensible Business Systems, 62	607-753-9482
Sentient Software, 54	415-595-2523
Sequel Development Corporation, 54	408-366-6900
Sequent Associates, 54	408-436-0111
Sequoia Computing Solutions, 98	603-888-5973
Seth Greenberg Computer Consulting, 98	212-431-9132
Seven Hills Software Corporation, 177	904-575-0566
SFC Desktop Business Systems, 94, **101**, 104	415-255-0200

Shaffstall Corporation, 188 — 317-842-2077

Shapiro & Company, 23, 106 — 805-962-8109 ▣

Shardonnay Audio Visual, Inc., 153 — 213-913-1238

Shattinger Interactive, 116 — 314-621-2408

Sheahan Productions, Inc., 149 — 609-497-1112

Shell Systems, Ltd., 23, **81**, 94, 104 — 910-996-1757 ▣

Sheridan Software, 54 — 206-331-1868

Shireman Software, 90 — 707-887-2809

Shoestring Engineering, 60 — 415-647-4107

Shoestring Multimedia, 140 — 415-487-6930

ShopKeeper Publishing International Inc., 62

904-222-8808

Shopware, Inc., 65 — 206-532-3392

Show & Tell Systems, Inc., 118 — 415-691-1077

ShowCase Corporation, 159 — 507-288-5922

Shuger Software Services, 54 — 708-228-2959

SIB Consulting, 72 — 617-341-8516

Sibony & Associates, 100 — 510-644-9322

Sigma 4, Inc., 98 — 505-382-8799

Sigmund Software, 65 — 717-566-9255

Sign Equipment Engineering Inc., 62 — 206-747-0693

Signal Science, Inc., 71 — 800-266-2020

SILC, Incorporated, 83 — 301-428-1439

Silicon Graphics Computer Systems, 54 — **800-770-3033**
415-390-3033

Silicon Valley Bus Company, 149 — 408-623-2300

Silk City Software Inc., 140 — 203-228-0091

Silva Systems, 72 — 718-488-7702

Silverberg, Katz, Thompson & Braun, 148 — 310-445-5858

SilverStar Enterprises, 117 — 404-880-5794

Simetra Systems, 24, 62 — 310-640-6878 ▣

Simon/Ross & Associates, Inc., 55 — 416-960-5647

Simone (C.) & Associates, 186 — 301-369-1990

Simple Software Development Company, 55

415-381-2650

Simply Software, Inc., 123 — 800-774-1123

Simulate Inc., 62 — 215-664-7433

Sinard Productions, 149 — 612-338-7771

Sisca, 71 — 819-564-4003

Skamp Computer Services Inc., 89 — 612-941-0696

Skapa Publishing AB, 177 — 46 8 140760

Skees Associates Inc., 55 — 703-250-0862

Skoog Software & Consulting, 68 — 408-265-7756

Skunk Works Multimedia, Inc., 37 — 610-489-0895

Skye Solutions Inc., 55 — 201-222-9006

Sligo Video, 152 — 310-837-5422

Slippery Disks, 55 — 310-274-3600

Small Business Computer Solutions, 98 — 415-897-4420

SMARTALK, 145 — 415-821-7722

smartNET Marketing Connections, **118**, 119

415-321-3868

SMG: Consulting, 117 — 415-928-2514

SmileSystems Inc., 74 — 215-663-9155

Sneakers Software, Inc., 98 — 201-798-3102

SoftEngine, 24, **54**, 55 — 619-549-0907▣

Soft•Letter, 176 — 617-924-3944

Soft Solutions, Inc., 95 — 404-457-9400

Soft Way Computer Software, 95 — 914-381-4626

Soft-One Corporation, 151 — 801-226-8611

SoftAnswer, 55 — 408-725-4041

SoftCare, 74 — 206-780-1729

Softcraft AG, 68 — 415-628-1116

Softeach, 191 — 617-244-0037

SoftEasy Software, Inc., 74 — 215-825-5510

Softek Design, Inc., 71 — 303-728-5252

SoftGuide, **142,** 148 — 214-306-2029

SoftKare, 100 — 203-221-2881

SoftMaven, 92 — 510-525-7532

Softrade International, **86**, 109, 120 — 408-927-6866

SoftShell International Ltd., 68 — 303-242-7502

Software By Design, Inc., 55 — 508-650-4273

Software by Mann, 83 — 408-426-0846

Software Company Legal Guide, 117 — 212-421-6000

Software Complement, 159 — 717-491-2492

Software & Consulting, 55, 98 — 49-611-400142

Software Corporation, 55 — 407-995-8436

Software Design Technologies, 95 — 914-634-2051

Software Designs Unlimited, Inc., 84 — 919-968-4567

Software Development Factory, 159 — 410-666-8129

Software Development Group, 69 — 303-444-8789

Software Engineering Consultants, Inc., 29,55

910-855-0922 ▣

Software Engineering Professionals, Inc., 108 — 317-843-1640

Software Export Corporation, 177 — 617-354-9600

Software Farm, 56 — 510-843-3331

Software Mart Incorporated, 153 — 512-346-7887

Software Masters, 90 — 206-483-2564

Software Packaging Associates, 121 — 800-837-4399

Software Performance Specialist, Inc., 102   708-430-0290
Software Production Alexander Fushs, 177   49-515003
Software Productivity Strategists, Inc., 56   301-670-2837
Software Publishing Manuals, 178   3271519024
Software Services Group, **152**, 153, **173**, 175
                                                      800-622-3873
Software Solutions, Inc., 30, 177   510-426-6751 ▣
Software Studio, 109   416-323-0871
Software Systems & Products Corporation, 71
                                                      313-453-3370
Software Systems Group, 56   703-534-2297
Software Transformation Inc., 108   408-973-8081
Software Usability Seminars, 112   201-267-6007
Softweaver, 56   707-987-9000
Solar Systems Software, 140   415-952-2375
Solo Systems, 37   214-612-8425
SoluProbe Limited, 56   303-460-8264
Solustan, Inc., 72   617-449-7666
Solution Development Services, Inc., 191   713-772-2128
Solutions..., Inc. of Racine, 188   414-791-2237
Solutions Unlimited, 104   209-668-0600
Somerville Associates, 62   302-678-8100
Sonalysts Inc., 56   203-442-4355
Sonic Byte, 145   800-505-9160
Sonnet Technologies, Inc., 100   714-261-2800
Soothsong, 92   415-931-1614
SophisTech Research, 112   800-487-7687
SophSupp Inc., 56   718-253-0444
Sound Logic, 84   212-533-0466
Sound-Arts Company Inc., 145   908-493-8666
South Florida Wire Service, 116, **120**, 121, **122**
                                                      800-741-SFWS
South Sound Software, 29, 162   206-456-4103 ▣
Southern Computer Systems, 36   205-251-2985
Southern Horizons Corporation, 24, 106
                                                      404-552-6875 ▣
Southwestern Pennsylvania Industrial
     Resource Centers, 186   412-469-3530
SpaceTime Systems, 95   617-354-4618
Spatial Data Architects, 153   415-397-6431
Specialty Software, 102   407-728-1199
SpectraLogic, Inc., 24, 108   404-874-4200 ▣
Spellbinder Systems Group, 84   818-760-3956
Spentech, Inc., 56   301-622-1076

Spherix Software, 98   415-241-0101
Spiral Communications, 117   603-424-0545
Spring Branch Software, 56   319-927-6537
Spring City Software, 84   215-469-4600
Sproul Consulting, 165   908-246-3749
Spyglass, Inc., 69   217-355-6000
SRS Integral, Inc., 100   415-765-6705
SSE, 191   314-997-4700
SSG/Skippack Systems Group, 140   215-699-9658
SSTi, 102   609-231-7711
Stafford Associates, Inc., 165   516-698-2827
Stage Research, 84   216-888-8295
Staging Techniques, 188   213-874-5106
Stanford Business Systems, Inc., 159, **161**   310-215-8444
Star-Byte, Inc., 175   800-243-1515
Starboard Inc., **106**, 109, 140   408-261-7570
Starlight Software Solutions, 84   201-405-1208
Stat™ Media, 140   714-779-8176
Steam Radio Limited, 56   44 71 267 2561
Steinberg Jones, 145   818-993-4091
Steinberg Media, 140   49-40211594
Stellar Solutions, 162   805-543-3744
Stephanas & Company, 95   409-297-6647
Stephanie Wong, 147   415-442-7915
Stephen Chinn Consulting, 175   312-871-4060
StepUp Software, 92   214-520-7717
Sterling Automation, Inc., 72   612-476-2700
Sterling International/Ambush Productions, 62
                                                      704-664-8400
Steve Blake Design, 92   617-341-8763
Steven Fine, 84   419-481-2538
Stewart Carl Engineering, 110   415-323-3022
STG Graphic Communications, Inc., 174   415-864-4567
STM Languages, Enterprises, 89   619-599-7922
Stokes Electronic Enterprises P/L, 104   03 509 2200
Stone House Systems Inc., 116   708-256-5813
Stonecutter Software, 24, 56   209-966-3066 ▣
Stony Brook Services Inc., 165   516-567-6060
StoryGame Software, 140   413-339-0246
Stow Lake Software, 56   415-665-9005
STR Corporation, 24, 30, **71**, 72, **102**, 104, 105, **107**, 189
                                                      703-758-1100 ▣
Strata Systems, 95   512-327-8334
Strategic Directions, Inc., 57   305-473-4161

Strategic Management Group Inc., 62	215-387-4000
Strategic Micro Systems, 24, 106	717-871-9126 ▣
Strategic Planning Systems, Inc., 74	203-255-2916
Strategic Support Systems, Inc., 162	214-690-8411
StrategicMedia, 117	510-658-0105
Strawberry Tree, Inc., 72	408-736-8800
Straylight Corporation, 112	908-580-0086
Strichman Medical Equipment, Inc., 74	508-359-5312
Strippit, 72	716-542-4511
Strong/Tyler Systems, 98	707-542-0545
Studer Dyaxis, 145	615-391-3399
Studio 4, 167	908-303-0962
Studio Graphics, 140	415-344-3855
STUDIOTECH, 175	214-979-9400
Subiacorp, 174	505-345-2636
Success Stories by Kris Newby, 116	415-329-8150
Suick Bay Technologies, 57	612-425-7025
Sumbolon Corporation, 84	617-576-0758
SUMERIA, Inc., 176	415-904-0800
Summit Business Systems- Macromedia VAR, 123	
	310-498-8006
Summit Computer Systems Inc., 69	212-334-8087
Sundgau Software Development, 57	416-175-1302
Sunset Laboratory, 69	503-357-5151
Super School Software, 65	310-594-8580
Superset '93 Inc., 57	619-587-6003
Support Central, 188	513-984-0015
Support Syndicate for Audiology, 65	412-481-2497
SupportNet, 188	303-654-4100
Susan B. Morison Writer, 178	313-824-7429
Susan Strumer, 140	203-791-4973
Sussex Informatics Limited, 63	613-789-5444
Sussman Media, 151	408-427-9579
SWeDE Corporation, 140	714-640-5584
Sylvan Software, 163	802-649-2231
Symantec Corporation, 57	800-441-7234
Symbionics, 90	408-353-2016
Symbolic Sound Corporation, 145	217-355-6273
Symplex Systems, 92	604-433-1795
Synapse Software Inc., 74	919-895-6301
Synaptic Micro. Solutions, 77	800-526-6547
Synaptica:, 175	303-499-8120
Synergetics, 188	602-428-4073
Synergy Group, 84	310-471-7897
Synth-Bank, 70	503-626-9084
Synthesis Design, 84	919-787 3571
Synthesis, Inc, 145	501-327-2517
Synthesis Software, 57	704-394-3094
SYS TECH, 186	089-425649
Systec Computer Services, 74	408-723-2264
System Consultants Group, 69	816-842-2233
System Oriented Solutions Corporation, 102	216-867-5881
SYSTEM REENG Inc., 95	805-388-0908
System Solvers Ltd., 102	313-588-7400
Systems Consulting, Inc., 175	701-795-9270
Systems Contracting, 163	303-321-1119
Systems Data Processing Associates, 57	603-881-3107
Systems Engineering Solutions Inc., 62	703-573-4366
Systems Imagineering, 102	708-420-2044
Systems InterAction, 98	303-321-1119
Systems Management Consulting, 188	510-547-2425

T

Tab Computer Systems, 36	203-286-8410
Tactical Marketing Group, 116	510-524-1356
Taft Development Group, 149	303-494-4575
TalCompany Systems Services, 178	619-549-4025
Tangram Enterprise Solutions, 57	919-851-6000
Tanner Research, Inc., 63	818-792-3000
Tanner Software Development, 36	303-689-0720
Taras Development Corporation, 65	801-225-0832
Target Technologies, Inc., 70	203-866-6010
TASCA, 174	818-577-1092
Task Force, Inc., 36	212-777-4280
TaskMan Business Systems, 95	714-502-9051
TBF Publications, 176	314-351-1729
TBP, Inc., 153	818-889-2870
Te Corporation, 179	603-726-7177
Team Development Corporation, 84	512-892-1095
TEC Computer Consultants, 95	212-274-9441
Tech Museum of Innovation, 151	408-279-7174
Tech Prose, 30, **176**, **177**, 179, 180, 189	
	510-975-0660 ▣
Techbridge, Inc., 84	619-224-4881
Technical Analysis, Inc., 116	206-938-0570
Technical Programming Services Inc., 89	214-241-9920
Technical Support Services, Inc., 175	414-276-4165

Technical Writing PLUS, **169**, 179   214-306-8387
Technical Writing Services, 179   503-656-8062
Technique, 102   818-718-9092
Technoliteracy Development Company, 37   206-856-6080
Technologies Plus, Inc., 104   908-475-8883
Technology Inc., 117   415-345-4018
Technology & Learning Magazine, 65   415-457-4333
Technology Locator, 84   800-275-4852
Technology Management Consultant, 72   612 3574777
Technology Research Limited, 71   0279-433822
Technology Works, Inc., 165   512-794-8533
Technovation Training Inc., 74   419-537-1122
TechSys Corporation, 163   305-854-5146
Techware Corporation, 65   407-695-9000
Techway Solutions, 89   06-256-3444
TechWriters Ink, 179   714-661-8861
Tecval Memories SA, 118   41-21-635-90-91
Teknosys Inc., 188   813-620-3494
Teknowledgey Design Corporation, 151   808-539-3667
Teknowledgy, 38, **142**, 148   612-946-0106
Telecom Planning, 165   407-725-9100
TeleMac Visualization, 110   214-423-2276
Telicon Aps, 63   45 65959444
Tellan Software, Inc., 71   408-274-1110
Telluride, 163   617-332-7177
Terry Brown, 147   408-974-0936
Terry Tufts & Associates, 189   708-577-7381
Teton Data Systems, 74   307-733-5494
Texas Learning Technology Group, 146   800-580-8584
Texas PrePress Systems Inc., 167   512-264-1690
Texceed Corporation, 69   714-432-7083
Textware Canada, 180   416-777-0400
Textware Corporation, 179   416-345-8487
Thank Evan For Desktop Video, 140   619-222-3861
The Acacia Group, 165   714-995-0606
The Adams Company, 120   415-325-9822
The AG Group Inc., 165   510-937-7900
The Alternate Approach, 38, **55**, 57   818-889-6035
The Ambit Group/TAG's Channel Compass, 123   415-957-9433
The American Multimedia Group, 140   916-887-1216
The Ansar Group, 38   410-997-0436
The Automation Group, 95   415-777-9167
The Carl Group Inc., 180   408-255-9171

The Choices Center, 151   914-937-3454
The Cobb Group, 179   502-491-1900
The Communication Studio, 110   212-924-3729
The Computer Evolution, 191   310-821-6184
The Computer Factory Limited, 57   44 488 57035
The Computer Lab, 140   703-894-0511
The Computer Learning Company, 179   203-222-7747
The Computer Workshop, Inc., 175   614-487-9505
The Conroy Company/Fulcrum Software, 65   305-235-6479
The Dawson Group, 57   602-496-6848
The Decision Support Group Inc., 74   818-683-3801
The Decisionworks, 71   415-348-2257
The Design Office, 63   407-747-9884
The Design Practice London Ltd, 140   071-493-3391
The DesignSoft Company, 57   800-426-0265
The Digital Artist, Inc., 150   206-935-4606
The Dreamers Guild Inc., 70   818-349-7339
The Dublin Group, Inc., 191   415-227-4777
The EDI Connection, 163   310-373-6675
The Epsilon Naught Company, 69   617-491-6428
The Farrell Company, 63   508-747-3565
The Federation of International Distributors, 186   617-742-5599
The Garrison Group, 74   619-731-5248
The Glyph Media Group Inc., 150   212-989-7026
The Graphic Resource Center, 149   405-840-4723
The Graphics Production Center, 174   404-903-0472
The Hartsook Letter, 120   510-521-4988
The Hiser Consulting Group, 110   61 3 521 3311
The Human Element, Inc., 27, 140   513-745-9204
The Hybrid Group, Inc., 90   201-540-1505
The Hypermedia Group, Inc., 141   510-601-0900
The Idea Bank, 117   206-842-5420
The Intelligent Games Company, 57   44-635-248042
The Interface Experts, 57   310-474-3850
The Katherine Company, 147   602-749-1560
The Learning Center/Computer Land, 191   208-345-8024
The Lerro Corporation, 150   215-223-8200
The Mac Consultants, 167   513-294-7447
The Macintosh Learning Center, 175   212-213-4960
The Management Services Group, Inc., 62   914-358-0070
The Masters Group, 141   615-499-0706
The Maverick Group, Inc., 57   206-672-2000
The MEGA MAC Company, 57   207-582-2442

The MIS Group Inc., 60 — 800-303-7339
The Morgan Agency, 120 — 801-539-1328
The Multimedia Library, 176 — 212-674-1958
The Newsletter People, 116 — 718-596-5225
The Oasis Group, 191 — 206-524-5903
The Orlando Mac Consulting Group Inc., 98 — 407-678-4580
The Oxbridge Group, 71 — 303-963-8933
The Pacific Group, 62 — 408-662-2325
The Pacific Marketing Group, 119 — 415-788-8764
The Philmont Software Mill, 89 — 518-672-4890
The Planet Group, Inc., 159 — 312-772-8333
The Registry, Inc., 84 — 800-248-9119
The Resource, 148 — 415-485-1447
The Salisbury Research Group, 63 — 206-364-7486
The Seroka Group, Inc., 117 — 203-862-9700
The Sleeter Group, **61**, 62, **92** — 510-614-8148
The Soft Programer, 84 — 510-841-6500
The Software Factory, 175 — 800-955-3475
The Software Resource Publications Inc., **174**,179,180 — 608-238-6644
The Stepstone Corporation, 57 — 203-426-1875
The SU5 Group, 24, **55**, 57 — 817-870-2557
The Systems Expert, Inc., 163 — 203-263-0216
The Systems Group, 106 — 515-278-9168
The Taylor Group, 191 — 603-644-2141
The Technical Edge, 57 — 408-438-2524
The Thought Shop, 89 — 612-447-8475
The Turnaround Team, Inc., 92 — 908-654-7117
The VALIS Group, 77 — 510-236-4124
The Vass Company, 121 — 800-424-8277
The Visaeon Corporation, 24, 90 — 914-939-2579
The VITAL Consulting Network, 60 — 408-255-6456
The Voice Emporium, 27, **141**, 145, — 718-522-7533
The Whitley Group, 141 — 404-843-8550
The Willowplace Group, 57 — 612-435-8025
The Word & Image Workshop, Inc., **135**, 141 — 319-332-6324
The Write Tech, 180 — 509-927-0202
The Write Thing, 151 — 916-872-7279
ThinkNet Inc., 165 — 416-585-9678
ThinkThink, 110 — 408-427-0956
Third Coast Multimedia Group, **139**, 141 — 214-826-9810
Third Wave Technologies, Inc., 175 — 205-880-1622

Thomas M. Basista, 147 — 412-548-7425
Thomson Financial Services, 71 — 617-345-2556
Thornhill Data Systems, 179 — 404-998-0802
Tilted Windmill Ltd., 117 — 708-887-5814
Tim Duncklee-Consultant, 177 — 407-562-3621
Timberfield Systems, 69 — 508-872-0796
Time Inc. Picture Collection, 147 — 212-522-8800
Timebox Inc, 153. — 908-782-5643
TM Computer Consulting, Inc., 95 — 203-359-3082
TNT Computing, 57 — 909-984-5775
Toby L. Sanderes, 151 — 212-956-0678
Tokerud Consulting Group, 100 — 415-388-8563
Tom Nicholson Associates, Inc., 141 — 212-274-0474
Tony & Meryl Perutz, 147 — 805-565-0925
Topstack AG, 177 — 052-382243
Total Automation, Inc., 57 — 612-535-2968
Total Integration, Inc., 77 — 708-776-2377
Total Solutions, 165 — 408-996-7850
Totem Graphics Inc., 77 — 206-352-1851
TouchMedia, 28, 141 — 804-464-2191
TPS Electronics, 167 — 415-856-6833
Trailblazer Productions, 141 — 707-795-3087
Training Access, 191 — 303-745-9600
Tranquility System Advisors, 90 — 801-967-0658
TRANS Pro Media, 141 — 212-989-4909
Translitera Media AB, 174 — 4618-12-56-30
TransPac Software, 57 — 408-261-7550
Tree Frog Studio, 144 — 415-856-3764
Tree House Computer Services, 28, 141 — 713-356-7926
Tree Media Digital Music Services, 145 — 617-926-4502
Tresidder Ltd, 71 — 718-858-9407
Tri Com Computer Systems, 168 — 401-739-9347
Triad International Corporation, 84 — 612-832-5574
Trillium Business Learning, Inc., 84 — 408-879-0111
TriLogic, Inc., 84 — 206-784-3117
Trilogy Development Group, 38 — 512-794-5900
Trio Systems Europe, 168 — 020-638-6507
Triple Point, Inc., 84 — 503-531-2890
Tripos Associates Inc., 69 — 314-647-1099
Triticom, 168 — 612-937-0772
Trivium Computer Systems Inc., 106 — 514-335-9080
Trix Systems, 57 — 46-302-464 79
Tronca Associates Inc., 117 — 414-785-5544
Tronvision, 163 — 361-1358291

True Ware, 57 — 403-483-5934
TSP Software, 57 — 714-731-1368
TT Productions, 147 — 510-420-1630
TTJ Data Processing Services, Inc., 187 — 503-363-2693
Tuesday Software, 57 — 805-962-7889
Tuffet AntiGravity Inc., 57 — 519-672-5120
Tulane University, 191 — 504-862-8555
Tulip Software, 57 — 508-475-8711
Tumble Interactive Media, Inc., 147 — 212-316-0200
Turning Point Development, Inc., 118 — 803-219-2552
Turning Point Software, 24, **48, 58,** 63, **68, 70,**
    75, 77, **82,** 85, 90, 108 — 617-332-0202 ▣
TurnKey Computer Systems, Inc., 16, **36,** 37
     — 212-779-8445 ▣
Turtle Creek Software, 63 — 607-589-4471
Tutorland, 108 — 408-973-0472
TW DESIGN, 141 — 404-237-3958
Twilight & Barking, 58 — 602-759-0857
Two Twelve Associates, Inc., 147 — 212-925-6885

U

U.S. Computer, 106 — 408-446-0387
U.S. Media Group, 152 — 415-274-8555
UniPress Software, 165 — 908-287-2100
United Data Corporation, 159 — 415-750-8068
Univenture CD Packing & Storage, 122 — 800-992-8262
Universal Imaging Corporation, 58 — 215-344-9410
Universal Management Accounting, 58 — 818-366-8344
Universal Medsoft, Inc., 74 — 408-286-7880
University of Oregon, 191 — 503-725-3058
Unlimited Access, 24, 28, 95, **96,** 99, **135,** 142
     — 415-255-8958 ▣
Unlimited Ink, 95 — 210-629-7483
Up & Running Systems Ltd., 165 — 613-232-6050
Update & More, 176 — 512-328-4621
Urban Software, 58 — 206-720-0590
User Active Media, 151 — 208-883-5548
User Group Connection, **119,** 121 — 408-461-5725
Using It buba, 179 — 32 2 230 02 21

V

V/March, Inc., 145 — 408-365-860
Valad Data Solutions, Inc., 95 — 703-820-4026
Valence, Inc., 144, 147, 174, 177 — 415-435-9252
Van Nostrand Reinhold, **87,** 109 — 800-544-0550
Vandellos Studios, 145 — 415-574-8446
Vanguard Media, 110 — 212-242-5317
Vanguard Research Inc., 58 — 703-934-6300
Varcon Systems Inc., 63 — 619-563-6700
Vector Systems, 85 — 219-478-8088
Vent, 110 — 408-559-4015
Ventana Studio, 180 — 619-751-2632
Ventura College & La Vie, 147 — 805-654-6400
Ventura Community College, 151 — 805-648-8906
Veridian, 150 — 415-386-0429
Vermont Software, 118 — 802-584-4020
Vernier Software, 65 — 503-297-5317
VGC Corporation, 167 — 714-639-1101
Victor Consulting, 90 — 415-964-9870
Video Arts Inc., 149 — 415-546-0331
Video Images, 123 — 414-785-8998
Video Simulations, 147 — 212-663-6812
Video-It Post, 149 — 310-280-0505
Videomation, 118 — 408-988-6100
Viewpoint Animation Engineering, 144 — 801-224-2222
Viewpoint Consulting, Inc., 103 — 313-647-9145
Vineyard Software, 58 — 714-930-1724
Vinko Enterprises, 58 — 905-338-7836
Vintage Consulting Group, **83,** 85, 95 — 707-939-8387 ▣
Virginia Systems, Inc., 72 — 804-739-3200
Viridis, **138,** 142 — 310-445-2055
Virtual Beauty, 142 — 212-675-0699
Virtual Company Visits, Inc., 152 — 415-777-3438
Virtual Image Inc., 99 — 508-772-4225
Virtual Reality Labs, 112 — 805-545-8515
Viscon, 63 — 214-422-8313
Vision Chips, 74 — 714-831-1994
Visions Edge, Inc., 77 — 904-386-4573
Visions Software, Inc., 25, 58, **67, 84,** 90, 108
     — 617-246-6260
Visual Business Systems Inc., 175 — 404-956-0325
Visual Impact!, 142 — 313-583-2080

Visual Interface Design, 110 — 415-327-5352
Visual Logic, 142 — 302-234-5707
Visual Programming, Inc., 90 — 408-865-6690
Visual Solutions, 149 — 404-365-0839
Vital, **81**, 85, 90 — 206-354-8120
Vitale Software Group, 65 — 415-663-9520
Vivid Publishing, 174 — 415-949-4933
Vividus Corporation, 144 — 415-321-2221
ViviStar Consulting, 25, **69**, 90, **112**, — 602-483-3123 ▣
Voldstad Interactive Design, **92**, 142 — 408-733-4116

W

W. M. Treadway & Associates, Inc., 167 — 713-840-8921
Wabash Medical Resources Inc., 74 — 317-579-5900
Wadsworth Data Systems AB, 102 — 46-42 140201
Wadsworth Publishing Company, 177 — 415-637-7528
Warever Computing, Inc., 29, **163** — 800-WAREVER ▣
Warner Cable, 145 — 414-963-1716
Warner-Cotter, 180 — 415-441-4011
Warren-Forthought, Inc., 63 — 409-849-1239
Wave Technologies Training, Inc., 121 — 314-878-2050
WaveForms, 142 — 510-848-2143
WaveMetrics, Inc., 69 — 503-620-3001
Waverly Software Design, 16, 38 — 413-322-4414 ▣
Way Cool Productions, 95 — 610-385-6080
Way Cool Productions, 142 — 518-346-3590
Wayne Media Group, 147 — 49-89-3595904
Wayne Norman Inc., 60 — 415-738-8475
Wayzata Technology, 153 — 218-326-0597
WegWeiser Macintosh Consulting, 100 — 617-945-3224
Weingarten Gallery, 77 — 513-435-0134
Wessex Corporation, 36 — 214-384-2894
West Side Electronics Inc., 85 — 818-884-4794
West Valley Engineering, Inc., **83**, 85, **89**, 90, **137**, 142, 148, 163, **164** — 408-744-1420
Western Software Associates, 63 — 510-932-3999
Wette Enterprises, 92 — 314-863-1248
WFT, 69 — 303-321-1119
White & Cromer Public Relations, 121 — 415-354-8800
White Creek Software, 95, **107, 172**, 174 — 518-686-1760
White Crow Software Inc., 63 — 802-658-1270
White Oak Software, 58 — 415-637-0222
White Pine Software, Inc., 58 — 603-886-9050
Wildware, 28, **146**, 151 — 415-367-3682 ▣
Wilkes University ITEC Center, 65 — 717-824-4651
William K. Bradford Publishing Company, Inc., 65 — 508-263-6996
William M. Mercer, Inc., 37 — 708-317-7615
William Rush Voice Consultants, 117 — 708-328-1753
Williams Cadco, 69 — 800-321-9193
Willow Solutions, 58 — 203-777-5634
WillStein Software, Inc., 58 — 708-256-2895
Wiltshire Computer Management, 106 — 207-967-2226
Windhorse Productions, 142 — 902-492-4523
Windom Health Enterprises, 74 — 510-848-6980
Winehouse Computer Company, 167 — 408-354-2500
Winston Advertising Inc., 116 — 408-982-3830
Winthrop-Lawrence Corporation, 58 — 413-786-0041
Wintress Engineering, 69 — 619-550-7300
WIS Computer Systems, 99 — 206-575-0965
Wisconsin Technical College System Foundation Incorporated, 151 — 608-849-2400
Wisdom Ware, 148 — 415-574-2683
Wizard Computers, 99 — 415-365-3818
Wizard Software, 103 — 216-582-0582
Wizard Works, 189 — 303-665-7085
Wizdom Micro Systems, Inc., 25, 95, **96** — 602-567-5011 ▣
WM Associates, 60 — 415-366-1548
WMP NJ Software, 58 — 206-578-9597
Wolf, Greenfield & Sacks, 118 — 617-720-3500
Wonderplay Inc., 142 — 212-595-7894
Wong, Pamela L., Macintosh Consulting Services, 30, **189**, 191 — 415-388-9668 ▣
Wood River Gallery, 148 — 415-388-6500
Woodbridge Information Solutions, 65 — 415-424-9051
Word Associates, Inc., 177 — 708-291-1101
Word Master, Inc., **103**, 104, 108 — 708-948-9600
WordPlay Communications, 179 — 505-243-6001
WordPlay Communications, 179 — 510-841-5858
Words & Deeds, 70 — 408-294-2974
WORDSTATION GmbH, **109**, 111 — 49-6102 31095
Wordswork, 179 — 415-826-4716
Wordwright Associates, 116 — 512-696-6868
Work Improvement Technologies Inc., 58 — 201-292-2736
Working Computer, 60 — 619-945-4334

Working Software Inc., 62 — 408-423-5696
WorkPlace, 25, **57**, 60 — 818-407-0010 ▣
Workstation Technologies, Inc., 149 — 714-250-8983
World Benders, Inc., 165 — 603-881-5432
World Company, 74 — 815-633-9205
World Ready Software, 109 — 415-957-1300
Worldata, 119 — 407-393-8200
Worthington Software Engineering, Inc., 104 — 612-525-5901
WOW Control Technology, 58 — 040-511-662
WPA Film Library, 176 — 708-535-1540
Wright Information Indexing Services, **176**, 179, 180 — 206-784-2895
Write Design, 179 — 503-648-7431
WSC, Inc., 60 — 800-776-5924
Wys System Ltd., 177 — 852-529-1831

X

X-Ray Scanner Corporation, 78 — 310-214-1900
Xante Corporation, 78 — 800-926-8839
Xenon Communications Corporation, 150 — 708-577-7057
Xerox Special Information Services, 108 — 818-351-2351
XMAN, 78 — 415-626-3359
Xpand, 177 — 408-279-8655
Xperience Consulting Inc., 58 — 408-983-1177
Xram Xpert Systems, 100 — 212-989-8559

Y

Yale University School of Medicine Biomedical Media Production, 90 — 203-785-4088
YARC Systems Corporation, 108 — 805-499-9444
Yellow Shark Software, 109 — 46-8-333-593
Yoh Information Technology Associates, 58 — 408-956-1611

Z

Z Mac Software Solutions, 58 — 206-448-4929
Zantos Control Systems, 165 — 714-960-9530
Zayante Creek Productions, 75 — 408-335-7412
Zeik Consulting, **56**, 58 — 201-444-5800
Zephron Corporation, 85 — 206-778-8396
Zeta Data, 179 — 603-643-6103

Zicon Software Corporation, 99 — 503-635-9622
Ziegler Ross, Inc., 165 — 415-386-0501
Zihua, 90 — 408-372-0155
Zocalo Engineering, 29, 165 — 510-540-8000 ▣
Zola Technologies Inc., 145 — 404-843-2972
Zona Corporation, 144 — 508-465-9632
Zuffoletto & Company, 71 — 415-543-8900
Zumwalt Environmental Systems, 69 — 310-375-7734
Zytech Marketing Party Ltd., 109 — 619-791-3622
ZZYZX Visual Systems, **146,** 152, 153 — 800-995-1025

Alabama

CUSTOM SOLUTIONS
Birmingham — Southern Computer Systems — 30
DEVELOPMENT & PROGRAMMING
Birmingham — KillerBytes Software — 74
Homewood — MonkWorks — 53
Mobile — Xante Corporation — 78
MULTIMEDIA
Birmingham — Adventures for Gifted & Talented, Inc. — 147
Birmingham — Digital Media Solutionz — 131
Huntsville — JAYCOR — 135
Huntsville — Morgan Research Corporation — 138
PUBLISHING
Huntsville — Third Wave Technologies, Inc. — 175
SUPPORT
Anchorage — Communications Software, Inc. — 187

Alaska

DEVELOPMENT & PROGRAMMING
Anchorage — Practical Computer Solutions, Inc. — 94

Arkansas

DEVELOPMENT & PROGRAMMING
Fort Smith — Gallaher & Associates, Inc. — 73
Hot Springs — Engineered Software Solutions Corporation — 90
MARKETING & DISTRIBUTION
Little Rock — Jann Greenland Communications — 119

MULTIMEDIA

Conway	Synthesis, Inc	145

PUBLISHING

Little Rock	H. K. Stewart Creative Services	173

Arizona

CUSTOM SOLUTIONS

Glendale	LRM Consultants International, LC	
		37
Mesa	American Software	36
Phoenix	corder associates, inc.	38
Tucson	ELB Consulting	**36**, 117

DEVELOPMENT & PROGRAMMING

Lake Montezuma	Wizdom Micro Systems, Inc.	
	25, 95, **96**	
Mesa	Concurrent Engineering Tools Inc.	
	19, 65	
Phoenix	AmeriChem Engineering Services Inc.	
		72
Phoenix	B-TEK	101
Phoenix	Desert Sky Software, Inc.	96
Phoenix	JP Imaging	79
Phoenix	MAX STAX, et cetera	64
Phoenix	MData Inc.	62
Phoenix	Paradise Software Corporation	53
Phoenix	The Dawson Group	57
Phoenix	Twilight & Barking	58
Scottsdale	Black & Ryan Engineering	65
Scottsdale	Cito, Inc.	70
Scottsdale	IC Optometrology Inc.	66
Scottsdale	Mastersoft Inc.	52
Scottsdale	Pensee Corporation	62
Scottsdale	ViviStar Consulting	
	25, **69**, 90, **112**	
Tempe	Class One Incorporated	73
Tempe	Evolution Computing	49
Tempe	Precision Computer Systems	53
Tempe	Re: Software	82
Tucson	Abacot Information Systems	43
Tucson	GEO Computing Systems	90
Tucson	HDS Systems	88
Tucson	MikroLogix Software Inc.	64

MARKETING & DISTRIBUTION

Tucson	ELB Consulting	**36**, 117
Phoenix	Cactus Computer Service	116
Phoenix	Modern Lines	38

MULTIMEDIA

Phoenix	EAR Professional Audio/Video	149
Phoenix	Khalsa Productions	136
Tempe	Communication Design	130
Tucson	Mediaware Development Group Inc.	
		149
Tucson	The Katherine Company	147

NETWORKING

Carefree	Corporate Advisory Group	163
Gilbert	MacWizards	164
Phoenix	Computer Advantage	166
Scottsdale	CalComp Digitizer Products Group	166
Tucson	Innovative System Design Ltd.	163

PUBLISHING

Chandler	Page Studio Graphics	179
Phoenix	Redrock Software Corporation	177
Sedona	Charles Rubin	178
Tempe	Merex Corporation	178
Thatcher	Synergetics	188

SUPPORT

Phoenix	Mac To School	190

California

CUSTOM SOLUTIONS

Agoura Hills	The Alternate Approach	38, **55**, 57
Alameda	Interlinear Technology, Inc.	36
Aptos	Rod Williams Resource Group	38
Berkeley	Bear River Associates, Inc.	
	16, 17, **36**, **38**, 43, **44**, **59**, 60, **86**, 90,	
	91, **98**, 99, **103**, 104, **105**, 106, 107,	
	108, **159**, **164**, 166, **167**, **168**, 188,	
	190	
Irvine	LeadingWay Corporation	38
Irvine	Read Technologies, Inc.	54
Palo Alto	Waverley Software Design	16, 38
San Diego	RSG International	37
San Francisco	Chrones Software, Inc.	45
San Francisco	Larry Wisch Associates	37
San Gabriel	Go Technology, Inc.	36
San Jose	Magna	38, **50**, 52, 186, 187

DEVELOPMENT & PROGRAMMING

Agoura Hill	The Alternate Approach	38, **55**, 57
Agoura Hills	Mainstay	62
Alamo	Alamo Computer	17, **86**, 110
Aliso Viejo	Memory International	77
Altadena	Baccus & Associates	99
Anaheim	Alpha Omega Systems Corporation	43
Anaheim	Cornerstone Data Systems	47
Anaheim	Dargon Development	66
Anaheim	Enlightened Software Corporation	90
Anaheim	Molecular Arts Corporation	**52**, 53
Anaheim	TaskMan Business Systems	95
Anaheim Hills	Golden Empire Publications	69
Aptos	n Dimensions Software House	53
Aptos	The Pacific Group	62
Atherton	Physicians' Educational Series	74
Belmont	Gary J. Hardy, Inc.	90
Ben Lomond	Dynamic Engineering	85
Berkeley	A. E. Wood Consulting	99
Berkeley	Bear River Associates, Inc. 16, 17, **36**, 38, 43, **44**, **59**, 60, **86**, 90, 91, **98**, 99, **103**, 104, **105**, 106, 107, **108**, **159**, **164**, 166, **167**, **168**, **188**, 190	
Berkeley	CCIC System Pacifica 108, **111**, 123, 160, **162**, **165**, 166	
Berkeley	CoDesign	107
Berkeley	Elefunt Software	103
Berkeley	Fresh Software & Instructional	20, 50
Berkeley	MetaTheory	64
Berkeley	MindStorm, Inc.	22, 81
Berkeley	Sibony & Associates	100
Berkeley	SoftMaven	92
Berkeley	Software Farm	56
Berkeley	Windom Health Enterprises	74
Beverly Hills	Chaparral Software	103
Brisbane	Balzer/Shopes Inc.	75
Burbank	Technique	102
Burlingame	The Decisionworks	71
Camarillo	Compas Technologies	96
Camarillo	SYSTEM REENG Inc.	95
Camino	Mountain Data Works	191
Campbell	Icon Medical Systems, Inc.	73
Campbell	IM Strategies	97
Campbell	Trillium Business Learning, Inc.	84
Campbell	Vent	110
Canoga Park	West Side Electronics Inc.	85
Capitola	E. J. Systems	105
Cardiff	Intuitive Design Engineering	110
Carlsbad	Biocomp	86
Carmel	Rhyton Software	23, 107
Chatsworth	Absolute Advantage, Inc.	65
Concord	Innovative Data Design, Inc.	63
Concord	Investment Research Institute	71
Concord	Maconsult	81
Costa Mesa	Maxwell Data Management, Inc.	77
Costa Mesa	QuickSilver Software, Inc.	92
Costa Mesa	Texceed Corporation	69
Costa Mesa	Vision Chips	74
Culver City	Lieberman & Associates	69
Cupertino	ACI US, Inc.	95
Cupertino	AI Consultants, Inc.	90
Cupertino	**Apple Computer Development Group** 43	
Cupertino	Berumen & Associates	90
Cupertino	Beta Research Inc.	110
Cupertino	CST Consulting	96
Cupertino	Microspot	68
Cupertino	Oakleaf Designs	81
Cupertino	Oxford & Associates Inc.	89
Cupertino	Rae Technology, Inc.	23, 94, **95**
Cupertino	S2 Software	**76**, 98
Cupertino	Sequel Development Corporation	54
Cupertino	SoftAnswer	55
Cupertino	Software Transformation Inc.	108
Cupertino	Symantec Corporation	57
Cupertino	The VITAL Consulting Network	60
Cupertino	Tutorland	108
Cupertino	Visual Programming, Inc.	90
Cypress	ESOFT	49
Danville	Fashoro Langhill Inc.	61
Danville	Hutchings Software Development	88
East Palo Alto	Alabanza Consulting	**92**, 106
El Segundo	Aura CAD/CAM, Inc.	65
El Segundo	Netcetera	81
El Segundo	Simetra Systems	24, 62
Elk Grove	Informant Communications Group **45**, 51, 161, **162**	

Encinitas	STM Languages, Enterprises	89
Englewood	Access Technologies, Inc.	78
Escondido	In Software	77
Escondido	MacSourcery	21, 81
Escondido	Pixel Perfect	77
Escondido	The Garrison Group	74
Felton	Zayante Creek Productions	75
Forest Knolls	Entropy	88
Foster City	Rhythm Technology	54
Fountain Valley	Impact Communication Group	107
Fountain Valley	Master Trainers' Consortium	191
Fremont	Desjardin Consulting	19, 96
Fremont	P. A. Christenson	82
Fremont	Professional Systems International	53
Fullerton	ESS Development Company	49
Glendale	In Phase Consulting	**49**, 50
Goleta	BIOPAC Systems Inc.	73
Goleta	Interactive Software Engineering	51
Granada Hills	HyperProject, Inc.	88
Granada Hills	The Dreamers Guild Inc.	70
Hermosa Beach	Business Solutions	96
Highland	OmniVision	82
Huntington Beach	Archway Systems	90
Huntington Beach	Jack Irby Consulting	71
Inverness	Bob Harris Consulting	59
Irvine	Bishop Development	44
Irvine	Custom Software Inc.	47
Irvine	Digital Thought	96
Irvine	Digital Vision Design & Automation	63
Irvine	Green Tree Software	72
Irvine	MicroComputer Technologies, Inc.	71
Irvine	OnBase Technology, Inc.	72
Irvine	Platinum Software Corporation	71
Irvine	Qube Software, Inc.	72
Irvine	Read Technologies, Inc.	54
Irvine	Sonnet Technologies, Inc.	100
Irvine	TSP Software	57
La Jolla	American Retail Consultants	92
Lafayette	Logisoft Inc.	104
Lafayette	Master Software Inc.	22, **50**, 52, **78**, 81
Lafayette	Roy Posner & Associates	103
Laguna Beach	DFC Enterprises Inc.	20, 101
Laguna Hills	Second Glance	77
Laguna Niguel	BlackMax	99
Lakewood	SophisTech Research	112
Livermore	Bernstein Design Services	65
Livermore	CPSA	107
Livermore	Molecular Solutions	89
Livermore	Problem Solving Tools	68
Long Beach	Super School Software	65
Los Altos	BAL Associates Inc.	107
Los Altos	EMA Software	64
Los Altos	Menlo Business Systems, Inc	62.
Los Angeles	Demometricka	19, 93
Los Angeles	Diehl.Volk Typographics	76
Los Angeles	Entertainment Solutions, Inc.	69
Los Angeles	IDOC, an International Documentation Company	109
Los Angeles	Interval Music Systems	88
Los Angeles	Modability Inc.	77
Los Angeles	MODACAD	63
Los Angeles	Slippery Disks	55
Los Angeles	Synergy Group	87
Los Angeles	The Interface Experts	57
Los Gatos	Bimillennium Corporation	65
Los Gatos	Paradigm Trading Systems	71
Los Gatos	Raymond Software Inc.	72
Los Gatos	Symbionics	90
Los Osos	Copious Systems	19, **46**, 47, **86**, 87
Manhattan Beach	Husk	79
Marina Del Rey	Prana Computing Inc.	53
Mariposa	Stonecutter Software	24, 56
Menlo Park	GreenSpring Computers	72
Menlo Park	Heidi C. Bowman, CPA	70
Menlo Park	Quorum Software Systems	107
Menlo Park	Robertson Associates	54
Menlo Park	Visual Interface Design	110
Middletown	Softweaver	32
Mill Valley	DataBright Management Systems	103
Mill Valley	Graphic Data Designs	103
Mill Valley	Greco & Associates	109
Mill Valley	Simple Software Development Company	55
Mill Valley	Tokerud Consulting Group	100
Milpitas	Korody-Coleman, Inc.	85
Mission Viejo	Acrobyte Software	99
Mission Viejo	Coyne Company	61

Mission Viejo	Lighthouse Technology	80
Modesto	DirectLine Technologies, Inc.	103
Modesto	Ed-Sci Development	79
Modesto	Robert F. Miller & Associates	94
Mohandessin	Arabic Information Systems	60
Monterey	LinksWare	88
Monterey	Sea Studios	65
Moor Park	Gibbs & Associates	72
Moorpark	Computer Results	87
Morgan Hill	BlackHawk Technology	65
Morgan Hill	Imagination Solutions Corporation	
	93, **159**, 166	
Mountain View	Brio Technology Inc.	61
Mountain View	MegaBase Inc.	94
Mountain View	PinPoint Solutions	23, 94, **95**, 98,
	99, **100**, 105, 106	
Mountain View	Ray Dream Inc.	77
Mountain View	Robert S. Lenoil	83
Mountain View	**Silicon Graphics Computer Systems**	
	54	
Mountain View	Victor Consulting	90
N. Hollywood	Spellbinder Systems Group	84
Napa	Napa Valley Computing Company	53
Nevada City	Breakthrough Productions	103
Newbury Park	YARC Systems Corporation	108
Newport Beach	Richards Consulting Enterprises	74
Northridge	Universal Management Accounting	
	58	
Novato	Chris Forden	86
Novato	Michael J. Harper	94
Novato	Small Business Computer Solutions	98
Oakland	EDP Consulting, Inc.	48
Oakland	Immersive Technologies	112
Oakland	Kansas Bay Systems, Inc.	62
Oakland	KidWare	107
Oakland	Montclair Data Services Corporation	
	105	
Oakland	The Soft Programer	84
Oceanside	Working Computer	60
Ontario	Vineyard Software	58
Orange	Career Publishing Incorporated	64
Orange	Data Technologies International	72
Orange	Ford Consulting	90
Orinda	Maxis	69
Oxnard	Maron Computer Services	74
Pacific Grove	Altura Software Inc.	106
Pacific Grove	Brooks/Cole Publishing Company	64
Pacific Grove	Zihua	90
Pacifica	Blue Tree Technology Inc.	86
Pacifica	Wayne Norman Inc.	60
Palo Alto	Arcadia Designs	110, **112**, 147
Palo Alto	AwareTech Design	92
Palo Alto	Charles B. Olson & Associates	105
Palo Alto	Grove Engineering--	
	A BWNT Company	66
Palo Alto	Stewart Carl Engineering	110
Palo Alto	Woodbridge Information Solutions	65
Pasadena	AceNet	17, 43
Pasadena	ASD, Inc.	101
Pasadena	CDBS-The Software Wizards	45
Pasadena	Help!	173
Pasadena	Natural Interface Lab	64
Pasadena	Neurodata Inc.	74
Pasadena	Off Key Microsystems	98
Pasadena	Tanner Research, Inc.	63
Pasadena	The Decision Support Group Inc.	74
Pasadena	Xerox Special Information Services	108
Petaluma	Seaborne Woodworking	60
Playa del Rey	JGI	79
Pleasanton	Prosoft Engineering Inc.	53, 54, 80, 82
Point Reyes Station	Vitale Software Group	65
Rancho Santa		
Marguerita	GroundZero Software Solutions	103
Redlands	Calliope Enterprises Inc.	86
Redlands	MedComp Consultants	101
Redondo Beach	Architectronica	90
Redondo Beach	PowerTraining	101
Redondo Beach	PSC Consultants	82
Redwood City	Brodie Lockard	69
Redwood City	Redwolf	82
Redwood City	Wizard Computers	99
Redwood City	WM Associates	60
Richmond	The VALIS Group	77
Riverside	NOVA Electronics & Software	53
Rohnert Park	Goodall Software Engineering	79
Sacramento	7 Star Computer Solutions	95
Sacramento	Laserpoint	77

San Anselmo	Ganesa Designs Inc.	90
San Anselmo	Masterplans	60
San Anselmo	Roy Sablosky Design	103
San Bernardino	Health Data Sciences Corporation	73
San Bruno	Bio-Logic, Inc.	73
San Carlos	Class Software	78
San Carlos	Elisabeth Waymire	110
San Carlos	Penny Bauersfeld Human Interface Design	110
San Carlos	Sentient Software	54
San Carlos	White Oak Software	55
San Diego	Acquired Knowledge Inc.	63
San Diego	Arcade Fonts	172
San Diego	CONSTAR	61
San Diego	Digital Science Corporation	48
San Diego	DreamTime™	48
San Diego	Engineerium	79
San Diego	KASA	88
San Diego	Medical Database Systems	22, 94
San Diego	NeuWorld Services	81
San Diego	Ocean Beach Communications	53
San Diego	Pacific Science & Engineering Group	110
San Diego	Quadrature	65
San Diego	RTS Corporation	83
San Diego	SoftEngine	24, **54**, 55
San Diego	Superset '93 Inc.	57
San Diego	Techbridge, Inc.	84
San Diego	Technology Locator	84
San Diego	Varcon Systems Inc.	63
San Diego	Williams Cadco	69
San Diego	Wintress Engineering	69
San Francisco	Albathion Software Inc.	64
San Francisco	All Star Computer Services	85
San Francisco	Allied Support	60
San Francisco	Chronos Software, Inc.	45
San Francisco	Digital Media Reality Labs	112
San Francisco	DNS, Inc.	88
San Francisco	Elrick & Lavidge	110
San Francisco	Finnegan O'Malley & Company Inc.	79
San Francisco	GEOPOINT Software	50
San Francisco	Globus Systems, Inc.	97
San Francisco	Human Resource Microsystems	62
San Francisco	Integrated Accounting Systems	71
San Francisco	InterOptica Publishing Limited	21, 107
San Francisco	Inventure Inc.	51
San Francisco	Jennie's Code Boutique	92
San Francisco	MacDesigns	97
San Francisco	Media In Motion	64
San Francisco	Micromega Systems, Inc.	94
San Francisco	NeoLogic Systems	89
San Francisco	Open Designs, Inc.	82
San Francisco	Oryx Associates	98
San Francisco	Prescience Corporation	68
San Francisco	Recommended Test Labs, Inc.	82
San Francisco	RJM Systems, Inc.	54
San Francisco	San Francisco Canyon Company Inc.	54
San Francisco	SFC Desktop Business Systems	94, **101**, 104
San Francisco	Shoestring Engineering	60
San Francisco	Soothsong	92
San Francisco	Spherix Software	98
San Francisco	SRS Integral, Inc.	100
San Francisco	Stow Lake Software	56
San Francisco	The Automation Group	95
San Francisco	Unlimited Access	95, **96**, 99
San Francisco	World Ready Software	109
San Francisco	XMAN	78
San Francisco	Zuffoletto & Company	71
San Jose	Accolade, Inc.	65
San Jose	Concept 2001	70
San Jose	Imagine That, Inc.	72
San Jose	Jeddak	62
San Jose	North Mountain Software	104
San Jose	Sequent Associates	54
San Jose	Skoog Software & Consulting	68
San Jose	Systec Computer Services	74
San Jose	Tellan Software, Inc.	71
San Jose	TransPac Software	57
San Jose	Universal Medsoft, Inc.	74
San Jose	Words & Deeds	70
San Jose	Yoh Information Technology Association.	58
San Juan Capistrano	Power Services of Ne Inc.	103
San Leandro	The Sleeter Group	**61**, **62**, **92**

San Luis Obispo	Virtual Reality Labs	112
San Marcos	Adept Solutions	75
San Mateo	Deltam Systems, Incorporated	47
San Mateo	Power Up Software Corporation	63
San Rafael	3D TV Corporation/Stereo Scopic Video	112
San Rafael	Opus Systems	98
San Rafael	Technology & Learning Magazine	65
Santa Barbara	Desktop Information	72
Santa Barbara	EDGE Environmental Development Group	79
Santa Barbara	Morton Associates Inc.	68
Santa Barbara	Shapiro & Company	23, 106
Santa Barbara	Tuesday Software	57
Santa Clara	CAPCOM USA Inc.	108
Santa Clara	Crystal Graphics Inc.	76
Santa Clara	FIT Software	61
Santa Clara	Integra Technologies Inc.	51
Santa Clara	Mark/Space Softworks	88
Santa Clara	Signal Science, Inc.	71
Santa Clara	Xperience Consulting Inc.	53
Santa Cruz	AMCI	112
Santa Cruz	Arturo Droguett	108
Santa Cruz	Central Coast Software	45
Santa Cruz	International Accessability Corporation	21, 109, **111**
Santa Cruz	Pacific Systems, Inc.	89
Santa Cruz	Software by Mann	83
Santa Cruz	ThinkThink	110
Santa Cruz	Working Software Inc.	62
Santa Monica	Fine Artist's Color & Ink	76
Santa Monica	Los Angeles Software Inc.	80
Santa Monica	M.I.B. Chock	52
Santa Monica	North Communications	62
Santa Rosa	Strong/Tyler Systems	98
Saratoga	U.S. Computer	106
Scotts Valley	The Technical Edge	57
Sebastopol	Chertov & Associates	101
Sebastopol	Cheshire Group	18, 78
Sebastopol	Shireman Software	90
Sherman Oaks	Art & Logic	16, 17, 26, **38**, **43**, **44**, 83, 85, 107, **109**, **129**, 130, 149
Sherman Oaks	Goldsoft Corporation	62
Sherman Oaks	ISIS International, Inc.	62
Sierra Madre	EPIC Systems Group Inc.	66
Simi Valley	Bitworks	86
Sonoma	Vintage Consulting Group	85, **87**, 95
Stamford	Envisage Ltd.	107
Sun City	AcutAbove Software	69
Sunnyvale	Charles Rogers & Associates Inc.	96
Sunnyvale	Claude J. Pany	45, **46**
Sunnyvale	Dapple Systems	66
Sunnyvale	Frederic M. Fowler & Assoc., Inc.	50
Sunnyvale	Inter/Action	91
Sunnyvale	Langley Autosystems	88
Sunnyvale	P.L. Kelly Engineering	68
Sunnyvale	Second Nature	92
Sunnyvale	Strawberry Tree, Inc.	72
Sunnyvale	Voldstad Interactive Design	**92**, 142
Sunnyvale	West Valley Engineering, Inc.	**83**, 85, **89**, 90, **137**, 142, 148, 163, **164**
Torrance	JTZ Engineering, Inc.	79
Torrance	X-Ray Scanner Corporation	78
Torrance	Zumwalt Environmental Systems	69
Truckee	NoteTaker Software	62
Turlock	Solutions Unlimited	104
Union City	Productivity Through Technology	51, 53
Upland	TNT Computing	57
Van Nuys	After Hours Software	92
Van Nuys	Howard Goldstein Design	112
Ventura	Dart Computing	96
Walnut Creek	PowerHouse Programmers	23, 67, 82
Walnut Creek	Western Software Associates	63
West Hollywood	Schindler Imaging	70
Woodacre	Castle Rock Software Development	45
Woodacre	Sean Hill Software Development	70
Woodland Hills	Berlitz International	108
Woodland Hills	Big Badge Productions	178
Woodland Hills	Dubl-Click Software Corporation	48
Woodland Hills	WorkPlace	25, **57**, 60
Woodside	Focal Point Systems, Inc.	79
Woodside	Kinetic Software Inc.	112

MARKETING & DISTRIBUTION

Alameda	The Hartsook Letter	120

Berkeley	Bay Graphics Design Inc.	119
Berkeley	CCIC System Pacifica	
	108, **111**, 123, 160, **162, 165**, 166	
Berkeley	General Parametrics	116
Berkeley	Goodlove & Moon	116
Berkeley	Griffin Dix Research Associates	120
Berkeley	Hunza Graphics	118
Berkeley	JPD Communications	**119**, 120
Campbell	CKS Partners	118
Campbell	Deborah Designs	119
Canoga Park	Grafica	119
Chatsworth	Baker & Taylor Software	123
Concord	Golden Gate Tax Service	117
Corte Madera`	Schweichler Associates, Inc.	121
Cupertino	Business Builders	118
Cupertino	Cogar, Melton & Associates	116
Cupertino	Planning Showcase	121
El Segundo	MaxSacks International	
	Professional Selling Clinic	121
Emeryville	New Science InterActive	118
Fairfax	Dennis Trager Associates	116
Fairfax	Multimedia Specialists	123
Foster City	Pillar Corporation	118
Foster City	Technology Inc.	117
Garden Grove	California Marketing Group	116
Half Moon Bay	Kearney Rietmann	121
Hayward	PSE Network Distribution Systems	119
Hillsborough	Elizabeth A. Strode	117
Hollywood	Bradley Group	123
Irvine	Gallup Organization	120
Irvine	Read Technologies, Inc.	54
Kensington	Tactical Marketing Group	116
Laguna Hills	Aster Services	119
Long Beach	McHale Design	121
Long Beach	Summit Business Systems-Macromedia	
Los Altos	Block Communications 118, **142**, 148	
Los Altos	Image Architects Computer	
	Graphic Slides	116
Los Altos	Live Marketing	117
Los Altos	Piic	121
Los Altos Hills	Crossfield Marketing	117
Los Angeles	Inbody Bruck & Company Advertising	
		116
Los Angeles	Maddocks & Company	121

Los Angeles	Peggi Sturm & Associates	123
Menlo Park	Crimson Consulting Group	121
Menlo Park	Olson & Company Strategy &	
	Marketing	117
Menlo Park	smartNET Marketing Connections	
	118, 119	
Milpitas	Calico Subscription Company	116
Monterey	Alexander & Lord	118
Mountain View	Ariel PSS Corporation	121
Mountain View	Sales Systems Development Inc.	117
Mountain View	Show & Tell Systems, Inc.	118
Oakland	Hunter Mail	118
Oakland	Marketing Research &	
	Consultant Services	121
Oakland	StrategicMedia	117
Palo Alto	Computer Learning Foundation	120
Palo Alto	Engineering Software Concepts, Inc.	
		121
Palo Alto	Fortune & Associates	25, 116
Palo Alto	Johnson Direct Advertising	118
Palo Alto	MWA Consulting	122
Palo Alto	Success Stories by Kris Newby	116
Palo Alto	The Adams Company	120
Palo Alto	White & Cromer Public Relations	121
Redwood City	Acknowledge Solutions	**122**, 178
Redwood City	Bindco	123
Rohnert Park	Direct Mailing Systems	118
South Pasadena	Land Graphics	120
San Carlos	Motivation Consultants Inc.	121
San Diego	Jack Fox Associates	117
San Diego	Progressive Allied Marketing Inc.	121
San Diego	Reardon & Wynn Associates	117
San Francisco	Addison Design	120
San Francisco	Albert Frank-Guenther Law	116
San Francisco	BBDO	116
San Francisco	Clement Mok Designs, Inc.	
	117, **119, 130**	
San Francisco	Earl Office	119
San Francisco	Hewitt/Katona International	121
San Francisco	Hi-Tech Public Relations Inc.	121
San Francisco	MacDaniels Henry & Sproul Inc.	121
San Francisco	Miller/Kadanoff Promotional	
	Marketing, Inc. 22, **59**, 60, 62, 119	
San Francisco	SMG: Consulting	117

San Francisco	The Ambit Group/	
	TAG's Channel Compass	123
San Francisco	The Pacific Marketing Group	119
San Jose	G. A. Bell & Associates	121
San Jose	Munday & Collins Rents	117
San Jose	Pacifico Inc.	116
San Jose	PRX Inc.	116
San Jose	Softrade International	86, 109, 120
San Mateo	McLean Public Relations	121
San Mateo	NVision3	120, 133, 136, 138
San Rafael	ADF Research	120
San Rafael	Marriner Associates	117
San Rafael	RSVP Publications	119
Santa Ana	Infotec Training Institute	121
Santa Ana	Michael Brandman Associates	120
Santa Barbara	MacTimes	118
Santa Clara	Access Education	117
Santa Clara	Creative Strategies Research	
	International	120
Santa Clara	Cunningham Communication, Inc.	
		121
Santa Clara	Lindsay Public Relations	121
Santa Clara	Pearson Communications Group	119
Santa Clara	Videomation	118
Santa Clara	Winston Advertising Inc.	116
Santa Cruz	Alben & Faris	119
Santa Cruz	Market Vision	120
Santa Fe Springs	Extron Electronics	116
Santa Monica	Kalb & Associates	117
Santa Rosa	Morgan Consulting Group	121
Sausalito	Carew Design	119
Scotts Valley	User Group Connection	119, 121
Solana Beach	Nisus Software	123
Sunnyvale	Endpoint Marketing	
	Information Systems	121
Sunnyvale	Hecht & Associates	121
Sunnyvale	Janal Communications	121
Upland	Cornice Graphics	121
Ventura	James Graca Design Group	119
Walnut Creek	Applied Business Communications	
	Inc.	116
Walnut Creek	Business & Technical	
	Communications	120
West Sacramento	JLH Direct Marketing	118

Westlake Village	Captured Images, Inc.	116
MULTIMEDIA		
Anaheim	Advanced Digital Imaging	148
Arcata	Redwood Software	140
Auburn	The American Multimedia Group	140
Belmont	Grafica Multimedia	133
Berkeley	Dan R. Sukiennik	143
Berkeley	InfoUse	26, 134
Berkeley	Peter Samis Art Services	146
Berkeley	WaveForms	142
Beverly Hills	Rosenfeld, Meyer & Susman	148
Burbank	21st Century Media	25, **151**
Burbank	Four Media Company	148
Burbank	Screenplay Systems	140
Burlingame	Maus Haus	144
Carson	ASR Recording	**143**, 144
Castro Valley	John Gammon Video Service	148
Chula Vista	3D Perception	147
Concord	Display Tech Multimedia, Inc.	148
Concord	Media Kinematics	137
Corona	Magneton Consulting	137
Culver City	Video-It Post	149
Cupertino	Mac Art Multimedia	136
Cupertino	Pixel Translations Inc.	147
Cypress	Sonic Byte	145
Danville	Multimedia Creation	144
Del Mar	Digital Vistas	132
Del Mar	Moov Design	138
El Granada	Medior Inc.	144
Emeryville	Aaron Marcus & Associates, Inc.	
		26, 147
Emeryville	The Hypermedia Group, Inc.	141
Encino	New Visions Media Works	138
Fairfax	EdgeWriter Film/Video Systems Inc.	
		149
Fairfax	The Resource	148
Felton	Lumigenic Media	136
Foster City	Wisdom Ware	148
Fremont	Cheryl L. Blundell	150
Fremont	Dale Komai	150
Fremont	Frame-by-Frame Media Services	133
Glendora	R & D Multimedia Productions	139
Grass Valley	Grass Valley Multimedia	133
Grass Valley	KnoSys	136

Half Moon Bay	Passport Designs, Inc.	145
Hayward	Computer Center of Hayward/San Jose	
		143
Irvine	After Hours Computer Group	129
Irvine	Procom Technology	153
Irvine	Workstation Technologies, Inc.	149
Lincoln	Claire Moore Instructional Design	
		26, 150
Long Beach	ASK International	146
Long Beach	Creative Enterprises	
	16, 19, **38**, 47, **129**, 130	
Long Beach	MultiTrain International	151
Los Altos	Parcway Software Inc.	139
Los Angeles	Anderson Soft Teach	150
Los Angeles	Bogner Entertainment Inc.	153
Los Angeles	Digital Development Corporation	149
Los Angeles	DigitalFacades Corporation	26, **131**
Los Angeles	DoremiLabs, Inc.	149
Los Angeles	Einstein's Bicycle	150
Los Angeles	Filmsonix, Inc.	145
Los Angeles	IME	146
Los Angeles	J. L.Cooper Electronics	135
Los Angeles	LeBlanc Design	136
Los Angeles	Leo Home Media	136
Los Angeles	Parallel Media	139
Los Angeles	R. Seide & Associates International	
		148
Los Angeles	Shardonnay Audio Visual, Inc.	153
Los Angeles	Silverberg, Katz, Thompson & Braun	
		148
Los Angeles	Sligo Video	152
Los Angeles	ZZYZX Visual Systems	**146**, 152, 153
Los Gatos	Ciphers	130
Los Gatos	Optical Media International	153
Malibu	Kasdin Productions	150
Menlo Park	CLE Group	150
Menlo Park	Wildware	**146**, 151
Mill Valley	Wood River Gallery	148
Monte Sereno	Easy Street Software	132
Morgan Hill	Koala Acquisitions, Inc.	149
Morgan Hill	Reflections Publishing, Inc.	152
Mountain View	Catalogic	153
Mountain View	David Anderson Consulting	147
Mt. Shasta	Andree R. Oreck	147
Newport Beach	SWeDE Corporation	140
North Hollywood	Learning Systems Sciences	150
Northridge	Greytsounds Sound Development	145
Northridge	Steinberg Jones	145
Novato	Broderbund Software	149
Novato	Inkman & Associates	134
Oakland	Elmo Productions	150
Oakland	Guillermo Pulido	148
Oakland	Hearing Voices	145
Oakland	Interdimensional Arts	134
Oakland	Judy Munsen	145
Oakland	Kallisto Productions, Inc.	135
Oakland	TT Productions	147
Orinda	**Morph's Outpost on the Digital**	
	Frontier	**42, 138**
Pacifica	Pulse Productions	145
Palo Alto	Animated Systems & Design	149
Palo Alto	Arcadia Designs	110, **111**, 147
Palo Alto	Avatar Numedia	150
Palo Alto	Cooley Godward	148
Palo Alto	DDLabs	150
Palo Alto	Dolphin Multimedia	26, **139**, 143
Palo Alto	HeyerTech-IICS	147
Palo Alto	Peter C. Reynolds & Associates	151
Palo Alto	Tree Frog Studio	144
Palo Alto	Vividus Corporation	144
Paradise	The Write Thing	151
Pasadena	Bussard & Associates	152
Pasadena	Electric Image, Incorporated	143
Petaluma	Adamsound	144
Pleasant Hill	Premier Design	147
Pleasant Hill	EXEGI	150
Pleasanton	Individual Software	150
Pleasanton	Parallax Technologies	146
Rancho Palos Verdes	Live Wire Productions™	144
Redondo Beach	Interface International	
	Communications	**140,** 148
Redwood City	Ames & Associates	144
Redwood City	Health & Education	
	Communication Consultants	150
Redwood City	Rodney Vaughan Associates	144
Redwood City	Schubert Media Design	151
Sacramento	Hill Productions	133

San Anselmo	Amazing Media	129
San Anselmo	Fulcrum Media Services	146
San Anselmo	Morphonix	138
San Bruno	Solar Systems Software	140
San Carlos	Glaser Media Group	153
San Diego	ad•hoc Technologies	129
San Diego	Aerie Animation	143
San Diego	Andersen Consulting	149
San Diego	Beachware	147
San Diego	Branfman & Associates	148
San Diego	Informania, Inc.	134
San Diego	Interactive Presentation Technology, Inc.	134
San Diego	Leland Interactive Media	151
San Diego	Media Designer	137
San Diego	Multi Lingual Media Presentations & Training	150
San Diego	Multimedia Scientific	150
San Diego	New Renaissance	151
San Diego	Presentations Plus	139
San Diego	Thank Evan For Desktop Video	140
San Francisco	Adair & Armstrong	148
San Francisco	Advance Reality Systems	149
San Francisco	Allied Film & Video	149
San Francisco	Anne Dorfman	146
San Francisco	Arborescence SF	130
San Francisco	Blue Waters	86
San Francisco	Bulldog Studios	146
San Francisco	C-Wave	130
San Francisco	Calypso Interactive	149
San Francisco	Clement Mok Designs, Inc.	117, 119, 130
San Francisco	Collosal Pictures	149
San Francisco	Cremer & Associates	148
San Francisco	David H. Lawrence	131
San Francisco	DC Productions	131
San Francisco	Digital Hieroglyphics	145
San Francisco	DK Digital Media	151
San Francisco	Dori Friend Design	132
San Francisco	Eileen Mullinaux	146
San Francisco	Eyejam/Earwax	132
San Francisco	Form & Function	133
San Francisco	Frank Scales Productions	148
San Francisco	Grahame-Harding Productions	133
San Francisco	Graphic Directions	147
San Francisco	Harappa Films	148
San Francisco	Haukom Associates	133
San Francisco	Howard Metzenberg Multimedia Consultant	148
San Francisco	Ikonic	153
San Francisco	Imaginia Inc.	133
San Francisco	Interactive Audio	145
San Francisco	Interplay Artists	147
San Francisco	Joe Czop Photography	135
San Francisco	Kristi Wachter	147
San Francisco	Latent Image Productions	136
San Francisco	LNS Communications	148
San Francisco	Long & Company	150
San Francisco	Luminaria	152
San Francisco	Magic Teleprompting Inc.	136
San Francisco	Media in Content	152
San Francisco	Media Synergy	137
San Francisco	MEDIUS IV	148
San Francisco	Minerva Interactive	148
San Francisco	Morgan Interactive	150
San Francisco	Morrison & Foerster	126, 148
San Francisco	Moving Media	144
San Francisco	Multimedia Business Presentations	148
San Francisco	Music Annex, Inc.	145
San Francisco	MW Productions	151
San Francisco	MZ Media Group	13, 146, 147, 175
San Francisco	Paoletti Technologies	151
San Francisco	Perkins/Boyer Advertising & Digital Productions	134, 139
San Francisco	Preview Media	149
San Francisco	Printz-Electronic Design	151
San Francisco	Quartet	150
San Francisco	ReadyToGo Presentations	140
San Francisco	Red Sky Interactive, Inc.	34, 137, 140, 150, 151
San Francisco	RPM Productions	140
San Francisco	Rusch Design	140
San Francisco	Shoestring Multimedia	140
San Francisco	SMARTALK	145
San Francisco	Spatial Data Architects	153
San Francisco	Stephanie Wong	147
San Francisco	U.S. Media Group	152

San Francisco	Veridian	150
San Francisco	Video Arts Inc.	149
San Francisco	Virtual Company Visits, Inc.	152
San Jose	Compression Labs, Inc.	148
San Jose	David Rose Design	131
San Jose	Frax Incorporated	150
San Jose	M2 Multimedia	146
San Jose	Media Concepts	137, **143**, 149
San Jose	New Media Entertainment	
		133, 138, 173
San Jose	Planet X Productions	139
San Jose	Starboard Inc.	**106**, 109, 140
San Jose	Tech Museum of Innovation	151
San Jose	V/March, Inc.	145
San Juan Bautista	Silicon Valley Bus Company	149
San Luis Obispo	Lindamood-Bell Learning Processes	136
San Mateo	Interactive Solutions, Inc.	148
San Mateo	NVision3	**120, 133, 136**, 138
San Mateo	Studio Graphics	140
San Mateo	Vandellos Studios	145
San Rafael	Presage Software Development	139
San Ramon	In-House Productions	133
Santa Barbara	Tony & Meryl Perutz	147
Santa Clara	Computer Modules Inc.	153
Santa Clara	Minerva Systems, Inc.	150
Santa Clara	Multimedia Computing Corporation	
		138
Santa Clara	Terry Brown	147
Santa Cruz	Media Group	147
Santa Cruz	Sussman Media	151
Santa Monica	Film Works Software, Inc.	147
Santa Monica	Incline Productions	151
Santa Monica	Main Street Multimedia	152
Santa Monica	Neotech Interactive	138
Santa Monica	Pacific Interactive Design Corporation	
		139
Saratoga	Imagetects	173
Sausalito	AlterNet Television, Inc	149
Sausalito	Communication Bridges	148
Sausalito	e Motion Technologies	149
Sausalito	Equilibrium	132
Sausalito	Flying Rhino	143
Sebastopol	Trailblazer Productions	141
Sherman Oaks	Art & Logic	
		16, 17, 26, **38, 43, 44**, 83,
		85, 107, **109, 129**, 130, 149
Spring Valley	Horizons Technology, Inc.	151
Stockton	AR Design	130
Studio City	Orpheum Productions	146
Sunnyvale	CD Technology Inc.	153
Sunnyvale	KAR Enterprises, Inc.	136
Sunnyvale	Multimedia Research Group	148
Sunnyvale	West Valley Engineering, Inc.	
		83, 85, 90, **137**, 142, 148, 163, **164**
Sunnyvale	Voldstad Interactive Design	92, 142
Tehachapi	Rampant Lyon	140
Thousand Oaks	Autologic Inc.	130
Thousand Oaks	Dave Saunders & Associates	131
Tiburon	Amuse Interactive	
	Learning Environment	150
Tiburon	Komenar Production	
	& Marketing Group	136
Topanga	Palamar Communications	139
Torrance	Image Smith	151
Union City	Ebook, Inc.	153
Ventura	i MEDIA Solutions, Inc.	133
Ventura	Mega Media	153
Ventura	Photo Library Management Services	
		152
Ventura	Ventura College & La Vie	147
Ventura	Ventura Community College	151
Walnut Creek	MarCole Enterprises	152
West Hollywood	Pacific Coast Sound Works	139
Westlake Village	Screen Media Software	140
Westlake Village	TBP, Inc.	153
Whittier	M3 Dimensions, Inc.	153
Woodacre	Harris Consulting	149
Woodside	Scott Mize Productions	150
Yorba Linda	Stat™ Media	140

NETWORKING

Agoura Hills	Brockman Consulting	**165**, 166, 172
Alameda	Farallon Computing, Inc.	165
Aliso Viejo	Advantage Memory Corporation	163
Aliso Viejo	MicroMac Technology	167
Aptos	Engage Communication, Inc.	163
Aptos	RWRAD	168

Berkeley	Bear River Associates, Inc.	
	16, 17, **36**, **38**, 43, **44**, 59, 60, **86**, 90,	
	91, **98**, **99**, **103**, 104, **105**, 106, 107, **108**,	
	159, **164**, 166, **167**, **168**, **188**, **190**	
Berkeley	CCIC System Pacifica	
	108, **111**, 123, 160, **162**, **165**, 166	
Berkeley	Information Access Technologies Inc.	
		168
Berkeley	Integral Information Systems	159
Berkeley	LanMinds	166
Berkeley	Zocalo Engineering	165
Cerritos	Network International	162
Culver City	Stanford Business Systems, Inc.	
		159, **161**
Cupertino	McComb Research	161
Cupertino	Rikei Corporation	167
Cupertino	Total Solutions	165
Elk Grove	Informant Communications Group	
	45, 51, 161, **162**	
Fairfax	Business Solutions For The Mac	160
Huntington Beach	**ResNova Software, Inc**	**170**, **175**
Huntington Beach	Zantos Control Systems	165
Irvine	LanSharks	161, **163**
Irvine	Richard Vallens Consulting	164
Irvine	Gateway Group Inc.	159
Laguna Hills	Evergreen Consulting, Inc.	160
Long Beach	The Acacia Group	165
Los Alamitos	Featherstone Communications	166
Los Angeles	Catalyst Computer Services	160
Los Angeles	Entertainment Solutions, Inc.	166
Los Angeles	MacMinn & Associates	166
Los Angeles	Warever Computing, Inc.	163
Los Gatos	JHAMCON Company	163
Los Gatos	Mactivity, Inc.	161
Los Gatos	Winehouse Computer Company	167
Los Osos	Copious Systems	**46**, 47, **86**, 87
Mountain View	First Floor Software	168
Oakland	Dana Shultz & Associates	165
Orange	RB Graphic Supply Company	167
Orange	VGC Corporation	167
Palo Alto	HeyerTech Inc.	166
Palo Alto	Jack Daley & Company	161
Palo Alto	KPMG • ExIS	161
Palo Alto	TPS Electronics	167
Pasadena	Comsul Ltd.	160
Redondo Beach	P.S.C. Consultants	82
San Francisco	Blue Waters	**130**, 163
San Francisco	Chronos Software, Inc.	45
San Francisco	eMedia	168
San Francisco	Entertainment Digital Network (EDNET)	168
San Francisco	Johnathon Freeman Technologies	164
San Francisco	**Pacific Telesis Electronic Publishing Services/Re:Source Network Solutions**	**158**, **162**
San Francisco	United Data Corporation	159
San Francisco	Ziegler Ross, Inc.	165
San Jose	AdvanTel, Inc.	165
San Jose	API Engineering	165
San Jose	Arcom Electronics, Inc.	28, 159
San Jose	Asanté Technologies, Inc	165
San Jose	Celan Technology	160
San Jose	MPI Engineering	168
San Luis Obispo	Information Presentation Technologies, Inc.	165
San Luis Obispo	Stellar Solutions	162
San Mateo	Mariette Systems International	166
Santa Ana Heights	Gordian	28, 161, **162**
Santa Barbara	Miramar Systems, Inc.	168
Santa Barbara	MultiAccess Computing Corporation	165
Santa Monica	Interconnect Networking Consulting Group Inc.	166
Sunnyvale	Computer Solutions & Innovations	160
Sunnyvale	West Valley Engineering, Inc.	85, 90, **83**, **89**, **90**, **137**, 142, 148, 163, **164**
Torrance	The EDI Connection	163
Walnut Creek	The AG Group Inc.	165
PUBLISHING		
Agoura Hills	Brockman Consulting	**165**, 166, 172
Anaheim	Computrend	172
Belmont	Wadsworth Publishing Company	177
Berkeley	Abacus Concepts, Inc.	177
Berkeley	Benainous Communications	172
Berkeley	Boardman & Associates	174
Berkeley	Douglas Pundick Technical	178

Berkeley	P. Heidi Beeler	178
Berkeley	Peachpit Press	176
Berkeley	WordPlay Communications	179
Buena Park	Brunner Professional Services	172
Carlsbad	Allenbach Industries, Inc.	175
Chico	Multi-Image Systems	177
Cloverdale	PEMD Education Group	175
Cupertino	Dave Meyers	178
Cupertino	MADA	177
Cupertino	The Carl Group Inc.	180
El Cerito	M/E Design	173
El Granada	Island Resources	179
El Sobrante	Morris Communications	176
Fairfield	Cindy Hamner Graphic Designer	172
Guerneville	Hoff Consulting	174
Half Moon Bay	Fog Press	173
Irvine	Graphix Zone, Inc.	176
Lafayette	Tech Prose **176, 177**, 179, 180, 189	
Laguna Niguel	TechWriters Ink	179
Long Beach	Creative Enterprises	
	16, 19, **38**, 47, **129**, 130	
Los Altos	Vivid Publishing	174
Los Angeles	Bertram Gader	174
Los Angeles	Custom Typographic Solutions	172
Los Angeles	Digiflex®	177
Los Angeles	Mac-nificent Services	173
Los Angeles	Michael Diehl Design	173
Menlo Park	Addison-Wesley Publishing	176
Modesto	Page Creations	173
Montclair	Devonian International Software	
	Company	172
Mountain View	In Writing	178
Mountain View	Lasselle-Ramsay Inc.	178
Oakland	Curves	172
Pacifica	Bridget Burke	179
Pacific Grove	Bottomline Communications. 36, 178	
Palo Alto	Live Oak Press	173
Placentia	Rachel Richards	174
Pleasanton	Software Solutions, Inc.	177
Redwood City	Acknowledge Solutions **122**, 178	
Redwood City	DeskTop Production Services	172
Sacramento	Emigre Fonts	177
San Diego	InnovaTech Corporation	175
San Diego	TalCompany Systems Services	178
San Francisco	Caryl International	178
San Francisco	Corporate Solutions	190
San Francisco	Grande Vitesse Systems	133
San Francisco	MZ Media Group **13,** 146, 147, 175	
San Francisco	Pacific Digital Image	173
San Francisco	Production First Software	177
San Francisco	Rapid Design Services	174
San Francisco	Semantic Imaging	178
San Francisco	STG Graphic Communications, Inc.	
		174
San Francisco	SUMERIA, Inc.	176
San Francisco	Warner-Cotter	180
San Francisco	Wordswork	179
San Jose	Certified Media Corporation	175
San Jose	Comtech Services Inc.	179
San Jose	Courseware Design Services	174
San Jose	International Datawares, Inc.	175
San Jose	New Media Entertainment	
	133, 138, 173	
San Jose	Xpand	177
San Marino	TASCA	174
San Mateo	ANDROS SoftWear	178
San Rafael	Full Circle Media	178
San Ramon	EnerAnalytics	178
Santa Barbara	In•Color Graphics	173
Santa Cruz	Miller Technical Publishing	178
Santa Cruz	Paul Hoffman	178
Santa Monica	Cinema Desktop Publishing	172
Scotts Valley	Great Ware Software	177
South San		
Francisco	Godar & Hossenlopp	
	Printing Company	178
Sunnyvale	HLS Duplication, Inc.	175
Sunnyvale	Linda Jay Brandt **174,** 176	
Torrance	Nadson & Terrill Communications	
		178
Valley Center	Ventana Studio	180
Venice	The Computer Evolution	191
Ventura	Graphic Traffic	174
SUPPORT		
Aliso Viejo	Mac Upgrade Specialists	187
Belmont	MacTraining House	191

Berkeley	Bear River Associates, Inc	
	16, 17, **36**, 38, 43, **44, 59**, 60, **86**, 90,	
	91, 98, 99, **103**, 104, **105**, 106, 107, **108, 159, 164,**	
	166,167, **168, 188**, 190	
Berkeley	BMUG	185
Berkeley	Dolphin Software	186
Berkeley	Flashpoint	189
Berkeley	Kagi Engineering Inc.	190
Carlsbad	Aaron's Computer Relief	189
El Dorado	Macintosh Movie Makers Guild	185
Fullerton	Media Res	189
Gilroy	Orca Software Solutions	186
Guerneville	Richey Software Training	189
Hollywood	Staging Techniques	188
Huntington Beach	Quick Start Technologies	189
Lafayette	Tech Prose **176, 177,** 179, 180, 189	
Larkspur	Notti & Company, CPAs	191
Mill Valley	Wong, Pamela L., Macintosh	
	Consulting Services **189**, 191	
Montclair	ASD Software, Inc.	186
Novato	DriveSavers, Inc. 30, **185,** 186, 187	
Oakland	Macaroni	175
Oakland	Systems Management Consulting	188
Ontario	Growing Minds Software	187
Palo Alto	Customer Service Solutions	187
Palo Alto	Emergent Behavior	**47**, 49
Palo Alto	International Association of Business	
	Communications	185
Palo Alto	Kramer Group	187
Redondo Beach	Motioneering	191
Redwood City	RSA Data Security, Inc.	187
Sacramento	Michael Zolen Macintosh Consulting	
		188
San Diego	Computer Conversions, Inc.	186
San Diego	Learnsoft, Inc.	190
San Diego	Microage of San Diego	191
San Diego	New Ledger	191
San Diego	Platt College	191
San Francisco	Abacus, Inc	187
San Francisco	AT&T Computer Users Group	185
San Francisco	Data Vision Technologies	189
San Francisco	Kolnick Consulting Services	190
San Francisco	The Dublin Group, Inc.	191
San Francisco	MacMentor	189
San Jose	Personal Training Systems	189
Santa Clara	800-WE-FIX-MACS	187
Santa Cruz	C. Olson & Company	190
Santa Monica	Santa Monica MicroAge	191
Sausalito	Baseline Software	186
Sunnyvale	DT & T Macintosh Services	30, 187
Walnut Creek	24-Hour Macintosh Service	187
Walnut Creek	MTC New Horizons	189
Westlake Village	PC Dynamics	187

Colorado

CUSTOM SOLUTIONS

Greenwood Village	Tanner Software Development	36

DEVELOPMENT & PROGRAMMING

Arvada	21st Century Graphics	75
Boulder	Data Solutions, Inc.	19, **46**, 47
Boulder	Imagine Better Software	88
Boulder	John Wong Systems Consultants	101
Boulder	Macreations Publishing	77
Boulder	Micro Analysis & Design, Inc.	68
Boulder	Plug-In Systems	77
Boulder	Rocky Mountain Translators Inc.	109
Boulder	Software Development Group	69
Broomfield	Bloom Software	86
Carbondale	The Oxbridge Group	71
Colorado Springs	1-Up Computing 16, **43, 76**, 78	
Denver	Brownstone Research Group	64
Denver	C4 Network, Inc.	76
Denver	Computer Help Services	90
Denver	Data, Design Engineering	78
Denver	Fred Pittroff	70
Denver	Preferred Technologies	98
Denver	Systems InterAction	98
Denver	WFT	69
Englewood	Advanced System Technologies, Inc.	
		65
Grand Junction	SoftShell International Ltd.	68
Highlands Ranch	Efficiency & Software	96
Highlands Ranch	Kentary, Inc.	92
Highlands Ranch	SanSoft	100
Lakewood	DataCraft	93
Lakewood	Infinity Digital, Inc.	50
Littleton	Debron Enterprises	79

Lon Mott	Digital Consultants	66
Parker	Legal Computer Solutions	72
Salida	Catspaw Inc.	90
Telluride	Softek Design, Inc.	71
Westminster	SoluProbe Limited	56
Wheat Ridge	RockWare, Inc.	68

MARKETING & DISTRIBUTION

Aurora	Denis Darby's Creative	119
Boulder	International Language Engineering Corporation	122
Boulder	The Vass Company	121
Colorado Springs	Laden Relations	121
Denver	PageWorks + TriDesign	120
Longmont	Coalescence	118
Louisville	Media Lab Inc.	118

MULTIMEDIA

Boulder	Taft Development Group	149
Denver	Centerline Productions	130
Golden	BOLDer MultiMedia	153
Lakewood	Macsimum Creative Enterprises	136

NETWORKING

Aurora	Cimarron International Inc.	165
Boulder	Cross International Corporation	160
Boulder	Diversified Computer Systems	160
Denver	Systems Contracting	163
Northglenn	MH Software	168

PUBLISHING

Boulder	Hal Chorpenning Communications	173
Boulder	Synaptica:	175
Englewood	Dream Maker Software	172
Evergreen	Bersearch Information Services	174
Littleton	Grafik Solutions	173
Longmont	Information Engineering Company	178

SUPPORT

Arvada	Aim High	187
Aurora	MacGraphics	190
Boulder	Martha S. Scheer, CPA: PC	188
Breckenridge	Alpine PC	189
Denver	Gibson Computer Associates	190
Denver	Training Access	191
Highlands Ranch	SupportNet	188
Littleton	A Little Computing, Inc.	189

Louisville	Wizard Works	189

Connecticut

CUSTOM SOLUTIONS

Bloomfield	Tab Computer Systems	36
Weston	Bottom Line Consulting	34

DEVELOPMENT & PROGRAMMING

Chesire	Acolyte Software Corporation	101
Glastonbury	Qualisys Inc.	68
Madison	CORGROUP	19, 61
New Haven	C.T.A. Inc.	61
New Haven	Willow Solutions	58
New Haven	Yale University School of Medicine Biomedical Media Production	90
Norwalk	Le Blanc Consulting Group, Inc.	21, **49**, 52
Norwalk	Target Technologies, Inc.	70
Orange	Advanced Decisions Inc.	43
Riverside	AFTECH Corporation	103
Sandy Hook	The Stepstone Corporation	57
Shelton	The MIS Group Inc.	60
Southport	Strategic Planning Systems, Inc.	74
Stamford	Concept Information Systems	46
Stamford	Image Systems	76
Stamford	TM Computer Consulting, Inc.	95
Stanford	HRF Associates, Inc.	50
Tariffville	Prompt, Inc.	53
Trumbull	OS Systems Group	53
Waterford	Sonalysts Inc.	56
West Haven	Rajni Malik	54
Westport	SoftKare	100
Wilton	Micro Trading Software Inc.	71
Wilton	Montage Software Systems	22, 97
Wilton	Odin Technologies, Inc.	94
Wilton	Richard D.Robbins, Independent Consultant	89

MARKETING & DISTRIBUTION

Farmington	Macsultants	117
Greenwich	Direct Media	118
Greenwich	The Seroka Group, Inc.	117
Guilford	Robert T. Coolidge, AIA	117
Meriden	Jam Software Limited	123
Oxford	Professional Business Assistance	120

| Rowayton | Howard M. Cutler | |
| | Productions | 116, **131**, 133 |

MULTIMEDIA

Brookfield	Susan Strumer	140
Hebron	Silk City Software Inc.	140
Marlborough	Computer Management	
	International, Inc.	130
Stamford	Burns, Connacher & Waldron	130

NETWORKING

Brookfield	Connexus	163
Cromwell	Ridgewood Software	168
Farmington	N:Deavor Group, Inc.	161
Norwalk	Next Age	167
Woodbury	The Systems Expert, Inc.	163

PUBLISHING

Branford	Cyberchrome	177
Stamford	Atticus Software Corporation	177
West Hartford	Electronic Pencil	178
Westport	Mac In Design	175
Westport	The Computer Learning Company	179

SUPPORT

Moodus	Parrothead Computercations	188
New Canaan	Benchmark Publications, Inc.	
		117, **118**, 188
New Canaan	Professional Support Services	191
New Haven	MicroServ	191
Norwalk	Cadre Systems	187
Southington	AM Computer Products	189
Wilton	Next Actions	191

D.C.

DEVELOPMENT & PROGRAMMING

| Advanced Laser Graphics | 95 |

MULTIMEDIA

| Avalon Integrated Services | 130 |
| Magnet Interactive Studios, Inc. | 137 |

SUPPORT

Future Enterprises, Inc.	190
Jane Mason, Computer Consultant	190
Simone (C.) & Associates	186

Delaware

CUSTOM SOLUTIONS

| Wilmington | Comacon, Inc | 38 |

DEVELOPMENT & PROGRAMMING

Dover	MacHelp Associates, Inc.	62
Dover	Somerville Associates	62
Wilmington	MicroStrategy Inc.	68

MARKETING & DISTRIBUTION

| Hockessin | Harris Design Office | 119 |

MULTIMEDIA

| Hockessin | Visual Logic | 142 |

NETWORKING

| Wilmington | General Information Services, Inc. | 165 |
| Wilmington | Laravela Associates, Inc. | 168 |

Florida

DEVELOPMENT & PROGRAMMING

Altamonte Springs	OakTree Software Specialists	53
Altamonte Springs	Techware Corporation	65
Apopka	Bartlett, Brandley & Lucky	92
Boca Raton	Boca On-Line Systems, Inc.	44
Boca Raton	Jackson Enterprises	107
Boca Raton	Software Corporation	55
Clearwater	Christopher Gross	18, 45
Clearwater	Kutoroff Development	90
Clearwater	Moonlighting Software Development	
		90
Coral Springs	Dimension Consulting, Inc.	61
Cross City	Seishin Creations	89
Davie	Strategic Directions, Inc.	57
Delray Beach	Dennis M. Nagel, Inc.	66
Delray Beach	Marisys Inc.	52
Delray Beach	Richard Battin	101
Fort Lauderdale	Macintosh Applications Consultants	
		62
Ft. Lauderdale	MLC Computer Services	52
Gainesville	Electronic Learning Systems Inc.	88
Jacksonville	Boxes & Arrows Inc.	17, 60
Jacksonville	Green Shades Software, Inc.	62
Jupiter	The Design Office	63
Longwood	Medina Software Inc.	64
Melbourne	Computer Science Innovations	18, 46

Melbourne Beach	Edu-Tech Associates, Inc.	20, 93
Melbourne Beach	Nedrud Data Systems	68
Melbourne Beach	OITC, Inc.	53
Miami	The Conroy Company/ Fulcrum Software	65
North Miami Beach	L & B Software	104
Naperville	Logikal Solutions	80
Niceville	JMT Technologies, Inc.	77
Orlando	The Orlando Mac Consulting Group Inc.	98
Shalimar	Lynch's Computer Services, Inc.	81
Tallahassee	ShopKeeper Publishing International Inc.	62
Tallahassee	Visions Edge, Inc.	77
Tampa	FoodStar Inc.	61
Tampa	WSC, Inc.	60
Winter Park	Advanced Data Systems	72

MARKETING & DISTRIBUTION

Boca Raton	Worldata	119
Bradenton	Atlantech, Inc.	121
Cape Canaveral	Empire RBDMS	117
Ft. Lauderdale	South Florida Wire Service	116, **120**, 121, 122
Miami	Mac, S.A.	123
Palm City	Jack Lewis & Associates	122

MULTIMEDIA

Cape Canaveral	Communications Concepts Inc.	148
Port St. Lucie	Buffalo Brothers Marketing	149
St. Petersburg	Image Technologies, Inc.	133

NETWORKING

Deerfield Beach	BCG, Inc.	163
Hollywood	MacInstitute	161
Melbourne	CSI, Inc.	163
Melbourne Beach	Telecom Planning	165
Miami	Corporate Systems Group	160
Miami	TechSys Corporation	163
Pensacola	Mark Pappas Development	168
Tampa	Custom Cable Industries	165

PUBLISHING

Boynton Beach	Cultural Technology	178
Dunedin	Jeff Tanner Artistic Concepts	174
Ft. Lauderdale	MacCreations Publishing	77
Lantana	KB Design	175
Miami	Dart Products, Inc.	178
Miami	Insight Communications Group	179
Naples	I.D.E.A.S.	174
Tallahassee	Seven Hills Software Corporation	177
Tampa	Marlene C. Semple Communication Services	178
Tampa	Teknosys Inc.	188
Vero Beach	Tim Duncklee-Consultant	177

SUPPORT

Boca Raton	MISCA	188
Cooper City	Elron Consulting Inc.	187
Coral Springs	Mac Generation Inc.	189
Ormond Beach	MacAcademy	186
St. Petersburg	Marketech Inc.	188

Georgia

CUSTOM SOLUTIONS

Atlanta	INFO grafix, Inc.	38

DEVELOPMENT & PROGRAMMING

Alpharetta	Southern Horizons Corporation	24, 106
Alpharettea	Richmond Software Corporation	103
Atlanta	AppleTree Technologies Inc.	174
Atlanta	Binders Computer Graphics	75
Atlanta	Databasics, Inc.	47
Atlanta	Laser Solutions Inc.	94
Atlanta	Mentor Software Innovations, Inc.	110
Atlanta	Productivity Point	53
Atlanta	Soft Solutions, Inc.	95
Atlanta	SpectraLogic, Inc.	24, 18
Decatur	IronMike Software Inc.	21, 79
Duluth	Grant Holland & Associates	90
Marietta	Fractal Solutions	93
Norcross	Peachtree Software	62
Smyrna	Printing Communications Associates, Inc.	107
Stone Mountain	Comprehensive Business Solutions Group, Inc.	65

MARKETING & DISTRIBUTION

Atlanta	Boardwalk Designs	116
Atlanta	Fain & Company	47, 49, **93**, 116, **131**, 133

Powder Springs	SilverStar Enterprises	117

MULTIMEDIA

Atlanta	Evenview Corporation	132
Atlanta	Galileo Inc.	133
Atlanta	General Picture	146
Atlanta	IBM	133
Atlanta	Presentation Technologies, Inc.	139
Atlanta	The Whitley Group	141
Atlanta	TW DESIGN	141
Atlanta	Visual Solutions	149
Atlanta	Zola Technologies Inc.	145
Decatur	Design Teknekh	147
Decatur	On-Line Design, Inc.	**135**, 138

NETWORKING

Atlanta	Personal Systems Services, Inc.	159

PUBLISHING

Lawrenceville	Network Publications, Inc.	176
Marietta	Encryption Technology Corporation/Prism Packaging	172
Norcross	The Graphics Production Center	174
Norcross	The Software Factory	175
Roswell	Thornhill Data Systems	179

SUPPORT

Atlanta	Visual Business Systems Inc.	175
Norcross	GE Rental/Lease	187

Hawaii

DEVELOPMENT & PROGRAMMING

Area	Info Dent	73
Honolulu	Coconut Info	78
Honolulu	Island Micro Solutions, Inc	59
Kailua-Kona	Daniel L. Roudelbush	61
Makawao	Maui Software	52
Paia	Morrison Consulting	81

MULTIMEDIA

Honolulu	Teknowledgey Design Corporation	151

PUBLISHING

Honolulu	Image Management	174

SUPPORT

Kailua-Kona	Easy	190

Idaho

DEVELOPMENT & PROGRAMMING

Moscow	From The Heart Software	64
Sandpoint	Clerk of the Works	70
Sun Valley	Analytix Group, Inc.	70

MULTIMEDIA

Moscow	User Active Media	151

SUPPORT

Boise	The Learning Center/Computer Land	191

Illinois

CUSTOM SOLUTIONS

Chicago	Cyborg Systems, Inc.	36
Deerfield	William M. Mercer, Inc.	37

DEVELOPMENT & PROGRAMMING

Arlington Heights	Apriori Inc.	99
Arlington Heights	MDG Computer Services	94
Arlington Heights	MTP Systems Consulting, Ltd.	94
Barrington	Infotech Information Services	51
Barrington	McClure Consultants Ltd.	52
Bolingbrook	Designed Data Company, Inc.	66
Buffalo Grove	DataBase Designs, Inc.	105
Carbondale	DxR Development Group, Inc.	64
Chicago	Alan George & Associates, Inc.	43
Chicago	Ariel Software Consultants, Inc.	17, 92
Chicago	Design Access, Inc.	63
Chicago	Doblin Group	61
Chicago	Fast, Cheap, Reliable Inc.	73
Chicago	Get Creative Technologies	101
Chicago	InfoMaker Inc.	93
Chicago	Kanbay Resources Inc.	79
Chicago	Kula Corporation	71
Chicago	Right Click!	54
Collinsville	Hurn Computing	91
Deerfield	Information Conversion Services, Inc.	88
Deerfield	Word Master, Inc.	**103**, 104, 108
Des Plaines	CF Software	18, 45
Des Plaines	Shuger Software Services	54
Elgin	Muirhead & Associates	97
Elmhurst	Blankenship Systems Consulting, Inc.	60

Evanston	DCI Integrated Computer Systems	70
Evanston	Q Technologies, Inc.	54
Evanston	Rittenhouse & Associates	105
Hanover Park	Catalyst Computer Systems	61
Hinsdale	Information Systems Technology, Inc.	21, 51, **67**
Lake in the Hills	Green Dragon Creations, Inc.	69
Marion	MTEC	53
Naperville	Systems Imagineering	102
Northbrook	Lipschultz Brothers, Levin & Gray	60
Oak Park	C4SI, Inc.	96
Palatine	Total Integration, Inc.	77
Palos Hills	Software Performance Specialist, Inc.	102
Peoria	Ron Wallace Enterprises Inc.	62
Rockford	World Company	74
Savoy	Spyglass, Inc.	69
Schaumburg	Compare Technologies, Inc.	46
Schaumburg	Meadows Information Systems, Inc.	77
Schaumburg	Michael Ericksen PC	52
Schaumburg	Personal Consulting Services	98
Skokie	Donald H. Kraft & Associates	70
Skokie	J. Schachter Enterprises	94
Springfield	Miller/Burns Associates, Inc.	62
Wheaton	The DesignSoft Company	57
Wheeling	Kracom Computer Services	94
Wilmette	WillStein Software, Inc.	53

MARKETING & DISTRIBUTION

Aurora	Hertrich Graphics	116
Chicago	Ahrens Creative Group, Inc.	116
Evanston	William Rush Voice Consultants	117
Hinsdale	Tilted Windmill Ltd.	117
Kenilworth	Stone House Systems Inc	116
River Forest	Michael R. Mizen & Associates, Inc.	118
Wheaton	Robis, Inc. Software Marketing	118

MULTIMEDIA

Arlington Heights	Xenon Communications Corporation	150
Champagne	Symbolic Sound Corporation	145
Chicago	850 Productions Inc.	25, **140**, 144
Chicago	Christopher L. Schneck	143
Chicago	Dynacom, Inc.	152
Chicago	Interactive Engineering	134
Chicago	Reactor Inc.	153
Elgin	CD-Press	152
Evanston	Alphabets Design Group Inc.	129
Western Springs	Adams Consulting Group	145
Wilmette	Oracle Multimedia	151

NETWORKING

Bensenville	Calumet Professional Imaging	166
Bolingbrook	Better Way Computing	168
Chicago	Computer Services & Consulting, Inc.	160
Chicago	Logic Plus Inc.	161
Chicago	Metamor Technologies	161
Chicago	MicroAge Solutions, Inc.	164
Chicago	R. A. Meyers & Associates	167
Chicago	The Planet Group, Inc.	159
Glen Ellyn	Oak Enterprises	159
Glenview	Lan Data Voice Technologies Inc.	166
Naperville	InfoTech	166
Naperville	Kustom Automated Technologies Inc.	161
Rockford	Ansan Industries, Ltd.	165
Warrenville	Alliance Consulting	163

PUBLISHING

Chicago	Monotype Typography, Inc.	173
Chicago	Sandra Pakin & Associates, Inc.	178
Chicago	Stephen Chinn Consulting	175
Northbrook	Word Associates, Inc.	177
Oak Forest	WPA Film Library	176
Peoria	Dynamic Graphics Inc.	172

SUPPORT

Addison	Flip Track OneOnOne Computer Training	189
Arlington Heights	Terry Tufts & Associates	189
Bensenville	Porter & Porter	**189**
Chicago	Computing Solutions	190
Chicago	McLaughlin Consulting	188
Oak Forest	8th Day Consulting, Training, & Software	189
Rosemont	Crawford & Associates, Inc.	185

Indiana

DEVELOPMENT & PROGRAMMING

Bloomington	Bibliogem Inc.	64

Bloomington	Computed Designs	61
Evansville	Specialty Software	102
Fort Wayne	Vector Systems	85
Indianapolis	Daniels Associates Inc.	78
Indianapolis	Software Engineering Professionals, Inc.	18
Indianapolis	Wabash Medical Resources Inc.	74
Pittsboro	Charles Cooper Consulting	18, 96
South Bend	Information Management Systems Inc.	104

MULTIMEDIA

Indianapolis	MSI	149

NETWORKING

Carmel	Dome Software Corporation	166
Indianapolis	Naval Air Warfare Center	161

PUBLISHING

Carmel	Que Software	177

SUPPORT

Indianapolis	Shaffstall Corporation	188

Iowa

DEVELOPMENT & PROGRAMMING

Cedar Rapids	Assembled Solutions, Inc.	43
Des Moines	The Systems Group	106
Fairfield	Clear Access-Fairfield Software	45
Fairfield	Script Software International	83
Iowa City	Computer Solutions, Ltd.	46
Manchester	Spring Branch Software	52
Marshalltown	Excel Software	49

MARKETING & DISTRIBUTION

Grinnell	Ferro Enterprises	121

MULTIMEDIA

Bettendorf	The Word & Image Workshop, Inc.	135, 141

PUBLISHING

Iowa City	Iowa Market Systems	177

SUPPORT

Fairfier	Maharishi International University	175

Kansas

DEVELOPMENT & PROGRAMMING

Haysville	Micro Solutions	81
Leawood	Independent Consultant	79
Olathe	Data By Design	101
Overland Park	Decision Technologies	61
Shawnee	Heritage Computer Consulting & Services	20, 50
Shawnee	Philip Davis & Associates	98
Shawnee Mission	RISM	54

MULTIMEDIA

Overland Park	Music & MIDI Sales	145

NETWORKING

Lawrence	Computer Support	160
Lawrence	Mac Systems	166
Manhattan	Jim Sharp & Associates	166

PUBLISHING

Kansas City	Gazlay Marketing Group	173

SUPPORT

Lawrence	Sampson & Associates	188
Wichita	Optimum Technology Consultants	188

Kentucky

DEVELOPMENT & PROGRAMMING

Lexington	Academic Software, Inc.	73
Lexington	Envent Group	76
Somerset	Delta Medical Shareware, Inc.	73

NETWORKING

Frankfort	Ky Housing Corporation	161

PUBLISHING

Louisville	The Cobb Group	179

Louisiana

DEVELOPMENT & PROGRAMMING

Baton Rouge	Camsoft Data Systems, Inc.	44
Baton Rouge	Fifth Generation Systems	49

MARKETING & DISTRIBUTION

Mandeville	Consult Rosen Communication	120
New Orleans	Computer Mentors	116
Renens	Tecval Memories SA	118

MULTIMEDIA

New Orleans	Bent Media, Inc.	118, 129, 130, 152

NETWORKING

New Orleans	NetSpec	168

SUPPORT

New Orleans	Tulane University	191

Maine

DEVELOPMENT & PROGRAMMING

Augusta	The MEGA MAC Company	57
Castine	Evergreen Technologics, Inc.	73
Kennebunkport	Wiltshire Computer Management	106

Maryland

CUSTOM SOLUTIONS

Columbia	The Ansar Group	38
Easton	CCS Enterprises, Inc.	37

DEVELOPMENT & PROGRAMMING

Annapolis	Navigation Technologies Inc.	89
Baltimore	Body CT Imaging Lab	73
Baltimore	Karow Associates, Inc.	21, 51
Baltimore	MK Consulting	68
Baltimore	Noetic Systems Inc.	68
Beltsville	Asgard Consulting	85
Bethesda	INTE-GREAT Corporation	51
Charlestown	Brinkmann Consultants	44
Columbia	Applied Computer Solutions, Inc.	43
Columbia	Business Computer Solutions Inc.	96
Columbia	Infinity Systems	50
Columbia	Ourtime Publishing	98
Columbia	RWD Technologies, Inc.	54, 80, 88
Derwood	Hypertek, Inc.	88
Frederick	Land Lord Software Inc.	51
Gaithersburg	Information Management Resources, Inc.	178
Germantown	Online Computer Systems Inc.	94
Germantown	SILC, Incorporated	83
La Plata	Pathos One Inc.	104
Montpelier	Company Seven Astro-Optics Division	65
Mt. Airy	DataMasters	19, 93
Owings Mills	ISM, INC.	69
Potomac	Info Serv Information Service Inc.	93
Riva	Reiter Consulting Services	60
Rockville	Charles E. Brault	78
Rockville	High Techsplanations, Inc.	112
Rockville	OGDEN Bio Services	53
Rockville	Personal Library Software	94
Rockville	Potomac Software Engineering, Inc.	68
Rockville	Software Productivity Strategists, Inc.	56
Silver Spring	Automated Accounting Solutions Inc.	70
Silver Spring	Cedrus Corporation	78
Silver Spring	Double Click Systems, Inc.	163
Silver Spring	Micro Dynamics Ltd.	62
Silver Spring	Spentech, Inc.	56
Upper Marlboro	Barnes Computer, Inc.	78

MARKETING & DISTRIBUTION

Silver Spring	Holmes Agency Inc.	116

MULTIMEDIA

Baltimore	Nighthawk Productions, Inc.	138
Bethesda	NDG Phoenix, Inc.	138
Columbia	Freq Sound/Workman Computer Services	145
Columbia	Rall & Company	140
Rockville	Forsight, Inc.	133

NETWORKING

Gaithersburg	Abernathy Business Consultants, Inc.	163
Glynoon	Bruce, Bruce, & Bruce	18, 159
Greenbelt	Enabling Technologies Corporation	160
Hunt Valley	Software Development Factory	159
Silver Spring	JPH Consultant Services	161

PUBLISHING

Baltimore	Foxglove Communications	74
Rockville	Khera Communications, Inc.	178

SUPPORT

Gaithersburg	M2 Ltd.	187

Massachusetts

CUSTOM SOLUTIONS

West Boxford	Cordant Imaging Systems	36

DEVELOPMENT & PROGRAMMING

Acton	Sandhill Systems	103
Acton	William K. Bradford Publishing Company, Inc.	65
Agawam	Winthrop-Lawrence Corporation	53

Allston	WegWeiser Macintosh Consulting	100
Amherst	James Pistrang Computer Resources	104
Amherst	JP Computer Resources	104
Andover	Tulip Software	57
Arlington	Good News Marketing Inc.	62
Ayer	Virtual Image Inc.	99
Belmont	Adventurer Software	90
Belmont	Language Engineering Corporation	52
Bernardston	Cressey Consulting & SW	47
Billerica	Automatix, Inc.	72
Boston	Adam Leffert	75
Boston	Avalon Engineering, Inc. 37, 38, 43, **44**, **74**, 75, **76**, 78, **85**, 86, 107, **110**	
Boston	Boston Systems Group Inc.	60
Boston	Cognitive Systems Inc.	61
Boston	Database International Inc.	61
Boston	KPMG Peat Marwick Management Consultants	72
Boston	Lara Consulting Group	77
Boston	Legal Computer Solutions, Inc.	72
Boston	Thomson Financial Services	71
Brighton	C & C Logic Engineering	93
Brookline	Beacon Export Systems, Inc.	72
Brookline	Informed Solutions Inc.	97
Burlington	Dimensional Insight, Inc.	61
Cambridge	Automated Business Management	65
Cambridge	Belmont Research	73
Cambridge	Bitstream Inc.	75
Cambridge	Database Designs	93
Cambridge	Drucker & Associates	110
Cambridge	JM Associates	97
Cambridge	John Shockey	79
Cambridge	Natural Intelligence Inc.	97
Cambridge	Relevant Technologies, Inc.	98
Cambridge	SEG	72
Cambridge	SpaceTime Systems	95
Cambridge	Sumbolon Corporation	84
Cambridge	The Epsilon Naught Company	69
Canton	Edo Communications	96
Chelmsford	Geni Inc.	79
Chelmsford	North Atlantic Publishing Systems, Inc.	77
Concord	Concord Consulting Group	65
Dedham	Cyber Viz	110
E. Douglas	DMP Associates	48
Falmouth	Pinehill Software Corporation	60
Framingham	E. E. S. Companies, Inc.	93
Framingham	Timberfield Systems	69
Holyoke	Computer Solutions!	46
Hyannis	Intramedia	93
Jophin	Digital Voice Inc.	73
Lincoln	HotCode Ltd.	50
Lincoln	Lincoln Software, Inc.	60
Littleton	Angiographic Devices Corporation	73
Medfield	Strichman Medical Equipment, Inc.	74
Medford	Bayle Collaborations	110
Medway	1ST Desk Systems	72
Natick	Applications Unlimited	101
Natick	Command Systems Inc.	103
Natick	Software By Design, Inc.	55
Needham	Database Associates	61
Needham	Emerging Information Technologies, Inc.	96
Needham	Solustan, Inc.	72
Needlham	NuLogic® Inc.	72
Newton	KTAADN Inc.	67
Newton	The Registry, Inc.	84
Newton	Turning Point Software 24, **48**, **58**, 63, **68**, **70**, **75**, 77, **82**, 85, 90, 108	
Newton Highlands	Morgenlender Associates	81
North Andover	Aries Systems Corporation	73
Plymouth	The Farrell Company	63
Rowe	Douglas Corarito	90
Somerville	Binary Techniques Inc.	60
Somerville	Flashpoint, Inc.	61
Stoughton	SIB Consulting	72
Stoughton	Steve Blake Design	92
Sudbury	Sackman Associates	77
Wakefield	Micro Alliance Inc.	89
Wakefield	Visions Software, Inc. 25, 58, **67**, **84**, 90, 108	
Walpole	Affinity Software Corporation	75
Waltham	David Spector Associates	79
Watertown	Intentional Educations	64
Wenham	Harvard Psychiatric Consultants	73

Westford	John Pyra Consulting	97
Weston	RTJ Corporation	74
West Tisbury	Deborah J. Mayhew & Associates	110

MARKETING & DISTRIBUTION

Boston	Wolf, Greenfield & Sacks	118
Cambridge	Media Map/Cambridge Communications	121
Huntington	Common Sense Computing, Inc.	116
Natick	International Communications Inc.	116
Worcester	Cirrus Technology	117

MULTIMEDIA

Amesbury	Complete Solutions/QTFX	148
Arlington	Open Eyes Video	138
Cambridge	Avid Corporation	148
Cambridge	In Context	147
Cambridge	Interactive Factory	134
Millis	Abbate Video, Inc.	148
Needham	GTE Hotel Interactive Television Services	152
Newburyport	Zona Corporation	144
Newton	Micro Visual Systems	137
Rowe	StoryGame Software	140
Watertown	Chedd-Angier Production Company	130
Watertown	Forman & Flack, Inc.	147
Watertown	Tree Media Digital Music Services	145
Woburn	Lynx System Developers, Inc.	149

NETWORKING

Boston	Education Catalysts Inc.	163
Boston	Frye Computer Systems, Inc.	166
Boston	Greenline Electronics	28, 161
Cambridge	Chris Hurley	163
Newton	Telluride	163
Stow	Integrated Management Resources	166
Woburn	Focus Enhancements	163

PUBLISHING

Andover	Landry Design Associates	173
Belmont	Graphic Arts Technology	173
Boston	Eric Hook Graphic Design	172
Cambridge	Drucker Documents	178
Cambridge	Haywood & Sullivan	173
Cambridge	Software Export Corporation	177
Lexington	Erica Kerwien	178
Lincoln	MindCraft Publishing Corporation	173
North Chelmsford	Pagecrafters	173
Pembroke	Mainstay Business Services Inc.	173
Watertown	Mark Siegel Creative Graphics	173
Watertown	Soft•Letter	176

SUPPORT

Amherst	Mac Resource	190
Boston	The Federation of International Distributors	186
Brookline	Computer Aided Results	190
Cambridge	Photon Inc.	188
Millbury	Omni Resources Corporation	175
Newton	RSH Consulting, Inc.	187
Newton	Softeach	191
Northampton	David Spound Associates	190
Peabody	CAST, Inc.	190
Topsfield	National Association of Desktop Publishers	186
Westford	Laser Publishing	187
Worcester	Consortium for Laboratory & Industrial Applications of the Macintosh	185
Worcester	Macintosh Scientific & Technical Users Association	185

Michigan

CUSTOM SOLUTIONS

Grand Rapids	InfoServices, Inc.	38

DEVELOPMENT & PROGRAMMING

Ann Arbor	Arbor Intelligent Systems, Inc.	106
Ann Arbor	Arborworks, Inc.	17, 85
Ann Arbor	B. W. Software	90
Ann Arbor	Cider Mill Software	78
Ann Arbor	Comshare	46
Ann Arbor	Cybernet Systems Corporation	112
Ann Arbor	DPK Software	90
Ann Arbor	Full News Information Service	76
Ann Arbor	Rock Ridge Enterprises	83
Ann Arbor	Rubicon, Inc.	98
Beverly Hills	Viewpoint Consulting, Inc.	103
Brighton	Frostbyte Software, Inc.	97
Dearborn	Guardianware	105

Dexter	Ralph Krug, P.E.	89
Farmington Hills	Klex Software	67
Frankfort	Orcutt/Oeflein Software	65, **67**, 90
Grand Rapids	Baudville Inc.	75
Madison Heights	System Solvers Ltd.	102
Midland	Holder, Egan & Company, Inc.	97
Milan	Arroyo Software	90
Orchard Lake	CompuMod Software	78
Plymouth	D. Kevin Rowe	101
Plymouth	Software Systems & Products	
	Corporation	71
Rochester Hills	Absoft Corporation	65
Southfield	Childs Consulting Associates Inc.	64
Troy	Second Difference	83
W. Bloomfield	Accountasystems Ltd.	60
Warren	Leviathan Media Corporation	69
Warren	Omicron Electronics Inc.	68

MARKETING & DISTRIBUTION

Southfield	Scott Satovsky, Sat's Graphics	117

MULTIMEDIA

Beula	Artist House	130
Bloomfirld Hills	Management Advisory Services	150
Royal Oak	Visual Impact!	142
Troy	Butler Graphics, Inc.	130

NETWORKING

Almont	Group 20/20 Ltd.	166
Ann Arbor	Network Express, Inc.	168
Farmington Hills	JEDtech Consulting	161

PUBLISHING

Ann Arbor	Desktop Technologies Inc.	172
Dearborn	Jacque Consulting, Inc.	173
E. Lansing	Number One Graphics	177
Grosse Pointe Park	Susan B. Morison Writer	178

Support

Ann Arbor	Peter David Lauwers	
	Macintosh Support	191
Southfield	MacTraining & Design, Inc.	191

Minnesota

CUSTOM SOLUTIONS

Eden Prairie	Teknowledgy	38, **142**, 148

DEVELOPMENT & PROGRAMMING

Blaine	Knowledge Bank, Inc.	80

Blaine	Liberty Computer	52
Bloomington	Business Brothers, Inc.	18, 44, **45**
Burnsville	Knowledge Factory	80, 121
Burnsville	The Willowplace Group	57
Chanhassen	Click Click, Inc.	93
Eden Prairie	Skamp Computer Services Inc.	89
Edina	Alexus Group Limited	43
Fridley	SCV Consulting, Inc.	54
Inver Grove	Business Software Applications	96
Maple Grove	Lawinger Consulting, Inc.	80
Maple Grove	Object Factory Inc.	89
Maple Grove	Suick Bay Technologies	57
Minneapolis	Antley Business Systems, Inc.	
		17, 58
Minneapolis	Hyper Active Software	21, 50, **91**
Minneapolis	management graphics	77
Minneapolis	Sapphire Systems	98
Minneapolis	Sterling Automation, Inc.	72
Minneapolis	Triad International Corporation	84
Minneapolis	Worthington Software Engineering,	
	Inc.	104
Minnetonka	HMS Computer Company	70
New Hope	Total Automation, Inc.	57
Northfield	MicroAssist, Inc.	101
Osseo	CEI Systems, Inc.	61
Plymouth	(M)agreeable software, inc.	52
Prior Lake	The Thought Shop	89
Roseville	Exact Systems, Inc.	**66**, 79, 90, **104**
Roseville	Micro Specials Inc.	68
St. Paul	Andante Systems	95
St. Paul	Applied Statistics, Inc.	72
St. Paul	Janus Technologies	88
St. Paul	Quantic Corporation	89
St. Paul	Sandpiper Software, Inc.	65
West St. Paul	Crown Communications	99
Wayzata	Manufacturing & Computer Systems	
		104
Wayzata	Sales Dominator Ltd.	62

MARKETING & DISTRIBUTION

Minneapolis	Martin & Wichmann	121

MULTIMEDIA

Chanhassen	KV Graphics	136
Grand Rapids	Wayzata Technology	153
Minneapolis	Excel Instruction	150

Minneapolis	ICONOS	133
Minneapolis	Sinard Productions	149
Minnetonka	Integrated Strategies, Inc.	150
Minnetonka	Intra-Active Designs	150
St. Paul	Emerging Technology Consultants Inc.	
		132

NETWORKING

Albert Lea	McHenry Consulting & Development	167
Eden Prairie	Triticom	168
Minneapolis	DataSoft Corporation	160
Minneapolis	Doradus Corporation	163
Minneapolis	Lanovation	168
Minneapolis	Mallin Consulting	164
Rochester	ShowCase Corporation	159

PUBLISHING

Richfield	Hagen MicroAge	190
Minneapolis	PROmote Communications	174
St. Paul	Keith Gilbert Consulting	175
St. Paul	Logical Solution	176

SUPPORT

Eden Prairie	Ontrack Data Recovery	186
Minneapolis	Application Developers Training Company	188
Minneapolis	MacCounting	190

Mississippi

NETWORKING

Southaven	Networkers	164

Missouri

CUSTOM SOLUTIONS

Blue Springs	Montgomery Consulting Group, Inc.	36

DEVELOPMENT & PROGRAMMING

Bridgeton	Calico Publishing	64
Clayton	Wette Enterprises	92
Concordia	Paradigm Software	89
Kansas City	Daystar Software Inc.	66
Kansas City	Ernst & Young	70
Kansas City	Greystone Computer Management, Inc.	50
Kansas City	System Consultants Group	69

Manchester	Armadillo Computer Services	96
Manchester	Excalibur Technologies	97
Maryland Heights	Cellular Hotline	45
Parkville	Northland Computer Services, Inc.	68
Rolla	McKune Consulting Services	107
St. Louis	Armo	78
St. Louis	Computer Consultants & Service Center, Inc.	61
St. Louis	IMS Information Management Solutions, Inc.	50
St. Louis	McDonnell Douglas Aerospace	67
St. Louis	Nelson Laffey Associates, Inc.	
	16, 22, **37**, 89, 161, **163**	
St. Louis	Richardson Technical Services	83
St. Louis	Tripos Associates Inc.	69

MARKETING & DISTRIBUTION

Marshall	Package Express Inc.	121
Marshall	Simply Software, Inc.	123
North Kansas City	Mendon & Associates	117
St. Louis	Shattinger Interactive	116
St. Louis	Wave Technologies Training, Inc.	121

MULTIMEDIA

Crofton	NB Engineering	**132, 133**, 138,
		143, 144, 149
Kansas City	Fearless Eye	133
St. Louis	Busch Creative Services Corporation	
		149
St. Louis	Drochelman Meng & Associates	**132**

NETWORKING

Florissant	DeskTop Consulting, Inc.	160
St. Louis	Creative Media Software Solutions Inc.	
		167
St. Louis	Creative Technologies	166
St. Peters	ComNet	160

PUBLISHING

St. Louis	TBF Publications	176

SUPPORT

Kansas City	Empower Trainers & Consultants, Inc.	
		189
Kansas City	MacHardware Ind.	187
St. Louis	Independent Computer Consultants Association (ICCA)	**185**
St. Louis	Productivity Plus, Inc.	191
St. Louis	SSE	191

Montana

DEVELOPMENT & PROGRAMMING

Big Sandy	CMJ Computers Inc.	61
Gardiner	CINNABAR Macintosh	93
Helena	Keep It Simple Software	62

Nebraska

DEVELOPMENT & PROGRAMMING

Lincoln	MacMinded Computer Specialists	99

MULTIMEDIA

Lincoln	CommGraphics	130

PUBLISHING

Omaha	Software Services Group	
	152, 153, **173**, 175	

Nevada

DEVELOPMENT & PROGRAMMING

Boulder City	GeoData Systems	66
Incline Village	Quansa	82
Las Vegas	Nedrud Data Systems	68
Stateline	Coral Research	47

PUBLISHING

Reno	Exact Art Design	173

SUPPORT

Reno	Professional Computer Training	189

New Hampshire

CUSTOM SOLUTIONS

Peterborough	Appropriate Solutions, Inc.	37
Salem	SaleMaker Corporation	38

DEVELOPMENT & PROGRAMMING

Amherst	Northstar Systems, Inc.	53
Condia	Minuti Software Consulting, Inc.	52
Derry	Microstar	52
Hampton Falls	Joel M. Bowers & Associates	99
Hanover	L & L Products, Inc.	92
Mount Vernon	Circle Noetic Services	76
Nashua	Campagne Associates Ltd.	61
Nashua	Circuit Research Corporation	78
Nashua	ComputerCrafts	107
Nashua	Custom Interfacing Solutions	96
Nashua	Sequoia Computing Solutions	98
Nashua	Systems Data Processing Associates	57
Nashua	White Pine Software, Inc.	58
Pelham	Alternative Systems Concepts	65
Plymouth	HDA Technical Services	101
Rindge	Peter F. Wells	72
Weare	KyTek, Inc.	77

MARKETING & DISTRIBUTION

Durham	Local Knowledge	117
Merrimack	Spiral Communications	117
North Hampton	Interconsult	120

NETWORKING

Hanover	Sassafras Software, Inc.	167
Lebanon	CMI (Corporate Microsystems, Inc.)	
		165
Nashua	Alexander LAN, Inc.	159
Nashua	World Benders, Inc.	165

PUBLISHING

Bedford	Paragon Publishing Systems	177
Campton	Te Corporation	179
Hanover	Zeta Data	179
Peterborough	New Edge Technologies	175
Warren	Falcon Software, Inc.	177

SUPPORT

Manchester	The Taylor Group	191

New Jersey

CUSTOM SOLUTIONS

Englewood Cliffs	Bizware Corporation	16, 36
Short Hills	Los-Lawrence Computer Systems	38

DEVELOPMENT & PROGRAMMING

Belvidere	Technologies Plus, Inc.	104
Bloomfield	Essex Systems Inc.	103
Boundbrook	Digital Objectives	79
Brick	Freewood Computer Services Inc.	50
Cherry Hill	Maximum Software	94, **99**
Clinton	Click Systems	93
Demarest	Avalon Computer	70
Edison	Command Line Corporation	72
Edison	Human-Computer	
	Systems, Company	110

Fair Lawn	Al Jen, Inc.	71
Fair Lawn	EDR Consulting Services, Inc.	20, 48
Flemington	Landgrove Associates	80
Franklin Park	Jersey Cow Software Company, Inc.	64
Garfield	Christine Maggio Consulting	99
Glen Rock	A. A. Gole, Consulting	60
Hightstown	Millstone River Systems, Inc.	105
Hoboken	Milesquare Associates	99
Hoboken	Skye Solutions Inc.	55
Jersey City	Sneakers Software, Inc.	98
Kearny	Prototype Systems, Inc.	23, **47**, 54, **55**
Lambertville	B & L Associates, Inc.	17, 43, **45**
Little Falls	Innovative Systems & Solutions	51
Matawan	CEO Software Solutions	64
Mendham	Software Usability Seminars	112
Montclair	Baltic Consulting & Computer Services	108
Morris Plains	Work Improvement Technologies Inc.	58
Mount Laurel	Drextec Inc.	93
Mt. Laurel	SSTi	102
North Brunswick	Hil Bren Consulting Services	70
Oakland,	Starlight Software Solutions	84
Pennsauken	A O-K Services, Inc.	109
Princeton	Biometallics	65
Princeton Junction	Lou Harrison & Associates, Inc.	81
Ridgewood	Zeik Consulting	**56**, 58
Rockaway	The Hybrid Group, Inc.	90
Secaucus	Projects in Knowledge Inc.	74
Short Hills	LCS-Lawrence Computer Systems	59
Summit	Creative Consulting Associates, Inc.	47
Sussex	Engineering Resources, Inc.	49
Trenton	DRW, Inc.	48
Trenton	Pine Grove Software	90
Voorhees	A to Z Computers, Inc.	65
Warren	Straylight Corporation	112
Westfield	The Turnaround Team, Inc.	92

MARKETING & DISTRIBUTION

Edison	Martin Goffman Associates	117
Manasquan	Computer Product Testing Services, Inc.	121
Princeton	American List Council Inc.	118
Trenton	Optima Design & Advertising	116

MULTIMEDIA

Clark	AGS Information Services, Inc.	129
Fairfield	MasterPiece Video	150
Flemington	Timebox Inc.	153
Morristown	Instructional Design Group, Inc.	**145**, 150
Mt. Laurel	NFL Films	149
Ocean	Sound-Arts Company Inc.	145
Ocean City	Glass Eye Productions	146
Princeton	Sheahan Productions, Inc.	149
Rahway	Philips Professional Products	139
South Amboy	Presentation Media	151
South Orange	Cooper Communications	146
Tenafly	Media Direct, Inc.	137, **141**
Upper Saddle River	Pioneer New Media Technologies, Inc.	139

NETWORKING

Allendale	Global Investment Technology	166
Edison	UniPress Software	165
Freehold	Studio 4	167
Hazlet	Compusoft, Inc.	163
Mahwah	Magic Solutions, Inc.	161
Marlton	Computer Methods Corporation	166
Marlton	PF Consulting	162
Mountainside	Cyberresources Corporation	160
North Brunswick	Sproul Consulting	165
Weehawken	Beyond Consulting, Inc	160
West Orange	Granite Graphics	161

PUBLISHING

Cranbury	Graphic Connexions, Inc.	173
Fair Lawn	Concepts & Keystrokes	174
Harrington Park	Maria L. Langer	178
Hoboken	Blue World Graphics	172
Jersey City	Gal Computer Imaging	175
Moorestown	Pearl Computer Systems, Inc.	177
Parsippany	Bureau of Electronic Publishing	17
Rockaway	CPS Technologies Inc.	172
Skillman	Decision Images Inc.	175
Voorhees	London Computing	173

SUPPORT

Freehold	DDP Training Center	190
Pennington	PCES Inc.- Express Train	189
Somerset	Personal Computers, Personal Solutions Inc.	189

New Mexico

DEVELOPMENT & PROGRAMMING

Albuquerque	Dana Wood & Associates	65
Las Cruces	Sigma 4, Inc.	98
Los Alamos	Mesa Graphics, Inc.	52
Penasco	Emanuele Corso & Associates, Inc.	59
Santa Fe	Acumen, Inc.	58

PUBLISHING

Albuquerque	Subiacorp	174
Albuquerque	WordPlay Communications	179

New York

CUSTOM SOLUTIONS

New York	Task Force, Inc.	36
New York	TurnKey Computer Systems, Inc.	**36**, 37
Plainview	Micro Business Software	36
Upper Mac	Agie Seife Associates, Inc.	38

DEVELOPMENT & PROGRAMMING

Akron	Strippit	72
Albany	Albany Micro Solutions	64
Bellerose	Opal Computing	71
Bohemia	E & C Manufacturing/Computer Supply Company	79
Brewster	Nexial	98
Brooklyn	adINFINITUM Development	95
Brooklyn	Nadcomp Systems Inc.	81
Brooklyn	Relational Paradigms, Inc.	71
Brooklyn	Silva Systems	72
Brooklyn	SophSupp Inc.	56
Brooklyn	Tresidder Ltd.	71
Buffalo	Digital Information Gallery	20, 48
Buskirk	White Creek Software	95, **107, 172**, 174
Clifton Park	Littauer Associates	77
Cortland	ManPower Corporation	97
Cortland	Sensible Business Systems	62
Farmington	QuesTech	89
Floral Park	Richard Soohoo Associates, Inc.	54
Forest Hills	Consulting Solutions, Inc.	19, **77**, 78
Glendale	Monarch Design Systems	77
Greig	Capital Transactions	73
Hauppange	Digital Systems Consulting, Inc.	48
Hempstead	D & A Infosystems Inc.	47
Islandia	Computer Associates International, Inc.	46
Ithaca	Exceller Software Corporation	64
Ithaca	Jovian Systems Development, Inc.	109
Lindenhurst	ForeFront Long Island	50
Mamaroneck	Datadyne Systems	103
Mamaroneck	Soft Way Computer Software	95
Mill Neck	Crisp Computer Corporation	47
New City	Software Design Technologies	95
New York	A la Carte Systems	95
New York	Admiral	43
New York	Applied Imagination Inc.	43
New York	Array Technologies, Inc.	72
New York	Baseline	69
New York	Berlitz Translation Services	108
New York	Beyond Technology	96
New York	Brumbaugh, Graves, Donohue & Raymond	72
New York	Craft Robot Company	65
New York	Fox & Mouse	101
New York	FutureSoft System Designs Inc.	88
New York	Graffio, Inc.	88
New York	Honeybee Software Inc.	20, 50, **56, 57**, 59, 60, **75,** **76, 97, 99, 100**, 101, 133, **134**
New York	Integrated Software Inc.	77
New York	Logicat	80
New York	Lucida Corporation	69
New York	MacTechnologies Consulting	94
New York	Marubeni America Corporation	52
New York	MicroWorks	52, 91, **94**
New York	MicroWorks Businessworld, Inc.	22, **59**, 60, 62
New York	Options Computer Consulting	98
New York	REBO Research	69
New York	SelectStar, Inc.	94
New York	Seth Greenberg Computer Consulting	98
New York	Sound Logic	84
New York	Summit Computer Systems Inc.	69
New York	TEC Computer Consultants	95
New York	The Communication Studio	110

New York	Van Nostrand Reinhold	**87**, 109
New York	Vanguard Media	110
New York	Xram Xpert Systems	100
Ossining	Bobcat Systems	78
Ossining	Knowledge Software, Inc.	77
Oyster Bay	Ahmac Associates, Inc.	60
Philmont	Philmont Software Mill	89
Philmont	The Philmont Software Mill	89
Pittsford	Consulting Resources & Design	99
Pittsford	Microlytics Inc.	52
Pittsford	Millennium Computer Corporation	**51**, 52
Pittsford	Peter B. Holler	68
Port Chester	The Visaeon Corporation	24, 90
Poughkeepsie	Quire Inc.	71
Rochester	Font World Inc.	108
Roslyn Heights	Cheyenne Software Inc.	107
Shokan	Braided Matrix, Inc.	17, **56**, 59, 96
Spencer	Turtle Creek Software	63
Tarrytown	Cutting Edge Computer Consulting	47
Unionville	COMPUTE-X	96
Utica	Critical Technologies Inc.	65
Valley Cottage	The Management Services Group, Inc.	62
W. Nyack	Marigold Database Systems Inc.	74
Webster	ANEXTEK	92
White Plains	DataLan	101
Williamsville	Desktop Paging Software, Inc.	47

MARKETING & DISTRIBUTION

Brooklyn	Rivanne Advertising	120
Brooklyn	The Newsletter People	116
Farmingdale	21st Century Marketing	118
Hanbassey Hills	Neo Directions Computer Support Ltd.	120
Millbrook	Delio Consulting	117
Naples	Hawks Associates	121
New York	AFM Associates	120
New York	Arete CA Incorporated	116
New York	InfoBase	118
New York	Our Designs, Inc.	120
New York	Software Company Legal Guide	117
Schenectady	MUG News Service (MNS)	119
Troy	Consultech Communications Inc.	120
White Plains	Machover Associates Corporation	117

MULTIMEDIA

Bedford Hills	Gerin Productions, Inc.	148
Bronxville	Mac Software Registry	152
Brooklyn	Mercury Multi Media	152
Brooklyn	Sam Adams	146
Brooklyn	The Voice Emporium	**141**, 145
Cornwall-on-the-Hudson	Digital United	149
East Chatham	Diversified Music Design Inc.	132
Garrison	Clarity	144
Lynbrook	Chazz Communications Company	148
Menands	Audio-Video Corporation	130
Nesconset	Fresh Cream Design Group	133
New York	Adam Gewanter Consulting	129
New York	Adrienne Schure	150
New York	Aesthetic Engineering	144
New York	Current Designs Corporation	131
New York	D S Simon Productions	152
New York	Dot Dash, Inc.	132
New York	E Ware	147
New York	Ellen Bari	149
New York	Flying Pictures/Mercuria Interactive	146
New York	Golden Branch Interactive Productions	147
New York	HOT-Tech Multimedia, Inc.	133
New York	Integrated Media, Inc.	134
New York	James Robinson Design & Production	135
New York	Jesse Sugarman	144
New York	Kamen Audio Productions/CD Archives	26, **132**, 136, **141**, 145
New York	LJR Communications, Inc.	152
New York	Multimedia Magic	150
New York	Polygram Special Markets	145
New York	Prelinger Associates, Inc.	149
New York	Richard L. Bergman	151
New York	Scholastic Software	151
New York	The Glyph Media Group Inc.	150
New York	Time Inc. Picture Collection	147
New York	Toby L. Sanders	151
New York	Tom Nicholson Associates, Inc.	141
New York	TRANS Pro Media	141
New York	Tumble Interactive Media, Inc.	147

New York	Two Twelve Associates, Inc.	147
New York	Video Simulations	147
New York	Virtual Beauty	142
New York	Wonderplay Inc.	142
Port Chester	The Choices Center	151
Rochester	Carousel Mediaworks, Inc.	130
Rochester	Insync Productions	148
Schenectady	Way Cool Productions	142
Troy	McGraw Advertising/Design	150
White Plains	Film Rite Entertainment Group, Inc.	148

NETWORKING

Bohemia	Innovative Information Concepts, Inc.	159
Bohemia	Stony Brook Services Inc.	165
Brooklyn	Centurion Software Associates, Inc.	160
Buffalo	Federal Software Inc	166
Cornwall-on-the-Hudson	Robert A. Frankel Management Consultants	167
DeLanson	Francis Tanner Inc.	159
Fairport	Dataman Services Inc.	166
Fairport	Excalibur Technologies	166
Flushing	Robert Gezelter Software Consultant	107, **112, 160**, 162
Nanuet	Micro Computer Networks	164
New York	Ablon Associates	168
New York	Altura Systems Integration Inc.	163
New York	Art Machines Inc.	166
New York	Infomax Corporation	166
New York	Information Resources	161
New York	Rossnick Consulting	164
North Woodmere	Alan M. Gordon Consulting	28,165, **187**
Pittsford	Real Time Enterprises Inc.	167
Rhinebeck	Crossroad Systems	28, 160, **164**
Selden	Stafford Associates, Inc.	165
Spring Valley	Micro Computer Networks	164

PUBLISHING

Brooklyn	Electronic Tablet Publishing Company, Ltd.	172, **176**, 178
Cazenovia	Jowaisas Design	173
Forest Hills	Business & Automation Consulting	179
Monroe	Martin L. Deutsch, Inc	173
New York	Ad Design Consulting	174
New York	Advanced Capabilities Design Group Inc.	172
New York	Al Luongo	**174**, 178, 179
New York	DocuClear	178
New York	Duggal Color Projects Inc.	172
New York	Electronic Directions	174
New York	I.M.A.G.E. Inc.	173
New York	Images Design Group Inc.	173
New York	Joseph Greco	175
New York	Magnetic Press	176
New York	Re:Design	174
New York	The Macintosh Learning Center	175
New York	The Multimedia Library	176
Salt Point	Black Gryphon Ltd.Writing	178
White Plains	Knowledge Industry Publications, Inc.	176

SUPPORT

Huntington	Computer Custom Services	190
New York	Arete	187
New York	PCLC	191
New York	Productivity Point/MicroTrek	191
Newtonville	LOG-N-COMPUTING	188
Rochester	Randamax Inc.	191

North Carolina

CUSTOM SOLUTIONS

| Boone | CIS Communication & Information Services | 37 |

DEVELOPMENT & PROGRAMMING

Boone	Info Systems, Inc.	51
Cary	German Localizations	108
Cary	Steven Fine	84
Chapel Hill	Business Tools, Inc.	44
Chapel Hill	Ninth Wave Computing, Inc.	74
Chapel Hill	Software Designs Unlimited, Inc.	84
Charlotte	Bootstrap Enterprises Inc.	44
Charlotte	NHG Inc.	53
Charlotte	Synthesis Software	57

Durham	Augment, Inc.	60
Durham	Creative Software	64
Durham	J.W.G. Enterprises, Inc.	51
Fayetteville	MEDformatics, Inc.	74
Henderson	ADS Designs	85, 106, **109**
Huntersville	Nancy A. Ridenhour, CDP	**94**
Kernersville	Shell Systems, Ltd.	23, **81**, 94, 104
Mooresville	Sterling International/Ambush Productions	62
Raleigh	Automated Analysis Corporation	63
Raleigh	COMPUTER: Applications Inc.	18, 78
Raleigh	Magenta Seven, Inc.	97
Raleigh	Sanders & Sanders, Inc.	102
Raleigh	Synthesis Design	84
Raleigh	Tangram Enterprise Solutions	57
Rockingham	Synapse Software Inc.	74

MARKETING & DISTRIBUTION

Raleigh	Image Associates, Inc.	121

MULTIMEDIA

Durham	Illuminati	143
Eden	Oxygen Farm	144
Raleigh	Graphic Detail, Inc.	152
Raleigh	Microspace Communications Corporation	138
Winston Salem	Paradigm Interactive, Inc.	139

NETWORKING

Falkland	A. L. Freeman, Jr. & Associates, Inc.	159
Hickory	DILAN	163

PUBLISHING

Raleigh	DaVinci Systems Corporation	160
High Point	Presentation Graphics	175

North Dakota

DEVELOPMENT & PROGRAMMING

Grand Forks	Aatrix Software Inc.	70

PUBLISHING

Grand Forks	Systems Consulting, Inc. Production Services	175

Ohio

DEVELOPMENT & PROGRAMMING

Akron	System Oriented Solutions Corporation	102
Canton	Prime Prodata, Inc.	72
Cincinnati	Brainchild Corporation	44
Cincinnati	Computer Graphics Group	76
Cincinnati	Computer Presentations, Inc.	46
Cincinnati	Electronic Catalog Corporation	61
Cincinnati	Exodus Software	20, 49
Cincinnati	FSCreations, Inc.	64
Cincinnati	Information Systems Research, Inc.	101
Cincinnati	Pharos Technologies	90
Cleveland	New Media, Inc.	16, 22, 29, **37**, 38, 53, **63**, 64, **79**, 81, **89**, **94**, **97**, **104**, 105, 106, 107, **108**, **111** 159, **160**
Cleveland	Wizard Software	103
Columbus	Adaptive Machine Technologies, Inc.	43
Columbus	BOOKUP	69
Columbus	Creative Computing	91
Columbus	Ernest De Gidio	93
Columbus	Pickering & Associates	98
Dayton	Gem City Software	79
Dayton	Weingarten Gallery	77
Gahanna	Quantum Solutions, Inc.	54
Hilliard	Productive Systems, Inc.	53
Milford	International TechnoGroup Incorporated	67
Palma Heights	Stage Research	84
Steubenville	EM Software, Inc.	76
Toledo	GSE Choice Ticketing Software	69
Toledo	HJM Computer Consulting Group, Inc.	93, 101
Toledo	Technovation Training Inc.	74
Willoughby Hills	Mundo Corporation	105

MARKETING & DISTRIBUTION

Bowling Green	Senecio Software, Inc.	121
Cincinnati	Software Packaging Associates	121
Dublin	Univenture CD Packing & Storage	122

MULTIMEDIA

Beachwood	EDR Media	149
Cincinatti	The Human Element, Inc.	140
Cincinnati	Magnagraphics, Inc.	149
Dublin	Metatec Corporation	153

NETWORKING

Cincinnati	DCA	166
Cincinnati	Mark One Computer Networks, Inc.	
		164
Dayton	Century Technologies, Inc.	166
Dayton	The Mac Consultants	167
Hilliard	Mac Solutions	161
Lakewood	Relational Systems, Inc.	162
Millbury	Electro Plasma Inc.	143

PUBLISHING

Columbus	Q1 Communicators	178
Columbus	The Computer Workshop, Inc.	175
Yellow Springs	Electronic Edge	174

SUPPORT

Cincinnati	Pro Train	189
Cincinnati	Support Central	188
Fairborn	Logtec	190

Oklahoma

DEVELOPMENT & PROGRAMMING

Comanche	Bliss Interactive Technologies	91
Durant	International Software Consultants	
	Inc.	135
Midwest City	Powers Hills, Inc.	101
Oklahoma City	New Visions	53
Oklahoma City	PSS Systems Design, Ltd.	107
Ponca City	Mayfield Information Services	52
Tulsa	PaperClip Products	23, 53

MARKETING & DISTRIBUTION

Tulsa	Multi-Impressions Corporation	117

MULTIMEDIA

Oklahoma City	The Graphic Resource Center	149
Tulsa	Quintessence Audio	145

PUBLISHING

Edmond	Free-lance Communications	173
Tulsa	Graphics Universal Inc.	173

SUPPORT

Norman	Alexander Technology	185
Oklahoma City	MacSpec	190

Oregon

CUSTOM SOLUTIONS

Portland	Phoenix Management, Inc.	38
Portland	Pierian Spring Software	39

DEVELOPMENT & PROGRAMMING

Amity	LC Resources	88
Beaverton	Architrion Oregon	65
Beaverton	Triple Point, Inc.	84
Bend	Blank-Hitchcock Associates	44
Camas Valley	Camtronics	65
Corvallis	Doktor Einrik's Software	48
Eugene	Datawindow Software	76
Eugene	Golden Avatar Software	103
Forest Grove	Sunset Laboratory	69
Hillsboro	Peripheral Visions Inc.	98
Hood River	Mind & Motion	52
Lake Oswego	Critical Path Software, Inc.	78
Lake Oswego	WaveMetrics, Inc.	69
Lake Oswego	Zicon Software Corporation	99
Philomath	BioTechnology Software	65
Portland	Abraxas Software, Inc.	85
Portland	Computer Information XP, Inc.	70
Portland	Decision Graphics	70
Portland	Electric Eye	66
Portland	European Languages Plus	**88**, 108
Portland	Image Builder Software	107
Portland	Inspiration Software, Inc.	62
Portland	Instantiations Inc.	88
Portland	KEA	92
Portland	MacEmpowered	99
Portland	MacSolutions Inc.	104
Portland	MLT Software, Inc.	51, 52, **79**, 81
Portland	Northwest Programming Inc.	101
Portland	Randy Schroeder	94
Portland	RDR Inc.	104
Portland	Reusable Solutions Inc.	23, **80**, 83
Portland	Synth-Bank	70
Portland	Vernier Software	65
Prospect	J. W. Havstad	67
Salem	Interactive Design Associates	63
Seaside	Easy Computing	103
Tualatin	Houlberg Development	103
Tualatin	Instant Information Inc.	51

Yachats	Alto Stratus	95

MARKETING & DISTRIBUTION

Lake Oswego	Novation Technology Inc.	116
Portland	McLaren Associates	118

MULTIMEDIA

Hood River	Burnette Multimedia Services	130
Portland	Ariel PSS Coporation	150
Portland	Binary Designs	147
Portland	Digital One	145
Portland	In Focus Systems	133
Portland	Planet Productions	151

NETWORKING

Clackamas	Media Systems	167
Portland	LDR, Litho Development & Research	161

PUBLISHING

Hillsboro	Write Design	179
Portland	Ace Communications	178
Portland	Blue Sky Research	179
Portland	Caduceus	175
West Linn	Technical Writing Services	179

SUPPORT

Aloha	Mark Prewitt Consulting	188
Beaverton	International Interactive Communications Society (IICS)	135, **184,** 185
Beaverton	Lightship Software	189
Portland	University of Oregon	191
Salem	TTJ Data Processing Services, Inc.	187

Pennsylvania

CUSTOM SOLUTIONS

Collegeville	Skunk Works Multimedia, Inc.	37

DEVELOPMENT & PROGRAMMING

Allentown	Niche Solutions	104
Bala Cynood	Simulate Inc.	62
Bensalem	DATATAG	93
Bloomsburg	Learning Tomorrow, Inc.	64
Bryn Mawr	Ashmead Computers	92
Catasauqua	Inpatients	73
Clairton	LSB Technology	67
Conshohocken	SoftEasy Software, Inc.	74
Darby	Digital Applications, Inc.	47, 48, **73, 77,** 79, **87,** 88
Devon	MacLaboratory Inc.	64
Douglassville	Way Cool Productions	95
Elkins Park	SmileSystems Inc.	74
Erie	Navaco	62
Exton	KKS Software Inc.	90
Harleyville	Candes Systems Inc.	44
Hatboro	Meyer Software	52
Hummelstown	Sigmund Software	65
Kennett Square	Perseus Systems Corporation	101
Lancaster	Cantrell Design Group	112
Lancaster	Cargas Systems, Inc.	96
Lancaster	Miracle Concepts, Inc.	81
Langhorne	Costanza & Associates	47
Malvern	Current Music Technology	47
Malvern	Merion Software Assoc., Inc.	72
Mansfield	Autograph Systems	102
Millersville	Strategic Micro Systems	24, 106
Norristown	Atkeison Consulting	99
Norristown	Conure Software	46
Orefield	Herrel Business Systems	93
Philadelphia	Macintosh Accounting Consultants	71
Philadelphia	Strategic Management Group Inc.	62
Pittsburgh	Eureka Software	49
Pittsburgh	Foxtron Systems	101
Pittsburgh	Impact Solutions Inc.	97
Pittsburgh	John Pane, Consultant	79
Pittsburgh	Microautomation Associates	104
Pittsburgh	Mysterium Tremendum	64
Pittsburgh	PCX Consulting	62
Pittsburgh	PMS Microdesign, Inc.	23, 68, **112, 134,** 139
Pittsburgh	R & L Office Systems	62
Pittsburgh	Support Syndicate for Audiology	65
Plymouth Meeting	IDR UniCom, Inc.	50
Southeastern	MG Management Group	62
Spring City	Spring City Software	84
State College	Compumation Inc.	76
Stroudsburg	Mintaka Technologies	81
University Park	Institute for the Study of Adult Literacy	63
Upper Darby	Eclipse Services	96
West Chester	Lapin Systems Inc.	80

West Chester	Universal Imaging Corporation	53
Wilkes Barre	Wilkes University ITEC Center	65
Willow Grove	Decision Software Systems	47
Yardley	Anzus	43

MARKETING & DISTRIBUTION

Northampton	Sales Automation, Inc.	121

MULTIMEDIA

Bellefonte	Design Mirage, Inc.	131
Blue Bell	Mixed Media Works	138
Kittanning	Thomas M. Basista	147
Langhorne	Nash Video Interactive	138
Malvern	Frontier Media Group, Inc.	149
Newtown	Dreamworks	149
North Wales	SSG/Skippack Systems Group	140
Philadelphia	MegaMedia Inc.	153
Philadelphia	The Lerro Corporation	150
Pittsburgh	Alan i Harris Group, Inc.	140, 151
Pittsburgh	All Night Media	129
Pittsburgh	Novette Incorporated	152
State College	Design Mirage, Inc.	152
Yardley	Rittenhouse Communications	152

NETWORKING

Berwyn	InfoTech Plus, Inc.	166
Horsham	Digilog	167
Landsdale	Jasnic Consulting Services	161
Matamoras	Software Complement	159
Philadelphia	MacSpecialists Inc.	161
Pittsburgh	Sargent Electric Company	166

PUBLISHING

Bala Cynooyd	Berkeley Education & Training Center	190
Chalfont	Klouda Communications	178
Elizabethtown	Continental Press, Inc.	172
Hatfield	Star-Byte, Inc.	175
Landenberg	Heliotrope Inc.	178
Monroeville	Rasmusson Graphics	175
Wayne	Centre Grafik Inc.	178
Wayne	Insonautics	175

SUPPORT

Duquesne	Southwestern Pennsylvania Industrial Resource Centers	186
West Conshohocken	Schulco Training Corporation	189

Puerto Rico

DEVELOPMENT & PROGRAMMING

Bayaman	Computing on Micro's	73

Rhode Isalnd

DEVELOPMENT & PROGRAMMING

Cumberland	Phase II Consulting Inc.	60
East Greenwich	AutoSoft	78

NETWORKING

Warwick	Tri com Computer Systems	168

South Carolina

DEVELOPMENT & PROGRAMMING

Greenville	Bunder Computer Services	61
Greenville	Datastream	105
Greenville	International Computer Systems	77

MARKETING & DISTRIBUTION

West Augusta	Turning Point Development, Inc.	118

MULTIMEDIA

Myrtle Beach	KnowledgeVision	144

South Dakota

DEVELOPMENT & PROGRAMMING

Rapid City	Scott Knudsen	83
Sioux Falls	Digital Designs Corporation	59, 61, 96, 97

Tennessee

DEVELOPMENT & PROGRAMMING

Cordova	Cordova Research Associates	64
Knoxville	Perceptics Corporation	107
Memphis	Computer Applications Corporation	46
Memphis	Memphis Area Computer Services	104
Memphis	Precision Data Corporation	53

MULTIMEDIA

Brentwood	A. W. Vidmer & Company	129
Chattanooga	The Masters Group	141
Knoxville	Computer Resource Sysems, Inc.	130

Nashville	Duthie Associates, Inc.	132
Nashville	NewOrder Media, Inc.	147
Nashville	Studer Dyaxis	145

NETWORKING

| Columbia | Advanced Integrated Technology | 159 |
| Memphis | ComTek | 160 |

PUBLISHING

| Memphis | Mac Solutions of Memphis | 173 |

SUPPORT

| Memphis | Jessica M. Morris | 187 |

Texas

CUSTOM SOLUTIONS

Austin	Trilogy Development Group	38
Dallas	Data Flow Systems	36
Dallas	GenText, Inc.	36
Dallas	Robert E. Nolan Company	38
Lufkin	Darmstadter Designs	36
Plano	Solo Systems	37
Richardson	Wessex Corporation	36

DEVELOPMENT & PROGRAMMING

Angleton	Warren-Forthought, Inc.	63
Arlington	Progressive Computing, Inc.	53
Austin	Amicus Software	95
Austin	Bureau of Economic Geology	65
Austin	Colleague Business Software Inc.	61
Austin	Complete Data Solutions	18, 46
Austin	Glenrose Systems	66
Austin	MacPeak	52
Austin	National Instruments	72
Austin	Optimization Alternatives	62
Austin	Parson Consulting	64
Austin	Pragma	89
Austin	Strata Systems	95
Austin	Team Development Corporation	84
College Station	Knowledge Based Systems Inc.	51
Dallas	Apeiron	110
Dallas	Desktop Dynamics	172
Dallas	Emphasys Technologies, Inc.	88
Dallas	Millennium Software Company	52
Dallas	Minerva Technology, Inc.	81
Dallas	Robert T. Culmer Consulting Services	83

Dallas	StepUp Software	92
Dallas	Technical Programming Services Inc.	89
Dallas	TeleMac Visualization	110
Denton	Computer Dynamics	93
Flower Mound	Concepts In Healthcare, Inc.	73
Fort Worth	The SU5 Group	24, 55, 57
Grand Prairie	Computer Survival	93
Houston	Applied Technology Associates, Inc.	17, 43
Houston	HV Consultants	79
Houston	MacMedic Publications, Inc.	74
Houston	MGlobal International Inc.	107
Houston	Scientific Placement Inc.	54
Lake Jackson	Stephanas & Company	147
Longview	Micro Management Associates	101
Lubbock	A * A Data	73
Marshall	CVSI	47
New Braunfels	Unlimited Ink	95
Plano	Déwí Development Corporation	79
Plano	G'Day Software, Inc.	50
Plano	G141J Systems Inc.	50
Plano	Viscon	63
Richardson	Actoris Software Corporation	103
Round Rock	Metric Systems	68
San Antonio	Architext Inc.	172
San Antonio	Datadesigns	59
Southlake Drive	Christensen Design	96
Waxahachie	Cottage Micro Services	47

MARKETING & DISTRIBUTION

Dallas	Absolute Inc.	117
Dallas	Harper House Inc.	116
Houston	C & A Graphics	116
Houston	Citadel Systems	116
Houston	Laser Set	116
Houston	RenderTech	123
Plano	RADX Corporation	117
San Antonio	Rivers Edge Corporation	122
San Antonio	Wordwright Associates	116

MULTIMEDIA

Austin	American Institute for Learning	149
Austin	AVCA	130
Austin	Graphics Edge	133
Austin	GXStudios	133

Austin	Human Code, Inc.	150
Austin	Interactive Multimedia Project	134
Austin	Optimal Sounds	138
Austin	Software Mart Incorporated	153
Austin	Texas Learning Technology Group	
146		
Dallas	Digital Designs	152, **172**, 174
Dallas	Panache Productions	146
Dallas	SoftGuide	**142**, 148
Dallas	Third Coast Multimedia Group	
	139, 141	
Houston	Computize	130
Houston	Engaging Media	132
Houston	Imagination Software Consultants	133
Houston	Kirk Mahoney	152
Houston	Michael Cowey	148
Houston	Treehouse Computer Services	141
Plano	Advanced Audioworks	144

NETWORKING

Austin	Passport Communications	162, 167
Austin	Second Wave, Inc.	167
Austin	Technology Works, Inc.	165
Dallas	Aztec Systems	166
Fort Worth	Entrepreneurial Technologies, Inc.	165
Houston	W. M. Treadway & Associates, Inc.	
	167	
Irving	Christopher Wesselman	166
Richardson	D & L Enterprises	166
Richardson	NetSpan Corporation	168
Richardson	Raindrop Software Corporation	168
Richardson	Strategic Support Systems, Inc.	162
San Antonio	Color System Support Group	
	(CSS Group)	**165**, 166
Spicewood	Texas PrePress Systems Inc.	167
Spring	New Technology Consulting	
	Associates	167
The Woodlands	KMS Systems, Inc.	
	26, 29, **132**, 136, 161	

PUBLISHING

Austin	Daniels & Mara Inc.	177
Austin	Kingdom Graphics	176
Austin	Update & More	176
Carrollton	MDF Associates, Inc.	175
Dallas	Merit Software	177

Dallas	STUDIOTECH	175
Dallas	Technical Writing PLUS	**169**, 179
El Paso	AWARE TECH	175
Houston	C. V. Rao Consultants	177

SUPPORT

Arlington	Mac Info-To-Go	190
Austin	Mac Systems Consultants	188
Bellaire	CLH Wares	189
Dallas	MBA Seminars, Inc.	191
Dallas	Pepperdine & Company, CPAs	191
Houston	Solution Development Services, Inc.	
	191	
Irvine	Digital Prepress Integration	187
Temple	MacD Enterprises	173

Utah

DEVELOPMENT & PROGRAMMING

Moab	Canyonlands Software	86
Orem	MicroCode Engineering	68
Provo	Taras Development Corporation	65
Provo	Salt Lake City Alpnet Inc.	108
Salt Lake City	Applied Informatics	73
Salt Lake City	COMPanion	64
Salt Lake City	Databases, Inc.	104
Salt Lake City	Footprints, Inc.	61
Salt Lake City	Franklin Estimating Systems	61
Salt Lake City	Green Arbor Software	79
Salt Lake City	Lion's Share	90
Salt Lake City	Revelar Software	54, 98
Sandy	Fundamental Software	88
West Jordan	Tranquility System Advisors	90

MARKETING & DISTRIBUTION

Salt Lake City	The Morgan Agency	120

MULTIMEDIA

Orem	Soft-One Corporation	151
Orem	Viewpoint Animation Engineering	
	144	

NETWORKING

Provo	Holmstead Partners	161
Salt Lake City	Micro Systems Internet Services	168

PUBLISHING

Provo	Digital Libraries	176

Salt Lake City	Mircro Security Systems, Inc.	187
Salt Lake City	Power Graphics	174
Sandy	New Heights	178

SUPPORT

Bountiful	Paw Computers, Inc.	191
Stansbury Park	Ron Allen Consulting Services	188

Vermont

DEVELOPMENT & PROGRAMMING

Burlington	Aardvark Research Group	60
Burlington	White Crow Software Inc.	63
Groton	Vermont Software	118

MULTIMEDIA

Brattleboro	International Software Products	135
Norwich	Bryten, Inc.	130
Waitsfield	InterMagic	134

NETWORKING

Norwich	Sylvan Software	163

SUPPORT

Barre	EMC2 Computer Solutions	187

Virginia

CUSTOM SOLUTIONS

Vienna	National Management Systems	38

DEVELOPMENT & PROGRAMMING

Annandale	Valad Data Solutions, Inc.	95
Arlington	Arlington Technology Group	96
Arlington	Highlighted Data Inc.	91
Arlington	M/Mac	90
Arlington	Software Systems Group	56
Ashland	Capitol Mac Consultants, Inc.	70
Burke	J P Systems	94
Centreville	Multimedia Design Group, Inc.	89
Dunn Loring	Systems Engineering Solutions Inc.	62
Fairfax	Air Land Systems	85
Fairfax	Globalink, Inc.	**85**, 109, **111**
Fairfax	LICA Systems Inc.	80
Fairfax	Positive Logic	89
Fairfax	Vanguard Research Inc.	58
Fairfax Station	Skees Associates Inc.	55
Falls Church	Carlow International Incorporated	65
Flint Hill	Blueridge Technologies, Inc.	60

Herndon	ITech, Inc.	51
Herndon	Language Systems Corporation	80
McLean	FMI Group, Ltd	97
McLean	Lester Ingber Research	71
McLean	Selfware	54
Middleburg	Hypermedia Solutions	63
Midlothian	Virginia Systems, Inc.	72
Norfolk	Corporate Computing Services	101
Reston	Open Systems Associates, Inc.	53
Reston	STR Corporation 24, 30, **71**, 72, **102**, 104, 105, **107**, 189	
Richmond	Broughton Systems Inc.	44
Richmond	MacXperts, Inc.	21, 78, 81
Sterling	InfoE	66
Vienna	Doctor Mac	79
Virginia Beach	Adjuvare, Inc.	92
Waynesboro	Eclipse Multimedia	110

MARKETING & DISTRIBUTION

Springfield	Aviation Management Associates, Inc.	117
Virginia Beach	Propaganda	120

MULTIMEDIA

Charlottesville	Creative Perspectives	131
Louisa	The Computer Lab	140
Richmond	Mediacom, Inc.	147
Richmond	Mind's Eye Graphics	144
Virginia Beach	TouchMedia	28, 141

NETWORKING

Sterling	Dulles Networking Associates, Inc.	160
Sterling	Open Network Solutions Inc.	164
Arlington	DT Software	186
Arlington	Gorman Consulting	190
Arlington	KANDU Software Corporation	186
Newport News	National Association of Macintosh Trainers	186
Reston	HFSI Education Services	190
Reston	STR Corporation 24, 30, **71**, 72, **102**, 104, 105, **107**, 189	
Richmond	1st Step Computers/MicroAge	189
Roanoke	Media Design & Images	191
Virginia Beach	League for Engineering Automation Productivity (LEAP)	186

Washington

CUSTOM SOLUTIONS

Mt. Vernon	Technoliteracy Development	
	Company	37

DEVELOPMENT & PROGRAMMING

Aberdeen	Shopware, Inc.	65
Bainbridge Island	Good Northwest	20, 79
Bainbridge Island	SoftCare	74
Bellevue	Match Data Systems	88
Bellevue	Sign Equipment Engineering Inc.	62
Bellingham	HyperDEX	62
Copalis Beach	General Systems	110
Edmonds	Linguist's Software, Inc.	77
Edmonds	Revision	54
Edmonds	The Maverick Group, Inc.	57
Ellensburg	Miles & Miles	77
Everett	KeyPeople Publishing, Inc.	64
Everett	Northwest Data Services, Inc.	22, 53
Forks	Hoh Humm Ranch	66
Freeland	Sheridan Software	54
Issaquah	Manley & Associates, Inc.	107
Kent	Ed Tech Northwest	64
Kirkland	Halley & Scott	97
Kirkland	Z Mac Software Solutions	58
Longview	WMP NJ Software	58
Lynden	Vital	**81**, 85, 90
Lynnwood	Zephron Corporation	85
Mercer Island	future tense	88
Mountlake Terrace	PC Consulting Services, Inc.	53
Mountlake Terrace	Randal Jones & Associates	82
Olympia	Computer Solutions	64
Pateros	Ariel Publishing, Inc.	43
Redmond	Comptrol, Inc.	93
Redmond	Phillips Associates	62
Richland	MicroAge Computer Center	52
Richmond	ORCA Software Company	74
Roy	Puget Pastings	105
Seattle	Azalea Software, Inc.	75
Seattle	Cederblom & Associates	61
Seattle	Clinical Information Systems, Inc.	73
Seattle	Data Dimensions, Inc.	96
Seattle	Diversified Computer Corporation	
		73, 105

Seattle	Footprints, Inc., NW Operations	61
Seattle	Intermedia	64, **122**, 123
Seattle	James Hays	51
Seattle	Remote Measurement Systems, Inc.	72
Seattle	Seawell Microsystems Inc.	68
Seattle	The Salisbury Research Group	63
Seattle	TriLogic, Inc.	84
Seattle	Urban Software	58
Tukwila	WIS Computer Systems	99
Tumwater	Totem Graphics Inc.	77
Vancouver	DataPak Software Inc.	78
Vancouver	DeNovo Systems, Inc.	72
Woodinville	Newhoff & Associates	97
Woodinville	Software Masters	90

MARKETING & DISTRIBUTION

Bainbridge Island	The Idea Bank	117
Edmonds	Scott Hysmith	122
Renton	Objectic Systems Inc.	121
Seattle	Levy & Wurz Channel Marketing	116
Seattle	Technical Analysis, Inc.	116
Vancouver	KB Communications	116

MULTIMEDIA

Bellevue	Center for Multimedia	150
Bellingham	Michael Feerer & Associates	149
Olympia	JRA Interactive	135
Redmond	Persuasive Presentations	147
Seattle	Digital Post & Graphics	148
Seattle	Interactive Design, Inc.	134
Seattle	Jane Sallis & Associates	135
Seattle	Lingua Service Associates	26, **128**, 136
Seattle	Power R, Inc.	139
Seattle	The Digital Artist, Inc.	150

NETWORKING

Bellevue	InterConnections, Inc.	168
Olympia	South Sound Software	29, 162
Seattle	EPIC Consulting Services	166
Seattle	Essential Systems Consulting	163
Seattle	Image Control Systems Inc.	166

PUBLISHING

Bellevue	PMC/Mac Seps	174
Gig Harbor	Letter Perfect	173
Monroe	Insight Systems, Inc.	175
Mt. Vernon	Age of Invention Computing	
	Resources Company	177

Seattle   Binary Graphics   174
Seattle   MultiCom Publishing   176
Seattle   Wright Information Indexing Services
                                        176, 179, 180
Spokane   The Write Tech   180
Tukwila   Communicating Ways™   172
SUPPORT
Bellevue   Online Press Inc.   191
Seattle   Pratt & Chew   191
Seattle   The Oasis Group   191

West Virginia

DEVELOPMENT & PROGRAMMING
Charleston   Mountain Software   63

Wisconsin

DEVELOPMENT & PROGRAMMING
Appleton   Synaptic Micro Solutions   77
Brookfield   Professional Systems   98
Cedar Grove   Kleinhans Systems   72
Hudson   Burton Computer Consulting   107
Lake Mills   by Design. Inc.   65
Madison   DEMCO, INC.   64
Middleton   Alpha Inc.   108
New Berlin   Minder Technologies, Inc.   62
MARKETING & DISTRIBUTION
Cedar Grove   Tronca Associates Inc.   117
Milwaukee   Other Company, Inc.   117
New Berlin   Reprographic Technologies   121
Waukesha   Video Images   123
MULTIMEDIA
Cedarburg   Ken Braband Business
                    Communications   146
Eau Claire   Computer Based Enterprises, Inc.   130
Milwaukee   21st Century Media 25, 129, **145,** 150
Milwaukee   MED.I.A. Inc.   150
New Berlin   Hartley Metzner, Huenink   150
Shorewood   Warner Cable   145
Waunakee   Wisconsin Technical College System
                    Foundation Incorporated   151
NETWORKING
Waukesha   Futurity Systems   166

PUBLISHING
Madison   Imagesetter Inc.   173
Madison   The Software Resource Publications
                    Inc.   174, 179, 180
Wauwatosa   Technical Support Services, Inc.   175
SUPPORT
Oshkosh   Don Barth Consulting   190
Racine   Solutions..., Inc. of Racine   188

Wyoming

DEVELOPMENT & PROGRAMMING
Boulder   Chalk Butte   64
Jackson   Teton Data Systems   74
NETWORKING
Jackson Hole   Moose Systems, Inc.   159

Argentina

DEVELOPMENT & PROGRAMMING
Buenos Aires   Maxim Software SA   62

Australia

DEVELOPMENT & PROGRAMMING
Beecroft   Deltra P/L   73
Bruce   Techway Solutions   89
Bunbury   Zytech Marketing Party Ltd.   109
Chatswood   Human Media Limited   110
Mawson   Learning Curve Pty Ltd.   63
Marayong   Database Techniques Pty, Ltd.   96
Parkville   Biomedical Teaching & Information
                                                     64
Prahan, Victoria The Hiser Consulting Group   110
Telopea   PacPics   89
Victoria   Stokes Electronic Enterprises P/L 104
Woolloomooloo   Technology Management Consultant
                                                     72
MULTIMEDIA
Queensland   Edge Technologies   149
NETWORKING
Wollonbean   Bailey Bailey & Bailey Pty. Ltd.   166

Austria

DEVELOPMENT & PROGRAMMING

Graz	Digi Media	108
Vienna	Libraries of the Mind	64
Wien	Microtrade	97
Wien	Icon EDV Informations-Systeme Gmb	
		88

Belgium

CUSTOM SOLUTIONS

Boncelles	Manex SPRL	37

DEVELOPMENT & PROGRAMMING

Angleur	Hermes Systems S.A.	76
Bassilly	Raymond Studer Communication Publicitaire	100
Dillbeek	DATABEHEER	103
Liege	Human Line Inc.	59
Lochristi	Colin-Data	45
Melen	DRAC'S Technologies	48
Mortsel	Athena Consult	108

MARKETING & DISTRIBUTION

Antwerpen	Medialine International	117

MULTIMEDIA

Brussels	Rigel Engineering S.A.	140
Diepenbeek	Limburgs University Centre	136
Verlaine	S.I.A. - Advanced Information Systems	153

PUBLISHING

Brussels	Using It buba	179
Montigny-le-Tilleul	Software Publishing Manuals	178

Canada

Alberta

DEVELOPMENT & PROGRAMMING

Barrhead	Alberta Education	64
Calgary	AccuWare Business Solutions Ltd.	103
Calgary	Andromeda Computer Systems Ltd.	65
Edmonton	EBA Engineering Consultants Ltd.	66
Edmonton	Jonoke Software Development, Inc.	74
Edmonton	True Ware	57

MARKETING & DISTRIBUTION

Calgary	Hybridge Inc.	120

MULTIMEDIA

Mayerthorpe	Opticon Pictures Corporation	138

NETWORKING

Calgary	Scovell Communications	165

PUBLISHING

Calgary	Image Club Graphics, Inc.	173

British Columbia

DEVELOPMENT & PROGRAMMING

Burnaby	Symplex Systems	92
Richmond	Metafact Technology Inc.	22, 87, 109
Trail	QLS (Int.) Inc.	54
Vancouver	Kinetic Sciences Inc.	112
Vancouver	Prodigy Technologies Corporation	89
Vancouver	Ruigrok Innovations Inc.	62
West Vancouver	Rodus International Corporation	103

MULTIMEDIA

Grantham's Landing	Folkstone Design Inc.	153
New Westminster	ATI Advertising Technologies Inc.	147
Vancouver	Class One Software	130
Vancouver	Motion Works International	138
Victoria	Drumlin Interactive Design	143

NETWORKING

Burnaby	Designed Information Systems	163
Vancouver	GXR Systems Services	161

New Brunswick

DEVELOPMENT & PROGRAMMING

Bass River	International Computer Group Inc.	69

Nova Scotia

DEVELOPMENT & PROGRAMMING

Dartmouth	Dover Technology Ltd	66
Wolfville	Core Business Systems	103

MULTIMEDIA

Halifax	Windhorse Productions	142

Ontario

CUSTOM SOLUTIONS

Concord	Account Ware Distributors	36

DEVELOPMENT & PROGRAMMING

Cambridge	Bannister Lake Software Incorporated	
		92
Kanata	Macsys Inc.	97
Kingston	Mentat Research Inc.	88
London	Tuffet AntiGravity Inc.	57
Markham	Plusware Inc.	104
Mississauga	Advantage Software Inc.	60
Mississauga	Delta Catalytic Corporation	72
Mississauga	Heartland Software Corporation	
	102, 103, 105	
Nepean	Globalogic Inc.	70
Norwich	Maintenance Master Limited	72
Oakville	HR Hi-Tech Inc.	60
Oakville	Vinko Enterprises	58
Ottawa	David Berman Developments Inc.	93
Ottawa	Megalith Technologies Inc.	71
Sudbury	F1 Consulting Services	49
Toronto	Chrysalis Software, Inc.	91
Toronto	CustomWare Inc.	96
Toronto	Get Info Computer Systems	
	Incorporated	101
Toronto	Peat Marwick Thorne/Strategic	
	Solutions Inc.	100
Toronto	Simon/Ross & Associates, Inc.	55

MULTIMEDIA

Downsview	Hahn Computer Institute	133
Ottawa	Animatics	130
Ottawa	Ottawa Researchers	139
Toronto	Dataway	131

NETWORKING

Ottawa	Up & Running Systems Ltd.	165
Toronto	ThinkNet Inc.	165

PUBLISHING

Downsview	Management Graphics Inc.	175
Toronto	Textware Canada	180
Toronto	Textware Corporation	179

SUPPORT

Embrun	Psychologi Logiciel Software	191
Toronto	ColorExpert Inc.	190
Toronto	Mac Help Canada	188

Quebec
DEVELOPMENT & PROGRAMMING

Montreal	Integration	51
Montreal	Le Groupe Micro-Intel Inc.	52
Montréal	Les Logiciels SYSTAMEX Inc.	62
Montreal	McGilly Information Systems Inc.	
	22, 71, **100**, 104	
Montreal	MESS/DGEC	64
Montreal	Trivium Computer Systems Inc.	106
Sherbrooke	Sisca	71
St. Lambert	Ex Software, Inc.	73
St. Lambert	LES lOGICIELS Macapa	97

MULTIMEDIA

Montreal	A. Visual	129
Montreal	Megafusion	137

NETWORKING

Montreal	Eicon Technology Corporation	160
Montreal	MPACT IMMEDIA	161
Pointe-Claire	Protec Microsystems Inc.	164

SUPPORT

Montreal	elan technologies inc.	185,186

Saskatchewan
NETWORKING

Saskatchewan	QCC Communications Corporation	
	164	

China

PUBLISHING

Singapore	Binary Magic	172

Denmark

DEVELOPMENT & PROGRAMMING

Odenses	Telicon Aps	63

MULTIMEDIA

Aalborg	GIS plan	133
Copenhagen K	Design Factory APS	131

England

CUSTOM SOLUTIONS

Cheshire	Consensus	37

Herts	Commstalk	38

DEVELOPMENT & PROGRAMMING

Avon	Micro Planning International Ltd.	62
Berkshire	The Computer Factory Limited	57
Berkshire	The Intelligent Games Company	57
Bradford	Computer Hyphenation LTD	46
Brighton	ARC Electronics	78
Cheltenham	Euronix Computing	76
Derbyshire	Imagination Technology	64
Essex	Technology Research Limited	71
Hornchurch	Another Dimension Ltd.	95
London	Steam Radio Limited	56
Northampton	Homeopathic Bicycle Company	73
Oxford	Oxford Molecular Ltd.	68
Scarborough	Pindar Graphics Systems	98
Suffolk	Freagra	59
Suffolk	Polymorph	89
Warrington	FSL Computer Services Division	76
York	Durrant Software Limited	93

MULTIMEDIA

London	IMAGIC	148
London	The Design Practice London Ltd	140
Oxford	Results Training Group Pic.	140
Surrey	Newton Design Co.	147

France

DEVELOPMENT & PROGRAMMING

Lille	New Line	97
Le Plessis	CFJ R & D	86
Paris	Logi 27	109
Pau	Christophe Vanhecke	87
Roven	La Solution Douce	71
Taverny	d-Log	47

NETWORKING

Aix les Orchies	B & L Parentheses	168
Lyon	Computer Answer Line	163

PUBLISHING

Puteaux	Duo Conseil	172

Germany

CUSTOM SOLUTIONS

Blenks International		37

DEVELOPMENT & PROGRAMMING

Berlin	Applied Technologies GmbH	85
Berlin	Century Software	86
Dortmund	ACK Software & Beratungs	78
Hamburg	Forty-Two Software	93
Hamburg	Promo Datentechnik +	
Systemberatung	GmbH	109
Hamburg	Med-I-Bit GmbH	109
Munich	Bergmann Und Langer GmbH	78
Munich	E.D.I.T.S.	108
Neu-Isenburg	WORDSTATION GmbH	109, 111
Wiesbaden	Extra Computer Services, GmbH	97
Wiesbaden	Software & Consulting	55, 98

MARKETING & DISTRIBUTION

Hamburg	LaRan Technologies	118

MULTIMEDIA

Berlin	ScreenDesign	147
Berlin	Buechting:Pieroth	130
Germering	Wayne Media Group	147
Hamburg	Steinberg Media	140
Munich	Medialab Information Design	137
Munich	RETINA	149
Nuernberg	Feldman Film Medien &	
	Kommunikation	133

PUBLISHING

Barsinghausen	Software Production Alexander Fushs	
		177
Oststewbek	CODESCO GmbH	172

SUPPORT

Hamburg	Mertens BDV-Beratung	191
Munchen	SYS TECH	186

Holland

DEVELOPMENT & PROGRAMMING

Postbus	Cart Systems	76
The Hague	BSO Management Support	161

MULTIMEDIA

Nuenen	InVision b.v.	135

NETWORKING

Amsterdam	Trio Systems Europe	168

Hong Kong

DEVELOPMENT & PROGRAMMING

Wanchai	Asia CD Ltd.	108

MULTIMEDIA

	Multimedia Asia Ltd.	153
Causeway Bay	Grid Media Limited	153,175
Tsuen Wan	Display Research Laboratory	148

PUBLISHING

	Compuserve Consultants Limited	177
Wanchai	Wys System Ltd.	177

Hungary

NETWORKING

Budapest	Tronvision	163

Israel

DEVELOPMENT & PROGRAMMING

Tel-Aviv	Panergy Ltd.	99

MULTIMEDIA

Ra'anana	QuickSoft	149
Holon	Eduself Multimedia Publishing Ltd.	175

Italy

DEVELOPMENT & PROGRAMMING

Milan	Desktop Edit	93
Milan	I-Per Media	148

MARKETING & DISTRIBUTION

Udine	D'Agostini Organizzazione	117

MULTIMEDIA

Reggio Emilia	IDEA sas	133

Japan

DEVELOPMENT & PROGRAMMING

Aoba-ku Sendai	Intersoft, Ltd.	109
Kamakura	Jirokichi & Company, Ltd.	51
Tokyo	Information & Mathematical Science Laboratory, Inc.	67
Yokohama	MarketSoft, Ltd.	71

MARKETING & DISTRIBUTION

Shibuya-Ku, Tokyo	Ring of Fire, Inc.	117

Korea

DEVELOPMENT & PROGRAMMING

Seoul	ELEX Computer, Inc.	48

Norway

CUSTOM SOLUTIONS

Tonsberg	Ra Data A.S	38

Scotland

MULTIMEDIA

North Berwick	Loch Moy	147

Singapore

MARKETING & DISTRIBUTION

inTouch Communications Pte Ltd	123

Spain

DEVELOPMENT & PROGRAMMING

Madrid	Digital Domain	108
Palma	FCS, S.L.	76

Sweden

DEVELOPMENT & PROGRAMMING

Goteborg	Punos Electronic AB	68
Solna	Sapia Mekatronik AB	68
Stockholm	CODA	96
Stockholm	PBM-Analys AB	82
Stockholm	Yellow Shark Software	109
Skurup	Kjell Ingvarsson Konsult hb	62
Vegby	Trix Systems	57

MARKETING & DISTRIBUTION

Goteborg	Double Click ab	123

MULTIMEDIA

Stockholm	MultiMedia AB	138

PUBLISHING

Enskede	Bildrummet/MacHelp	172

Stockholm   Skapa Publishing AB   177
Uppsala   Translitera Media AB   174

Switzerland

DEVELOPMENT & PROGRAMMING

Basel   Ecosophon®   48
Rodersdorf   Sundgau Software Development   57
Langenthal   Software Studio   109
Le Mont   Micro Consulting S.A.   52
Montreux   DDESIGN SA   108
Rossenaison   PRODUCTEC SA   63
Untersiggenthal Softcraft AG   68
Winkel   Michael Bodmer   99
Winterthur   Pepa Informatik   94
Zurich   LGH Informati Zurich   97

MULTIMEDIA

Basel   bopp productions inc.   147
Montreux   MontreuxMedia c/o DDESIGN SA
                                                 138

NETWORKING

Féchy   ITI SA Intégration texte et images 166

PUBLISHING

                 Topstack AG   177
Rolle   ITI SA   177

The Netherlands

DEVELOPMENT & PROGRAMMING

                 AJ Oss Document Partners Nederland
                                                  76
Schiedam   Learning Associates International bv
                                                 185
Eindhoven   WOW Control Technology   58

MULTIMEDIA

Utrecht   Raphael & De Jong   145

PUBLISHING

Zeist   MacVONK•International B.V.   177

Turkey

DEVELOPMENT & PROGRAMMING

Ankara   Komili Teknik Hiz. ve Sanayi AS. 67

AGORA DIGITAL MARKETPLACE

TALENT SOURCEBOOK™

◇   ◇   ◇

WHAT IS IT?

The Essential Directory of Computer and Multimedia Development Professionals

WHO GETS IT?

- Developers
- Bookstores
- Corporations
- Ad Agencies
- Influencers

WHO NEEDS IT?

Anyone interested in locating creative and technical service providers

HOW MUCH IS IT?

$14.95 first copy; $9.95 additional copies

WHERE'S MINE?

To Order Call 1-800-927-1200 or Simply Fill Out the Order Form

◇   ◇   ◇

Return to:

AGORA / MZ Media, Inc.
221 Main Street, Suite 700
San Francisco, CA 94105

Name _____

Title _____

Company _____

Address _____

City, State, Zip _____

Phone _____

Fax _____

◇   ◇   ◇

CHECK ONE:

____ 1 copy @ $14.95   _____

____ # of additional copies @ $9.95   _____

Postage and Handling:

1 copy - $4.95   _____

4-9 copies - $7.55   _____

More than 10 copies - $10.65   _____

Tax (8.5% CA only)

Total   _____

PAYMENT METHOD:

☐ Visa   ☐ Mastercard

☐ Amex   ☐ Check *(Make payable to MZ Media Group)*

_____

Card Number / Expiration

_____

Card Holder Name

_____

Signature

PHONE: FAX: EMAIL
415-543-8290, x140   415-543-5613   agora@delphi.com

FREE ON-LINE PREVIEW:

____ Yes, please sign me up for a sneak preview of AGORA Digital Marketplace ON-LINE!

Platform and computer configuration:

☐ Macintosh   ☐ SGI

☐ Windows   ☐ Other _____